The Evolution of Biological Disarmament

Nicholas A. Sims

sipri
Stockholm International Peace Research Institute

OXFORD UNIVERSITY PRESS
2001

OXFORD

UNIVERSITY PRESS

Great Clarendon Street, Oxford OX2 6DP
Oxford University Press is a department of the University of Oxford.
It furthers the University's objective of excellence in research, scholarship,
and education by publishing worldwide in
Oxford New York
Athens Auckland Bangkok Bogotá Buenos Aires Cape Town
Chennai Dar es Salaam Delhi Florence Hong Kong Istanbul Karachi
Kolkata Kuala Lumpur Madrid Melbourne Mexico City Mumbai Nairobi
Paris São Paulo Shanghai Singapore Taipei Tokyo Toronto Warsaw
and associated companies in Berlin Ibadan

Published in the United States
by Oxford University Press Inc., New York

© SIPRI 2001

First published 2001

British Library Cataloguing in Publication Data
Data available

Library of Congress Cataloguing-in-Publication Data
Data available
ISBN 0-19-829578-2

Typeset and originated by Stockholm International Peace Research Institute
Printed in Great Britain on acid-free paper by
Biddles Ltd., Guildford and King's Lynn

Abstract

Sims, N. A., *The Evolution of Biological Disarmament*, SIPRI Chemical & Biological Warfare Studies, no. 19 (Oxford University Press: Oxford, 2001), xii + 203 pp. (Stockholm International Peace Research Institute). ISBN 0-19-829578-2.

The evolution of the disarmament regime of the 1972 Biological and Toxin Weapons Convention (BTWC) is described from 1980, when the first BTWC Review Conference was held, until 1998. The author analyses the results of the first four review conferences; the meetings of the Ad Hoc Group of Governmental Experts to Identify and Examine Potential Verification Measures from a Scientific and Technical Standpoint; the 1994 Special Conference; the current negotiations of the Ad Hoc Group to produce an additional protocol to the BTWC, which may include verification measures; handling of the 1997 Cuban allegation of US biological warfare; and the implementation of Article X of the BTWC on international transfers and cooperation for peaceful purposes. The strength of the BTWC regime is assessed in the light of its evolution through the review process and its changing contexts, including Russia's admission that it had inherited an offensive biological weapon programme. The book applies an original sector-by-sector approach to its analysis of the BTWC, studied in a long-term perspective. 7 chapters, 4 annexes.

Contents

Preface

In this volume Nicholas A. Sims sketches the emergence of various aspects of the Biological and Toxin Weapons Convention (BTWC) regime and analyses their respective strengths and weaknesses. The treaty entered into force on 26 March 1975. In addition, the author provides an in-depth historical analysis of several issues that will be at the heart of the future protocol. Following the successful conclusion of the negotiation of the protocol the legal relationship between the BTWC and the protocol will be subject to uncertainties, and the membership of both agreements will vary. The existing BTWC regime therefore will remain of critical importance for several years.

The BTWC was negotiated in a period during which détente contributed to greater cooperation between the Soviet Union and the United States. However, upon its entry into force the BTWC immediately faced major challenges, including the emergence of genetic engineering as a biotechnology that could contribute to the development of a new generation of biological warfare agents and the worsening relations between East and West. The advances in biotechnology challenged the assumption about the limited military value of BW, and the accidental release of anthrax from a secret Soviet military laboratory near Sverdlovsk (now Yekaterinburg) in 1979 woefully exposed the lack of mechanisms to verify compliance.

Currently, an Ad Hoc Group of States Parties to the BTWC is negotiating a legally binding protocol, which, among other things, will include mechanisms to monitor and enforce compliance with the BTWC. However, over the past quarter of a century the BTWC has proved able to adapt to technological challenges. The scope of its prohibition has been extended to include new techniques and processes, and in periodic review conferences measures have been developed to enhance transparency and confidence in compliance by states parties. While these mechanisms are imperfect and politically rather than legally binding, they have contributed to the development of a viable treaty regime that sets norms of state behaviour and governs the expectations of the parties to the convention.

This work could not have been accomplished without the tireless efforts of SIPRI editor Jetta Gilligan Borg to whom we would like to express our special thanks. SIPRI hopes that this volume will contribute to the deeper understanding of the relevance and future importance of the BTWC treaty regime.

Dr Jean Pascal Zanders
Project Leader
Chemical and Biological Warfare Project

Dr Adam Daniel Rotfeld
Director, SIPRI
April 2001

Acknowledgements

The involvement of this author with this subject over 30 years has benefited greatly from the university setting in which I have been enabled to pursue the specialist study of biological and chemical disarmament. As a member since 1968 of the Department of International Relations at the London School of Economics and Political Science (LSE), University of London, I have received much encouragement from staff and students in developing an individual perspective of which the latest expression is the present volume.

The generosity of the Joseph Rowntree Charitable Trust has nurtured my writing on the Biological and Toxin Weapons Convention (BTWC) since a first typing grant in 1977. In particular, by providing full replacement funding for a temporary lecturer to be appointed, the Trust enabled my university department to release me on special writing leave for the academic year 1991/92. This was a time of turbulence and rapid change in the evolution of biological disarmament. Although much of my writing on current issues in the BTWC was published at the time, the chapters of the present volume are also derived from work made possible by the Trust in 1991/92. I gratefully acknowledge the major contribution which the Trust thereby made to the genesis of this book.

My distinctively sectoral analysis of the BTWC, in terms of a regime of compliance, a regime of development and a regime of permanence, took shape in 1991 and was first presented in a guest lecture at the Free University of Brussels (Vrije Universiteit Brussel, VUB). I thank my hosts on that occasion, the VUB Centre for Polemology (now the Centre for Peace and Security Studies) and the Centre for United Nations Law, for their encouragement and in particular for publishing the text of the lecture in *Vredesonderzoek* (no. 6, March 1992).

Short research visits to Geneva were made possible by the International Studies Research Division of LSE. I gratefully acknowledge the financial support of the Division and the cooperation of government delegates and non-governmental specialists in enabling me to use these visits to stay in touch with the diplomacy of the BTWC through the 1990s. I owe special thanks to Peter Herby, for many years Associate Representative for Disarmament at the Quaker United Nations Office, Geneva, and to his successors, David Maggs and David Atwood, for their never-failing patience and helpfulness in collecting documents and arranging meetings.

In common with many of those who attempt to pursue the complexities of biological and chemical disarmament, I remain much indebted to the wide-ranging and critical scholarship of Julian Perry Robinson, Senior Fellow in the Science and Technology Policy Research Unit at the University of Sussex, and to the exemplary generosity which he has always shown to other students of this subject. I have warmly appreciated also the helpfulness of Dr John Walker, Principal Research Officer in the Arms Control and Disarmament Research Unit of the Foreign and Commonwealth Office, London, in answering requests for information and providing unobtrusive encouragement for my work over many years. Neither they, nor any of the other people thanked in these acknowledgements, are committed in any way to the views expressed in this volume, for which I alone am responsible.

Many other people have contributed ideas and information on which I have drawn in writing this book. In particular, I thank for their help Professor Malcolm Dando, Dr Erhard Geissler, Dr Jozef Goldblat, Dr Johan Lundin, Professor Matthew Meselson, Dr Graham Pearson, Dr Barbara Hatch Rosenberg, Dr Amy Smithson, Dr Oliver Thränert, Dr Susan Wright, Dr Jean Pascal Zanders; Professor Vivienne Nathanson, Ms Marcia Darvell and Dr Catherine Hobday of the British Medical Association; and the diplomatic representatives of many governments in ministries of foreign affairs and at Geneva. None bears any responsibility for the uses I have made of ideas and information provided.

I thank Elaine Childs, Judy Weedon and Susan McGurk for their patience in typing successive drafts of these chapters in the Department of International Relations at LSE and Dr Jean Pascal Zanders and Jetta Gilligan Borg for the care with which they have taken this volume through the editorial process at the Stockholm International Peace Research Institute.

Nicholas A. Sims
April 2001

Acronyms and abbreviations

Acronyms not defined in this list are defined in the chapters of this volume.

ACDA	Arms Control and Disarmament Agency (USA)
AIDS	Acquired immunodeficiency syndrome
BL	Biosafety level
BMA	British Medical Association
BTW	Biological and toxin weapon
BTWC/BWC	Biological and Toxin Weapons Convention
BW	Biological weapon
CBM	Confidence-building measure
CCD	Conference of the Committee on Disarmament
CD	Conference on Disarmament
CDA	Centre for Disarmament Affairs
CMEA	Council for Mutual Economic Assistance
CPI	Commercial proprietary information
CRG	Council (earlier Committee) for Responsible Genetics
CSBM	Confidence- and security-building measure
CSCE	Conference on Security and Co-operation in Europe
CW	Chemical weapon
CWC	Chemical Weapons Convention
DDA	Department for Disarmament Affairs
DNA	Deoxyribonucleic acid
EC	European Communities
EU	European Union
FAO	Food and Agriculture Organization
FAS	Federation of American Scientists
FOA	Swedish Defence Research Establishment
FRG	Federal Republic of Germany
GDR	German Democratic Republic
HIV	Human immunodeficiency virus
ICGEB	International Centre for Genetic Engineering and Biotechnology
ICRC	International Committee of the Red Cross
NATO	North Atlantic Treaty Organization
NBR	National biological register

NGO	Non-governmental organization
NIEO	New International Economic Order
NNA	Neutral and non-aligned (states)
NPT	Non-Proliferation Treaty
ODA	Office for Disarmament Affairs
OPCW	Organisation for the Prohibition of Chemical Weapons
ProCEID	Programme for Countering Emerging Infectious Diseases
ProMED	Program for Monitoring Emerging Diseases
R&D	Research and development
UNCED	United Nations Conference on Environment and Development
UNDP	United Nations Development Programme
UNESCO	United Nations Educational, Scientific and Cultural Organization
UNICEF	United Nations Children's Fund
UNIDIR	United Nations Institute for Disarmament Research
UNIDO	United Nations Industrial Development Organization
UNSCOM	United Nations Special Commission on Iraq
VEREX	Ad Hoc Group of Governmental Experts to Identify and Examine Potential Verification Measures from a Scientific and Technical Standpoint
VFP	Vaccines for Peace
WHO	World Health Organization
WIPO	World Intellectual Property Organization
WTO	Warsaw Treaty Organization

1. A treaty regime in full evolution

I. Introduction

A treaty regime may be traced chronologically through its peaks and troughs. That approach was adopted in *The Diplomacy of Biological Disarmament*, which focused on the 10 years after the entry into force, in 1975, of the 1972 Biological and Toxin Weapons Convention (BTWC).[1] The March 1980 First Review Conference of the BTWC, the central diplomatic event of that period, was examined in detail and comprised the main part of that book. The First Review Conference was pivotal in that the 5 years leading up to it were generally successful ones for the BTWC, while the 5 years which followed it were its worst.

In this volume the treaty regime is broken down into three sectors: a regime of compliance, a regime of development and a regime of permanence. Each is examined in turn, with particular attention to the composition of each sector, its strengths and weaknesses, and its capacity for evolution.

II. Compliance

Chapters 2, 3 and 4 in this volume explore the evolution of the regime of compliance with the central obligations of the BTWC in three different modes. Chapter 2 analyses the original elements of the BTWC that served as functional substitutes for verification, including contingency mechanisms and procedures, one of which was first tested in 1997. Chapter 3 traces the attempt to supplement those elements with confidence-building measures (CBMs); chapter 4 discusses the addition of a new verification apparatus. Since 1992 various efforts have been made to strengthen the BTWC. These include the 1992–93 VEREX exercise;[2] the 1994 Special Conference; and the Ad Hoc Group,[3] which has been active in this area since 1995, and its negotiations which have been conducted since 1997 to conclude a legally binding instrument to strengthen the BTWC. However, long before VEREX the main elements needed to strengthen the BTWC had been identified in the literature reviewed in this volume.

III. Development

The regime of development is a set of principles and norms that lead to practical economic and social benefits, particularly in the developing countries that are parties to the BTWC. It derives from Article X of the BTWC, which combines the promotion of international cooperation in the peaceful applications of microbiology for health and other purposes with the obligation to avoid ham-

[1] Sims, N. A., *The Diplomacy of Biological Disarmament: Vicissitudes of a Treaty in Force, 1975–85* (Macmillan: London and St Martin's Press: New York, 1988). The text of the Convention on the Prohibition of the Development, Production and Stockpiling of Bacteriological (Biological) and Toxin Weapons and on their Destruction is available at the SIPRI Chemical and Biological Warfare Project Internet site, URL <http://projects.sipri.se/cbw/cbw-mainpage.html>. It is reproduced as annexe A in this volume.

[2] The Ad Hoc Group of Governmental Experts to Identify and Examine Potential Verification Measures from a Scientific and Technical Standpoint (VEREX) was established after the 1991 review conference.

[3] The Ad Hoc Group was established by the 1994 Special Conference of the BTWC and is open to all states parties.

pering economic or technological development. Chapter 5 discusses the relation of the regime to Article X.

The evolution of a regime of development has been apparent throughout the review process, but it has suffered from diffusion of effort and disparity between aspiration and achievement. This has been aggravated by North–South disagreement over the implications of the regime as regards 'free trade' in bio-technology. The notion of a development orientation to the convention has also been contested. Activities which are or may be of relevance to Article X have become more complex and numerous, and the parties to the BTWC have yet to determine which of these fall under the auspices of the convention.

IV. Permanence

An emergent regime of permanence is identified in chapter 6. This regime combines legal and diplomatic elements which reinforce the permanent character of the BTWC and render it more irreversible. These elements are evolving and their evolution could strengthen the regime. Convergence of the compliance and development regimes is likely to be facilitated by the emergence of a robust regime of permanence. This will promote the durability of the BTWC as a well-balanced treaty regime.

V. Perspective

The elements of the BTWC disarmament regime that are analysed in this volume are traced chronologically through the BTWC review conferences of 1980, 1986, 1991 and 1996, and the 'strengthening' process that has taken place since 1992. This enables the identification of unresolved issues or unadopted proposals that are related to each element. The image underlying this analysis is that of an international regime in evolution, flowing from the conclusion of the BTWC in 1972, and the first disarmament treaty regime created at the global level. Each of its sectors has evolved independently and at a different pace. The potential of each sector for further evolution is discussed below in sections I–III of chapter 7; this, in turn, raises the question of how that potential might best be realized by collective action on the part of governments.

The Diplomacy of Biological Disarmament addressed the 'unfinished business' of the First Review Conference, the erosion of credibility and the necessity for 'friends of the convention' to combine their efforts to restore trust in the regime. Various proposals for strengthening the regime and an agenda for recovery were presented in that volume.

The perspective of the late 1990s is different. The efforts of friends of the convention and international developments have increased the willingness of governments to devote attention to strengthening the BTWC. Many of the proposals in *The Diplomacy of Biological Disarmament* have been adopted, but the proposal for 'supportive institutions' has not. While the creation of a verification organization has been discussed since 1994, and under active negotiation in the Ad Hoc Group since 1997, proposals for supportive institutions for the BTWC as a whole have not succeeded despite advocacy in 1991 from governmental and non-governmental organizations. The regime still has no permanent secretariat or interim intersessional committee. Without at least a modest infrastructure of supportive institutions the regime is unlikely to realize its full potential for cross-sectoral evolution. This, in turn, will impede the strengthening of the BTWC. Chapter 7, the concluding chapter, discusses this lack.

VI. Setting the scene

This chapter, first, outlines the negotiating history of the BTWC, its obligations, reinforcement in review conferences, geographical coverage and the extent of participation. Seventy-five per cent of the states that are eligible to join are now parties to the BTWC.[4] The question remains of how to attract the additional 25 per cent. Second, the changing context (beyond the review process) within which the convention has evolved since 1991 is presented, with special attention paid to the trilateral process related to the 1992 Moscow Joint Statement.[5] Third, the concept of biological disarmament as a treaty regime is discussed. It is increasingly used by academics and diplomats in discussion of strengthening the BTWC.

VII. A short negotiating history of the BTWC

The BTWC was negotiated between 1969 and 1971 at the Conference of the Committee on Disarmament (CCD) in Geneva. In 1968 the United Kingdom had proposed strengthening the ban in the 1925 Geneva Protocol[6] on the use of bacteriological methods of warfare by extending it to all microbiological warfare and by also banning the weapons with which such warfare might be waged.[7]

The draft convention, which was submitted by the UK in 1969, was the first such document to address exclusively the abolition of biological weapons (BW) and the prohibition of biological warfare.[8] Canada and some West European states supported the draft, but other states opposed it, favouring the complete prohibition of both biological and chemical weapons (CW). Concurrently, the United Nations was seeking the achievement of a single treaty to ban both BW and CW simultaneously.

---

[4] This calculation assumes a total of 192 states in the world and takes the status of the BTWC as at 20 July 1999, when the United Nations listed alphabetically 143 parties and 18 signatory-only states. UN document BWC/AD HOC GROUP/INF.20, 20 July 1999. The UN lists of parties and signatory-only states exclude Taiwan, which signed in 1972 and ratified in 1973 as the 'Republic of China' in Washington, DC. US rosters have accordingly always been higher than others because of this addition.

Also absent from the UN lists, but on the US roster of parties, is Kyrgyzstan. The US Arms Control and Disarmament Agency included it in an updated list of parties issued on 17 Feb. 1999, although its date of accession to the BTWC is not known. It is surmised that its status must be based on the Bishkek declaration of 1992, by which Kyrgyzstan expressly included the BTWC among the international obligations of the former USSR to which it succeeded, and on its participation in the 1993 round of BTWC CBMs. *CBW Conventions Bulletin*, no. 44 (June 1999), p. 25.

[5] Joint Statement on Biological Weapons by the Governments of the United Kingdom, the United States and the Russian Federation, cited in *Chemical Weapons Convention Bulletin*, no. 18 (Dec. 1992), pp. 12–13.

[6] Protocol for the Prohibition of the Use in War of Asphyxiating, Poisonous or Other Gases, and of Bacteriological Methods of Warfare, signed at Geneva 17 June 1925, entered into force 8 Feb. 1928. The text of the protocol is available at the SIPRI Internet site, URL <http://www.sipri.se/cbw/docs>. It is also reproduced as annexe B in this volume.

[7] Eighteen-Nation Disarmament Committee document ENDC/231, 6 Aug. 1968.

[8] Eighteen-Nation Disarmament Committee document ENDC/255, 10 July 1969.

On 25 November 1969 the conclusions of a national policy review by US Secretary of State Henry Kissinger and other US policy makers led President Richard Nixon to announce the unilateral renunciation of all biological weapons by the USA; on 14 February 1970 toxin weapons were also renounced. There was no equivalent renunciation of chemical weapons, only a voluntary halt to production and a promise never to be the first to use the existing CW stockpile, which would be retained for its deterrent value. The policy review had separated biological from chemical weapons, with BW but not CW candidates for early disarmament.

The British initiative gained first US and then (30 March 1971) Soviet support in the CCD. However, its content was considerably diluted in a bilateral negotiation between the superpowers, which rushed into a deal—in part, it seems, to clear the way for the first bilateral Strategic Arms Limitation (SALT I) agreements the following spring. Apparently, the chief negotiators deemed it more important to reach agreement quickly rather than to worry about details. Consciously or unconsciously, in their bilateral negotiation the superpowers gutted the draft treaty of some of its most valuable components between April and August 1971. On 5 August 1971 identical US and Soviet drafts emerged,[9] co-sponsored by the Soviet Union's allies but by no Western state apart from the USA. The drafts were criticized for their inadequacies by the neutral and non-aligned (NNA) delegations at Geneva. Together with the Western delegations, they attempted to salvage what they could. Ultimately, four Western states—Canada, Italy, the Netherlands and the UK—acquiesced in the 'less ambitious objective' adopted by the superpowers and agreed to co-sponsor the final redraft on 28 September 1971.[10] They had, as British Ambassador Henry Hainworth remarked, 'reflected [the] spirit of compromise to the maximum extent'.[11]

Egypt, India, Mexico, Sweden, Yugoslavia and the other states of the NNA group at the CCD refused to co-sponsor the 28 September redraft, as did Japan. Attempts to strengthen the text in the First Committee of the UN General Assembly were unsuccessful; all committee amendments proposed were withdrawn after debate.

The draft BTWC was commended by the General Assembly, on 16 December 1971, by a vote of 110–0–1. France abstained, and China was among the UN members absent from the vote. (Of the 21 absentees, 3—including Iraq, but not China—later advised the UN Secretariat that they had intended to vote in favour of the commendatory resolution.[12])

The convention lacked the explicit ban on the *use* of the prohibited weapons that had been contained in Article I in the UK's original proposal and in subsequent drafts up to 1971.[13] In addition, the UN Secretary-General was no longer assigned an investigatory role and no mention was made of *research* or of con-

[9] Conference of the Committee on Disarmament documents CCD/337 (Soviet), 5 Aug. 1971; and CCD/338 (US), 5 Aug. 1971.

[10] Conference of the Committee on Disarmament document CCD/353, 28 Sep. 1971.

[11] Conference of the Committee on Disarmament document CCD/PV.542, 28 Sep. 1971.

[12] UN General Assembly Resolution A/RES/2826 (XXVI), 16 Dec. 1971; and 'UN General Assembly resolutions on disarmament and related matters, 1970–1971', *World Armaments and Disarmament: SIPRI Yearbook 1972* (Almqvist & Wiksell: Stockholm, 1972), p. 564.

[13] ENDC/231 (note 7); ENDC/255 (note 8); Conference of the Committee on Disarmament document CCD/255/Rev.1, 26 Aug. 1969; and Conference of the Committee on Disarmament document CCD/255/Rev.2, 18 Aug. 1970.

straining research that could threaten the integrity of the BTWC. Had these measures been kept, they would have provided stronger functional substitutes for verification than those which were retained. Verification provisions, as normally understood, were absent. The full array of functional substitutes for verification would have strengthened the convention and made it a more comprehensive ban.[14]

The weakened convention was signed by 80 states when it was opened for signature in London, Moscow and Washington on 10 April 1972. It entered into force on 26 March 1975.

VIII. Obligations

Most of the obligations of the BTWC are summarized in table 1.1. Two additional provisions are of importance. Article VIII ensures that nothing in the BTWC may be interpreted as limiting or detracting from the authority of the Geneva Protocol, which bans the use in war of chemical weapons (defined in the French text as 'gaz asphyxiants, toxiques ou similaires' but in the equally authentic English text more comprehensively as 'asphyxiating, poisonous or other gases') together with 'bacteriological methods of warfare'. It was of great importance that the authority of this ban on the use in war of *both* biological *and* chemical weapons should not be diminished by the temporary division of the negotiations to prohibit all activities logically prior to their use into two stages: first, the BTWC, and second, a CW disarmament treaty. In 1968–71 this had been a controversial division, despite Article VIII which explicitly reaffirmed the Geneva Protocol in its entirety.

Article XII, which provides the authority for states parties to meet in review conferences, is also important. Although only *one* review was formally required (fixed for 1980, five years after entry into force) the parties chose to hold review conferences not only in 1980, but also in 1986, 1991 and 1996. Review conferences will continue to take place at intervals of no more than five years. This review sequence has been essential to the reinforcement of the BTWC because it does not have committees that meet regularly or a secretariat. Continuing responsibilities have been shared, at a minimal level of activity, by the Department for Disarmament Affairs (DDA)[15] of the UN Secretariat and the three depositary governments (the UK, the USA and the Russian Federation, as successor to the USSR).[16] The depositaries were designated in the BTWC for

---

[14] Sims, N., 'Biological disarmament: Britain's new posture', *New Scientist*, 2 Dec. 1971, pp. 18–20.

[15] On 29 Feb. 1992 the (1983–92) Department became the Office for Disarmament Affairs and was subsumed under the Department of Political Affairs. In 1994 it became the Centre for Disarmament Affairs. Their predecessors within the UN Secretariat, during the lifetime of the BTWC, had been the Disarmament Affairs Division of the Department of Political and Security Council Affairs (to 1976) and the Centre for Disarmament (1977–83), before Disarmament Affairs was upgraded for 9 years into a full department with its own Under-Secretary-General. It returned to this status under Secretary-General Kofi Annan's reform of the UN Secretariat in 1997–98, with Ambassador Jayantha Dhanapala (formerly the Permanent Representative of Sri Lanka to the Conference on Disarmament, subsequently Director of the United Nations Institute for Disarmament Research and President of the 1995 Review and Extension Conference of the Nuclear Non-Proliferation Treaty) as Under-Secretary-General for Disarmament Affairs from 2 Feb. 1998.

[16] The triple depositary mechanism was used in 5 multilateral treaties, bearing on arms control and disarmament, between 1963 and 1972: the BTWC was the last of the five. The others were the 1963 Partial

Table 1.1. Obligations of the 1972 Biological and Toxin Weapons Convention

BTWC article	Obligations
Article I	Never in any circumstances to develop, produce, stockpile, or otherwise acquire or retain, biological or toxin weapons (defined as: (*a*) microbial or other biological agents, or toxins whatever their origin or method of production, of types and in quantities that have no justification for prophylactic, protective or other peaceful purposes; and (*b*) weapons, equipment or means of delivery designed to use such agents or toxins for hostile purposes or in armed conflict)
Article II	To destroy them, or divert them to peaceful purposes, not later than 9 months after the entry into force of the convention
Article III	Not to transfer them to any recipient whatsoever, and not in any way to assist, encourage or induce anyone else to acquire them
Article IV	To take any necessary measures to give domestic legal effect, within each state party, to its international obligations under the convention
Article V	To consult and cooperate as necessary, bilaterally and multilaterally, in solving any problems that may arise, including the use of 'appropriate international procedures within the framework of the United Nations and in accordance with its Charter'
Article VI	To cooperate with the UN Security Council in any investigation which it may 'initiate' (English text) or 'entreprendre' (French text),[a] should it receive a complaint that one state party finds another state party to be acting in breach of its obligations
Article VII	To assist victims, again in cooperation with the Security Council, if biological or toxin weapons are used against a state party
Article IX	To continue negotiations in good faith 'with a view to reaching early agreement' on a chemical disarmament treaty
Article X	To pursue international cooperation in the peaceful uses of micro-biology, through the 'development and application of scientific discoveries' for the prevention of disease and for other peaceful purposes; and to implement the BTWC in such a way as 'to avoid hampering the economic or technological development of States Parties to the Convention' or international cooperation in the peaceful uses of microbiology

[a] This inexact correspondence of terms was pointed out by Ambassador Michel Van Ussel of Belgium in the UN First Committee when the draft BTWC was under consideration, but the mistranslation remained uncorrected. United Nations document A/C.1/PV.1841, 1 Dec. 1971, para. 40.

Source: The Convention on the Prohibition of the Development, Production and Stockpiling of Bacteriological (Biological) and Toxin Weapons and on their Destruction, which is available at the SIPRI Chemical and Biological Warfare Project web site, URL <http://projects.sipri.se/cbw/cbw-mainpage.html>. It is reproduced as annexe A in this volume.

the formal purposes of receiving and circulating notifications of ratification, accession, and so on. This inadequate allocation of wider and continuing responsibilities has meant that, apart from ad hoc meetings, the regime only

Test Ban Treaty, the 1967 Peaceful Uses of Outer Space Treaty, the 1968 Nuclear Non-Proliferation Treaty and the 1971 Sea-Bed Treaty. It was also used in other multilateral treaties.

receives the sustained attention it needs from governments when a review conference is imminent.

IX. Review and reinforcement

The first two review conferences were hampered by East–West differences but some reinforcement measures were adopted. The 1980 review conference laid foundations which could be built on in 1986, when Soviet policy was evolving rapidly in the direction of greater openness under General Secretary Mikhail Gorbachev and Foreign Minister Eduard Shevardnadze. The Second Review Conference in September 1986 was one of the earliest beneficiaries. The Third Review Conference in 1991 made further progress, although as East–West tensions diminished, the North–South differences (which had always been present) increased. This affected the Fourth Review Conference in 1996 as did concerns about compliance and the prospect that verification machinery would be introduced through a supplementary protocol.

One early measure of reinforcement, a 'consultative meeting open to all States Parties at expert level',[17] was intended to address disputes over compliance with obligations under the convention. It was based on the Article V formula 'appropriate international procedures within the framework of the United Nations and in accordance with its Charter' and defined a contingency mechanism which could be used on the request of any party. This formal consultation procedure was introduced in 1980 and elaborated on in 1986 and 1991. It was intended to allow a party to use Article V multilaterally, rather than to take a compliance dispute to the Security Council (where it might encounter a permanent member's veto) under the complaints procedure outlined in Article VI.

This Article V contingency mechanism was not tested until 1997 when Cuba invoked it following an insect infestation that was detected in December 1996.[18] The credibility of the convention had, however, already been reinforced by establishing a specific way to apply Article V (i.e., by defining and elaborating a mechanism to clarify that provision of the BTWC).

The convention has also been reinforced by the development of agreements at successive review conferences to achieve greater transparency by means of voluntary unilateral declarations, annual data exchanges and other CBMs. The term 'confidence-building measures' was borrowed from the Helsinki process of the Conference on Security and Co-operation in Europe (CSCE). Since 1987 it has been used to describe a range of agreements which attempt to improve the transparency of permitted activities in order to detect the impermissible.

In 1980 the parties to the BTWC were urged to declare that they had never possessed biological and toxin weapons (BTW) or, if they had, to declare that they had now destroyed them. In both 1980 and 1986 the parties were also encouraged to provide the United Nations with legislative or other texts relevant to the convention for consultation purposes. Such texts provide a measure of confidence that obligations are being taken seriously and are being translated into laws or decrees in the process of national implementation.

---

[17] Final Declaration, First Review Conference document BWC/CONF.I/10, 21 Mar. 1980, p. 8.
[18] The episode is discussed in detail in section VII of chapter 2 in this volume.

The 1986 review conference was able to address issues which had been politically controversial in 1980. International cooperation in the peaceful application of microbiology was linked to compliance assurance, reflecting provisions of articles V and X. Politically binding commitments were made to provide initial declarations to the UN Department for Disarmament Affairs (for subsequent distribution to the parties) and thereafter annually to exchange information on: high-containment facilities (medical, veterinary, agricultural and military) for handling the most dangerous pathogens; unusual outbreaks of diseases; and publications, exchanges and conferences in fields relevant to the BTWC. Greater openness was meant to enhance international cooperation, decrease the number of ambiguous activities and suspect locations, and potentially to reveal violations of the convention or clarify concerns about a party's compliance.

Despite disappointment that the information-exchange response rate in 1987–90 was 15–26 per cent (with most parties ignoring their CBM commitments altogether),[19] the Third Review Conference continued to support data exchange as the most promising mode for reinforcing the regime. In the hope of increasing the number of responses, the CBMs were enhanced and expanded, their focus sharpened and the procedure for annual reporting made easier. States were also encouraged to submit nil returns in order to complete the picture.

Of the first three review conferences, the second was freer than the first, and the third was freer than the second, to negotiate CBMs and other measures designed to strengthen the BTWC. At the First Review Conference the word 'strengthen' was considered provocative and 'clarification' was used instead. The ingenuity and determination of several delegations ensured that modest reinforcement of the regime was achieved nonetheless, even as early as 1980.

The reviews have contributed greatly but unevenly to the reinforcement process, which is clarified in the sectoral analysis in chapters 2–6. The regime of development has lagged behind the regime of compliance in terms of reinforcement despite strenuous, but insufficiently focused, efforts. The emerging regime of permanence is only now benefiting from the reinforcement process.

X. Participation

Seventy-five per cent of the states in the world are currently bound by the BTWC. There have always been geographical imbalances in participation. This section discusses this situation and what can be done to increase participation.

The BTWC did not enter into force until 26 March 1975 because the USA and the USSR—which completed their internal procedures for ratification on 22 January and 11 February 1975, respectively—were only then ready to exchange certificates of deposit of their instruments of ratification with each other and with the third depositary, the UK. The UK had enacted the necessary national legislation in the winter of 1973–74 and had been ready to ratify since the Biological Weapons Act had received the Royal Assent on 8 February 1974.

Although only those 3 depositary states and any 19 other signatories were required to ratify the BTWC to bring it into force, 46 states were original

---

[19] For the basis of these calculations, see section III in chapter 3.

parties.[20] Several of the states that did not then ratify the BTWC were signatory states which supported the convention but whose complicated internal procedures had not been completed by the time of entry into force of the convention. Belgium, the Netherlands, Japan and the Federal Republic of Germany (FRG) were committed from the outset to becoming parties but experienced delays. Belgium's domestic legislation was not enacted until 1978, six years after its government had initiated the process. It became a party to the BTWC in 1979. The Netherlands experienced similar delays but ratified in 1981. In Japan there were definitional problems over the objects to be covered in its legislation. It became a party in 1982. The FRG had constitutional problems related to the status of West Berlin, and it took until 1983 for it to ratify the convention.

Other states did have objections of principle. France disapproved of the absence of effective verification procedures. China found the verification procedures insufficient and was displeased that the explicit ban on BTW use had been removed from the draft text of the BTWC in 1971. China also objected to the US decision to allow Taiwan to sign the convention in 1972 and ratify it in 1973 as the 'Republic of China'. The triple depositary mechanism could have enabled the People's Republic of China to sign and ratify the BTWC in the UK and the USSR, but for many years it chose to treat the US roster of parties as an insuperable obstacle. Eventually, France and China reconsidered their objections and decided to join the BTWC and strengthen it from the inside. France acceded in March 1984 and China, as the one-hundredth state party, in October 1984.[21]

The number of parties grew fastest in the early years of the BTWC, as is shown in table 1.2. It shows the total at entry into force (26 March 1975), at the end of each year up to 1979, thereafter on the occasion of each review conference, and at 20 July 1999.[22] For the purposes of this analysis, 5 February 1992 has been taken as the date of ratification by Botswana[23] and 17 May 1993 as the date of accession by Slovakia.[24] Neither Kyrgyzstan nor Taiwan is included.[25]

The Middle East may be a special case. Israel remains the most prominent of the non-signatories in that region, and it is likely that Egypt and Syria will remain signatory-only states unless Israel accedes to the convention. Concerted

[20] They were in Europe: Austria, Bulgaria, the Byelorussian Soviet Socialist Republic, Cyprus, Czechoslovakia, Denmark, Finland, the German Democratic Republic, Hungary, Iceland, Ireland, Norway, Poland, San Marino, Turkey, the UK, the Ukrainian Soviet Socialist Republic, the USSR and Yugoslavia; in North America: Canada and the USA; in Latin America and the Caribbean: Barbados, Brazil, Costa Rica, the Dominican Republic, Ecuador, Guatemala, Mexico and Panama; in Africa: Mauritius, Niger, Nigeria, Senegal and Tunisia; in Asia: Afghanistan, India, Iran, Kuwait, Laos, Lebanon, Mongolia, Pakistan, the Philippines and Saudi Arabia; and in Oceania: Fiji and New Zealand. In addition, Taiwan had ratified as the 'Republic of China' in Washington, DC, only, a controversial ratification not counted in this total of 46 original parties.

[21] Lists of signatures to and ratifications of the BTWC are given in annexes C and D in this volume.

[22] See note 4.

[23] Botswana had been included in some lists of parties on the notification of one depositary (the USA) before the Third Review Conference, but the basis of this purported ratification was unclear to other depositaries or to the UN Secretariat. The Office of the Attorney-General of Botswana had earlier informed the present author of Botswana's ratification in 1977. The act of 1992 may therefore be regarded as confirmation or regularization of a treaty status it had already assumed, in its own eyes, long before.

[24] The Czech Republic had confirmed on 1 Jan. 1993 its effective succession to the BTWC obligations of Czechoslovakia by agreeing to adhere to the convention. In some lists it is shown as having acceded on 5 Apr. 1993.

[25] The status of Kyrgyzstan and Taiwan is discussed in note 4.

Table 1.2. Number of states parties to the BTWC, 26 March 1975–20 July 1999

Date	Number of states parties
26 Mar. 1975	46
31 Dec. 1975	63
31 Dec. 1976	73
31 Dec. 1977	76
31 Dec. 1978	79
31 Dec. 1979	87
First Review Conference (1980)	87
Second Review Conference (1986)	102
Third Review Conference (1991)	121
Fourth Review Conference (1996)	138
20 July 1999	143

Source: Compiled by the author.

entry into the BTWC could form part of a comprehensive regional agreement enabling these states to become parties not only to the BTWC, but also to the 1968 Treaty on the Non-Proliferation of Nuclear Weapons (NPT) and the 1993 Chemical Weapons Convention (CWC),[26] as suggested in Peter Herby's study of the CWC in relation to the Middle East.[27]

Participation rates for the BTWC have been highest in Europe and lowest in Africa. In 1990–91 the depositaries and the 12 members of the European Communities (EC) conducted a campaign to recruit new parties. Three African accessions (Burkina Faso, Swaziland and Zimbabwe), two other accessions (Liechtenstein and Saint Kitts and Nevis) and a ratification (Malaysia) are credited to these initiatives by Germany's delegation to the Third Review Conference.[28] Australia may also have been influential in persuading Malaysia to ratify. However, the following countries, which had signed the BTWC in 1972, did not ratify: Burundi, the Central African Republic, Côte d'Ivoire, Egypt, Gabon, Haiti, Liberia, Madagascar, Malawi, Mali, Morocco, Myanmar (Burma), Nepal, Somalia, Syria, Tanzania and the United Arab Emirates. Guyana, which signed in 1973, also failed to ratify. In addition to those 18 states, which have still not ratified their signatures, a further 30 states have not yet signed the BTWC, including 13 in Africa. Altogether 25 of the 48 non-parties are in Africa.

[26] The Convention on the Prohibition of the Development, Production, Stockpiling and Use of Chemical Weapons and on their Destruction (corrected version), 8 Aug. 1994, is reproduced on the SIPRI Chemical and Biological Warfare Project Internet site at URL <http://www.sipri.se/cbw/docs/cw-cwc-texts.html>. The proposed 31 Oct. 1999 amendment to Part VI of the CWC is reproduced at URL <http://projects.sipri.se/cbw/docs/cw-cwc-verannex5bis.html>.

[27] Herby, P., *The Chemical Weapons Convention and Arms Control in the Middle East* (International Peace Research Institute, Oslo (PRIO): Oslo, 1992), p. 80.

[28] Beck, V. and Salber, H., 'The Third Review Conference of the Biological Weapons Convention: results and experience', ed. O. Thränert, *The Verification of the Biological Weapons Convention: Problems and Perspectives* (Friedrich Ebert Stiftung: Bonn, 1992), p. 21.

Possible means of increasing participation

Great reliance has been placed on regional initiatives. Australia, in particular, has made efforts to convince more Asia–Pacific states to join or ratify the BTWC.[29] Following a joint proposal by Belgium, the Netherlands and Italy, the Third Review Conference encouraged further regional initiatives.[30] Its Final Declaration 'particularly welcome[d]' such initiatives in its Article XIV section, as did the Final Declaration of the Fourth Review Conference.[31] Whether such initiatives will be effective in Africa or the Middle East remains to be seen.

Some non-parties are hampered by administrative overload in understaffed foreign ministries. 'Many of the governments contacted' in the 1990–91 initiatives 'were not aware of the problems'.[32] The BTWC has not been brought to their attention on a sufficiently continuous basis to overcome inertia and competition with other policy priorities. Isolated initiatives are inadequate. There has been no counterpart to the outreach programmes to encourage states to join the CWC which have been organized by the Organisation for the Prohibition of Chemical Weapons (OPCW) and, prior to entry into force of the CWC, by the Provisional Technical Secretariat (PTS). A BTWC secretariat which provided assistance to non-parties (e.g., by supplying them with user-friendly accession/ratification material) could expect to meet with a reasonable degree of success in encouraging participation. The political authority already exists in the Article XIV section of successive final declarations which, most recently in 1996, 'requests States Parties to encourage wider adherence to the Convention'.[33]

For some states, such as those in the Middle East, non-participation in the BTWC cannot be attributed to organizational difficulties. Security concerns may be a factor. Such a state may fail to sign or ratify the BTWC if there is no incentive in terms of improving its regional security position or if remaining outside the convention does not appear to worsen its security. Jean Pascal Zanders has observed that 'the Convention offers few potential absolute gains in terms of social and economic benefits, so that few other incentives to become a party are available'.[34] Zanders is one of few scholars to have subjected the patterns of participation and non-participation in the BTWC and the CWC to analysis in relation to regional security complexes and their dynamics.

Participation in the convention is unlikely to reach 100 per cent soon, although that goal should not be abandoned. Participation could certainly be increased above the current 75 per cent, if the parties to the BTWC were to organize a continuous, collective effort to persuade non-parties to join (recognizing particular concerns or administrative problems), and were to entrust the detailed implementation of this mandate to a secretariat acting on their behalf.

---

[29] Australia may have helped to persuade Brunei Darussalam to accede, and Malaysia and Indonesia to ratify. It was unable to convince Nepal to ratify. Information from the Australian delegation to the Third Review Conference, Personal communication with the author, 19 Sep. 1991.

[30] Third Review Conference document BWC/CONF.III/17, 24 Sep. 1991, p. 73.

[31] Fourth Review Conference document BWC/CONF.IV/9, 6 Dec. 1996, p. 28.

[32] Beck and Salber (note 28), p. 21. This was also the present author's experience in 1977.

[33] Fourth Review Conference document BWC/CONF.IV/9 (note 31), p. 28.

[34] Zanders, J. P., 'Biological disarmament in the global versus regional interface: some insights from the Chemical Weapons Convention', *Proceedings of the Sixth International Symposium on Protection Against Chemical and Biological Warfare Agents, Stockholm, Sweden, May 10–15 1998*, FOA-R-98-00873-862-SE (Swedish Defence Research Establishment: Umeå, Sweden, Nov. 1998), pp. 29–41.

XI. The 1992 Moscow Joint Statement and the trilateral process

The Third Review Conference did not directly address Western concerns regarding the 1979 Sverdlovsk Incident[35] and other suspicions of Soviet BTW activity in violation of the BTWC between 1975 and 1991. However, it enjoined 'a positive approach in questions of compliance' under the Article I section of its Final Declaration and stressed 'the need for all states to deal seriously with compliance issues' in the Article V section.[36] These phrases held special significance for the UK, the USA and Russia because, as deputy leader of the US delegation to the review conference Michael Moodie revealed: 'Even prior to the conference, as well as subsequently, the United States and the United Kingdom had been working with the government of the Soviet Union and later Russia to resolve their concerns with compliance.'[37]

In 1991 this British–US activity was not publicized. Only after Gorbachev's fall from power and the dissolution of the Soviet Union did it become clear that the UK and the USA had been granted a measure of access to help Gorbachev clear up doubts over the actions (or inaction) of previous Soviet governments. In 1992, on the other hand, President Boris Yeltsin and the newly independent Russian Federation seemed to court publicity for their compliance concerns. The reasons for this contrast may be found in the personalities of the two leaders and in the change of president and political authority: it was in Yeltsin's interest to emphasize allegations of non-compliance against the regime which he had replaced. There was also a transition within the CBM programme of the BTWC from the limited declarations of 1987–91 to the enhanced and expanded declarations that were required from 15 April 1992. This transition coincided with the ending of the Soviet era of Russian history.

US officials apparently used this change, which required parties to disclose more information about past and current BTW activities, to urge Russia to redraft the CBM declaration that was due to be submitted on 15 April 1992. In addition, Yeltsin had publicly declared his unhappiness with the alleged failure of the USSR to close down offensive programmes and acknowledge that it had 'lagged' behind in implementing the BTWC, even 'crossing the line' into violation of its obligations.[38] These disclosures were regarded in the USA as 'a very positive first step'.[39] They were followed by a presidential decree, on 11 April 1992, outlawing all activities in contravention of the BTWC. Speculation

[35] An outbreak of anthrax among the human population of Yekaterinburg, the Russian city then known as Sverdlovsk, occurred in Apr. 1979 and was the subject of repeated démarches by the USA in 1980–81 under Article V of the BTWC. Commonly known as the Sverdlovsk Incident, this event and its supposed causes have generated an extensive journalistic and scientific literature. Some of the major academic contributions include: Towle, P., 'The Soviet Union and the Biological Weapons Convention', *Arms Control*, vol. 3, no. 3 (Dec. 1982), pp. 31–40; Perry Robinson, J. P., 'The Soviet Union and the Biological Weapons Convention' and 'Guide to sources on the Sverdlovsk Incident', *Arms Control*, vol. 3 no. 3 (Dec. 1982), pp. 41–56; Harris, E. D., 'Sverdlovsk and Yellow Rain: two cases of Soviet non-compliance?', *International Security*, vol. 11, no. 4 (spring 1987); and Leitenberg, M., 'A return to Sverdlovsk: allegations of Soviet activities related to biological weapons', *Arms Control*, vol. 12, no. 2 (Sep. 1991), pp. 161–90. The definitive post-Soviet scientific study, by a joint Russian–US team, is by Meselson, M. *et al.*, 'The Sverdlovsk anthrax outbreak of 1979', *Science*, vol. 266 (1994), pp. 1202–8.

[36] Third Review Conference document BWC/CONF.III/23, 27 Sep. 1991, pp. 11, 18.

[37] Moodie, M., 'Arms control programs and biological weapons', ed. B. Roberts, *Biological Weapons: Weapons of the Future?* (Center for Strategic and International Studies: Washington, DC, 1993), p. 52.

[38] Roberts, B., 'New challenges and new policy priorities for the 1990s', ed. Roberts (note 37), p. 79.

[39] Moodie (note 37), p. 52.

mounted that some such activities might have survived as late as March 1992 (after the demise of the Soviet Union). It was felt that, even after his April decree, Yeltsin might have had difficulty ensuring that all institutions were fully complying with the BTWC obligations inherited by Russia.[40]

It was important to the USA that the Russian CBM declaration should be so drafted as to vindicate the charges long levelled at the Soviet Union by US officials, 'not just because it was some compensation for the abuse heaped on them at various times during the 1980s for making such charges, but also because it meant that the compliance problem in Russia may begin to be resolved and the BWC set free of this fundamental problem'.[41] Controversy over the final content of the Russian CBM declaration continued in the summer of 1992. It came to a head when US Acting Secretary of State Lawrence Eagleburger visited Russian Foreign Minister Andrey Kozyrev in August 1992.

The Eagleburger–Kozyrev conversations were followed a fortnight later by a trilateral negotiation out of which emerged the Moscow Joint Statement of 11 September 1992.[42] Russia was represented by Deputy Foreign Minister Grigory Berdennikov, who had been closely involved in the Third Review Conference as deputy leader of the Soviet disarmament delegation in Geneva. The USA was represented by Under-Secretary of State Frank G. Wisner and the UK by Paul Lever, an Assistant Under-Secretary of State at the Foreign and Commonwealth Office. All three led inter-agency delegations in which defence and foreign ministries were represented.

The Moscow Joint Statement proceeded from a simple but necessary premise: 'The three governments confirmed their commitment to full compliance with the Biological Weapons Convention and stated their agreement that biological weapons have no place in their armed forces.'[43] Eight steps already taken by Russia 'to resolve compliance concerns' were listed together with four further steps to which it had agreed 'as a result of these exchanges'. The steps already taken comprised:

(*a*) the presidential decree of 11 April 1992 and the creation of a presidential committee entrusted with supervising BTWC implementation in Russia;

(*b*) confirmation of the termination of offensive research, the dismantlement of experimental technological lines for the production of biological agents, and the closure of the BW testing facility;

(*c*) a 50 per cent reduction in the number of personnel involved in military biological programmes;

(*d*) a 30 per cent reduction in the funding of military biological research;

(*e*) the dissolution of the Defence Ministry department responsible for the offensive biological programme and the creation of a new department for radiological, biological and chemical defence;

(*f*) submission of the Russian CBM declaration to the United Nations;

[40] Roberts (note 38), p. 80.
[41] Moodie (note 37), p. 52.
[42] Joint Statement on Biological Weapons . . . (note 5).
[43] Text supplied by the Foreign and Commonwealth Office, London.

(g) an investigation into activities at the Institute of Ultra-Pure Biological Preparations (Biopreparat) in St Petersburg, ordered by Yeltsin in response to concerns raised by the UK and the USA;[44] and

(h) a recommendation by the Russian Parliament to Yeltsin that he propose legislation to enforce Russia's obligations under the BTWC.

The first of the four additional steps was potentially far-reaching. It encouraged openness but was dependent upon subsequent negotiations regarding access and restrictions. Russia announced that it would accept 'visits to any non-military biological site at any time in order to remove ambiguities, subject to the need to respect proprietary information on the basis of agreed principles. Such visits would include unrestricted access, sampling, interviews with personnel, and audio and video taping. After initial visits to Russian facilities there will be comparable visits to such UK and US facilities on the same basis.' Diplomatic reciprocity was thus incorporated into the agreement, but it was intended to take effect only after initial visits to Russian facilities had first been carried out by the UK and the USA. The symmetry was not meant to be immediate. This deliberate postponement of reciprocity was not long respected in practice.

The other three new steps agreed by Russia were the provision, on request, of information about the dismantlement Russia had accomplished; the supplying of further clarification of its CBM declaration regarding past offensive and/or defensive programmes;[45] and an invitation to 'prominent independent scientists' to participate in the investigation of cases concerning compliance.

In addition to these new commitments, the Moscow Joint Statement encompassed a programme of trilateral activity. Working groups, including experts, were created: to address the possibility of extending the acceptance of visits from the civilian to the military sector ('visits to any military biological facility, on a reciprocal basis, in order to remove ambiguities, subject to the need to respect confidential information on the basis of agreed principles'); to review potential measures to monitor compliance and enhance confidence in compliance; to assess potential modalities for testing such measures; to examine the physical infrastructure of biological facilities in the UK, the USA and Russia to determine jointly whether specific equipment or excess capacity seemed inconsistent with the stated purpose of those facilities; to consider cooperation in developing defence against BW; to examine ways to promote cooperation and investment in the conversion of BW facilities, including visits to already converted facilities; to consider an exchange of information on a confidential, reciprocal basis concerning past offensive programmes not recorded in detail in the CBMs; and to consider the provision of periodic reports to their legislatures and publics, describing biological research and development activities, and the encouragement of long-term exchanges of scientists at biological facilities.

Michael Moodie saw the main purpose of the Moscow Joint Statement as allowing visits 'as a way to begin to define the extent of the Soviet BW program and to investigate suspect sites'. He added: 'Over the long term this agreement should—it is hoped—put compliance concerns to rest. Thus it must be

---

[44] 'UK, US, and other experts are invited to take part in the investigation, including a prompt visit to this facility, and the report will be made public.' Joint Statement on Biological Weapons . . . (note 5).

[45] UN Department for Disarmament Affairs document DDA/4-92/BWIII/Add.3, 3 July 1992.

understood as an exercise in compliance broadly conceived rather than verification narrowly defined. This is an effort designed specifically to generate confidence that Russia is now fully compliant with the BWC and that noncompliant activities have been terminated.'[46] According to Brad Roberts, the Moscow Joint Statement 'commits Russia to opening suspect facilities to inspection . . . as intrusive as necessary to resolve concerns'.[47] However, it was predictable that obstacles would arise and that Russian implementation would prove slower than desired by the other parties to the Moscow Joint Statement.

The trilateral process rapidly re-established symmetry regarding visits in spite of the intention to postpone symmetry: a British–US delegation visited Russian sites in October 1993 and January 1994, and a Russian delegation visited three US sites and one British site in February and March 1994. Expert working groups held their first session in London in April 1994 and another in Moscow in October 1994. The trilateral process then encountered obstacles which slowed it down before concerns about Biopreparat's activities and other questions had been resolved. The early impetus was apparently lost in bureaucratic inertia: 'Despite an intervening period of four years, little official information was available at the time of the Fourth Review Conference to suggest that Western concerns had been resolved. [US Arms Control and Disarmament Agency (ACDA) reports make] clear that little progress is being made in resolving compliance concerns about the former Soviet Union's offensive BW program.'[48]

A major 1996 study of the trilateral process and its subject matter by arms control expert Milton Leitenberg gave little cause for optimism,[49] and ACDA stated in its 1997 compliance report to the US Congress that:

Previous assessments of Russian compliance have highlighted the dichotomy between what appears to be the commitment from President Yeltsin and other members of the Russian leadership in attempting to resolve BWC issues and the continued involvement of 'old hands' in BWC Protocol negotiations and in what Russia describes as its defensive BW program.

With regard to former Soviet biological weapon related facilities, some research and production facilities are being deactivated and many have taken severe personnel and funding cuts. However, some facilities, in addition to being engaged in legitimate activity, may be maintaining the capability to produce BW agents. The Russian Federation's 1993–1997 BWC data declarations contained no new information and its 1992 declaration was incomplete and misleading in certain areas.[50]

The report concluded the section on Russia and the BTWC thus: 'With regard to the trilateral process that began in 1992, while there has been progress toward achieving the openness intended in the Joint Statement (which calls for a series of confidence-building visits and information exchanges), the progress has not resolved all U.S. concerns.'

[46] Moodie (note 37), p. 52.

[47] Roberts (note 38), p. 93.

[48] Dando, M. R. and Pearson, G. S., 'The Fourth Review Conference of the Biological and Toxin Weapons Convention: issues, outcomes, and unfinished business', *Politics and the Life Sciences*, vol. 16, no. 1 (Mar. 1997), pp. 113–14.

[49] Leitenberg, M., 'Biological weapons arms control', *Contemporary Security Policy*, vol. 17, no. 1 (Apr. 1996), pp. 1–79.

[50] The report is available at Arms Control and Disarmament Agency, Adherence to and Compliance with Arms Control Agreements, URL <http://dosfan.lib.uic.edu/acda/reports/annual/comp97.htm>.

US scepticism increased in 1998 when former First Deputy Director of Bio-preparat Dr Kenneth Alibek testified before the US Congress that the 'size and scope [of the Soviet programme] were enormous' and that, although a party to the BTWC, the USSR/Russia 'continued a high-intensity program to develop and produce biological weapons through at least the early 1990s'.[51]

It is possible that the trilateral process exacerbated existing difficulties. In 1998 Amy Smithson wrote:

All totaled, the Russians visited eight facilities in America under the umbrella of the trilateral agreement. In return, US and British teams made four trips to Russia, visiting ten facilities. Over the course of these on-site exchanges, the American participants felt that the purpose of the exercise shifted from building confidence in Russian compliance with the BWC to an effort by Russian participants to allege offensive activities in the United States. Many US officials were therefore content to allow the trilateral process to disintegrate.[52]

Smithson quoted a US government official, interviewed on 5 January 1998, as saying that the trilateral process had degenerated into 'a big farce, with American officials playing right into their [Russian] hands'.[53]

The original agreement that visits to UK and US facilities would be made only after initial visits to Russian facilities had been carried out had eroded. Perhaps this was inevitable. One of Smithson's interviewees 'noted that the trilateral process took a wrong turn at the outset, when the US and British agreed to reciprocal visits . . . even though the situations in the three countries were sharply different' and that 'the Russians played the diplomatic situation very well, trying to compel the Americans to reveal sensitive national security and commercial information during each visit'.[54]

Until the trilateral process is reactivated its contribution to satisfying British and US doubts with regard to Russian compliance is questionable, and it is too early to attempt to assess it. Its effect on US policy related to the inspection provisions of a verification regime may have been negative, producing a 'hardening of viewpoints within different parts of the US government'.[55] Its contribution to the evolving multilateral regime of compliance will be positive only if Russia, the UK and the USA can revive the process and introduce the lessons which have been learned about resolving compliance concerns.

Although the parties appeared to be acting in the spirit of Article V of the BTWC ('to consult one another and to cooperate in solving any problems which may arise') the Moscow Joint Statement does not refer to Article V. This suggests that it was intended to be distanced from the compliance procedures that are made available to the parties to the BTWC (such as those examined in chapter 2 of this volume). Roberts may be right to see the trilateral process as a special case, rather like the United Nations Special Commission on Iraq

---

[51] Statement by Dr Kenneth Alibek, Program Manager, Battelle Memorial Institute, before the Joint Economic Committee, US Congress, 20 May 1998, URL <http://www.house.gov/jec/hearings/intell/alibek.htm>.

[52] Smithson, A. E., 'Man versus microbe: the negotiations to strengthen the Biological Weapons Convention', in ed. A. E. Smithson, *Biological Weapons Proliferation: Reasons for Concern, Courses of Action*, Report no. 24 (Henry L. Stimson Center: Washington, DC, Jan. 1998), p. 120.

[53] Smithson (note 52).

[54] Smithson (note 52).

[55] Smithson (note 52), p. 119.

(UNSCOM); he regards both as '*ad hoc* mechanisms [which] will also be help-ful in resolving compliance concerns in instances where circumstances permit measures beyond those in a multilateral treaty'.[56]

The trilateral process may be presumed to have had a powerful contextual effect on the evolution of the BTWC regime. It represents the spirit, if not the letter, of Article V in demonstrating a willingness—if carried forward in good faith—to consult and cooperate on compliance questions. Russia, the UK and the USA can report on their experience of the trilateral process at the Fifth Review Conference. Any lessons which may have been learned from the trilateral experience and from UNSCOM should be utilized to strengthen the BTWC. Their ad hoc nature should not be allowed to limit the wider appli-cability of such mechanisms.

XII. The evolving concept of a disarmament treaty regime

The concept of a disarmament treaty regime was uncommon at the time the BTWC was negotiated. Its negotiators apparently gave little thought to its implementation beyond the immediate actions required of its parties: the prompt enactment of national legislation and, if applicable, the completion of BTW disarmament within nine months after entry into force of the convention. Fulfilment of obligations was not perceived as a problem. This was guaranteed either by the appropriate governmental institutions of each party to the conven-tion (the Soviet position,[57] in accordance with its version of Marxism-Leninism) or by the pressure of world opinion through the United Nations[58] in the event the consultative provisions of Article V or the complaints procedure of Article VI were invoked.[59]

It was not expected that the convention would give rise to its own process of reinforcement to remedy its perceived weaknesses. The opening for signature and the entry into force of the BTWC were regarded as the end of a negotiation, not the beginning of the life of a treaty in force. However, the convention was destined to evolve and adapt in order to survive.

As the norms, rules, procedures and expectations associated with the BTWC developed, the concept of a treaty regime evolved. The review mechanism undoubtedly contributed to the process. At the First Review Conference there was general insistence that it was the operation of the convention which was being reviewed, not the convention itself. The focus was on review, not

[56] Roberts (note 38), p. 93.

[57] E.g., the leader of the Soviet delegation to the Second Review Conference, Ambassador Viktor Issraelyan, stated: 'His country had ratified the Convention by the decree of the Presidium of the Supreme Soviet of 11 February 1975 and compliance with its provisions was guaranteed by the relevant State institutions in accordance with Soviet legislation and practice.' Second Review Conference document BWC/CONF.II/SR.3, 9 Sep. 1986, para. 35.

[58] This expectation, although seldom clearly stated, can be traced to the origins of the BTWC. E.g., in its Working Paper on microbiological warfare the UK stated: 'Consideration should be given to the possi-bility of including in the Convention an article under which the parties would undertake to support appro-priate action in accordance with the United Nations Charter to counter the use, or threatened use, of micro-biological methods of warfare.' Eighteen-Nation Disarmament Committee document ENDC/231 (note 7), para. 10.

[59] From 1968 to 1972 it was the consistent intention of the authors of the BTWC that the complaints procedure should be reinforced by the passage of an 'accompanying resolution' which would constitute a declaration of intent on the part of the UN Security Council. The fate of the project and the prospects of its revival are discussed in section IX of chapter 2 in this volume.

revision.[60] This approach aimed, in part, to reassure the Soviet Union, whose invasion of Afghanistan less than three months earlier had significantly alienated the non-aligned world. At the Second Review Conference the object of review was the operation of the convention as interpreted and clarified in 1980 (in addition to the statutory Article XII requirements to review scientific and technological developments relevant to the convention and the implementation of Article IX on chemical disarmament negotiations). By the Third Review Conference the review process had to address the operation of the convention as interpreted and clarified in 1980 and as strengthened in 1986.[61] The same was true of the Fourth Review Conference. The treaty regime was defined and developed by a process of cumulative diplomacy and accretion; each review conference built on its predecessor.

In 1986, delegate Dr Günter Birbaum of Austria emphasized 'the fundamentally dynamic character of arms control regimes, which needed to be continuously adapted to technological developments, changes in military–strategic thinking and the evolving political scene'. He stressed that the 'regime on the prohibition of bacteriological (biological) weapons' should be strengthened and become 'genuinely universal'.[62] Ambassador Rolf Ekéus of Sweden also referred to 'some practical steps that could be taken within the framework of the existing regime'.[63]

President of the Second Review Conference Ambassador Winfried Lang presented the idea of a legal regime flowing from the convention.[64] He outlined four elements of such a regime: the BTWC, the Final Declarations of the 1980 and 1986 review conferences, and the data exchange approved in 1986–87.[65] These elements represent a blending of 'hard' and 'soft' law (i.e., of legally binding obligations and politically binding commitments). Lang went far towards assimilating the latter in the former, thereby comprising a continuum of obligation within a single regime. He wrote: '. . . the new commitments still were political rather than legal by nature. However, because these new commitments have to be considered as "subsequent practice" agreed upon by the parties in the application of the BWC, the obligations contained in the Convention itself have to be interpreted in light of the new understanding of the text as contained in the final declaration of the Second Review Conference.'[66]

In addition, Lang noted: 'In 1991 the next Review Conference could follow two different courses of action: (1) A fifth element may be added to the present regime that more explicitly covers the situation created by the rapid development of biotechnologies. (2) An entire restructuring of the regime to remedy most of its deficiencies may be initiated, albeit not formally concluded.'[67] He

[60] Sims (note 1), pp. 175–76.

[61] Sims, N. A., *Reinforcing Biological Disarmament: Issues in the 1991 Review*, Faraday Discussion Paper no. 16 (Council for Arms Control: London, 1991), p. 2.

[62] Second Review Conference document BWC/CONF.II/SR.5, 10 Sep. 1986, paras 31, 34, 38, 41.

[63] Second Review Conference document BWC/CONF.II/SR.7, 15 Sep. 1986, para. 16.

[64] Lang, W., 'Taking the pulse of the biological weapons regime', *Disarmament*, vol. 10, no. 1 (1986–87), pp. 44–51. Lang was Professor of International Law and International Relations at the University of Vienna, led the Austrian delegation to the First Review Conference, presided over the Second Review Conference and chaired the credentials committee of the Third Review Conference.

[65] Lang, W., 'The role of international law in preventing military misuse of the biosciences and biotechnology', *Politics and the Life Sciences*, vol. 9, no. 1 (Aug. 1990), p. 38.

[66] Lang (note 65), p. 41.

[67] Lang (note 65), p. 38.

favoured the second course: 'There is little doubt that this regime should be overhauled, that in the present state of international affairs the high amount of trust being built up between the superpowers should be used to reorganize the biological weapons regime.'[68]

Lang's paper is significant in that it admits both a political and a sociological dimension to the disarmament regime concept:

The contribution of international law to preventing the military misuse of the biosciences and biotechnology is certainly a modest one. Legal concepts cannot replace the political will necessary to establish a viable regime. Legal concepts cannot prevent scientific and technological advances which may erode confidence in a regime. Legal concepts cannot do away with incentives for violation of existing obligations . . .

International law can, however, assist in drawing up a relatively tight system of checks and balances, a system of surveillance related to peaceful research, a system which is likely to detect at an early stage attempts to channel the results of this research into weapons development.

To play its role, international law needs to be implemented by national rules and regulations, by courts and administrative agencies applying these rules and regulations. International law must also build on the support of public opinion and the media which are frequently the first ones to be alerted in case of violation and misuse of existing facilities for non-peaceful purposes.[69]

The same awareness of the role of law and its limits informs Lang's 1990 treatment of the regime concept. Previously, it had a firmly legal connotation: 'sets of rules linked to specific and locally defined situations' (e.g., navigation on the Danube).[70] However, in the theoretical development of international relations, which is linked in part to an older tradition of international political economy, the concept of regime encompasses networks or clusters of rules, norms and procedures for the patterning or regularization of international behaviour. These change over time in response to economic and political pressures.[71] Such regimes may be nebulous with their very existence open to question, unlike clear-cut regimes such as river navigation commissions.

A major body of literature focuses on analysis of international regimes.[72] This volume does not assess the validity of such analysis or the debate that questions its usefulness.[73] The use of 'regime language' in international relations has led to discussion of the BTWC regime in terms of expectations, enhancement, adaptation and reinforcement, drawing on the vocabulary and concepts of such an approach. The BTWC remains, however, essentially an international *legal* regime, somewhat removed from the mainstream of 'regime theory' in the literature of international political economy.

---

[68] Lang (note 65), p. 42.

[69] Lang (note 65), pp. 43–44.

[70] Lang (note 65), p. 38.

[71] Lang (note 65), p. 38, citing Keohane, R. and Nye, J., *Power and Interdependence* (Scott, Foresman: Glenview, Ill., 1989), p. 19; and Young, O., *International Co-operation: Building Regimes for Natural Resources and the Environment* (Cornell University Press: Ithaca, N.Y., 1989), p. 22.

[72] E.g., Haggard, S. and Simmons, B. A., 'Theories of international regimes', *International Organization*, vol. 41, no. 3 (summer 1987), pp. 491–517.

[73] E.g., Strange, S., '*Cave! hic dragones*: a critique of regime analysis', ed. S. Krasner, *International Regimes* (Cornell University Press: Ithaca, N.Y., 1983), pp. 337–54.

Even before the Birbaum contribution to the Second Review Conference,[74] the BTWC was being discussed by the academic community as a legal regime which could be weakened or strengthened. In 1986 Richard Falk, for example, had advocated the 'informal enhancement' of the convention through 'the adoption of an informal network of reassurance obligations';[75] later he wrote of 'strengthening the setting of the legal regime' by developing the support of professional constituencies and the commitment of governments and by maximizing the advantages enjoyed by the BTWC.[76] He summarized these as 'cultural revulsion tied to a framework endorsed by all major governments, political ideologies, and social institutions, that prohibits possession and development of biological weaponry, as well as their threat or use'.[77]

The flexibility of the concept, which links law with the factors that determine the regime's strength or weakness, was reflected in a 1989 paper by the present author which examined one aspect of the Second Review Conference.[78] The BTWC might cover every new scientific and technological development in its legal aspect, but it could be weakened in its wider aspect if expectations of compliance were diminished. Incentives and disincentives to comply with the BTWC have a greater influence than the legal comprehensiveness of the convention. Compliance expectations may be affected as much by changing assessments of military threat and utility as by the status under the BTWC of potential BTW agents.[79]

The 'expectations element' is stressed in Stephen Krasner's widely accepted definition of international regimes: 'sets of implicit or explicit principles, norms, rules, and decision-making procedures around which actors' expectations converge in a given area of international relations'.[80] Expectations of future behaviour are a strong determinant of the strength of the BTWC, because much of it has never been tested. Erosion of confidence in the regime is a function of expectations that, put to the test, it would fail. Law alone cannot determine the course of expectations, but legal provisions can influence them. Governmental actions may do even more to determine them, since international regimes are 'usually the result of accretion and incremental choices' rather than 'deliberate design'.[81]

A biological disarmament regime can also be regarded as an entity that is subject to change: 'The primary purpose of each review [conference] is to take the pulse of the treaty regime in question. Is it in good health? Is it operating as well as intended? And, if not, what remedy should be prescribed?'[82]

---

[74] Second Review Conference document BWC/CONF.II/SR.5 (note 62).

[75] Falk, R., 'Strengthening the Biological Weapons Convention of 1972', ed. E. Geissler, SIPRI, *Biological and Toxin Weapons Today* (Oxford University Press: Oxford, 1986), pp. 113, 114.

[76] Falk, R., 'Inhibiting reliance on biological weaponry: the role and relevance of international law', ed. S. Wright, *Preventing a Biological Arms Race* (MIT Press: Cambridge, Mass., 1990), pp. 260–64.

[77] Falk (note 76), p. 263.

[78] Sims, N. A., 'Diplomatic responses to changing assessments of scientific and technological developments relevant to a disarmament regime: the Second Review Conference of the 1972 Convention on Biological and Toxin Weapons, Geneva 1986', ed. H. G. Brauch, *Military Technology, Armaments Dynamics and Disarmament* (Macmillan: London and St Martin's Press: New York, 1989).

[79] Sims (note 78).

[80] Krasner, S., 'Structural causes and regime consequences: regimes as intervening variables', ed. Krasner (note 73), p. 2.

[81] Kratochwil, F. V., *Rules, Norms, and Decisions* (Cambridge University Press: Cambridge, 1989), p. 59.

[82] Sims, N. A., *Biological and Toxin Weapons: Issues in the 1986 Review*, Faraday Discussion Paper no. 7 (Council for Arms Control: London, 1986), p. 1.

In the 1980s the notion of 'a treaty regime in trouble' was much empha-sized,[83] which encouraged the use of health/illness metaphors. A 1986 paper, written during the latter stages of preparation for the Second Review Confer-ence, was pessimistic: 'Its 102 States Parties face the urgent task of restoring this sickly and debilitated treaty regime to health, engendering renewed confi-dence that the ban on biological and toxin weapons will survive and be respected. But the patient's ailments must be diagnosed, and appropriate pre-scriptions dispensed, before it can be set on the road to recovery.'[84] A more optimistic use of organic metaphors described the aftermath of that conference and its 'appendix' expert meeting, on 31 March–15 April 1987, to finalize the modalities of the CBM declarations in 1987:

The wider significance of the 1986–87 outcome lies in its exemplary effect. It shows that a disarmament regime can survive many tribulations and come through strengthened. It demonstrates the value of the review process. It points up the recovery potential of endangered agreements, as treaty regimes wax and wane and endure all the vicissitudes arising from international contention. The experience of biological disarmament reveals *this* treaty regime, at least, as an organism capable of adapting to changes in its environment.[85]

The concept of an international biological disarmament regime has been used not only by international law and international relations scholars, but also by BTW disarmament experts in the natural sciences, such as molecular biologists and geneticists. In 1990, Meselson, Kaplan and Mokulsky wrote of 'the pro-gress that has been made and is expected to continue in strengthening the inter-national regime for verifying compliance with the BWC' and subsequently abbreviated this to 'the international biological disarmament regime'.[86]

XIII. The Canadian concept: a compliance regime

The concept of an international biological disarmament regime gained accept-ance in academic literature and resulted in numerous policy recommendations to the Third Review Conference. This is reflected in the 10 September 1991 plenary statement by Ambassador Peggy Mason of Canada invoking the con-cept of a compliance regime (régime de conformité):

It has been said many times that verification is a process, just as confidence-building is a process, whereby States Parties can focus attention on compliance matters of concern and work together to address these concerns. That is why my Delegation prefers to speak in terms of the creation of a *compliance regime* for the Convention that will encompass not only confidence-building measures but also verification measures— with the latter, perhaps, focussed on particular situations.

What is the difference in a name? Most importantly, the title of *compliance regime* conveys very clearly that it is the obligation of States Parties *to demonstrate compli-ance* with the Convention/*démontrer que la Convention a été respectée*. In this way,

---

[83] Sims (note 82), p. 2.

[84] Sims (note 82), p. 3.

[85] Sims, N. A., 'The Second Review Conference on the Biological Weapons Convention', ed. Wright (note 76), p. 284, emphasis in the original.

[86] Meselson, M., Kaplan, M. M. and Mokulsky, M. A., 'Verification of biological and toxin weapons', eds F. Calogero, M. L. Goldberger and S. P. Kapitza, *Verification, Monitoring Disarmament* (Westview Press: Boulder, Colo., 1990), pp. 157, 158.

we mean to put the emphasis on co-operative approaches to the resolution of any concerns that may occur.

Such a *compliance regime* could combine:

– the politically binding commitments of States Parties on confidence-building measures;

– a provision for 'fact-finding' in circumstances when one or more States Parties may desire clarification, and this coupled with a strengthened consultation mechanism; and

– the establishment of institutional/procedural arrangements necessary for effective implementation.

Canada believes that such an integrated approach would constitute a practical and positive contribution to strengthening the international security regime of which we are all a part. My Delegation is prepared to co-operate with others in moving forward in each of these areas.[87]

XIV. The convergence of sectoral regimes

This volume develops the Canadian concept through an extended treatment, first, of the compliance regime and, then, of other sectors of the treaty regime. The regime of compliance is explored in three modes, followed by discussion of the regimes of development and permanence. If it is accepted that a disarmament treaty regime embraces several subsidiary or sectoral regimes, two questions about its evolution and internal structure can be asked:

1. Is the regime evolving at a constant rate across all sectors, or is one sector evolving rapidly while the others show no capacity for evolution?
2. Are the lines along which the different sectoral regimes are evolving *convergent* or *divergent*?

It is reasonable to suppose that the overall strength of a disarmament treaty regime requires an internal structure in equilibrium or a balanced evolution in which no sector outstrips another for long. The goal is a well-integrated treaty regime. However, its overall health and survival appear to require a strong likelihood of early convergence in the evolution of each sector.

---

[87] Department of External Affairs and International Trade, Canada, *Disarmament Bulletin*, no. 17 (fall 1991), p. 21. The text of the statement, reproduced in full on pp. 19–21, had earlier been made available in Geneva by the Canadian Delegation to the Third Review Conference; the quotation is from pp. 8–9 of that text, emphasis in both languages in the original text.

2. The regime of compliance: the original elements

I. Introduction

The central disarmament obligations of the 1972 Biological and Toxin Weapons Convention are set out in articles I, II and III. With articles IV, V, VI and VII they constitute the original elements of the regime of compliance. Together articles IV, V, VI and VII provide functional substitutes for verification; they are discussed in this chapter as the regime of compliance in Mode A. The addition of confidence-building measures—Mode B—and verification—Mode C—are addressed in chapters 3 and 4, respectively.

The regime of compliance is not equivalent to verification. Its relationship to verification is one of the most contentious issues in the new international climate, which has prevailed since 1986, that favours tight controls in arms control and disarmament. The parties to the BTWC seek to adapt its operation to changing circumstances, but compliance assurance and control are easier to approve in principle than to apply in practice.

It is widely agreed that a stronger compliance regime is needed to improve the effectiveness of the convention. A regime of compliance is the essence of the BTWC. The difficulty lies in elaborating operational rules for governments, and agreed procedures for their interaction, which give effect to the regime's norms and expectations.

II. Functional substitutes for verification

The BTWC, as finally adopted, contained a number of elements which offered *functional substitutes* for verification. Verification in the traditional sense had meant openness to inspection or, in the new 'strategic arms limitation sense', a mutual obligation not to interfere with the exercise of 'national technical means of verification' of strategic arms limitations (which would have made little sense in the biological and toxin weapons context). The term 'functional substitutes' was not used at the time, but the concept is inherent in the British initiative of 1968:

No verification is possible in the sense of the term as we normally use it in disarmament discussions [so] we must make a choice—balance the risks of evasion if we go ahead with the formulation of new obligations, against the risks for the world if we do nothing and allow the fears of eventual use of microbiological methods of warfare to continue and intensify. My choice is emphatically to go ahead; we cannot afford to do nothing. While we cannot offer a fully effective system of verification and we believe it is beyond the wit of man to devise one, we can provide arrangements which should satisfy States, given the intractable nature of the problem, that they will not be exposing themselves to unacceptable risks.[1]

---

[1] Mulley, F. W., United Kingdom, Eighteen-Nation Disarmament Committee document ENDC/PV.387, 6 Aug. 1968.

The 'arrangements' to which the United Kingdom referred were further developed in its 1969 draft convention[2] and carried forward into the multilateral negotiations of 1971.[3] They were, in effect, functional substitutes for unattainable verification and praised as such by former US Under Secretary of the Army and Assistant Director of the US Arms Control and Disarmament Agency (ACDA) Archibald Alexander: 'The British Draft Convention as a whole represents a careful effort, in short compass, to deal with the major problems involved in eliminating BW in a world composed of countries of many different kinds and sizes, with varying degrees of reluctance to submit to on-site verification.'[4]

These arrangements were central to the United Kingdom's 1968–69 approach to biological disarmament, to an extent which has been obscured by the UK's now long-established advocacy of adding a verification protocol to the BTWC. For the authors of the original British draft convention it was a matter of pride that the BTWC could be achieved without recourse to verification as normally understood.

The functional substitutes on which they chose to rely instead would have been more prominent in the BTWC as finally agreed had the British draft convention not been subjected to drastic dilution by the USA and the USSR in their bilateral negotiation. Between March and August 1971 some of the strongest components were discarded, and it is because of this that the convention's regime of compliance was initially so weak. Some would say that it still is. The task of restoring to the convention elements which *ought* to have been integral to its regime of compliance all along is still far from complete.

Nonetheless, the regime of compliance has been built up, slowly and painstakingly, on the basis of those functional substitutes for verification which were retained. Rules, expectations and procedures were elaborated, first cautiously in 1980, then more confidently in the warmer political climate of 1986 and the more favourable diplomatic environment of 1991. Indirectly, the process of elaboration restored some of the lost British elements to the regime of compliance, albeit gradually and with difficulty, and on a less secure legal basis than if they had always formed part of the convention.

In the 1980s and 1990s the BTWC was reinforced by the deliberate strengthening of rules, expectations and procedures in its regime of compliance. This chapter examines the compliance regime in Mode A (the original elements) by identifying and analysing four principal elements, each derived from a particular article of the convention, and tracing their evolution through the first four review conferences as a regime-building process. Chapter 3 examines the origins and implementation of the compliance regime in Mode B (with CBMs added), as enhanced and expanded by the Third Review Conference. Chapter 4 addresses the prospective transformation of the compliance regime into Mode C (with verification added) and analyses the relevant diplomatic efforts up to 1998. The difficult question of the precise relationship between verification and

---

[2] Eighteen-Nation Disarmament Committee document ENDC/255, 10 July 1969.

[3] Eighteen-Nation Disarmament Committee document ENDC/255/Rev.1, 26 Aug. 1969; and Conference of the Committee on Disarmament document CCD/255/Rev.2, 18 Aug. 1970.

[4] Alexander, A. S., 'Limitations on chemical and biological warfare going beyond those of the Geneva Protocol', Carnegie Endowment for International Peace, *The Control of Chemical and Biological Weapons* (Carnegie: New York, 1971), p. 102.

a regime of compliance which has grown accustomed to relying on functional substitutes for verification is unresolved. It goes to the heart of the controversial relationship between the convention and any eventual protocol.

III. Original elements in the regime of compliance

In place of verification the BTWC contains four elements upholding the practice of compliance with its central obligations. These obligations relate to the prohibitions laid down in Article I (on development, production, stockpiling, acquisition and retention) and Article III (on transfer, assistance, encouragement and inducement) together with, for states possessing BTW, the stockpile destruction provision of Article II.

The practice of compliance in Mode A (without CBMs or verification) is supported by: (*a*) national implementation (Article IV), the obligation to ensure national implementation of the convention through legislation or other constitutional processes as necessary to give it legal effect; (*b*) consultation and cooperation (Article V), the obligation 'to consult one another and to cooperate in solving any problems which may arise in relation to the objective of, or in the application of the provisions of, the Convention'; (*c*) complaint (Article VI), the right to lodge a complaint with the UN Security Council; and (*d*) assistance (Article VII), the obligation to provide or support assistance to a victim of BTW attack 'if the Security Council decides that such Party has been exposed to danger as a result of violation of the Convention'.

Through the interpretation of these provisions and the elaboration of procedures deriving from them the regime of compliance has evolved to its current state. It is, however, questionable how many of these derivative measures can truly be called *rules* since they consist of voluntary measures, subject to varying expectations of fulfilment. Some of these measures have acquired the status of politically binding commitments. They were promulgated in the consensually agreed final declarations of the review conferences, but they are not legally binding as are the obligations contained in the text of the convention.

However, the politically binding commitments are far from worthless. There is much to be said for the endogenous development of a treaty regime where the principle of equality and the practice of consensus impose the same degree of obligation upon every state party (even if that obligation is political rather than legal). The major objection to this approach comes from those who regard it as essential that parties to the BTWC be as legally bound to comply with the new obligations as they are by those of the original treaty text.

The alternative route, the adoption of legally binding additional or supplementary protocols, has only slowly come to be accepted (notably in the third and fourth review conferences and at the 1994 Special Conference), and then only conditionally, as one possibility among others. It was feared that a differentiated or many-tiered structure of obligation would be created if only some parties to the BTWC adopted the changes. It remains to be seen whether all or only some parties would be willing to be bound by a protocol to strengthen the convention or by other measures which emerge from the work of the Ad Hoc Group on strengthening the convention which has been meeting since 1995. In addition, if the regime of compliance can evolve satisfactorily through exploration of the possibilities latent in the existing articles, then, theoretically, effort need not be expended on supplementing the text of the BTWC.

It may be argued that the convention's functional substitutes for verification can, in principle, be developed and elaborated so that verification is redundant. Alternatively, the regime of compliance might perhaps be extended to embrace certain forms of verification without the need for a legally binding protocol to the convention. In the latter eventuality, the compliance regime could be said to have evolved to its fullest extent and to have done so endogenously.

The following sections examine the four principal elements which make up Mode A of the existing compliance regime.

IV. National implementation: Article IV

Article IV obliges each party to ensure national implementation in the broadest possible terms: 'Each State Party to this Convention shall, in accordance with its constitutional processes, take any necessary measures to prohibit and prevent the development, production, stockpiling, acquisition or retention of the agents, toxins, weapons, equipment and means of delivery specified in Article I of the Convention, within the territory of such State, under its jurisdiction or under its control anywhere.'

Although the word 'legislation' does not appear in Article IV, the commonest response to this obligation has been to pass national legislation to comply with the prohibitions contained in Article I or to determine that existing laws are adequate. (However, few parties have shared information about such activities.) National implementation also embraces government decrees, regulations and administrative memoranda to law enforcement agencies, but little is known about the actions which parties have taken under those headings. It is understandable therefore that national implementation has come to be identified with the adoption of new legislation.

Such legislation ties the convention into national legal systems in the clearest possible way, and it contributes to the regime of compliance by expanding the number of institutions which have an interest in the success of the convention. National legislation also builds the treaty regime into structures at the national level in the form of rules and expectations and procedures for upholding them. These, in turn, support their counterparts at the international level. They shore up the international treaty regime and help (even if only marginally) to ensure its survival by constituting one more obstacle to violation of the convention.

In 1980 the United Kingdom, with the support of Belgium and Finland, persuaded the First Review Conference to invite 'States Parties which have found it necessary to enact specific legislation or take other regulatory measures relevant to this Article to make available the appropriate texts to the United Nations Centre for Disarmament, for [the] purposes of consultation'.[5] In 1986 this invitation was repeated, as was the 1980 call 'upon all States Parties which have not

---

[5] First Review Conference document BWC/CONF.I/9, 21 Mar. 1980, p. 9. The intrusive 'the' was deleted when the invitation was repeated in 1986. The Australian delegation, in editing the text for the Drafting Committee, restored the original British language of 1980 at the request of its author.

yet taken any necessary measures in accordance with their constitutional processes, *as required by the Article*, to do so immediately'.[6]

The Second Review Conference took a modest step forward by building an element of the regime of compliance on the foundation of Article IV. On the initiative of the German Democratic Republic (GDR), it widened the range of national implementation actions which were given international commendation. After repeating the invitations in the 1980 declaration it added a new passage:

The Conference notes the importance of
– legislative, administrative and other measures designed effectively to guarantee compliance with the provisions of the Convention within the territory under the jurisdiction or control of a State Party,
– legislation regarding the physical protection of laboratories and facilities to prevent unauthorized access to and removal of pathogenic or toxic material, and
– inclusion in textbooks and in medical, scientific and military education programmes of information dealing with the prohibition of bacteriological (biological) and toxin weapons and the provisions of the Geneva Protocol
and believes that such measures which States might undertake in accordance with their constitutional process[es] would strengthen the effectiveness of the Convention.[7]

In 1991 Goldblat and Bernauer reported in a United Nations Institute for Disarmament Research (UNIDIR) Research Paper prepared for the Third Review Conference that 'very few' parties had adopted national legislative or administrative measures to implement the convention.[8] It was impossible to ascertain how few had sent their legislative or other appropriate texts to the Department for Disarmament Affairs—before 1983, the UN Centre for Disarmament—because the relevant file had been mislaid in New York.[9]

At the Second Review Conference the Netherlands reported that it had submitted the text of its implementing regulations to the United Nations when it ratified the BTWC in June 1981.[10] Apparently, only four other parties had shared their texts in this way. Goldblat and Bernauer reproduced the UK's 1974 Biological Weapons Act; Australia's 1976 Crimes (Biological Weapons) Act; New Zealand's 1987 New Zealand Nuclear Free Zone, Disarmament, and Arms Control Act; and the United States' 1989 Biological Weapons Anti-Terrorism Act in facsimile as annexes to their research paper,[11] together with France's

[6] Second Review Conference document BWC/CONF.II/13/II, 26 Sep. 1986, p. 4. The emphasized words were added in 1986.

[7] BWC/CONF.II/13/II (note 6). 'Process' seems to have been a typographic error in the Final Declaration carried through to the Final Document. It was corrected to 'processes' when the 1986 text was repeated in 1991. The 1986 GDR proposal (which used the plural 'processes') is reproduced in Second Review Conference document BWC/CONF.II/9, 22 Sep. 1986, annex, pp. 16–17.

[8] Goldblat, J. and Bernauer, T., *The Third Review of the Biological Weapons Convention: Issues and Proposals*, UNIDIR Research Paper no. 9 (United Nations: New York, 1991), p. 22.

[9] Personal communication with the author, 4 June 1991. The 1980 British proposal (Statement by the United Kingdom in the Committee of the Whole, First Review Conference document BWC/CONF.I/C/SR.2, 11 Mar. 1980, p. 5) had specified that the designated recipient of such texts, for purposes of consultation, be the Research and Reference Collection in the Geneva Unit of the UN Centre for Disarmament (which could make copies for the Centre's Treaties and Resolutions Section in New York so that duplicate collections could be maintained in both cities). At the insistence of the UN Secretariat, this provision was dropped during the First Review Conference. Sims, N. A., *The Diplomacy of Biological Disarmament: Vicissitudes of a Treaty in Force, 1975–85* (Macmillan: London and St Martin's Press: New York, 1988), pp. 80–81, 136–37.

[10] Second Review Conference document BWC/CONF.II/SR.5, 10 Sep. 1986, para. 56.

[11] Goldblat and Bernauer (note 8), pp. 62–75.

pioneering law of 9 June 1972.[12] This had anticipated the Article IV legislation of parties at a time when it appeared unlikely that France would accede to the convention. (It acceded in 1984.) The text of Belgium's law of 10 July 1978 had already been included in Belgium's national compliance report for the First Review Conference, the only such text which was submitted *in extenso* by the parties contributing to that 1979–80 compilation.[13] The process, in 1972–78, by which the Belgian legislation came about has been recounted elsewhere,[14] as has the protracted legislative process (1973–89) in the USA.[15]

Goldblat and Bernauer commented forcefully on the lack of attention paid by the overwhelming majority of parties to Article IV:

Since each State Party must ensure the observance of the BW Convention on its territory and anywhere else under its jurisdiction and control, it is *imperative* that it take the necessary national measures of legislative, administrative or regulatory nature. Such measures must specify the prohibitions and obligations to be observed by the natural and legal persons of the country concerned, and provide for the prosecution, trial and punishment of offenders.

The parties should *commit themselves* to send all pertinent information and documentation to the UN Secretariat, as recommended by the First and Second Review Conferences. This material, *to be distributed to all parties*, might serve as an incentive as well as guidelines for those States which have not yet adopted the required national measures.[16]

The Third Review Conference continued the process of regime building in this area, repeating the declarations of 1980 and 1986 and adding a new CBM entitled 'Declaration of legislation, regulations and other measures'.[17] This sought to put into effect the recommendations made by Goldblat and Bernauer. The new CBM, labelled 'E', went beyond simply addressing those parties which *had* legislated or taken other implementing action in this area. It asked every state party to complete a straightforward annual questionnaire answering four questions 'yes' or 'no':

1. Do you have legislation?
2. Do you have regulations?
3. Do you have other measures?
4. Has there been any amendment since last year to your legislation, regulations or other measures?

These four questions were applied to three areas of policy, requiring 12 answers altogether. The first area of policy was the direct concern of Article IV with the national application of the prohibitions in Article I. The second and third policy areas related to export and import controls, respectively

[12] France, Law No 72-467, Prohibiting the development, production, possession, stockpiling, acquisition and transfer of biological or toxin weapons, 9 June 1972. It is reproduced in SIPRI, *The Problem of Chemical and Biological Warfare*, vol. 3, *CBW and the Law of War* (Almqvist & Wiksell: Stockholm, 1973), pp. 178–79. The series is available on a CD-ROM, which is described at URL <http://editors.sipri.se/cd.cbw.html>.

[13] First Review Conference document BWC/CONF.I/4, 20 Feb. 1980, para. 30, pp. 17–18.

[14] Sims (note 9), pp. 81–85.

[15] Isaacs, J., 'Legislative needs', ed. S. Wright, *Preventing a Biological Arms Race* (MIT Press: Cambridge, Mass., 1990), pp. 291–99, and legislative texts appended at pp. 406–11.

[16] Goldblat and Bernauer (note 8), pp. 23–24. All emphases added.

[17] Third Review Conference document BWC/CONF.III/22/Add.2, 27 Sep. 1991, pp. 4–5, 7.

('the export and import of micro-organisms pathogenic to man, animals or plants, or of toxins, in accordance with the Convention'). These controls were of particular concern to the UK, which successfully proposed their addition to a CBM that would otherwise have been limited to making more universal and peremptory the invitations issued in 1980 and 1986.

In addition, the Third Review Conference stated that, from 15 April 1992, parties to the BTWC under CBM E 'shall be prepared to submit copies of the legislation or regulations or written details of other measures on request to the UN Department for Disarmament Affairs or to an individual State Party'.[18] Each party could now request these details bilaterally under the authority of the Third Review Conference, instead of depending solely upon the circulation of texts made available to the United Nations.

Future regime-building work in this area is likely initially to consist of the organization of a coherent international response to the replies elicited by CBM E. The areas to be dealt with might include: policy for addressing 'defaulters' (i.e., non-respondents); queries to parties which conscientiously file a nil return as to why they have no legislation, regulations or other measures to report; annual reminders (via the annual reporting requirement) to encourage more parties to legislate in this area; and concerted attempts at the application of 'quality control' to national implementation measures.

There may also be a loophole to be closed in order to ensure that the penal legislation enacted or other measures taken by parties is as comprehensive as possible. The USA already asserts, in respect of an offence under its Biological Weapons Anti-Terrorism Act, 'extraterritorial Federal jurisdiction over an offense under this section committed by or against a national of the United States'.[19] In its Final Declaration, the Third Review Conference restated the convention formula that any national implementation measures taken in accordance with Article IV 'should apply within the territory of a State Party, under its jurisdiction or under its control, *anywhere*'.[20] The extended formulation (compared to 1986) was restored at Ukraine's request. On a US initiative, the review conference invited 'each State Party to consider, if constitutionally possible and in conformity with international law, the application of such measures to actions taken anywhere by natural persons possessing its nationality'.[21]

This formulation corresponds closely to paragraph 1(c) of Article VII in the national implementation provisions of the 1993 Chemical Weapons Convention. The USA is not the only state whose legislation contains an extraterritorial provision. A German working paper issued during the Third Review Conference described the German War Weapons Control Act of 5 November 1990, which emphasizes *inter alia* that its 'penal provisions not only apply in Germany, but also to acts committed abroad by natural persons possessing German nationality'.[22]

The German working paper foreshadowed the new CBM and was of particular interest for its comprehensive account of national legislative and administra-

---

[18] Third Review Conference document BWC/CONF.III/22/Add.3, 27 Sep. 1991, pp. 18–19.
[19] Section 175(a) is reproduced in Goldblat and Bernauer (note 8), p. 71.
[20] BWC/CONF.III/22/Add.2 (note 17), p. 4, emphasis added.
[21] The Ukrainian proposal is reproduced at page 20 and the US proposal at page 21 of Third Review Conference document BWC/CONF.III/17, 24 Sep. 1991.
[22] Germany, Working Paper: legislation in the Federal Republic of Germany on the prohibition of biological weapons, Third Review Conference document BWC/CONF.III/7, 10 Sep. 1991, p. 3.

tive measures against BTW and for its description of an entire regulatory framework embracing export controls, lists of pathogens and the War Weapons Control Act, including its supporting ordinances and schedules. This example of a full national report could establish a benchmark for other parties to emulate in describing the national implementation measures they have taken as a regulatory framework.

Initially, however, the legislation reported under CBM E was not extensive or (save in one or two cases) particularly informative. By 1 June 1992, fewer than 20 parties had taken note of this new CBM even to the extent of ticking a 'Nothing to declare' box on the cover sheet; even fewer had completed Form E or made an equivalent declaration.[23]

Several parties were able to report that they had legislated or regulated in respect of the three matters addressed by this CBM (i.e., export and import controls, and Article IV national implementation of the Article I obligations).[24] The level of detail varied greatly. Hungary, the Netherlands and New Zealand offered the titles of relevant laws and regulations; Australia presented a three-page description of seven different legal instruments (adding that it was currently considering the imposition of export controls on dual-use biological equipment as well, already the subject of non-statutory guidelines); and the United States reproduced 30 pages of texts and supporting documents. Finland, Germany (which had reported fully in 1991), Mongolia and the United Kingdom simply ticked the appropriate 'yes' boxes, with the UK adding a mention of its Biological Weapons Act under another CBM.[25] Canada stated that: 'Under current legislation, Canada regulates or has the capacity to regulate' all three matters, but it did not expand on that statement, in contrast to the detail it provided elsewhere in the 52 pages of its CBM declarations.[26]

Austria and Belarus reported that they had legislation under review and might have more information to provide later; Sweden and Switzerland presented legislation and regulations on the national implementation of obligations but not on export or import controls.[27] Norway stated that both legislation and regulations on export controls would probably be introduced by the end of 1992; legislation and regulations on the other two matters were already in place.[28] Japan had legislated on everything except import controls.[29] Bulgaria offered a detailed narrative, including long lists of pathogenic strains kept in its national microbial collection and those provided in 1989–91 to foreign laboratories, as well as the relevant provisions in its domestic legislation and penal code. It added that these provisions were currently under examination in the light of other countries' legislation.[30]

---

[23] UN Department for Disarmament Affairs document DDA/4-92/BWIII, 30 Apr. 1992, and Add.1, 12 June 1992.

[24] DDA/4-92/BWIII (note 23), pp. 19–21 (Australia), p. 124 (Germany), p. 137 (Mongolia), p. 148 (New Zealand), p. 245 (the UK), pp. 364–94 (the USA), Add. 1, p. 53 (Finland), p. 65 (Hungary), and p. 94 (the Netherlands).

[25] DDA/4-92/BWIII (note 23), p. 246.

[26] DDA/4-92/BWIII (note 23), p. 77.

[27] DDA/4-92/BWIII (note 23), p. 25 (Austria), p. 181 (Sweden), p. 210 (Switzerland), and Add.1, p. 23 (Belarus).

[28] DDA/4-92/BWIII (note 23), p. 167 (Norway).

[29] DDA/4-92/BWIII/Add.1 (note 23), p. 70 (Japan).

[30] DDA/4-92/BWIII/Add.1 (note 23), pp. 35–37 (Bulgaria).

The Fourth Review Conference underlined the importance of Article IV, reaffirmed the commitment to taking 'the necessary national measures' and added recognition of 'the need to ensure, through the review and/or adoption of national measures, the effective fulfilment of their obligations under the Convention in order, *inter alia*, to exclude use of biological and toxin weapons in terrorist or criminal activity'.[31] This addition followed a recommendation from the G8 (the Group of Seven leading industrialized nations, plus Russia) Ministerial Conference on Terrorism, held in Paris on 30 July 1996.[32]

Article IV may be further strengthened by a corresponding provision which the Ad Hoc Group has included in the rolling text of the BTWC protocol as draft Article X (National Implementation Measures). It would be legally binding and would consolidate the progressive reinforcement of the 1980, 1986, 1991 and 1996 review conferences.

V. Consultation and cooperation: Article V

A system of compliance diplomacy depends upon the willingness of the parties to a treaty to engage in problem-solving activities. They must be ready to demonstrate their full compliance with the treaty obligations in such a manner as to generate reassurance, resolve ambiguities and allay suspicion. The health of the treaty regime will depend on this aspect of its regime of compliance. Article V obliges parties to consult and cooperate and is therefore important to the evolution of the BTWC treaty regime. The extent of those obligations, the procedures that can be elaborated, and the mechanisms which can be made available by clarification of Article V will determine its regime-building potential.

Article V does not distinguish between bilateral and multilateral problem-solving, but its first sentence has been understood as initially prescribing bilateral diplomacy: 'The States Parties to this Convention undertake to consult one another and to cooperate in solving any problems which may arise in relation to the objective of, or in the application of the provisions of, the Convention.' The second sentence is more clearly multilateral in its intent: 'Consultation and cooperation pursuant to this article may also be undertaken through appropriate international procedures within the framework of the United Nations and in accordance with its Charter.' Most regime-building efforts have focused on multilateral cooperation, which is discussed in section VI. Bilateral cooperation is addressed in section VIII.

VI. The multilateral dimension of Article V

The interpretation by the second and third review conferences of multilateral consultation and cooperation built on foundations laid in 1980 when the First Review Conference pioneered the clarification of Article V.[33] Working out the implications of that first clarification and filling in the procedural gaps in the contingency mechanism that was created has been a slow process. This has

---

[31] Fourth Review Conference document BWC/CONF.IV/9, 6 Dec. 1996, p. 17.

[32] Dando, M. R. and Pearson, G. S., 'The Fourth Review Conference of the Biological and Toxin Weapons Convention: issues, outcomes, and unfinished business', *Politics and the Life Sciences*, vol. 16, no. 1 (Mar. 1997), p. 118.

[33] A detailed account of the 1980 clarification of Article V is given in Sims (note 9), pp. 168–225.

been, in part, because of the need to establish consensus and, in part, because of concern associated with the process, particularly in its early years. Governments did not want to be put at a political disadvantage or become enmeshed in new procedures or institutions.

This latter consideration probably explains Soviet resistance in 1980 to the Swedish proposal that multilateral compliance diplomacy under Article V should be institutionalized in a Consultative Committee of Experts. This would have been a standing contingency mechanism, to be activated when needed by the UN Secretary-General and chaired by him or his representative, with every state party having the right to designate an expert. It was modelled on Article V of the 1977 Enmod Convention.[34] By 1980 the provisions of Article V of the Enmod Convention had not been invoked (nor have they since), and the concept of a Consultative Committee of Experts remains untried.

Article V of the Enmod Convention was also weaker than the concept originally proposed for it by the Netherlands and Sweden.[35] Sweden was therefore anxious to ensure that a similar body for the BTWC should be at least as strong as the Enmod Convention's Consultative Committee of Experts. At the First Review Conference Sweden and other neutral and non-aligned (NNA) states, together with several NATO members—notably, Canada—pursued the goal of instituting a Consultative Committee of Experts. They were only partially successful in 1980, and the group had to moderate its aims because the Soviet Union and its allies opposed the plan while the UK and the USA were unenthusiastic for this particular way of institutionalizing compliance diplomacy. Nonetheless, the 1980 Final Declaration stated: 'The Conference, noting the concerns and differing views expressed on the adequacy of Article V, believes that this question should be further considered at an appropriate time.'[36] In 1991 a similar proposal for a BTWC Consultative Committee of Experts modelled on the Enmod Convention was made by the UNIDIR experts Goldblat and Bernauer.[37]

On 20 March 1980, however, the First Review Conference *did* approve a contingency mechanism in which all parties could participate. A proposal was made by the British delegation to elaborate on the 'appropriate international procedures' formula in the second sentence of Article V. The agreed text read: 'These procedures include, *inter alia*, the right of any State Party subsequently to request that a consultative meeting open to all States Parties be convened at expert level'.[38] The 'British clause', based on an academic paper,[39] avoided the word 'committee' while preserving the essence of a consultative meeting at expert level open to all parties. It tied this new contingency mechanism to the

[34] The Enmod Convention was based on an earlier US–Soviet initiative and negotiated largely in a working group of the Conference of the Committee on Disarmament in 1976. The text of the Convention on the Prohibition of Military or Any Other Hostile Use of Environmental Modification Techniques, opened for signature at Geneva 18 May 1977, entered into force 5 October 1978, can be accessed from the United Nations Treaty Series Internet web site at URL <http://www.un.org/Depts/Treaty/collection/series/search3.htm>.

[35] The original proposal was for a Consultative Committee of Experts which would meet regularly, for continuous supervision of the Enmod Convention. After tough negotiation in the CCD Working Group the most that could be agreed was a contingency mechanism that would be used only in a crisis situation.

[36] BWC/CONF.I/9 (note 5).

[37] Goldblat and Bernauer (note 8), pp. 25–26.

[38] BWC/CONF.I/9 (note 5).

[39] Sims, N. A., 'Prospects for the Biological Weapons Convention review conference', Jan. 1980, Memorandum subsequently published by the University of Sussex Armament and Disarmament Information Unit in *ADIU Report*, vol. 2, no. 1 (Mar. 1980), pp. 6–7.

'appropriate international procedures' formula in Article V, which had been commended in earlier (Soviet-drafted) paragraphs of the Final Declaration.

This identification of a specific procedure was a modest advance but the most that could be achieved at the First Review Conference. It was little noticed outside Geneva, and its significance was generally regarded as slight. The United States declined to use it in the case of the Sverdlovsk incident,[40] preferring bilateral démarches. Although this diplomatic breakthrough was underrated, it served as the basis for a more substantial procedure that was devised and agreed in the second and third review conferences. In addition, this clarification of the possibilities open to parties under Article V was included when Norway submitted a follow-up resolution on the First Review Conference to the UN General Assembly.[41]

In 1986 the Second Review Conference again referred to 'appropriate international procedures', reproducing the 1980 language with the omission of the word 'subsequently', which had proved ambiguous.[42] The new text read: 'confirms the conclusion in the Final Declaration of the First Review Conference that these procedures include, *inter alia*, the right of any State Party to request that a consultative meeting open to all States Parties be convened at expert level'.[43]

Attempts were made to strengthen the contingency mechanism established by the First Review Conference because it had not been deemed usable since its creation six and one-half years earlier. The section of the Final Declaration which aimed to remedy the problem was based on a longer draft submitted by Sweden.[44] It read:

The Conference, taking into account views expressed concerning the need to strengthen the implementation of the provisions of Article V, has agreed:

– that a consultative meeting shall be promptly convened when requested by a State Party,

– that a consultative meeting may consider any problems which may arise in relation to the objective of, or in the application of the provisions of the Convention, suggest ways and means for further clarifying, *inter alia*, with assistance of technical experts, any matter considered ambiguous or unresolved, as well as initiate appropriate international procedures within the framework of the United Nations and in accordance with its Charter,

– that the consultative meeting, or any State Party, may request specialized assistance in solving any problems which may arise in relation to the objective of, or in the application of the provisions of, the Convention, through, *inter alia*, appropriate international procedures within the framework of the United Nations and in accordance with its Charter,

---

[40] The Sverdlovsk incident refers to the suspicious 1979 release of anthrax in Sverdlovsk (now Yekaterinburg). Questions were raised about the origin of the anthrax and whether it was evidence of an offensive Soviet biological warfare programme. See also section XI in chapter 1, section VIII in this chapter and section III in chapter 4 in this volume.

[41] UN General Assembly Resolution 35/144A, 12 Dec. 1980.

[42] Note 5. In this case, too, credit is due to the Australian delegation for using its chairmanship of the 1986 Drafting Committee to remove a word which had accidentally been inserted into the 1980 Final Declaration. The ambiguity of 'subsequently' (which 'may have conveyed the notion that no action should be taken automatically') was criticized by, among others, Goldblat and Bernauer (note 8), p. 16.

[43] BWC/CONF.II/13/II (note 6), p. 5.

[44] BWC/CONF.II/9 (note 7), p. 21.

The Conference considers that States Parties shall co-operate with the consultative meeting in its consideration of any problems which may arise in relation to the objective of, or in the application of the provisions of the Convention, and in clarifying ambiguous and unresolved matters, as well as co-operate in appropriate international procedures within the framework of the United Nations and in accordance with its Charter.[45]

This new text strengthened the contingency mechanism by assuring potential users that the consultative meeting would convene promptly with wide terms of reference and that the parties could request specialized assistance, suggest ways and means for further clarifying any matter considered ambiguous or unresolved, and initiate other procedures.

Regime building in the Article V sector of the regime of compliance had made considerable progress in 1980–86. However, there was still no agreement on the convening or chairing of the consultative meeting, and explicit mention was not made of the need for it to have fact-finding powers. Sweden and the UK had emphasized this as vital at the First Review Conference.[46] Barend ter Haar commented on the 1986 text that 'it was not clear how the consultative meeting would make its decisions. If the initiation of an investigation would have to be decided by consensus, the veto power would in fact have proliferated to all powers'.[47] The decision-making procedure remained unresolved in 1986.

The Final Declaration addressed the duty of parties to cooperate with the consultative meeting by introducing an *expectation* if not *obligation* (a distinction drawn by Marie Isabelle Chevrier[48]) for a state party whose compliance had been questioned to be represented.[49] This language was stronger than the 'open to all States Parties' language of 1980. The consultative meeting would still not necessarily be a meeting *of* all parties (the unadopted 1980 formula which had been changed in the 'British clause' to the words 'open to all States Parties') since attendance could not be guaranteed. Chevrier concluded in her analysis of the 1980 and 1986 texts that: 'The Final Declaration agreements go a long way to clarify the vague language of Article V. Nevertheless, they do not satisfy the goals of many reformers. That an *expectation* to co-operate with an investigation is created does not mean that an *obligation* to co-operate is established.'[50]

There had earlier been support for the UN Secretary-General (although not the depositary for the BTWC) to be the convener, if not the chairman, of the consultative meeting. By the Third Review Conference in 1991 there was instead a consensus in favour of addressing requests to the depositaries (the UK, the USA and the USSR).[51] In 1986 the United Kingdom had co-sponsored (with Canada, France, the Federal Republic of Germany, Norway, Spain and Turkey)[52] a proposal to designate the Secretary-General as the recipient of such

[45] BWC/CONF.II/13/II (note 6), pp. 5–6.

[46] Lidgard, C., Sweden, BWC/CONF.I/SR.12, 21 Mar. 1980, paras 24–25; and Summerhayes, D. M., UK, BWC/CONF.I/SR.12, para. 22.

[47] ter Haar, B., Center for Strategic and International Studies (CSIS), *The Future of Biological Weapons*, Washington Paper no. 151 (Praeger: New York, 1991), p. 34.

[48] Chevrier, M. I., 'Impediment to proliferation? Analysing the Biological Weapons Convention', *Contemporary Security Policy*, vol. 16, no. 2 (Aug. 1995), p. 86.

[49] 'The Conference considers that States Parties shall co-operate with the consultative meeting . . .' BWC/CONF.II/13/II (note 6), pp. 5–6.

[50] Chevrier (note 48), emphasis in original.

[51] Goldblat and Bernauer (note 8), p. 25.

[52] BWC/CONF.II/9 (note 7), p. 18.

requests; it now returned to its earlier preference for requests go to depositaries. In 1980 it would have been inconceivable that the three depositaries could have been so designated as a collectivity. The NNA states preferred to designate the Secretary-General (based on the precedent set by the Enmod Convention), and relations between the Soviet Union and the other depositaries were too frosty to engender confidence in joint action. On British initiative, the possibility was left open that, if the request were made to *depositaries* (the definite article was purposely omitted), just one depositary might be in a position to act. It might even have to convene a consultative meeting to consider a compliance dispute between the other two depositaries.[53] The Final Declaration of the Third Review Conference stated that it:

reaffirms the agreement reached at the Second Review Conference, and agrees that in order to strengthen the implementation of the provisions of Article V the following provisions should be adopted:

– A formal consultative meeting could be preceded by bilateral or other consultations by agreement among those States Parties involved in the problems which had arisen;

– Requests for the convening of a consultative meeting shall be addressed to the Depositaries, who shall immediately inform all States Parties of the request and shall convene within 30 days an informal meeting of the interested States Parties to discuss the arrangements for the formal consultative meeting, which shall be convened within 60 days of receipt of the request;

– With regard to the taking of decisions, the consultative meeting shall proceed in accordance with rule 28 of the rules of procedure of the Review Conference;

– The costs of the consultative meeting shall be met by the States Parties participating in accordance with the United Nations assessment scale prorated to take into account differences between the United Nations membership and the number of States Parties participating in the meeting;[54]

Paragraphs from the 1986 Final Declaration were repeated,[55] and a reference to the UN Secretary-General was inserted between the last two of those paragraphs: 'the States Parties agree that, should the consultative meeting, or any State Party, make use of such procedures within the framework of the United Nations, including lodging a complaint with the Security Council under Article VI of the Convention, the Secretary-General may be kept informed'.[56] This last insertion is of doubtful value because, since it is not a state party, the consultative meeting does not have the option to use Article VI. Should a party use it, the Secretary-General can hardly fail to be aware of the fact, given the range of his responsibilities under the UN Charter, which include the secretaryship of the Security Council.

Both the 1986 and the 1991 texts refer often to 'appropriate international procedures within the framework of the United Nations and in accordance with its Charter' without the prefatory adjective 'other'. This may be an inadvertent omission, but it suggests by default that the consultative meeting is regarded as deriving its legitimacy exclusively from successive review conferences. However, in 1980 and 1986 it had been identified as one among several possible

[53] Sims (note 9), pp. 193, 202.
[54] BWC/CONF.III/22/Add.2 (note 17), pp. 8–9.
[55] BWC/CONF.II/13/II (note 6), pp. 5–6.
[56] BWC/CONF.III/22/Add.2 (note 17), pp. 8–9.

Article V 'appropriate international procedures'. Its implied autonomy from the legal category cited in Article V weakens that original conceptual linkage.[57] While it is encouraging that a mechanism which was first identified in 1980 has become securely established as part of the treaty regime and been carried forward from one review to the next through successive stages of elaboration, it can be questioned whether there has been some loss of constitutional rectitude.

The costs formula in the fourth of the newly agreed paragraphs also raises concerns. If *only* 'the States Parties participating', and no others, have to pay for a consultative meeting, this creates a further incentive for governments not to become involved. It would be better to make all parties to the BTWC pay.

These criticisms apart, the 1991 text (which was substantially reaffirmed but not extended in 1996[58]) represents a further stage in the cumulative elaboration of the contingency mechanism based on the 1980 clarification of Article V. It should be more difficult now than it was in 1980 for a government to criticize this procedure on the grounds that it is too nebulous. The procedure still lacks details on chairmanship and fact-finding, but it is more concrete than before. In 1997 it was invoked for the first time, as recounted in section VII.

VII. The Article V contingency mechanism in action: *Thrips palmi* in Cuba

Until 1997 it was impossible to evaluate the adequacy of the contingency mechanism, because no party to the BTWC had invoked it. It had been available in its essential form since 1980 and in its current state since 1991. The basic element established by the First Review Conference was a consultative meeting at expert level, open to all parties, to be convened at the request of any party with compliance concerns, and defined as one of the 'appropriate international procedures' for cooperation and consultation under Article V. As noted above, the second and fourth review conferences consolidated the procedural advances of 1980 and 1991. They added a more explicit fact-finding mandate, an emphasis on the obligation to cooperate in resolving compliance concerns, a procedure for convening the consultative meeting, decision-making rules and time limits. These provided for an informal essentially procedural meeting to be held within 30 days—and the formal consultative meeting within 60 days—of the invocation of the contingency mechanism.

The First Review Conference had been deadlocked over whether depositaries should be authorized collectively or individually to convene the consultative meeting. The Second Review Conference was inclined to entrust this function to the UN Secretary-General (although its Final Declaration did not address the issue). The third and fourth review conferences formally committed the convening responsibility to the depositaries. Accordingly, the depositaries activated the contingency mechanism after Cuba invoked it on 30 June 1997.

[57] Sims, N. A., 'Consultative committees as "appropriate international procedures" in disarmament-related treaties', *Transnational Perspectives* (Geneva), vol. 4, nos 1–2 (1978), pp. 15–19; and Sims (note 39).
[58] BWC/CONF.IV/9 (note 31), pp. 18–19.

The nature of the compliance concern

A compliance concern arose from Cuban suspicions that two events were causally connected: an overflight of Cuba on 21 October 1996 by an aeroplane, registered to the US State Department, in transit from Florida to Grand Cayman, and the appearance of the first signs of a crop infestation by the insect *Thrips palmi* (palm thrips) in Cuba, which was detected on 18 December 1996. The *Thrips palmi* infestation had spread to the whole of western Cuba by the time Cuba made its suspicions public in two letters to the United Nations Secretary-General.[59]

From the outset there was uncertainty over three factors of significance for the establishment of a causal connection between the two events. The first was the number of reproductive cycles of the insect which had occurred before the *Thrips palmi* population was detected on 18 December; this affected determining the date of infestation. The second factor was the likelihood of the infestation having been caused by natural forces, such as insects being carried by the wind from other Caribbean islands or Florida. The third element was the content and purpose of an emission from the US aeroplane which had been interpreted by Cuban observers as spraying, but which the USA claimed had been warning smoke generated for safety purposes, because the pilot had wanted to make his presence known.

The only certainties were that something had been emitted by a US aeroplane while overflying Cuba on an approved flight path (the Giron air corridor) on 21 October 1996, and that a *Thrips palmi* infestation of crops in western Cuba had occurred before 18 December 1996, when it was first detected.

The early stages of the complaint process

Cuba formally invoked Article V on 30 June 1997. It approached the Russian Federation and requested that a consultative meeting be convened in accordance with the procedures agreed at the third and fourth review conferences.

Russia held informal consultations with the other two depositaries in the margins of the BTWC Ad Hoc Group, which held its seventh session in Geneva on 14 July–1 August 1997. Russia then circulated a note to the parties which had deposited their instruments of ratification or accession in Moscow, informing them of Cuba's request. The next stage of the multilateral procedure, the informal meeting of parties, was set for 31 July 1997.

Upon receiving the Russian notification, the UK and the USA sent equivalent notes to the parties which had deposited their instruments of ratification or accession in London and Washington, respectively. In this way every party received at least one notification. The triple-depositary mechanism achieved its original purpose of ensuring universality within the convention, irrespective of cold-war era or other problems of recognition.

---

[59] UN document A/52/128, 29 Apr. 1997; and UN document A/52/213, 27 June 1997. The US version of events was presented on 6 May: 'Transcript: State Department noon briefing, May 6, 1997', *Washington File* (United States Information Service, US Embassy: Stockholm, 7 May 1997), URL <http://www.sis.usemb.se/wireless/300/eur303.htm>. According to the State Department, the aeroplane flew over Cuba on its way to Bogotá via Grand Cayman Island. Wright, S., 'Cuba case tests treaty', *Bulletin of the Atomic Scientists*, vol. 53, no. 6 (Nov./Dec. 1997), p. 18.

A simple procedural meeting was held on 31 July 1997 to agree arrangements for the Formal Consultative Meeting of States Parties to the Convention. Decision-making rules and time limits had been laid down in the contingency mechanism as elaborated in 1991. The Formal Consultative Meeting had to be held within 60 days from invocation of the mechanism. It was scheduled for 25–27 August 1997, and the United Kingdom was chosen to chair the meeting. On 8 August the depositaries issued a note to all parties confirming the arrangements agreed on 31 July.

The Formal Consultative Meeting of the States Parties to the Convention

Three sessions of the Formal Consultative Meeting were held under the chairmanship of Ambassador Ian Soutar of the UK, and 74 parties and 3 signatory-only states participated. Surprisingly, in view of where the incident had occurred, the western hemisphere was represented only by 12 parties (Argentina, Belize, Brazil, Canada, Chile, Colombia, Ecuador, Mexico, Panama, Peru, Uruguay and Venezuela), in addition to Cuba and the United States, and by no Caribbean islands other than Cuba.

Cuba and the USA were given 30 minutes each for their statements. Deputy Minister of Foreign Affairs Maria Florez represented Cuba, and Acting Assistant Director of ACDA Ambassador Donald Mahley represented the USA.

At its first session, the Formal Consultative Meeting elected six vice-chairmen, one each from Africa, Asia, North America, South America, Eastern Europe and Western Europe. They were the ambassadors or other representatives of Nigeria, Iran, Canada, Brazil, the Russian Federation and the Netherlands. All these states had been parties to the BTWC for many years. (The Netherlands had been a party since 1981, and the other five states were original parties to the convention.) The election of these six vice-chairmen determined the composition of the Bureau of the Formal Consultative Meeting, which played an important role later in the application of this consultative mechanism.

In the words of the official report: 'The meeting heard statements by the delegation of Cuba and the delegation of the United States, the texts of which were circulated to all States Parties participating in the meeting. Both delegations then made a further statement amplifying points raised in their formal statements.'[60]

Cuba based its case on assertions that the timing and location of the first insect infestation (calculated from when it was detected on 18 December 1996) coincided exactly with the overflight; that there was no other way the insect could have arrived in Cuba; and that the US arguments, that the aeroplane had emitted smoke to signal its presence to a nearby Cuban aeroplane, were false since the US aircraft was not normally equipped to do so and it was not a normal procedure.

The USA responded that the coincidence of time and location could not be proven; that the spread of this and other insects through the Caribbean region followed a similar pattern and was often either wind-borne or caused by the import of goods; and that the US aeroplane which overflew Cuba on 21 October

---

[60] Formal Consultative Meeting of States Parties to the Convention document BWC/CONS/1, 27 Aug. 1997, para. 3.

1996 had standard smoke-emission equipment, used it regularly and, on that flight, did not have the necessary equipment fitted to spray anything else.

Both Cuba and the USA agreed that the US aeroplane had received clearance from the Cuban authorities for its flight path and that a substance of some kind had been released from it while it flew over Cuba. The official report noted:

In subsequent discussion, States Parties welcomed the fact that the delegations of Cuba and [the] United States had sought to clarify their positions with regard to the concerns raised by the Government of Cuba. States Parties noted that the consultation was fully in conformity with the conclusions of the final document of the Third Review Conference relevant to the application of Article V of the Convention. A number of States Parties, however, considered that in the time available the meeting had not fully been able to resolve all matters considered ambiguous or unresolved arising from the request of the Government of Cuba. A number of other States Parties considered that the obligation to consult and cooperate in relation to any problems which might arise in relation to the objective of, or in the application of the provisions of, the Convention had been fulfilled by the holding of the formal consultative meeting.[61]

It was therefore agreed that by 27 September the parties who wished to do so should submit to the chairman their 'observations, including from national technical experts' on the information provided by the governments of Cuba and the United States. The chairman and the vice-chairmen, together, would consult on the basis of the information supplied at the August meeting and by the additional submissions in order, as far as possible, to clarify and resolve any outstanding issues related to the concerns raised by Cuba. The chairman was to report in writing on these consultations to all parties by 31 December 1997. (He and the vice-chairmen continued to hold office until 31 December 1997.)

Procedural options

The Formal Consultative Meeting broke new ground as it decided the time limit for receiving observations and what should be done (and at what pace) with the observations submitted by interested states parties. The Third Review Conference had left those matters unspecified, presumably in the hope that the Formal Consultative Meeting would clarify ambiguities and resolve the compliance concerns which had led to invocation of the mechanism.

However, the three sessions on 25–27 August 1997 did not suffice, and further procedures had to be devised. These included the 27 September and 31 December deadlines noted above and the requirement that the bureau meet at least once between those two dates. (It met on 7 October, 27 November and 15 December.)

Interestingly, the Formal Consultative Meeting did not take up two of the options offered by the Third Review Conference to 'initiate appropriate international procedures within the framework of the United Nations and in accordance with its Charter' and to 'request specialized assistance in solving any problems that may arise', although the reference to 'observations, including from national technical experts' is similar to the phrase 'assistance of technical

---

[61] BWC/CONS/1 (note 60), para. 4.

experts' in the Final Declaration of the Third Review Conference.[62] These were the procedural options open to the Formal Consultative Meeting. In addition, three procedural options were open to Cuba which it did not invoke.

First, Cuba might have pursued its concern at the UN General Assembly, and initially it submitted several documents to it. Second, Cuba could have gone to the UN Security Council with a complaint under Article VI of the BTWC. In the first instance, there was no obvious procedure in the General Assembly for Cuba to follow; in the Security Council the likelihood of a US veto would have curtailed consideration of the complaint. This might have proved politically embarrassing for the USA and given the Cuban concern wider publicity, but at the expense of politicizing the matter irretrievably. Third, Cuba might have considered invoking the 1925 Geneva Protocol.

Both Cuba and the United States are parties to the Geneva Protocol. Under a 1982 French resolution the UN Secretary-General is requested by the General Assembly 'to investigate, with the assistance of qualified experts, information that may be brought to his attention by any Member State concerning activities that may constitute a violation of the [Geneva P]rotocol or of the relevant rules of customary international law in order to ascertain thereby the facts of the matter, and promptly to report the results of any such investigation to all Member States and to the General Assembly'.[63]

Cuba chose not to avail itself of any of these options, so no United Nations organ became directly involved. The subsequent involvement of UN organs was at the discretion of the parties to the BTWC. The Formal Consultative Meeting could have gone to the United Nations but did not. Significantly, the communications that were submitted by the parties (in response to the invitation contained in paragraph 5 of the 27 August 1997 text) were addressed not to the Secretary of the Formal Consultative Meeting (the same official of the UN Secretariat who had served as Secretary-General of the 1996 Fourth Review Conference and Secretary of the Ad Hoc Group) but to its chairman, Ambassador Soutar, at the Permanent Representation of the UK to the Conference on Disarmament (CD).

The later stages of the complaint process

By the 27 September 1997 deadline, Soutar had received submissions from 13 parties (fewer than 10 per cent of the total). Their content is analysed below.

Ambassador Soutar convened a meeting of the Bureau of the Formal Consultative Meeting on 7 October. They decided to send the 11 new submissions to the Cuban and US governments and 'enquire whether, in their view, the further submissions had assisted in clarifying or resolving the concerns raised by Cuba'. They also extended the process of consultation in respect of those two governments by making clear that the chairman 'was available, if they

---

[62] There would have been a logical problem in having the Formal Consultative Meeting initiate 'appropriate international procedures' since it is the central element in a contingency mechanism which itself constitutes the only 'appropriate international procedure' so far specifically defined as such (in 1980 and 1986) in the elaboration of Article V.

[63] UN General Assembly Resolution 37/98D, 13 Dec. 1982, para. 4.

wished, to meet their representatives to receive any further comments which they might wish to make'.[64] Soutar's report continued:

I subsequently received replies from Ambassador Mahley of the United States, dated 20 October, and from Ambassador Amat of Cuba, dated 22 October. . . . The former stated the view of the Government of the United States that no causal linkage between the infestation in Cuba and the overflight by a US aircraft has been demonstrated and that no further action on this issue was warranted or required. The latter stated the view of the Government of Cuba that the arguments put forward by the United States at the Formal Consultative Meeting were inadequate, lacking in objectivity and had done nothing to dispel the Cuban concerns. I also had a short meeting with the Deputy Minister of Foreign Affairs of Cuba, Señora Maria Florez, at her request, at which she reiterated that her Government continued to adhere to the suspicions which had given rise to the original complaint.[65]

The next meeting of the bureau, on 27 November 1997, was its most important. The agenda included the latest communications from Ambassador Mahley, Ambassador Carlos Amat and Deputy Minister Florez, as well as further examination of the information contained in the earlier submissions (i.e., the input from the 'national technical experts'). The conclusions of that meeting are discussed in the next subsection. A final meeting of the bureau was held on 15 December to agree on the chairman's report.

The conclusions of the bureau: fact-finding

The bureau was split between those who regarded the United States as fully exonerated and those who remained uncertain. In the words of the report: 'Some members of the Bureau stated that further examination in their capitals had confirmed their view that there was no causal link between the overflight of the US aircraft and the insect infestation in Cuba. Other members of the Bureau stated that the technical complexity of the issue and the lack of further detailed information made it impossible to draw any definitive conclusions.'[66]

The submissions received strongly favoured the first view—exoneration of the United States—because there was no causal link between the overflight and the infestation. Japan 'could not identify any relationship'. Australia found no 'sufficient evidence of a causal link'. Canada, whose submission included an analysis of the entomological and epidemiological literature on *Thrips palmi*, concluded that the evidence 'does not support the Cuban allegation of biological aggression', and New Zealand stated that the allegation 'can not be substantiated'.

Even stronger in support of US innocence were the conclusions of four European states. Hungary stated that its Ministry of Foreign Affairs:

is of the view that the Government of the United States of America provided for consideration by all delegations in the [Formal Consultative] Meeting factual, relevant and accurate information about both the actions of the American Aircraft transiting Cuban

---

[64] Report of the Chairman, contained in a letter to the states parties from the CD Permanent Representation of the UK, 15 Dec. 1997, para. 4. Statements by individual countries in this and subsequent subsections are from the Report of the Chairman unless otherwise specified.

[65] Report of the Chairman . . . (note 64), para. 5.

[66] Report of the Chairman . . . (note 64), para. 6.

airspace on 21 October 1996, as well as several reasoned and logical scenarios about how insect infestations of the kind described by the Cuban Government could have occurred on the island. The Ministry of Foreign Affairs believes that the material presented by the Government of the United States of America was comprehensive and demonstrates that the American Aircraft did not dispense *Thrips palmi* over the territory of the Republic of Cuba. Therefore, the Ministry of Foreign Affairs sees no link between the overflight and the infestation.

Denmark expressed the opinion that:

it has been convincingly argued that the United States aircraft in question could not have dispersed live insects. The United States' explanation of why the US pilot released smoke is credible and consistent with the observations of the pilot of the Cuban aircraft. Similarly, the United States has convincingly demonstrated that the occurrence of *Thrips palmi* in the Matanzas province of Cuba in late 1996 could have resulted from a number of causes including natural phenomena as well as the normal movement of trade and goods. In the light of the above, we find the available evidence sufficiently well-documented and credible to indicate beyond reasonable doubt that the infestation of *Thrips palmi* in Cuba was unrelated to the United States aircraft in question.

Germany responded: 'insects such as *Thrips palmi* couldn't be dispersed from an aircraft as dry substance, in a way that would correspond to the described picture of "spraying and sprinkling unknown substances"; the insects would drown after having been dispersed in a liquid; the dispersion of eggs of insects in a liquid is in principle possible to a limited extent, but would make no sense in the case in question because *Thrips palmi* places its eggs in living plant tissue needed for its metamorphosis'. Germany concluded that: 'after a thorough examination of the arguments put forward by both sides . . . on the basis of the available evidence there is no relationship between the observed overflight of the US aircraft in question and the infestation of *Thrips palmi* in Cuba'.

The Netherlands, 'having further studied the submission of the United States in America, considers it to be established adequately that it has not been possible for the US aircraft in question to have dispersed live insects *Thrips palmi Karny*, while flying over Cuban territory on its way from Florida to the Cayman Islands. Also the reasons for the US aircraft for giving smoke signals are acceptable and in conformity with the observations made from the Cuban aircraft.' It concluded that: 'no causal link can be established between the above-mentioned events and that the infestation of Cuba with *Thrips Palmi Karny* is not related to the US aircraft overflying Cuban territory'.

With the exception of the Cuban response, only two submissions dissented. China listed five matters which had been 'clarified' (points which were uncontentious, apart possibly from the crucially significant 'possibility that *Thrips palmi* may spread through airflow' and the significance of its presence in Haiti, the Dominican Republic and Jamaica in proximity to Cuba) and three on which 'the Chinese experts find it hard to draw conclusions'. These were: (*a*) whether or not the US aircraft carried *Thrips palmi* when it overflew the Cuban air space on 21 October 1996; (*b*) whether or not the US aircraft sprayed *Thrips palmi* while overflying the Cuban air space; and (*c*) whether or not the *Thrips palmi* plague in Cuba was caused by the *Thrips palmi* sprayed from the US aircraft, or by the spread of the insect by other means.

The Democratic People's Republic of Korea (DPRK) had no doubts: 'It is regrettable that the incident of spraying of biological substances by the United States against Cuba has taken place. This delegation considers that the incident cannot be tolerated in the light of international laws and that this issue should be impartially addressed in any case'.

The bureau had to take into account this diversity of views. It may be assumed that within the bureau there was some resistance to declaring the USA unconditionally innocent on the facts available at that time, which may explain why some members found it 'impossible to draw any definitive conclusions'.[67] The report also noted: 'On the basis of the above, I wish to report to States Parties that, due *inter alia* to the technical complexity of the subject and to the passage of time, it has not proved possible to reach a definitive conclusion with regard to the concerns raised by the Government of Cuba.'[68]

The conclusions of the bureau: fulfilment of Article V requirements

Six respondents (Australia, Canada, Denmark, Germany, Hungary and Japan) stated that the requirements of Article V as regards the obligation to consult and cooperate had been fulfilled. Australia added that the procedures laid down for the Article V contingency mechanism 'have been properly and fully followed in response to Cuba's request for the procedures to be invoked'. For Canada and Japan explicitly, and for others by implication, no further action was warranted.

Three respondents disagreed. China ended its communication with the hope 'that the Bureau of the Formal Consultative Meeting will continue to consult together with Cuba and the United States to further explore ways to clarify and resolve any outstanding issues relating to the concern raised by Cuba'. Viet Nam, complaining that too little time had been allowed for study of the complex technical documentation 'provided by both sides', stated that it 'therefore would support the Bureau's follow-up role in further consulting States Parties and experts specialized in the field with a view to resolving the issue in a satisfactory manner'. North Korea called for a 'practical step' to be taken 'which will include forming an expert group and undertaking on-site inspection'. It recalled that 'During the Korean War in the 1950s, a large number of civilians and military servicemen suffered live [*sic*] death from the brutal atrocities of biological warfare by the United States in the DPRK. It was proven to be true by the on-site inspection of the International Inspection Group of that time'.

The bureau did not agree that further consultation was needed and proceeded to 'emphasize that there has been general agreement throughout the process that the requirements of Article V of the convention and of the consultative process established by the Third Review Conference have been fulfilled in an impartial and transparent manner'.[69]

[67] Report of the Chairman . . . (note 64), para. 6.
[68] Report of the Chairman . . . (note 64), para. 7.
[69] Report of the Chairman . . . (note 64), para. 8.

The conclusions of the bureau: the need for a protocol

Denmark expressed the belief 'that the experience of this use of these consultation mechanisms demonstrates the need for early agreement on a protocol to the Convention, which will establish an effective and permanent regime for dealing with any such issues and thereby strengthen compliance with the Convention'. Similar statements were made by the Netherlands and Germany, with the latter specifying a verification protocol.

Australia continued to support the Article V consultative processes developed at the review conferences while expressing interest in additional verification measures: 'Australia is fully supportive of the consultative processes. . . . We believe that it is in the interests of all States Parties to the BWC to ensure that these procedures are applied in the spirit and for the purposes for which they were intended. Given the limitations of the existing consultative mechanisms, we believe the current matter has underlined the need to develop clear mechanisms for dealing with, and satisfactorily resolving, concerns about compliance with the BWC. This reinforces the urgent need to develop an effective verification regime for the Convention.'

Although the bureau avoided making a premature identification of the protocol with verification (as opposed to a general 'strengthening' of the BTWC), it concurred with Australia, Denmark, Germany and the Netherlands: 'The Bureau agreed that the experience of conducting this process of consultation had shown the importance of establishing, as soon as possible, an effective protocol to strengthen the convention which is being negotiated in the Ad Hoc Group.'[70]

BTWC coverage of use

When Cuba alleged the *use* against it of a biological weapon the objection could have been made that its allegation was outside the range of activities prohibited in Article I. The prohibition of use had, controversially, been dropped in 1971 from the convention then being finalized.[71] However, the Third Review Conference had declared in its extensive interpretation of Article V and the procedures available under it that: 'The State Parties agree to consult, at the request of any State Party, regarding allegations of use or threat of use of bacteriological (biological) or toxin weapons'.[72]

The context of this part of the 1991 Final Declaration is the conduct by the UN Secretary-General of investigations into allegations of use. However, it is possible to regard this declaration as agreement that allegations of use or threat of use could be assimilated to the existing consultative procedure if questions of compliance are raised for multilateral consideration.

By 1997, when the Cuban allegations were made, there was even less reason to exclude use allegations from the Article V contingency mechanism. This was because, in 1996, the Fourth Review Conference had declared BTW use a breach of Article I.[73] This had been done in the context of an Iranian proposal

---

[70] Report of the Chairman . . . (note 64), para. 9.
[71] Sims, N., 'Biological disarmament: Britain's new posture', *New Scientist*, vol. 52 (2 Dec. 1971), pp. 18–20.
[72] BWC/CONF.III/22/Add.2 (note 17).
[73] BWC/CONF.IV/9 (note 31). See also section VI of chapter 7 in this volume.

for formal amendment of Article I and of the title of the convention (to add the ban on use). The 1996 Final Declaration had made explicit what had been logically implicit in Article I (use presupposes at least one prohibited activity, since BTW must have been developed, produced, stockpiled, acquired, retained or transferred before becoming available for use).

The 1996 text opened the way for allegations of use to be raised by states parties as 'problems which may arise in relation to the objective of, or in the application of the provisions of, the Convention'.[74] These problems under Article V are the subject matter of the obligation to consult and cooperate—and hence of the contingency mechanism developed through the final declarations of 1980, 1986 and 1991. The mechanism therefore *does* cover BTW use.

BTWC coverage of insect infestation

Denmark and the Netherlands expressed doubt, which other parties are known to have shared, over the question of whether insects or other pests such as *Thrips palmi* fall within the scope of the BTWC. Both states included statements that their participation in the consultative process was without prejudice to their national positions on this question.

Although insects as a class are not specifically named as possible vectors in the convention (as they are, for example, in Protocol III to the Revised Brussels Treaty of the Western European Union[75]), plague-carrying fleas—the 'classic' vectors of biological warfare which Japan used against China in the early 1940s—are covered by the language of Article I: 'weapons, equipment or means of delivery designed to use such prohibited agents or toxins for hostile purposes or in armed conflict'. However, insects which are destructive of crops, like *Thrips palmi*, without causing disease are far removed from the central concerns of the convention with microbiological agents (bacteria, viruses, fungi and rickettsiae) and toxins, and it is questionable whether they fall within its scope. They may have more in common with the concepts of environmental or economic warfare, if they are (as alleged by Cuba) susceptible to use for hostile purposes where deliberately introduced.

Infestation is not infection, and perhaps Cuba was legally mistaken in its invocation of any procedure under the BTWC. However, for the USA to have sought refuge in this argument would have been politically maladroit. It could easily have found itself accused of using a legal quibble to evade investigation. It was better to accept this use of the Article V contingency mechanism and produce a persuasive explanation to exonerate itself. There are, however, three arguments for regarding infestation by insects as falling within the boundaries of the convention. These arguments are persuasive but not conclusive.

First, there is the link with the Geneva Protocol. Article VIII of the BTWC states: 'Nothing in this Convention shall be interpreted as in any way limiting or detracting from the obligations assumed by any State under the [Geneva]

[74] Article V of the BTWC.

[75] Treaty for Collaboration in Economic, Social and Cultural Matters for Collective Self-defence (Brussels Treaty), opened for signature at Brussels on 17 March 1948, entered into force on 25 Aug. 1948, *United Nations Treaty Series*, vol. 19; and Protocols to the 1948 Brussels Treaty (Paris Agreements on the Western European Union), opened for signature at Paris on 23 October 1954, entered into force on 6 May 1955, *United Nations Treaty Series*, vol. 211.

Protocol'. These obligations had been defined by the UN General Assembly in 1969 (i.e., only two years before it commended the BTWC) as extending to any biological warfare agents 'which are intended to cause disease or death in man, animals or plants'.[76]

Second, there are indications that the authors of the convention originally intended to ban anti-crop BW and, from 1969, to encompass infestation equally with infection. Article I of the British draft convention of 10 July 1969 read: 'Each of the Parties to the Convention undertakes never in any circumstances, by making use for hostile purposes of microbial or other biological agents causing death or disease by infection or infestation in man, other animals, or crops, to engage in biological methods of warfare.'[77] Subsequent amendments left 'by infection or infestation' and the inclusion of 'crops' unchanged.[78]

The BTWC as finally negotiated had no equivalent to Article I of the 1969 draft convention and its successors. However, the negotiators in 1971 did not drop 'infestation' and keep 'infection'; instead both words disappeared along with the entire formulation from 1969. This was done out of solicitude for the Geneva Protocol, it being argued that a 'use clause' in the BTWC might detract from the authority of the Geneva Protocol by default.[79] The method of waging biological warfare was no longer specified, and thus it can only be assumed that actions preparatory to *both* infection and infestation are prohibited.

Third, the evolution of the treaty regime is, in fact, consistent with this supposition. The Third Review Conference reaffirmed: 'that the Convention prohibits the development, production, stockpiling, other acquisition or retention of microbial or other biological agents or toxins harmful to plants and animals, as well as humans, of types and in quantities that have no justification for prophylactic, protective or other peaceful purposes'.[80]

Plants were not mentioned in the final declarations of the first two review conferences. 'Other biological agents . . . harmful to plants' would appear to embrace insects harming plants by infestation; and the general purpose criterion ensures that, subject to establishing their types and quantities, their development, production, stockpiling, acquisition or retention, for any purpose other than prophylactic, protective or other peaceful purposes, must constitute a breach of the convention.

---

[76] UN General Assembly Resolution 2603A(XXIV), 16 Dec. 1969.

[77] ENDC/255 (note 2). Infestation was not mentioned in the UK's Working paper on microbiological warfare, Eighteen-Nation Disarmament Committee document ENDC/231, 6 Aug. 1968. However, it was mentioned (as 'crop-destroying insects such as locusts or Colorado beetles') by British Minister of State for Foreign and Commonwealth Affairs Frederick Mulley when he introduced ENDC/255: Mulley stated: 'The Convention is, of course, aimed at prohibiting the use for hostile purposes of disease-carrying microbes . . . However, it is possible to envisage the use in war of biological agents which are not microbes; hookworm, for instance, or the bilharzia worm, or even crop-destroying insects such as locusts or Colorado beetles.' Eighteen-Nation Disarmament Committee document ENDC/PV.418, 10 July 1969.

[78] ENDC/255/Rev.1 (note 3) made two changes to Article I: 'in man' became 'to man', and the words 'insofar as it may not already be committed in that respect under Treaties or other instruments in force prohibiting the use of chemical and biological methods of warfare' were inserted after 'Each of the Parties to the Convention undertakes'. 'Toxins' were added in CCD/255/Rev.2 (note 3).

[79] The argument, criticized in Sims (note 71), was that, despite Article VIII of the BTWC, any reference to *use* would highlight the ban on bacteriological methods of warfare in the Geneva Protocol to the detriment of its ban on chemical warfare, and that the latter would suffer a loss of authority by default.

[80] BWC/CONF.III/22/Add.2 (note 17), p. 3.

The future of the Article V contingency mechanism

Assuming that a compliance concern involving *Thrips palmi* can properly be handled within the BTWC, would it have benefited from a different procedure? The 'finding of fact' paragraph of the 15 December 1997 report cited 'the technical complexity of the subject' and 'the passage of time' as being among the reasons why it had been impossible to reach a definitive conclusion.[81] This sub-section discusses what might have been different under a new procedure, such as the protocol now being negotiated by the Ad Hoc Group.

The technical complexity of the subject would have been the same, so it is presumably the passage of time which proponents of the new protocol reckon their instrument could have mitigated, had it been in force. However, the protocol could not have been used until Cuba chose to invoke the convention and its protocol. At that point, the procedure for launching an investigation would have been activated with the inspectorate at the core of the Technical Secretariat of the Organisation for the Prohibition of Biological and Toxin Weapons responding to Cuba's invitation to investigate. (For convenience, CWC-equivalent terminology is used here; the titles, functions and composition of future BTWC protocol organs remain to be determined.)

The process would have been facilitated by the ready availability of permanent inspectors and the possibility of convening any necessary meetings of the Executive Council more quickly than the informal and formal meetings— 30 and 60 days, respectively—which were held after Cuba invoked Article V. The institutions under the proposed protocol, however, would have faced the same problems as the Formal Consultative Meeting did in 1997. For whatever reasons, including attempts by Cuba to resolve the issue on a bilateral basis, six and one-half months elapsed between the date on which Cuba first detected *Thrips palmi* in Matanzas Province and the date on which it invoked the convention multilaterally for the first time and addressed its Article V request to one of the depositaries.

If the protocol, a legally binding instrument, were in effect cooperation would become mandatory. However, cooperation was not a problem in the 1997 case. On the contrary, Ambassador Soutar received full cooperation in his conduct of the consultative procedures.

Had it been in effect, the protocol would not have made technical assistance more readily available from other agencies, such as the Food and Agriculture Organization and its Plant Protection Commission for the Caribbean, whose notifications were adduced in evidence by Cuba. The Formal Consultative Meeting could have brought in expertise from the international organizations of the UN system and elsewhere, as could the new organization and its Technical Secretariat.

The institutions of a protocol would also have had to consult the scientific literature of entomology, epidemiology and, possibly, meteorology. They would still have faced the dilemma (discussed in the Canadian analysis) of whether to regard the insects detected on 18 December 1996 as third or fourth generation, which was critical for the success of determining the date of infestation.

[81] Report of the Chairman . . . (note 64), para. 7.

It is difficult to see any other respects in which the 1997 experience could have been improved by the existence of the protocol, beyond the advantages of speed once Cuba had invoked the convention and its protocol. This does not mean that a protocol is unnecessary, only that its benefits are more likely to be seen in other circumstances, with other kinds of compliance concern. It might, for example, have advantages in cases where investigations need to take place on the territory of the state whose compliance is the object of concern. In 1997 nothing would have been gained from an investigation on the territory of the United States.

The protocol might also have advantages in cases where cooperation between parties regarding a voluntary procedure might be limited or non-existent, or where one party had difficulties with the state whose ambassador was conducting the consultations. In 1997 cooperation was forthcoming and the British chairman was an acceptable choice. The UK was arguably the most appropriate depositary by virtue of its 1980 authorship and 1991 elaboration of the contingency mechanism, but it also enjoyed satisfactory relations with both Cuba and the United States.

Whatever the potential advantages of the protocol, until and unless it is in force for all parties to the BTWC, there will remain a need for Article V to be implemented as it stands. However, it is reassuring that the contingency mechanism has passed its first test, 17 years after it was first outlined. The procedures which the Third Review Conference had added to the foundations laid at the earlier review conferences were carried out faithfully. Some, such as the extended decision-making procedure, were not needed. Where guidance was lacking, the parties to the BTWC filled the gaps in ways which provide useful precedents for future use of the contingency mechanism.

Three decisions in particular strengthened the mechanism in 1997 and are helpful for any future use. The first was the election of geographically representative vice-chairmen to constitute the Bureau of the Formal Consultative Meeting. Its subsequent meetings provided the chairman with valuable collective legitimization for his report. The second decision that strengthened the contingency mechanism was the one-month time limit for parties to submit their observations, with the assistance of national technical experts if the process of analysis and assessment necessitated their participation. The third decision was the choice to invite the two states in dispute to comment on the observations submitted, thereby, in effect, recognizing their special need for a second round of written comments after the deadline for the other states had expired. (The second round of comments on 20–22 October 1997 confirmed the success of the procedure.)

US Ambassador Mahley wrote that 'In our view, the provisions of Article V of the Convention have been met; the allegation has been examined and reviewed to the fullest extent practicable and no causal linkage between the infestation in Cuba and the authorized overflight of Cuba by a US State Department aircraft on 21 October 1996 has been demonstrated. Accordingly, the United States does not believe any further action is warranted or required.'

Ambassador Amat of Cuba reiterated his country's view that 'the only thing which could explain the appearance of the *Thrips palmi* plague in December 1996 is the spillage of a substance as yet unknown by a United States aircraft when overflying the territory of the Republic of Cuba', and expressed surprise that the United States had not addressed the 'significant lacunae, omissions and uncertainties' of its 27 August response by making an additional submission. Cuba continued to adhere 'to its justified suspicions, which have now been strengthened by the silence on the part of the United States at this stage of discussions'. However, Cuba concluded its 22 October 1997 statement with a reference to the Article V mechanism which, taken in conjunction with the overall tone of the letter, signalled a certain level of procedural satisfaction even though substantive vindication had not been achieved:

The Government of the Republic of Cuba has at all times during this exercise demonstrated its flexibility and its total willingness for some kind of mechanism to be established, within the framework of the consultation and cooperation provided for in Article V of the Convention, which can help to clarify the situation experienced by Cuba, thereby strengthening the mechanism of the Convention, its integrity and the full reliance of all States Parties on the Convention as a guarantee for the international community.

For a variety of reasons it may be surmised that Cuba was not overly displeased with the outcome. Cuba did not make a formal denunciation or give notice of withdrawal from the convention under Article XIII, and it did not initiate the complaints procedure under Article VI. It also did not request a further stage of the Article V procedure (e.g., by adopting Viet Nam's proposal for 'follow-up' by the bureau or the similar suggestion from China), and it did not force a vote, after the mandatory pre-voting consultation period, in a resumed session of the Formal Consultative Meeting.

Summary

The contingency mechanism emerged strengthened from its first test. Useful precedents were established which can serve if it is used again. Although the 'finding of fact' was indeterminate, there was general satisfaction that the requirements of Article V had been fulfilled. However, there was also an agreed statement from the bureau that the indefinite outcome showed the need for a protocol, although it is not entirely clear in which respects the handling of Cuba's concern would have been improved had the protocol been in force.

Inconclusiveness is one of the difficulties inherent in proving allegations of biological warfare in some circumstances. During the negotiation of the convention the long incubation period for certain infectious diseases and the incidence of naturally occurring epidemics were seen as most likely to mask—or complicate the task of proving—a biological warfare attack.[82] The *Thrips palmi* episode demonstrated analogous problems in a case of insect infestation.

Compliance credibility is more likely to be enhanced or eroded according to the strength of the evidence presented to support an accusation and the plausibility of alternative explanations than it is to be completely vindicated or destroyed. This suggests that indeterminate findings, such as those issued by the bureau and the chairman of the Formal Consultative Meeting on 15 December

---

[82] Alexander (note 4), pp. 100–101.

1997,[83] will often be the most that can be expected. However thorough the investigation into an allegation of use—and whether it is conducted under UN procedures to uphold the Geneva Protocol, by using the Article V contingency mechanism or through the new institutions created by the future protocol to the BTWC—inconclusiveness is rooted deep in the nature of biological warfare and the challenge of proof of its use.

VIII. The bilateral dimension of Article V

There has been less development of the bilateral dimension of Article V than of its multilateral dimension, and by its nature it may be incapable of systematic development. Review conferences have repeatedly exhorted parties to the BTWC to resolve their differences, but have not defined the limits of an obligation to consult and cooperate bilaterally.

In 1980–81 the United States made three démarches in an attempt to secure clarification from the Soviet Union of the April 1979 Sverdlovsk (Yekaterin-burg) incident.[84] The USSR felt it had fulfilled its obligation by explaining how an outbreak of anthrax in the human population had occurred. The USA did not find the explanation satisfactory and insisted that it would only regard consultation and cooperation as having taken place in satisfaction of the Soviet Union's Article V obligation when its compliance concerns over Sverdlovsk had been met with an explanation it could accept.

Various explanations were proffered for the Sverdlovsk incident. The responses to it, the démarches of 1980–81, demonstrated the subjective nature of the Article V obligation in its bilateral dimension. The USA and the USSR each had its own view of what constituted fulfilment of that obligation.[85]

With multilateral consultation and cooperation, the parties to the BTWC can devise a procedure with rules and expectations that govern its observance. A party is expected to follow the set procedure and is in some sense 'breaking the rules' if it does not. However, in the bilateral dimension a party is required to do all that it reasonably can to demonstrate compliance with its obligations under the convention. The implication is that it should continue in consultation with its interlocutor until the latter is satisfied, subject to a criterion of 'reasonableness'. So long as consultation is pursued in a problem-solving mode this should present little problem; if it is or becomes adversarial, problems can arise.

Despite the efforts of the Soviet delegation to explain the Sverdlovsk incident, the Second Review Conference could not unite in accepting the Soviet explanation. This division of opinion is reflected in one of the Article I paragraphs of the 1986 Final Declaration:

The Conference notes statements by some States Parties [i.e., the USA and its allies] that compliance with Articles I, II and III was, in their view, subject to grave doubt in some cases and that efforts to resolve those concerns had not been successful. The Conference notes the statements by other States Parties [i.e., the USSR and its allies] that such a doubt was unfounded and, in their view, not in accordance with the Convention. The Conference agrees that the application by States Parties of a positive

83 Report of the Chairman . . . (note 64).
84 Note 40.
85 Sims (note 9), pp. 235–48.

approach in questions of compliance in accordance with the provisions of the Convention was in the interest of all States Parties and that this would serve to promote confidence among States Parties.[86]

The Final Declaration, in the fourth and fifth paragraphs of its Article V paragraphs, 'stresses the need for all States to deal seriously with compliance issues and emphasizes that the failure to do so undermines the Convention and the arms control process in general' and 'appeals to States Parties to make all possible efforts to solve any problems which may arise in relation to the objective of, or in the application of the provisions of, the Convention with a view towards encouraging strict observance of the provisions subscribed to. The Conference further requests that information on such efforts be provided to the Third Review Conference'.[87]

The 1991 Third Review Conference received no additional information on the compliance concerns which the UK and the USA maintained had not yet been dispelled by the USSR. The Article I section of its Final Declaration notes:

The Conference emphasizes the vital importance of full implementation by all States Parties of all provisions of the Convention and expresses concern at statements by some States Parties that compliance with Articles I, II and III has been, in their view, subject to grave doubt in certain cases and that efforts since the Second Review Conference to resolve these problems have not been successful. The Conference agrees that the application by States Parties of a positive approach in questions of compliance in accordance with the provisions of the Convention is in the interest of all States Parties and that continued non-compliance with its provisions could undermine confidence in the Convention.[88]

In the Article V section it repeated the 1986 paragraphs quoted above, but the final sentence was replaced by the following expanded text: 'In this connection, the States Parties agree to provide a specific, timely response to any compliance concern alleging a breach of their obligations under the Convention. Such responses should be submitted through the procedures provided for under the Convention. The Conference further requests that information on such efforts be provided to the Fourth Review Conference'.[89] Providing 'a specific, timely response' is an improvement on a vague and dilatory response, but it does not guarantee acceptability. An explanation can be both specific and timely but it may not be believed. Neither is it clear what procedures are provided for bilateral exchanges under the convention.

It would help if a future review conference could record an agreed procedure for implementing the consultative obligation bilaterally in the future. One possibility is suggested by the equivalent and more detailed provision in the second paragraph of the CWC's Article IX (Consultations, Cooperation and Fact-Finding), where governments are reminded that, without prejudice to the right of any party to *that* convention to request a challenge inspection, 'States Parties should, whenever possible, first make every effort to clarify and resolve, through exchange of information and consultations among themselves, any mat-

[86] BWC/CONF.II/13/II (note 6), p. 3.
[87] BWC/CONF.II/13/II (note 6), p. 5.
[88] BWC/CONF.III/22/Add.2 (note 17), p. 3.
[89] BWC/CONF.III/22/Add.2 (note 17), p. 11. Repeated (with slight variation in the references to review conferences) in 1996 in BWC/CONF.IV/9 (note 31), p. 20.

ter which may cause doubt about compliance with this Convention, or which gives rise to concerns about a related matter which may be considered ambiguous'. On receipt of a request for such clarification, there is a specific obligation to 'provide the requesting State Party, as soon as possible, but in any case *not later than 10 days after the request*, with information sufficient to answer the doubt or concern raised *along with an explanation of how the information provided resolves the matter*'.[90]

The phrases emphasized above would have helped the parties to the BTWC to handle BTW compliance concerns more expeditiously and satisfactorily had they been included with full legal effect in Article V. It is not too late to agree procedures along these lines and to endow them with the political authority of a final declaration from a review conference.

The bilateral consultation and cooperation required under Article V perhaps can be developed by integrating it with similar multilateral efforts. One possibility, foreseen in the 1991 elaboration of the consultative meeting as a contingency mechanism, is to encourage bilateral diplomacy as a preparatory procedure before the consultative meeting takes place in hope of amicable settlement. Another possibility is that bilateral consultation and cooperation will become more common and less adversarial as CBMs generate increasing volumes of data exchanged multilaterally among all parties, and as reciprocal programmes of visits by scientific and technical personnel develop.

IX. The significance of Article V

In the regime-building Final Declaration of the Third Review Conference Article V is central to the regime of compliance, with one established new element (CBMs) and one potential new element (verification) grouped under it. The Article V section of that text covers more than five pages—one-third of the document. However, the importance of CBMs and verification[91] should not obscure the continuing significance of the process deriving from the original Article V clarification of 1980. It was 'the first, all-important step' in offering 'an institutional means whereby problems could be aired, and their resolution attempted, by states concerned for the implications of any secret BW or toxin rearmament—without, however, bringing the very treaty regime which banned such rearmament crashing down around their ears'.[92] That diplomatic breakthrough opened the way to further regime building by the endogenous route, developing possibilities latent in the text of the BTWC.[93] This is where the progress of the treaty regime in evolution can be most clearly traced through the history of the convention in force.

[90] Article IX, para. 2, emphasis added. The Convention on the Prohibition of the Development, Production, Stockpiling and Use of Chemical Weapons and on their Destruction (corrected version), 8 Aug. 1994, is reproduced on the SIPRI Chemical and Biological Warfare Project Internet site at URL <http://www.sipri.se/cbw/docs/cw-cwc-texts.html>. The proposed 31 Oct. 1999 amendment to Part VI of the CWC is reproduced at URL <http://projects.sipri.se/cbw/docs/cw-cwc-verannex5bis.html>.

[91] They are discussed in chapters 3 and 4, respectively, in this volume.

[92] Sims, N. A., *Biological and Toxin Weapons: Issues in the 1986 Review*, Faraday Discussion Paper no. 7 (Council for Arms Control: London, 1986), p. 10.

[93] Sims (note 92), pp. 10–11.

X. The complaint procedure: Article VI

Article VI constitutes the only complaint procedure in the BTWC. It reads:

1. Any State Party to this Convention which finds that any other State Party is acting in breach of obligations deriving from the provisions of the Convention may lodge a complaint with the Security Council of the United Nations. Such a complaint should include all possible evidence confirming its validity, as well as a request for its consideration by the Security Council.

    2. Each State Party to the Convention undertakes to cooperate in carrying out any investigation which the Security Council may initiate [entreprendre], in accordance with the provisions of the Charter of the United Nations, on the basis of the complaint received by the Council. The Security Council shall inform the States Parties to the Convention of the results of the investigation.[94]

During negotiation of the convention in 1971 Article VI was criticized as too weak by those who felt that certain permanent members of the UN Security Council would be among the parties most likely to give rise to suspicion that led to use of the complaint procedure. A permanent member which had been accused could be expected to veto any proposal to investigate the complaint made against it. If this happened regularly, complaints would remain unresolved and either no investigation under Article VI would be allowed to take place or, worse still, some would occur and others would not. The principles of sovereign equality and non-discrimination would be violated if investigations were allowed when parties not protected by the veto power were involved, but not when permanent members (or their political friends or allies) were suspected of engaging in equally dubious activities. The inequity of the resulting discrimination would harm the BTWC.

Attempts were made, in vain, to amend the draft provision which was to become Article VI so that investigations could not be blocked by a permanent member's use of the veto power. Under the failed proposal a suspected breach of any of the convention prohibitions by any party would have been susceptible to investigation, even though the *outcome* of such an investigation could hardly have hoped to escape the veto if it offended one of the permanent members.

In the British draft convention, investigation of alleged *use* of BTW (as distinct from other prohibited BTW activities) would have been exempt from the risk of veto because the investigation would have been carried out by the UN Secretary-General under the direct authority of the convention. However, in the course of the 1971 negotiations both the prohibition of BTW use and any mention of the Secretary-General were dropped from the emerging BTWC.

It was proposed that complaints brought under Article VI should be considered by the Security Council in two stages, with agreement by the permanent

---

[94] This article has been much criticized, and not just for certain textual deficiencies. 'Initiate' and 'entreprendre' mean different things, as Ambassador Michel Van Ussel of Belgium pointed out when the English- and French-language drafts were under scrutiny in the First Committee of the General Assembly in 1971. UN document A/C.1/PV.1841, 1 Dec. 1971, para. 40.

    The English-language text should have been changed to 'undertake', or the French to 'initier'. Neither change was made. Moreover, the choice of the verb 'finds' in the first line of the first paragraph, in preference to 'alleges', 'believes' or 'suspects', introduces a note of inappropriate finality. It sets a standard of proof more appropriate to the Security Council when it deliberates on the outcome of an investigation than to the party making the initial accusation. Almost any complaint that can be envisaged would fail to fulfil the stringent criterion set by the word 'finds', if the latter is interpreted strictly.

members that they would not resort to using their veto power in the first (fact-finding) stage. This was rejected by the permanent members taking part in the negotiation, who argued that their veto powers ought not to be constrained beyond the limits set by the UN Charter (in the negotiation of which 'the inflexible attitude of the Great Powers on the issue of the veto' had been noteworthy[95]). The notion of a self-denying ordinance in this or any other area was deemed unrealistic.

Article VI appeared to offer little in support of a regime of compliance unless (which did not appear likely) the party whose behaviour gave rise to a complaint was out of favour simultaneously with all five permanent members and with a sufficient number of other, non-permanent members of the Security Council to allow the passage of a resolution initiating an investigation. The Second Review Conference in its Final Declaration therefore recognized 'the need to further improve and strengthen this and other procedures to enhance greater confidence in the Convention'.[96] A Colombian addendum, much diluted, suggested using the World Health Organization (WHO) to advise the Security Council; nothing else was done regarding Article VI.[97]

The credibility of Article VI as an element in the regime of compliance would have been bolstered if the Security Council initially had declared its intent to do what was being asked of it. This would not have eradicated the severe problems discussed above, but it could have made it more difficult for a permanent member to utilize its veto prematurely or irresponsibly in order to curtail consideration of a complaint brought under Article VI.[98]

Such a declaration was envisaged in each of the draft conventions between 1969 and 1971 as both necessary and feasible. It was presented as an Accompanying Resolution to be adopted by the Security Council at the time the BTWC was opened for signature.[99] The Accompanying Resolution was intended to proclaim the readiness of the Security Council to allow the Article VI complaint procedure to be activated, should a complainant apply to it for redress. The BTWC was opened for signature on 10 April 1972; 15 days later three members of the Security Council introduced the Accompanying Resolution. Under the resolution the Security Council was:

(i) to declare its readiness (a) to consider immediately any complaints lodged under Article VI of the Convention; (b) to take all necessary measures for the investigation of a complaint; (c) to inform the States Parties to the Convention of the results of the investigation; and

[95] Goodwin, G. L., Royal Institute of International Affairs, *Britain and the United Nations* (Oxford University Press: London, 1957), p. 30.

[96] BWC/CONF.II/13/II (note 6), p. 7.

[97] Colombia failed to secure the inclusion in the Final Declaration of its more radical proposals—BWC/CONF.II/13/II (note 6), p. 7—which would have given parties without the means to obtain evidence of a breach of the convention the right to entrust the necessary investigations to the WHO in addition to the possibility of investigations to evaluate evidence being entrusted to the WHO by the Security Council. BWC/CONF.II/9 (note 7), p. 25.

[98] The difficulty would have been political or psychological for any government concerned with its reputation for consistency—placing it under a moral, although not a legal, obligation to be sparing in its use of the veto to prevent an investigation.

[99] The Accompanying Resolution was a British initiative that originated in 1968 and was developed in 1969. ENDC/231 (note 77), para. 10; and ENDC/255 (note 2).

(ii) to call upon all States Parties to co-operate for the purpose of implementing the provisions of this Resolution.[100]

Poland, the UK and Yugoslavia sponsored the Accompanying Resolution.[101] They represented the three main political groups in the United Nations, as they had in the Conference of the Committee on Disarmament, where each had taken an active part in negotiating the BTWC. Article VI had originated as a Polish proposal on 14 April 1970, with Hungary and Mongolia as co-sponsors.[102]

The Accompanying Resolution was never adopted. It was withdrawn before it came to a vote because of a threatened Chinese veto. The People's Republic of China (PRC) had taken over the Chinese representation in the United Nations only a few months earlier. It was displeased that the Taipei authorities had been allowed to sign the BTWC in Washington on 10 April 1972 as the 'Republic of China'. The PRC did not want the Security Council to have anything to do with what it regarded as a 'tarnished' convention. There may also have been apprehension that the Taipei authorities, still in control of the large island of Taiwan (Formosa) and some offshore islands, might try to use Article VI to re-establish a toehold in UN proceedings. The PRC may have feared that the Republic of China would invoke its Washington signature (which the Republic of China subsequently ratified on 9 February 1973) and the Accompanying Resolution.

The PRC acceded to the BTWC in 1984, declaring the signature and ratification by the Republic of China to be 'illegal and null and void'.[103] It appears that China no longer regards the events of 1972 and 1973 as obstacles to its acceptance of the convention, and it seems reasonable to assume that there is no longer a threat that China would veto S/10619.

One useful way of reinforcing Article VI as an element in the regime of compliance would be to reintroduce the resolution and secure its passage. The Third Review Conference implicitly endorsed such an effort in the last three paragraphs of the Article VI passage of its Final Declaration (which was repeated, with minor additions, by the Fourth Review Conference[104]). It indicated to the Security Council that it expected it to encourage UN investigation of alleged BTW activity under Article VI.

The Conference invites the Security Council to consider immediately any complaint lodged under Article VI and to initiate any measures it considers necessary for the investigation of the complaint. The Conference reaffirms the undertaking of each State Party to cooperate in carrying out any investigations which the Security Council may initiate.

The Conference recalls, in this context, United Nations Security Council resolution 620 of 1988, which encouraged the United Nations Secretary-General to carry out prompt investigations, in response to allegations brought to his attention by any Member State concerning the possible use of chemical and bacteriological (biological) or toxin weapons.

---

[100] UN Security Council document S/10619, 25 Apr. 1972.

[101] UN Security Council document S/10619 (note 100).

[102] It was presented by Deputy Foreign Minister of Poland Jozef Winiewicz. Conference of the Committee on Disarmament document CCD/285, 14 Apr. 1970, and Corr.1; and Winiewicz, J., Poland, Conference of the Committee on Disarmament document CCD/PV.464.

[103] Sims (note 9), pp. 260–61; and Fan Guoxiang, China, BWC/CONF.II/SR.5 (note 10), para. 46.

[104] BWC/CONF.IV/9 (note 31), pp. 20–21.

The Conference invites the Security Council to inform each State Party of the results of any investigation initiated under Article VI and to consider promptly any further action which may be necessary.[105]

Until the Security Council acts by adopting S/10619 or a similar declaration of intent it remains in the anomalous position of having declared its readiness to launch investigations of alleged instances of BTW use (which is not explicitly banned by the convention) but not of those BTW activities which, unlike use, *are* explicitly prohibited. Another anomaly, considered noteworthy by Goldblat and Bernauer, is 'that the signatories to the BW Convention have assigned important functions to the Security Council—namely, to consider, receive and act upon complaints of breaches—without formally asking the Council for consent'.[106] A declaration of intent, such as S/10619, would constitute that consent.

In 1991 Cuba and Nigeria each sought unsuccessfully to modify the Article VI procedure, although in quite different ways.

Cuba wanted the Final Declaration to include, as a corollary to the injunction in Article VI that 'Such a complaint should include all possible evidence confirming its validity', a new undertaking: 'Each State Party undertakes not to abuse the procedures foreseen in Article VI and to act always in good faith and within the scope of Article I of the Convention.'[107]

The motivation for this proposal (also unsuccessfully proposed by Russia in 1996[108]) is unclear. It may have been connected with long-standing Cuban fear of US aggression involving the use of biological warfare agents. These were the subject of complaint in various international forums, including the Committee on Disarmament,[109] but they were not taken through the procedure of the BTWC. So Cuba never, for example, employed Article VI of the BTWC to present to the Security Council its allegations (reported in the Soviet press) that dengue fever outbreaks among the island's pigs had been caused by covert US introduction of the virus. Whether a US veto would have prevented investigation and thereby vitiated the Article VI procedure therefore will never be known.[110] On the other hand, in 1991 Cuba may have been protecting its future interests with a view to lodging a complaint under Article VI in the event the alleged activities recurred. (In 1997, however, it chose Article V for its *Thrips palmi* complaint.) Whatever the motivation, the proposal did not succeed.

Nigeria suggested a more radical change: a return to the two-stage complaint procedure (which had been proposed in 1971 as a way of delaying, if not preventing, the imposition of a veto). In 1991, Nigeria revived a 1986 proposal in

---

[105] BWC/CONF.III/22/Add.2 (note 17), pp. 12–13. Although the use of BTW was not documented in the 1980–88 Iraq–Iran War, Security Council Resolution 620 addressed Iraq's use of chemical weapons. UN Security Council Resolution 620, 26 Aug. 1988. Iran accused Iraq of using CW from 1983 until the end of the war. In 1984, 1986, 1987 and 1988 the United Nations had verified such use.

[106] Goldblat and Bernauer (note 8), p. 10.

[107] BWC/CONF.III/17 (note 21), p. 62.

[108] BWC/CONF.IV/9 (note 31), pp. 49–50. Russia sought to confine the Ad Hoc Group to the limits set by Article VI and not permit any other procedures: a position effectively negated by the Fourth Review Conference in para. 6 of the Article VI section of its Final Declaration which 'notes that the procedure outlined in this Article is without prejudice to the prerogative of the States Parties to the Convention to consider jointly the cases of alleged non-compliance with the provisions of the Convention and to make appropriate decisions in accordance with the Charter of the United Nations and applicable rules of international law'. BWC/CONF.IV/9 (note 31), p. 21

[109] Committee on Disarmament document CD/211, 13 Aug. 1981.

[110] Falk, R., 'Strengthening the Biological Weapons Convention of 1972', ed. E. Geissler, SIPRI, *Biological and Toxin Weapons Today* (Oxford University Press: Oxford, 1986), p. 109.

which the fact-finding stage would have been sharply separated from the 'stage of political consideration and decision by the Security Council'. This separation would have provided 'an effective compliance procedure' which was needed 'to attract greater confidence and eliminate possible political controversy on its application'.[111] Had Nigeria's proposal succeeded, the operative paragraph in the 1991 Final Declaration would have read: 'The Conference therefore agrees that the complaints of violations should be lodged with the Secretary-General of the United Nations who *should initiate* investigations through a Consultative Committee of Experts to be appointed by him. The result of such investigations should be conveyed to States Parties for consideration and decision.'[112]

It is hard to see how such a radical change could come about on the sole authority of a review conference, since it would amount to the restoration of a putative procedure that was lost in the 1971 negotiations. As such, it could only be reintroduced constitutionally by means of the formal amendment procedure laid down in Article XI.

Future regime building on the basis of Article VI is likely to be increasingly linked to the Security Council's evolving practice in the exercise of its responsibility under the UN Charter for the maintenance of international peace and security. This is indicated in the third paragraph quoted above from the 1991 Final Declaration, in which the Third Review Conference invited the Security Council to 'consider promptly any further action which may be necessary'.[113] Its significance lies in its acknowledgement of the dramatic revolution of rising UN expectations which had seen the Security Council, just five months before, impose 'further action' on Iraq under Resolution 687,[114] in the form of disarmament obligations and stringent supervision which extended to the BTW sector of the category 'weapons of mass destruction'. By the time of the Third Review Conference the likelihood of enforcement action being ordered by the Security Council had increased.

In addition, the parties to the BTWC could act individually on their own initiative. The deterrent effect of declarations of intent to consider sanctions was asserted in a joint Canadian–US paper on 17 September 1991. It proposed, unsuccessfully, that the following warning be added to the Article V section of the Final Declaration:

The Conference notes declarations by States Parties of their intention to consider individually the application of sanctions against any State which uses biological or toxin weapons as well as to consider individually appropriate measures, including sanctions, in response to any violations of the Convention. Such measures might include cessation of scientific and technical collaboration on any biological activity, trade restrictions or denial of economic assistance.[115]

The objects of possible sanctions were not only other parties to the BTWC, but also non-parties. The distinction between use and other BTW activities ('violations of the Convention') paralleled an Iranian paper on BTW verifica-

111 BWC/CONF.II/9 (note 7), p. 25.
112 BWC/CONF.III/17 (note 21), p. 62. This emphasis in the original was probably intended to highlight the only textual alteration from 1986, where the words used were 'should be empowered to initiate'.
113 BWC/CONF.III/22/Add.2 (note 17), pp. 12–13.
114 UN Security Council Resolution 687, 3 Apr. 1991.
115 BWC/CONF.III/17 (note 21), p. 25.

tion in treating use as the gravest BTW event, necessitating immediate investigation on site or, in this case, sanctions.[116]

The Italian paper, from which the paragraph concerning 'any further action which may be necessary' was drawn, envisaged the Security Council making a Chapter VII determination (of a threat to the peace, a breach of the peace or an act of aggression) under Article 39 of the UN Charter; thereafter it would proceed to 'act accordingly'.[117] The word 'sanctions' was not used in the Italian paper,[118] but the intention was evidently to strengthen the credibility of Article VI as a deterrent to any violation of the convention by hinting that investigation would not end the matter once the Security Council found a complaint to be justified.

XI. Assistance: Article VII

Article VII was intended to add an additional functional substitute for verification by introducing a further disincentive to contravention of the BTW ban. It empowers the UN Security Council not only to investigate complaints (with an obligation on all parties to the BTWC 'to co-operate in carrying out any investigation which the Council may initiate [entreprendre]'), but also to make a determination which would trigger assistance to the victim of a violation, provided both states were parties to the BTWC. This provision was an expression of international solidarity that was intended to threaten a potential BTW aggressor with the prospect of united opposition from all other parties. It might also deter BTW use by diminishing its military utility, if international assistance from other parties were to take the form of anti-BTW protection for troops and humanitarian aid for civilians.

Article VII was not only the last ingredient to be restored to the BTWC (it had been included in the UK's proposal in 1968–71, but dropped in the Soviet[119] and US[120] drafts of March and August 1971), but also one of the shortest: 'Each State Party to this Convention undertakes to provide or support assistance, in accordance with the United Nations Charter, to any Party to the Convention which so requests, if the Security Council decides that such Party has been exposed to danger as a result of violation of the Convention.' The First Review Conference noted 'with satisfaction' that it had not proved necessary to invoke the provisions of Article VII, and the Second Review Conference simply noted that they had not been invoked.[121]

By 1991 the equivalent but much more detailed provision of the draft CWC had been largely finalized under the heading Assistance and Protection against Chemical Weapons; eventually it became Article X of the CWC and comprised 11 paragraphs. Through their delegations in the CD, Argentina, Iran, Mexico, Pakistan, Sweden and the UK all had a strong influence on the content of the

[116] BWC/CONF.III/17 (note 21), pp. 61–62.

[117] BWC/CONF.III/17 (note 21), p. 61.

[118] However, Italy and Nigeria had used it, as had Canada and the USA jointly, in separate and unsuccessful proposals for strengthening the regime through Article V. BWC/CONF.III/17 (note 21), p. 32 (Italy), p. 34 (Nigeria), and p. 25 (Canada and the USA).

[119] Conference of the Committee on Disarmament document CCD/325, 30 Mar. 1971; and Conference of the Committee on Disarmament document CCD/337, 5 Aug. 1971.

[120] Conference of the Committee on Disarmament document CCD/338, 5 Aug. 1971.

[121] BWC/CONF.I/9 (note 5); and BWC/CONF.II/13/II (note 6), p. 7.

CWC's Article X, and all were present at the Third Review Conference of the BTWC. It met less than six months after the end of the 1991 Persian Gulf War, in which the Coalition forces of Desert Shield and Desert Storm had taken prophylactic and protective precautions against what they perceived to be a serious threat of BTW attack by Iraq. Although BTW were not used, the level of threat perception influenced the Third Review Conference to place more emphasis on Article VII than had its predecessors. The relevant passage of the 1991 Final Declaration read:

The Conference notes with satisfaction that these provisions have not been invoked.

The Conference reaffirms the undertaking made by each State Party to provide or support assistance in accordance with the Charter of the United Nations to any Party to the Convention which so requests, if the Security Council decides that such Party has been exposed to danger as a result of violation of the Convention.

The Conference takes note of desires expressed that, should a request for assistance be made, it be promptly considered and an appropriate response provided. In this context, pending consideration of a decision by the Security Council, timely emergency assistance could be provided by States Parties if requested.

The Conference considers that in the event that this article might be invoked, the United Nations, with the help of appropriate intergovernmental organizations such as the World Health Organization (WHO), could play a coordinating role.[122]

These paragraphs were repeated (with one paragraph added on the initiative of Iran) by the Fourth Review Conference in 1996.[123]

More might be done to bolster the effectiveness of Article VII as an element in the regime of compliance. Goldblat and Bernauer suggested in their UNIDIR Research Paper that:

Since the drafters of the relevant provision had in mind mainly action of a humanitarian nature, the parties may decide to establish an international humanitarian fund to be resorted to whenever the stipulated assistance is required. The proposed fund, possibly based on voluntary contributions, could be administered by the UN Disaster Relief Organization or by the International Committee of the Red Cross. The proposed measure would supplement the aid that may be offered by individual States following an appropriate UN Security Council decision.[124]

Supplementing in contemporary vein the original, compliance-encouraging intention of Article VII in 1971, they added: 'Reinforcing the pledges of assistance to parties threatened with biological weapons or harmed by their use may perhaps help attract new States to the Convention, especially in conflict areas of the world'.[125]

Along the same lines, Iran proposed an addendum, without success, to the 1991 Final Declaration. It would have asked the United Nations and the specialized agencies to prepare a list of potential forms of assistance which different countries could provide in time of emergency.[126] These proposals all followed closely the developing consensus on the content of the CWC's draft Article X

[122] BWC/CONF.III/22/Add.2 (note 17), p. 13. The words 'with satisfaction' in the first line were restored, on the initiative of the Netherlands, having been omitted in 1986. BWC/CONF.III/17 (note 21), p. 63.
[123] BWC/CONF.IV/9 (note 31), pp. 21–22.
[124] Goldblat and Bernauer (note 8), pp. 26–27.
[125] Goldblat and Bernauer (note 8), pp. 26–27.
[126] BWC/CONF.III/17 (note 21), p. 63.

on assistance and protection. They, however, went further than Article VII by encompassing assistance and protection against chemical weapon attack on a party to the CWC by *any* state, not just by another party (as logically implied in the BTWC, where Article VII can only be triggered by a chain of events taking their origin from 'violation of the Convention').[127]

At the Fourth Review Conference Iran proposed that the Final Declaration state: 'that the Ad Hoc Group needs to discuss the detailed procedure for assistance in order to ensure that timely emergency assistance would be provided by States Parties if requested'.[128] In a slightly weakened form ('The Conference takes note of the proposal that the Ad Hoc Group might need to discuss . . .') the text was included in the Final Declaration of 1996.[129]

Article VII is the least substantial of the four original elements of the regime of compliance discussed in this chapter. Its last-minute restoration to the text of the draft convention in September 1971 was intended as compensation to the United Kingdom and like-minded governments for the evisceration of the stronger treaty which they had promoted since 1969. It was supposed to show that all was not lost,[130] despite the UK's having 'reflected [the] spirit of compromise to the maximum extent' in accepting this 'less ambitious objective'.[131]

Article VII, relatively insubstantial as it is, does hold potential for regime-building efforts, as the greater attention paid to it by the third and fourth review conferences suggests. Goldblat and Bernauer indicated that this process could be taken further. In fact, in the relevant part (Article VI) of the rolling text of the BTWC protocol, the Ad Hoc Group has taken both the title of its draft provisions (Assistance and Protection Against Biological and Toxin Weapons), and much of the language negotiated by mid-2000, from Article X of the CWC.[132]

The idea of entering into a treaty obligation to supply humanitarian assistance to any country attacked with chemical or biological weapons goes back to 1930.[133] It is an expression of the common international interest in preventing chemical and biological warfare. It is also a vital part of the normative framework that contributes to the formal and practical repudiation of such methods of warfare.

XII. Conclusions

Chapters 3 and 4 examine the regime of compliance with CBMs added (Mode B) and with verification added (Mode C), respectively. These additions are important, but they should not eclipse the continuing relevance and evolutionary potential of those compliance elements which, originally intended as functional substitutes for verification, have been part of the treaty regime all along.

[127] CWC (note 90). The relevant provision is Article X, para. 8(c).

[128] BWC/CONF.IV/9 (note 31), p. 51

[129] BWC/CONF.IV/9 (note 31), p. 22.

[130] The main elements, which were lost in Mar.–Aug. 1971 and not restored in Sep., were the original Article I banning BTW use, the constraint on research aimed at BTW production, the role of the UN Secretary-General, and the three-month time-limit from entry into force for the completion of BTW disarmament.

[131] Hainworth, H. C., UK, Conference of the Committee on Disarmament document CCD/PV.542, 28 Sep. 1971.

[132] Procedural Report of the Ad Hoc Group, Twentieth Session, BWC/AD HOC GROUP/52, 11 Aug. 2000, part I, pp. 96–98.

[133] Goldblat and Bernauer (note 8), p. 10.

3. The regime of compliance: the addition of confidence-building measures

I. Origins of the subsidiary regime of confidence-building measures

The parties to the Biological and Toxin Weapons Convention have agreed to an expanding programme of international openness about past activities and current legitimate peaceful applications of microbiology under articles V and X of the convention. This simultaneously strengthens the regime of compliance by maximizing the transparency of national patterns of normal activity. In 1986–92 this subsidiary regime of confidence-building measures became the most visible component of the regime of compliance, and it remains important. It consists of voluntary politically binding commitments to pool information on a regular basis in a multilateral data exchange through the United Nations. This chapter focuses on the regime of compliance in 'Mode B'—with CBMs but without verification.

The first precursor to a CBM, proposed by the United Kingdom in 1980, focused on past military activities rather than on current peaceful programmes. The British initiative was supported by Australia, Canada, New Zealand and the United States. In its statement on Article II of the BTWC the First Review Conference declared that it 'welcomes the declarations of several States Parties to the effect *either* that they do not possess and have never possessed agents, toxins, weapons, equipment or means of delivery specified in Article I of the Convention, *or* that having possessed them they have destroyed them or diverted them to peaceful purposes'. It continued: 'The Conference believes that such voluntary declarations contribute to *increased confidence* in the Convention and believes that States not having made such voluntary declarations should do so.'[1]

Only the USA had made a declaration of the latter kind, but the hope was that other states that had formerly possessed biological and toxin weapons would follow suit to compensate somewhat for the uncertainty regarding compliance with Article II. Obviously, only BTW-possessor states which were still in possession of BTW stockpiles when the BTWC entered into force for them were covered by Article II. However, questions remained about which states belonged in that category and about when they would announce their completion of the process of BTW disarmament, which should have taken place within nine months at most from the entry into force of the convention for them. In 1971 there had been an expectation in the Conference of the Committee on Disarmament, where the BTWC was negotiated, that reports would be made on compliance with Article II, as the USA was then doing regarding its unilateral destruction of BTW stockpiles from 13 July 1971 under the policy announced by President Richard Nixon on 25 November 1969. No requirement to report on implementation of Article II was, however, written into the BTWC.

---

[1] First Review Conference document BWC/CONF.I/9, 21 Mar. 1980, p. 9, emphasis added.

In 1979 the Preparatory Committee for the First Review Conference invited the parties to the BTWC to report on their compliance with several articles of the convention, including Article II. The few responses received did little to clarify the situation. The First Review Conference therefore stated that: 'States not having made such voluntary declarations should do so' and thereby 'contribute to increased confidence in the Convention'.[2] This statement was based on the British proposal which was, in effect, a CBM prototype.

However, the Second Review Conference missed the point of the proposal. Instead of asking parties irrespective of date of ratification or accession to declare their status in one category ('never possessed') or the other ('having possessed'), the 1986 Final Declaration merely welcomed statements by *new* parties and conflated the two categories into a single ambiguous one ('do not possess'). The British proposal had aimed to clarify the ambiguity of 'do not possess'—in Soviet statements, in particular.[3] This need to distinguish between the two categories was lost in the 1986 formulation: 'The Conference notes the importance of Article II and welcomes the statements made by States which have become Parties to the Convention since the First Review Conference that they do not possess agents, toxins, weapons, equipment or means of delivery referred to in Article I of the Convention. The Conference believes that such statements enhance confidence in the Convention.'[4]

In 1991 the 1986 formulation was repeated verbatim with only 'First' replaced by 'Second'. This was done on the suggestion of France and Bulgaria,[5] but it made even less sense in 1991 than it had in 1986. In the early 1980s a number of major powers had become parties to the BTWC—among them China (1984), the Federal Republic of Germany (1983), France (1984) and Japan (1982). They were of such military significance in other (nuclear or conventional) types of armament that their declarations of non-possession of BTW had some reassurance value, even if those declarations only confirmed a status enshrined in earlier agreements in the cases of the FRG and Japan. Between the 1986 and 1991 review conferences, however, the only new party which declared itself a non-possessor of BTW was Iraq, which did so after it ratified the BTWC in April 1991. That declaration commanded so little credence that it was being subjected to uniquely intrusive investigation at the same time as the Third Review Conference was in session.[6] The relevant units of the UN Secre-

[2] Sims, N. A., *The Diplomacy of Biological Disarmament: Vicissitudes of a Treaty in Force, 1975–85* (Macmillan: London and St Martin's Press: New York, 1988), pp. 132–34.

[3] Sims (note 2).

[4] Second Review Conference document BWC/CONF.II/13/II, 26 Sep. 1986, p. 3.

[5] Third Review Conference document BWC/CONF.III/22/Add.2, 27 Sep. 1991, p. 3. The French proposal of 13 Sep. 1991 and the Bulgarian proposal of 16 Sep. 1991 are reproduced in Third Review Conference document BWC/CONF.III/17, 24 Sep. 1991, p. 15.

[6] The second United Nations Special Commission on Iraq inspection concerned with BTW (UNSCOM 15) took place on 20 Sep.–3 Oct. 1991. It inspected 10 sites in Iraq: 6 declared under CBMs in May 1991 and 4 undeclared but suspect sites to be inspected without advance notice. The 10 sites included a pharmaceutical plant, a blood bank, vaccine production facilities, and research and development laboratories with fermentation capabilities and specially designed facilities allowing work with hazardous pathogens. No biological weapons or facilities for filling such weapons were found. The inspection team, however, did conclude that 3 vaccine production facilities, which had the capacity to produce sufficient quantities of biological agents to meet weapon requirements, should be covered by the future compliance monitoring regime (see chapter 7 in this volume) as should the embryonic fermentation plant at Al Hakam designed for single-cell protein development and production, primarily for use in animal feeds. UN document S/23165, 31 Oct. 1991; UN press statement, 31 Oct. 1991; and *Chemical Weapons Convention Bulletin*, no. 14 (Dec. 1991), pp. 12, 14.

tariat were not notified that any other state had ratified or acceded to the convention since 1986 and had made statements of non-possession of BTW. (If the depositaries had received such information with a state's instrument of ratification or accession, it ought to have been forwarded to the UN Secretariat.)

The Third Review Conference did nothing directly to restore the original purpose of the prototype CBM under Article II but did adopt a French proposal (confidence-building measure F).[7] It required all parties to declare whether or not they had conducted any offensive and/or defensive biological research and development (R&D) programmes since 1 January 1946. If a party answered yes to the first question, information on 'the destruction programme of such agents and weapons' was to be supplied under this CBM.[8]

First identification of the main elements of the subsidiary regime

The main elements of the subsidiary regime of CBMs were identified in 1984–86. They joined articles V and X together by encouraging peaceful international cooperation in those areas where transparency was most necessary for the avoidance of ambiguity and suspicion that could give rise to concerns over compliance. A paper delivered by Robert P. Mikulak to the Symposium on Biological Research and Military Policy at the Annual Meeting of the American Association for the Advancement of Science (AAAS) on 26 May 1984 was a rich source of ideas.[9] Mikulak had been the principal scientific specialist on chemical weapons and BTW in the Bureau of Multilateral Affairs of the US Arms Control and Disarmament Agency since 1971 and was a key member of the US delegation to the First Review Conference. He was also to be a key member of the US delegation at the Second Review Conference. The BTWC had fallen into disfavour in the US and other Western governments since 1979–80. Mikulak was one of the first to suggest ways in which the treaty regime might develop, and the current CBM programme owes much to his tenacity and foresight.

The key to this approach was openness. Mikulak united with US domestic critics of military secrecy, such as the Committee (now Council) for Responsible Genetics (CRG), on the issue of genetic engineering as an actual or potential threat to the BTW disarmament regime.[10] He argued that military research on recombinant DNA should not be designated as officially secret. In the USA all such research was unclassified, and Mikulak maintained that this should be the case in all countries. Open publication policies in this field would generate greater confidence in the convention by dispelling exaggerations of the threat posed to it by genetically modified organisms that had military applications.

Mikulak foreshadowed the CBM programme in other areas, including: (*a*) information on past and current BTW activities with data reporting requirements, including information on such activities conducted before the BTWC

---

[7] Third Review Conference document BWC/CONF.III/17, 24 Sep. 1991, pp. 52–53. The French proposal of 1991 is further discussed in section VI of this chapter.

[8] BWC/CONF.III/22/Add.2 (note 5), p. 7, and Add.3, pp. 20–21.

[9] Mikulak, R. P., 'Possible improvements in the Biological Weapons Convention', Paper delivered to the Symposium on Biological Research and Military Policy at the AAAS Annual Meeting, Philadelphia, 26 May 1984.

[10] Sims, N. A., *Biological and Toxin Weapons: Issues in the 1986 Review*, Faraday Discussion Paper no. 7 (Council for Arms Control: London, 1986), p. 20.

was negotiated; (*b*) information on unusual or large-scale outbreaks of disease; (*c*) information on biological research facilities that were handling particularly dangerous materials; and (*d*) exchange of personnel between such facilities, perhaps through a programme of fellowships under Article X of the convention.

It was Mikulak's conviction that: 'Greater openness about past and present activities, in the form of data reporting requirements, could help to minimize unwarranted concerns.'[11] Sufficient transparency would minimize apprehension about establishments and occurrences which, unexplained, might be misperceived as evidence of offensive BTW intent or capability.

This approach was strongly influenced by the BTWC's absence of constraints on research. Greater transparency in research on topics of relevance to the convention was intended to compensate to some extent for this deficiency. In 1984 this approach was more likely to succeed than the direct assault on the problem advocated by the CRG. At the time the CRG was circulating a petition among US scientists to subject all research on BTW to justification by the criteria ('of types and in quantities . . . [justified] . . . for prophylactic, protective or other peaceful purposes') which already were applied when permission was sought to develop research findings.[12] Mikulak's approach was indirect and accepted that research could not be dealt with in the same way as development. This was necessary since the BTWC covered development but not research, and it was unlikely that it would be amended to cover research.

II. The Second Review Conference, 1986

The Second Review Conference did not use the term 'confidence-building measures'. In 1986 it was too narrowly associated with the military dimension of the Helsinki Process, initiated by the 35-member Conference on Security and Co-operation in Europe (CSCE), to be applied with ease to a global treaty regime. However, although (out of consideration for parties from other parts of the world) the CSCE states did not impose this term on the voluntary measures of international mutual cooperation to which the participants in the Second Review Conference committed all parties to the BTWC, they pursued adoption of the concept. It was a fortunate coincidence that the successful conclusion of the 1984–86 Conference on Confidence- and Security-Building Measures and Disarmament in Europe (the Stockholm Conference)[13] occurred just as the Second Review Conference entered its final week.

The CSCE states played a leading part at the BTWC review conference, and the success of the Stockholm Conference made a significant impression. The review conference adopted four cooperative measures, which subsequently became known as confidence-building measures A, B, C and D. The current CBM programme derives its original authority from the 1986 Final Declaration:

---

[11] Mikulak (note 9), p. 5.

[12] Committee for Responsible Genetics (CRG), *Petition Concerning the Military Use of Biological Research* (CRG: Boston, Mass., 1984).

[13] The Stockholm Conference extended the CBMs agreed at the 1975 Helsinki Conference on Security and Co-operation in Europe into new confidence- and security-building measures subject to challenge inspection. A good account of the 1984–86 Stockholm Conference is Borawski, J., *From the Atlantic to the Urals: Negotiating Arms Control at the Stockholm Conference* (Pergamon-Brassey's: London and New York, 1988).

The Conference, mindful of the provisions of Article V and Article X, and determined to strengthen the authority of the Convention and to enhance confidence in the implementation of its provisions, agrees that the States Parties are to implement, on the basis of mutual co-operation, the following measures, in order to prevent or reduce the occurrence of ambiguities, doubts and suspicions, and in order to improve international co-operation in the field of peaceful bacteriological (biological) activities:

1. Exchange of data, including name, location, scope and general description of activities, on research centres and laboratories that meet very high national or international safety standards established for handling, for permitted purposes, biological materials that pose a high individual and community risk or specialize in permitted biological activities directly related to the Convention.

2. Exchange of information on all outbreaks of infectious diseases and similar occurrences caused by toxins that seem to deviate from the normal pattern as regards type, development, place, or time of occurrence. If possible, the information provided would include, as soon as it is available, data on the type of disease, approximate area affected, and number of cases.

3. Encouragement of publication of results of biological research directly related to the Convention, in scientific journals generally available to States Parties, as well as promotion of use for permitted purposes of knowledge gained in this research.

4. Active promotion of contacts between scientists engaged in biological research directly related to the Convention, including exchanges for joint research on a mutually agreed basis.

The Conference decides to hold an *ad hoc* meeting of scientific and technical experts from States Parties to finalize the modalities for the exchange of information and data by working out, *inter alia*, appropriate forms to be used by States Parties for the exchange of information agreed to in its Final Declaration, thus enabling States Parties to follow a standardized procedure. The group shall meet in Geneva for the period 31 March–15 April 1987 and shall communicate the results of the work to the States Parties immediately thereafter.

Pending the results of this meeting, the Conference urges States Parties to promptly apply these measures and report the data agreed upon to the United Nations Department for Disarmament Affairs.

The Conference requests the United Nations Department for Disarmament Affairs to make available the information received to all States Parties.[14]

On 15 April 1987 the Ad Hoc Meeting of Scientific and Technical Experts—chaired by Director of the Swedish Defence Research Establishment (FOA) Dr Bo Rybeck—agreed the text of the forms and set 15 October 1987 as the date by which initial declarations were to be submitted to the Department for Disarmament Affairs in New York. Thereafter, annual declarations were to be made by 15 April each year for the preceding calendar year (i.e., the declarations due on 15 April 1989 would cover events in 1988, and so on).[15]

[14] BWC/CONF.II/13/II (note 4), p. 6.
[15] Second Review Conference document BWC/CONF.II/EX/2, 21 Apr. 1987, p. 10. The Ad Hoc Meeting constituted an 'appendix' to the conference. Its 'Modalities for the exchange of information' were reproduced in facsimile as an appendix in Goldblat, J. and Bernauer, T., *The Third Review of the Biological Weapons Convention: Issues and Proposals*, United Nations Institute for Disarmament Research (UNIDIR) Research Paper no. 9 (United Nations: New York, 1991), pp. 51–60. The title 'Confidence-Building Measures' began to replace 'exchange of information and data' in 1987.

III. Implementation of the first CBMs, 1987–91

By early 1991 it was clear that the CBM programme was not working well. Even though China, France and Italy (which initially failed to do so) had begun to file returns in 1989, there were still none from the Middle East and only three from Asia. The 1987–90 response rate was 15–26 per cent;[16] by 1 March 1991 only 33 per cent of the parties—not even a majority of those which had participated in the Second Review Conference—had filed either an initial or annual return.[17] Confidence-building measure B (unusual outbreaks of disease) was almost universally ignored, despite the evidence in reports made separately to the World Health Organization (WHO) by governments' health departments that data existed which might reasonably have been expected to qualify for declaration under this CBM.[18] For confidence-building measures A, C and D, the criterion common to all three, 'activities/research directly related to the Convention', was interpreted in widely divergent ways, for reasons which have been closely analysed by Barend ter Haar in his critique of the 1987–91 CBMs and their origins and shortcomings in practice.[19] This divergence thwarted the aim of the 1987 agreed modalities: to enable respondents 'to follow a standardized procedure'.[20]

During 1990 and 1991 proposals were devised to make the CBM programme a more significant part of the compliance regime. It was widely agreed that the existing CBMs ought to focus more sharply on data that would build confidence, particularly those which conveyed a fuller picture of states' BTW defence programmes than the listing of high-containment facilities under confidence-building measure A had done. Too much of marginal relevance to confidence building had been declared, and too little of the more useful types of information. As ter Haar pointed out, 'Participation in the exchange of information is not the same as full implementation of the agreed-upon measures. Doubts exist whether the parties that took part in the data exchange all noted everything they should have declared.'[21]

Many parties ignored the entire exercise, especially in Africa, Asia and Latin America. Nil (or null) returns were made by New Zealand and Togo, but few parties followed their example. Perhaps it had not been stressed adequately that such returns would be welcomed for the sake of reassurance and completeness. A more 'user-friendly' questionnaire would have made it easier for busy min-

---

[16] In this period the number of parties increased from 109 to 112. The number of respondents varied from 16 to 29, with 15% responding in 1987, 19% in 1988, 16% in 1989 and 26% in 1990. In view of the diversity of CBM returns and their variable quality, limited significance should be attached to these figures. A careful analysis of the information exchanges up to 31 Aug. 1989 is presented in Geissler, E. (ed.), *Strengthening the Biological Weapons Convention by Confidence-Building Measures*, SIPRI Chemical & Biological Warfare Studies no. 10 (Oxford University Press: Oxford, 1990) in the following chapters: Geissler, E., 'The first three rounds of information exchanges', pp. 71–79; Geissler, E. and Brunius, G., 'Information on high-risk laboratories', pp. 80–104; Woodall, J. P. and Geissler, E., 'Information on outbreaks of infectious diseases and intoxinations', pp. 105–24; Brunius, G. and Geissler, E., 'Information on publication of results and promotion of contacts', pp. 125–30; Geissler, E., 'Supplementary information', pp. 131–33; and Geissler, E. *et al.*, 'Discussion', pp. 134–46.

[17] Goldblat and Bernauer (note 15), pp. 21–22, record participation on one or more occasions (up to 1 Mar. 1991) by 37 parties, based on information provided by the DDA.

[18] Woodall and Geissler (note 16), pp. 105–24.

[19] ter Haar, B., Center for Strategic and International Studies (CSIS), *The Future of Biological Weapons*, Washington Paper no. 151 (Praeger: New York, 1991), pp. 38–48, 70–75.

[20] BWC/CONF.II/EX/2 (note 15), pp. 4, 7, 10.

[21] ter Haar (note 19), p. 71.

istries of foreign affairs to join in the exchange of data, but the fact remains that the non-respondents were defaulting on a politically binding commitment.

There were other reasons for dissatisfaction. The DDA simply photocopied the documents submitted to it (even a handwritten fax, in one case)[22] and distributed them 'in the form received' in the original language only to the parties and to the WHO. The DDA had been asked to do so by the 1987 Meeting of Experts, and its limited resources did not allow it to do more.[23]

In a 1990 SIPRI study a small group of scientific experts, led by Professor Erhard Geissler of the German Democratic Republic Academy of Sciences, analysed the data reported in the initial and annual declarations made up to 1989 and presented it in a more accessible form.[24] The volume's recommendations for rationalizing and improving the 1987 CBM procedures were reinforced by discussions among government experts on BTW defence at an international symposium in Umeå, Sweden.[25] A consensus favoured making drastic changes to the CBM programme when the Third Review Conference met. Conferences held in the first six months of 1991—at Moscow, Noordwijk-aan-Zee near The Hague, and Bossey near Geneva—widened the consensus and encouraged governments to plan detailed improvements.[26]

IV. The Third Review Conference, 1991

The United Nations was expected to analyse and assess the implementation of the CBMs since 1987 and report to the Third Review Conference, as requested by the UN General Assembly in 1990.[27] However, the UN Secretariat produced a 958-page compilation of the material it had already circulated. (An additional 52 pages were added in a 12 August addendum.) Not surprisingly, the Preparatory Committee in April 1991 recommended that the material remain in the original languages of submission of each item and that only two copies per party should be printed.[28]

The UN Secretariat and governmental and non-governmental specialists expressed disappointment with the results. Instead of an analytical report on the implementation of the decisions of the Second Review Conference and the 1987 Ad Hoc Meeting of Experts' modalities, previously circulated national declarations were reproduced. These were arranged by year and CBM type with a table

---

[22] 'The author, for example, who was until 1989 responsible for the data provided by the Netherlands, once received handwritten information on one of the institutes of the Netherlands. To expedite delivery of the data, he faxed the information in the form received to the Netherlands Permanent Representation to the UN in New York with the request to forward the data to the UN Department of Disarmament Affairs. The fax was handed over to a UN official, photocopied, and in the photocopied handwriting, distributed to all parties. This was a minor thing, but it probably did not stimulate reading.' ter Haar (note 19), pp. 179–80.

[23] BWC/CONF.II/EX/2 (note 15), p. 10.

[24] Geissler (note 16).

[25] FOA hosted an international symposium, Improving Confidence-Building Measures for the Biological Weapons Convention, at Umeå, Sweden, on 28–30 May 1990. There were participants from the high-containment laboratories declared under the CBM exchanges and from the defence and foreign ministries of Bulgaria, Canada, Czechoslovakia, France, the FRG, the GDR, the Netherlands, Sweden, the UK, the USA and the USSR. *Chemical Weapons Convention Bulletin*, no. 9 (Sep. 1990), p. 11.

[26] They were organized, respectively, by UNIDIR, with financial assistance from the governments of Austria and the USSR; by the Government of the Netherlands; and by the Quaker United Nations Office, Geneva.

[27] UN General Assembly Resolution 45/57B, 4 Dec. 1990.

[28] Report of the Preparatory Committee, Third Review Conference document BWC/CONF.III/1, 15 Apr. 1991, para. 21.

listing which parties had made CBM declarations in 1987–91.[29] Of the 115 states listed in this table, which extended to 12 August 1991, only 12 had reported in each of the five rounds; 71 states had not participated in the CBM programme at all. The nature of the report led to discussion of the limited role of the DDA, the result both of its narrow mandate and lack of resources. However, extra resources were not allocated for processing future CBM data, although, initially, it appeared that the UN Secretariat would be assigned the task or that a comparable improvement would be decreed by the Third Review Conference.

The review conference made greater progress on the contents of the CBMs, which were sharpened, enhanced and expanded in a special 'technical' group.[30] The main sponsors of intended improvements presented detailed proposals which aided the work of the technical group. Some of the CBM proposals made by Canada, Finland, France, Germany, Sweden and the UK were adopted, and aspects of proposals made by Hungary, Nigeria, Peru, the Soviet Union and Yugoslavia were also incorporated.[31]

V. CBMs not adopted at the Third Review Conference

The conference adopted all but three of the new CBMs and improvements to existing CBMs which had been submitted as committee papers. The three which were not adopted in 1991 are discussed in this section.

The first of these was a German proposal for a confidence-building measure on open-air release. It would have required parties to report initially and annually 'on open-air release of micro-organisms and viruses or simulants for defence hazard assessment, testing of detection equipment and decontamination procedures/equipment'. The form for returns under this CBM would have required information for every such release, the location and approximate area affected; the type of micro-organism, virus or simulant released; and the purpose (whether hazard assessment, test of detection equipment, or decontamination procedure) of the release.[32]

Although the proposal was not adopted, Germany succeeded in persuading the review conference to insert a new paragraph on open-air release in the Article I section of the 1991 Final Declaration: 'The Conference notes that experimentation involving open-air release of pathogens or toxins harmful to man, animals or plants that has no justification for prophylactic, protective or other peaceful purposes is inconsistent with the undertakings contained in Article I.'[33] Arguably, parties ought to be able to explain any open-air release if a request is made for clarification of its compatibility with Article I as interpreted in the new text. Such a request could be made under the Article V obligation to cooperate in problem-solving consultations.

---

[29] Third Review Conference document BWC/CONF.III/2/Add.1, 12 Aug. 1991, pp. 3–7.

[30] It was chaired by Minister-Counsellor in the Peruvian Delegation to the Conference on Disarmament and Alternate Representative of Peru Dr Félix Calderón, who also served as Friend of the Chairman of the Committee of the Whole and of the Drafting Committee, 'co-ordinating technical consultations' on CBMs. Report of the Committee of the Whole, BWC/CONF.III/17 (note 7), para. 4; and Report of the Drafting Committee, BWC/CONF.III/22/Add.2 (note 5), para. 4.

[31] Proposals put before the Committee of the Whole, BWC/CONF.III/17 (note 7), annex 1.

[32] BWC/CONF.III/17 (note 7), p. 50.

[33] BWC/CONF.III/22/Add.2 (note 5), p. 2.

The second unadopted CBM proposal, made by Finland, was a CBM on military vaccination programmes. (It had originally been proposed by France in 1986.[34]) The CBM would have required lists of vaccines (noting the agent or disease being vaccinated against) used in 'standard and/or regular peacetime vaccination programmes concerning active-duty military personnel, including conscripts, but excluding *ad hoc*, short-notice vaccinations for military personnel on special assignment (such as UN peace-keeping duties)'.[35]

France supported the Finnish proposal and made one of its own on 'information on the regular pattern of military vaccination programmes for troops as prescribed by their military health authorities'.[36] However, agreement could not be reached on the CBM, probably because of the 'balance of risks' argument that the risk of exposing vulnerability to a BTW aggressor outweighed the confidence-building value of openness in an area of high-security sensitivity for armed forces.[37]

The third CBM that was not adopted was a proposal by Hungary for opening declared facilities. It was a different kind of CBM proposal which could have formed an important link between the CBM programme and the introduction of verification (limited to declared facilities) in a regime of compliance. Under the proposal the review conference would have welcomed:

the initiative by which States Parties—which are ready to do so—wish to open their declared facilities on a reciprocal basis to verify on-site the information provided in their respective national reports. Such voluntary undertakings would greatly enhance efforts aimed at elaborating a verification regime and would also represent a means of demonstrating compliance. Should such an initiative gather wider support from States Parties, it could possibly form a basis for a multilateral CBM.[38]

An additional proposal for 'an indicative list of micro-organisms, viruses and toxins which are capable by their very nature of being used as a means of warfare' was not acted on by the Third Review Conference. Canada, Germany and the Netherlands proposed that such a list be annexed to the 1991 Final Declaration in order 'to improve the awareness of States Parties and to improve the participation in, and quality of, the exchange of information under Article V'. A similar list was separately proposed by Romania.[39] Although its supporters emphasized that the list would be merely indicative and would not 'diminish or reduce the scope of Article I of the Convention',[40] fear that such a list might be misconstrued as exhaustive (thereby unwittingly encouraging the exploitation of supposed loopholes in the scope of the BTWC) prevented its adoption.

[34] France had unsuccessfully proposed a CBM on military vaccination programmes limited to parties already under investigation in exceptional circumstances. Second Review Conference document BWC/CONF.II/9, 22 Sep. 1986, p. 25. The French proposal was made under the heading of Article VI; it envisaged that 'within the framework of an enquiry into an unusual or dubious situation or an alleged use, the States Parties shall provide information on the vaccinations undergone by their military personnel or laboratory staff in the region in question. The State to which the request is addressed shall co-operate fully in supplying the appropriate evidence'.

[35] BWC/CONF.III/17 (note 7), p. 36.

[36] BWC/CONF.III/17 (note 7), p. 29.

[37] Sims, N. A., *Reinforcing Biological Disarmament: Issues in the 1991 Review*, Faraday Discussion Paper no. 16 (Council for Arms Control: London, 1991), pp. 12–14.

[38] BWC/CONF.III/17 (note 7), p. 44.

[39] BWC/CONF.III/17 (note 7), pp. 16–17.

[40] BWC/CONF.III/17 (note 7), pp. 25–26.

The above discussion illustrates how fluid the subsidiary regime of CBMs is, with a continuing agenda capable of constructive exploitation in this evolutionary process. Ideas which were unacceptable in 1986 (such as the US proposal for declaration of past BTW involvement[41]) were adopted in 1991. This may also be the case in future with one or more of the CBMs which were proposed in 1991. However, no new CBMs were added at the 1996 Fourth Review Conference. The ultimate limits of CBM development remain to be seen. Perhaps the most ambitious proposal is the 'interim' CBM suggested by Pakistan in 1986 whereby parties should 'open all their establishments engaged in research in biological agents to interested scientists'.[42]

VI. CBMs adopted, enhanced or expanded at the Third Review Conference

The Third Review Conference adopted, enhanced or expanded a number of CBMs. The CBM technical group developed and formally organized the CBM programme into seven CBMs. These were labelled A to G, and a single-sheet questionnaire made nil (null) returns easy to complete by ticking boxes for each of the seven CBMs in columns 'Nothing to declare' (for initial declarations) and 'Nothing new to declare' (for annual declarations). The redesigned forms gave those parties which did have something to declare greater assistance in compiling their national declarations. The new forms approximated a questionnaire format as closely as possible; in some cases detailed notes provided guidance.

The Third Review Conference repeated the text from the Second Review Conference that authorized the measures: 'the Conference . . . agrees that the States Parties are to implement, on the basis of mutual co-operation, the following measures'; the rationale was also reiterated: 'in order to prevent or reduce the occurrence of ambiguities, doubts and suspicions, and in order to improve international co-operation in the field of peaceful bacteriological (biological) activities'. As at the Second Review Conference articles V and X were linked. However, at the Third Review Conference the words 'set out in the annex to this Final Declaration' were inserted between the authority and the rationale text.[43] This insertion was significant because it gave the detailed contents of the CBMs the same status as the Final Declaration. Those details had to be negotiated and agreed in the three weeks of the conference (9–27 September 1991) and could not be delegated to a Meeting of Experts like the one which had worked out modalities in 1987 as an 'appendix' to the Second Review Conference.

The toughest negotiation took place over confidence-building measure A; it was originally just a declaration of high-containment facilities but now

---

[41] The USA proposed in 1986 'that States Parties should declare whether or not they possessed, at any time during the ten years prior to the entry into force of the Convention for them, any facility designed and used for activities prohibited by the Convention and, if so, the current status of the facility'. BWC/CONF.II/9 (note 34), p. 15.

[42] BWC/CONF.II/9 (note 34), p. 23.

[43] BWC/CONF.III/22/Add.2 (note 5), p. 6. The new text read: 'the Conference agrees . . . that the States Parties are to implement, on the basis of mutual cooperation, the following measures set out in the annex to this Final Declaration, in order to prevent or reduce the occurrence of ambiguities, doubts and suspicions, and in order to improve cooperation in the field of peaceful bacteriological (biological) activities'. Third Review Conference document BWC/CONF.III/23, Geneva, 1992, p. 14.

extended into a comprehensive disclosure of national BTW defence arrangements. Following the 1990 meeting in Umeå, Sweden, the British, Canadian, French, Soviet and Swedish governments each developed detailed adaptations of CBM A which they promoted energetically at Geneva. China, Germany, the UK and the USA also engaged in hard bargaining on, for example, the extent to which individual facilities to which defence work was subcontracted (e.g., as only part of their overall activity such as a university or commercial laboratory) need be included in national reports. According to Barbara Hatch Rosenberg, 'the United Kingdom and Germany stood in the way of requiring that the names and locations of the latter be declared, fearing that this might upset or endanger their university or commercial contractors'.[44] A compromise was eventually reached, so that instead of a fixed percentage of BTW defence work being defined as the threshold above which a facility must be declared, the criterion became: 'each facility, both governmental and non-governmental, which has *a substantial proportion* of its resources devoted to the national biological defence research and development programme, within the territory of the reporting State, or under its jurisdiction or control anywhere'.[45] CBM A was divided into two parts: 'Part 1, Exchange of data on research centres and laboratories'; and 'Part 2, Exchange of information on national biological defence research and development programmes'.

Confidence-building measure B ('exchange of information on outbreaks of infectious diseases and similar occurrences caused by toxins, and on all such events that seem to deviate from the normal pattern as regards type, development, place, or time of occurrence') was retained, although there was little enthusiasm for it, in an amended form proposed by Germany.[46] The only substantial change was the addition of a form for reporting background information on the number of cases of reportable infectious diseases for each of the five years 1988–92 (this information had been volunteered by Canada, China and Sweden in their responses) so that deviations from the normal pattern could more readily be identified.[47]

Confidence-building measure C ('encouragement of publication of results and promotion of use of knowledge') was left unchanged. In an important reaffirmation of the 1984 'Mikulak proposition',[48] from which the main principles of openness guiding this CBM programme originally derived, the Third Review Conference repeated a recommendation first formulated at the 1987 Meeting of Experts: 'It is recommended that basic research in biosciences, and particularly that directly related to the Convention, should generally be unclassified; and that applied research to the extent possible, without infringing on national and commercial interests, should also be unclassified.'[49]

[44] Rosenberg, B. H., 'North vs. South: politics and the Biological Weapons Convention', *Politics and the Life Sciences*, vol. 12, no. 1 (Feb. 1993), p. 70.

[45] Question 7 on Form A, Part 2 (ii), of the newly enhanced confidence-building measure A. Third Review Conference document BWC/CONF.III/22/Add.3, 27 Sep. 1991, p. 7, emphasis added.

[46] German proposal on confidence-building measure B (improved), second revised version, 13 Sep. 1991, reproduced in BWC/CONF.III/17 (note 7), pp. 45–47.

[47] BWC/CONF.III/22/Add.3 (note 45), p. 12.

[48] Mikulak (note 9).

[49] BWC/CONF.II/EX/2 (note 15), p. 9; and BWC/CONF.III/22/Add.3 (note 45), p. 15. In both documents this recommendation constituted the first of the modalities agreed under CBM C, encouragement of publication of results and promotion of use of knowledge.

Confidence-building measure D ('active promotion of contacts between scientists engaged in biological research directly related to the Convention, including exchanges for joint research on a mutually agreed basis') was retained and slightly extended on the initiative of France ('other experts and facilities' were now added to 'scientists', and 'visits' were added to 'exchanges').[50] The form on which 'international conferences, symposia, seminars and other similar forums [fora in 1987] for exchange, and information regarding other opportunities' were to be reported remained unchanged.[51]

Three new CBMs were added. The first, confidence-building measure E ('declaration of legislation, regulations and other measures'), was a further stage in the regime-building process derived from Article IV (national implementation). It was added on the initiative of the UK,[52] whose delegation at the First Review Conference had initiated the efforts to build on Article IV.

Confidence-building measure F ('offensive and/or defensive biological R&D programmes') was a French initiative, which was based on an unsuccessful US proposal from the Second Review Conference.[53] The French proposal added detailed reporting requirements.[54] It went beyond a British proposal from 1980 that parties declare their BTW status as 'never possessed/having possessed' and read: 'In the interest of increasing transparency and openness, States Parties shall declare whether or not they conducted any offensive and/or defensive biological research and development programmes since 1 January 1946.'

If a party had conducted an offensive programme it was now required to state the period(s) of such activities and to provide a 'summary of the R&D activities, indicating whether work was performed concerning production, test and evaluation, weaponization, stockpiling of biological agents, the destruction programme of such agents and weapons, and other related research'. If it had carried out defensive activities the party was now required to state the period(s) of such activities and to provide a 'summary of the R&D activities, indicating whether or not work was conducted in the following areas: prophylaxis, studies on pathogenicity and virulence, diagnostic techniques, aerobiology, detection, treatment, toxinology, physical protection, decontamination, and other related research, with location if possible'.[55]

The date 1 January 1946 was adopted instead of the US proposal, made in 1986, that the reporting period should extend back in time only 10 years prior to the entry into force of the convention for the state concerned. If the US proposal had succeeded, it would have meant, for example, that the UK, the USA and the USSR would have been obliged to report only activities subsequent to 1965. Similarly, France and China would have only had to report on activities after 1974, Iraq only on activities subsequent to 1981, and so on. (In 1991 France sought to extend this period to 20 years prior to entry into force.[56]) The 1946

[50] French proposal of 13 Sep. 1991 on confidence-building measure D, as revised on 17 Sep. 1991, reproduced in BWC/CONF.III/17 (note 7), p. 51.

[51] BWC/CONF.II/EX/2 (note 15), p. 11; and BWC/CONF.III/22/Add.3 (note 45), p. 17.

[52] UK proposal of 13 Sep. 1991, Confidence-building measure on declaration of legislation, regulations and other measures, reproduced in BWC/CONF.III/17 (note 7), p. 27. CBM E is also discussed in chapter 2, section IV in this volume.

[53] BWC/CONF.II/9 (note 34), p. 15.

[54] French proposal of 18 Sep. 1991, Past activities, reproduced in BWC/CONF.III/17 (note 7), pp. 52–53.

[55] BWC/CONF.III/22/Add.3 (note 45), pp. 20–21.

[56] BWC/CONF.III/17 (note 7), p. 52.

date excludes the offensive BTW programmes of certain states in and before World War II but encompasses all post-1945 programmes.

Confidence-building measure G ('vaccine production facilities'), was adopted on the initiative of Canada and Finland. It read: 'To further increase the transparency of biological research and development related to the Convention and to broaden scientific and technical knowledge as agreed in Article X, each State Party will declare all facilities, both governmental and non-governmental, within its territory or under its jurisdiction or control anywhere, producing vaccines licensed by the State Party for the protection of humans.'[57]

The form for reporting on CBM G required information on the name and location of every such facility and a general description of the types of disease covered. The CBM as agreed was less extensive than the original proposal, which included vaccines for the protection of animals and requested more detailed information on each vaccine production facility from the reporting governments.[58] Nevertheless, it was an important first move into an aspect of compliance assurance—the transparency of commercial production in industries applying advanced techniques of biotechnology in the private sector—which may be further explored in future.

The adoption of this new, enhanced and expanded subsidiary regime of CBMs was a major part of the success of the 1991 review conference in agreeing a Final Declaration aimed at strengthening the BTWC, which 'can be partly attributed to the spectre of germ warfare which haunted the hostilities in the [Persian] Gulf and sharpened the determination of the international community to exclude the very possibility of resorting to biological and toxin weapons'.[59]

However, the absence of enabling machinery, such as a dedicated unit of the UN Secretariat to facilitate the processing of CBMs, appeared unlikely to encourage participation in the information exchange. Rosenberg noted that because of the failures of the review conference on the institutional front 'there is no reason to expect much change in the poor record of participation'.[60]

VII. Expectations of the enhanced CBM programme

As 15 April 1992 approached there was an expectation that the CBM programme would be transformed and that improvement would occur quantitatively and qualitatively in the national reports to be submitted by that date to the UN Office for Disarmament Affairs.[61] More parties were expected to report than in the past, and the additional information would increase confidence in compliance with the convention. However, only 11 parties—less than 10 per cent of the total roster—submitted their CBM declarations on 15 April 1992 or before.[62] By the end of April there were 6 additional submissions,[63] and by

---

[57] BWC/CONF.III/22/Add.3 (note 45), p. 22.

[58] BWC/CONF.III/17 (note 7), p. 36 (Finland); and pp. 36–37 (Canada).

[59] Goldblat, J. and Bernauer, T., 'Towards a more effective ban on biological weapons', *Bulletin of Peace Proposals*, vol. 23, no. 1 (Mar. 1992), p. 1.

[60] Rosenberg (note 44), p. 71.

[61] The Department for Disarmament Affairs (DDA) was replaced by the Office for Disarmament Affairs (ODA) on 29 Feb. 1992. It, in turn, was superseded by the Centre for Disarmament Affairs (CDA) in 1994. In 1998 it again became the Department for Disarmament Affairs.

[62] They were Australia, Austria, Canada, Czechoslovakia, Germany, Mongolia, New Zealand, Sweden, the UK, the USA and Yugoslavia.

[63] They were Norway (21 Apr.), Switzerland (23 Apr.), Cyprus and Japan (28 Apr.), and Hungary and Malta (30 Apr.).

1 June 1992 another 6 declarations had been made,[64] making a total of 23 reports. The substance of the national reports was so diverse and the rate of return so low that only tentative conclusions can be drawn from them.[65]

VIII. Analysis of the first returns under the new CBM programme

The most easily compared and aggregated data were presented in response to confidence-building measure G, on vaccine production facilities. By 1 June 1992, 19 parties had submitted declarations listing the names and locations of 69 production facilities and giving a general description of the vaccines being produced at each facility. Table 3.1 lists those facilities by country and the three countries which declared that they had no vaccine production facilities.

There was some uncertainty over what should be declared under CBM G. Czechoslovakia's description of work at the Research Institute of Viral Medicine in Brno ('reference laboratory for Teschen disease, development of diagnostics antisera, collection of micro-organisms'[66]) did not qualify it for inclusion on the list as clearly as the other five facilities it declared. The director of the Norwegian Defence Microbiological Laboratory, Professor Bjørn P. Berdal, listed four facilities actively producing vaccines (in Oslo, Overhalla, Stavanger and Tromsø) and added: 'There is also the National Institute of Public Health, N-0462 Oslo, where there are vaccine production facilities. However, earlier activities with influenza, whooping cough, tetanus and meningococcal group B-vaccine have presently been closed down. Some of these may be taken up again at a later stage, and will be reported then.'[67] Berdal's reporting of this 'latent' facility drew attention to the fine distinction between vaccine production facilities and 'facilities . . . producing vaccines'; only the latter were required to be declared, but it was necessary to declare the former in order to provide the full picture and allay concern.

Several governments went beyond the agreed limit: 'for the protection of humans'. Norway, for example, declared two facilities producing vaccines for fish-farming purposes and one aimed at the protection of cattle. The USA took as its criterion for inclusion establishments holding unsuspended, unrevoked product licences, and included one (the Frederick Cancer Research and Development Center of the National Cancer Institute of the National Institutes of Health) even though its vaccine production, against anthrax, was not scheduled to start until August 1992.

The new requirement to declare, in the interests of increased transparency and openness, whether or not parties had conducted any offensive or defensive biological R&D programmes since 1 January 1946 produced information on 3 offensive and 12 defensive programmes. In addition, Belarus noted, after

---

[64] They were South Korea (1 May), Tunisia (7 May), Belarus (14 May), the Netherlands (22 May), Bulgaria (26 May) and Finland (1 June).

[65] UN Department for Disarmament Affairs document DDA/4-92/BWIII, 30 Apr. 1992, contains the first 15 national reports. The returns under CBM E are discussed in chapter 2, section IV in this volume.

[66] UN Department for Disarmament Affairs document DDA/4-92/BWIII, 30 Apr. 1992, p. 102 (Czechoslovakia).

[67] UN Department for Disarmament Affairs document DDA/4-92/BWIII, 30 Apr. 1992, p. 169 (Norway).

Table 3.1. Vaccine production facility declarations under confidence-building measure G of the BTWC, as of 1 June 1992

Country	Number of facilities
USA[a]	23 (15 on US territory, 2 in south-east England, 1 each in Belgium, Canada, France, Italy, Japan and Switzerland)
Japan	10
Czechoslovakia	6
United Kingdom	6
Norway	5
Hungary	4
South Korea	4
Canada	2
Germany	2
Australia	1
Bulgaria	1
Finland	1
Mongolia	1
Netherlands	1
Sweden	1
Switzerland	1
Belarus	0
New Zealand	0
Tunisia	0

[a] The US facilities were run by US government agencies or commercial enterprises.

Source: UN Department for Disarmament Affairs document DDA/4-92/BWIII, 30 Apr. 1992, pp. 406–27 (USA); p. 128 (Japan); p. 102 (Czechoslovakia); pp. 249–52 (UK); p. 169 (Norway); pp. 67–69 (Hungary); p. 97 (South Korea); pp. 79–80 (Canada); p. 126 (Germany); p. 24 (Australia); p. 37 (Bulgaria); p. 53 (Finland); p. 139 (Mongolia); p. 95 (the Netherlands); p. 184 (Sweden); p. 212 (Switzerland); Add. 1, p. 25 (Belarus); p. 149 (New Zealand); and p. 98 (Tunisia).

reporting that it conducted no programmes of either kind: 'The Republic of Belarus does not have any information as to whether such programmes have been conducted on its territory.'[68] The implication was that the Soviet Union, of which the Byelorussian Soviet Socialist Republic had been part until 1991, might have carried out activities on Byelorussian territory to which the government of the newly independent Belarus was not privy.

Russia's declarations under CBMs A, F and G, in particular, were eagerly awaited, but no CBW information was received by 15 April 1992 (or in the subsequent weeks) from the Russian Federation, which had assumed the legal obligations of the former Soviet Union as its successor state.[69] The Russian declarations were submitted in the summer of 1992. The UK and the USA were dis-

[68] UN Department for Disarmament Affairs document DDA/4-92/BWIII/Add.1, 12 June 1992, pp. 24–25 (Belarus, 14 May).

[69] The Soviet Union had made the longest initial CBM declaration in 1987, providing 33 of the 79 pages of UN Department for Disarmament Affairs document DDA/20-87/BW/I, 16 Oct. 1987. It continued to make declarations annually until its dissolution in Dec. 1991.

satisfied with the Russian information, and intense trilateral diplomacy resulted in the Moscow Joint Statement of 11 September 1992, which established a reciprocal visits programme in Russia, the UK and the USA.[70]

Three offensive R&D programmes which had existed in the past were declared under confidence-building measure F.[71] Canada declared that it had maintained an offensive programme for 11 years after the operative date (1 January 1946), and had terminated it on 31 December 1956. The UK declared an offensive programme which was conducted from 1940 to 'the late 1950s': 'Whilst some research on offensive aspects continued for a few years after World War II, by 1957 the UK had abandoned work on an offensive capability'. The United States conducted such a programme from 1941 to 1969, and it was described in a chronology combined with the narrative account of US defensive programmes in that period.[72] Canada's report was the most concise:

In the above period [1946–56] offensive work undertaken by Canada included: studies of improved procedures for production of certain toxins (e.g. botulinum and diphtheria); studies on the use of insects as vectors for pathogenic bacteria; test and evaluation of munitions, including performance in cold weather; studies of weapon-produced aerosols of potential BW agents; fundamental work related to field trials, dealing with the dispersion and properties of solid particulates, preparation of finely divided solids for munitions charging and sampling of toxic particulates; development of tissue culture processes for large scale cultivation of viruses; and development of *M. mallei* and *M.1 pseudomallei* as new potential BW agents. There was no large scale production, stockpiling or weaponization of BW agents, and no work was aimed at determining the suitability of specific agents as weapons. When necessary, BW agents are destroyed by autoclaving.[73]

Subsequent declarations under this CBM by other parties might shed light on the implementation (if any) of Article II, as states which disarmed later or which carried out offensive programmes for a longer period might reveal when and how they disposed of their BTW stockpiles.

Defensive programmes were declared and described by Australia, Canada, Czechoslovakia, Finland, Germany, Mongolia, the Netherlands, Norway, Sweden, the UK and the USA.[74] None of these states had abandoned its defensive programme so current as well as past activity had to be declared—in some cases only current activity. For several parties much of the relevant information was already being provided under the new, third part of CBM A, and the two declarations had to be read together. Often the information was supplemented by lists of relevant publications to exemplify the research pursued by defence scientists involved in the programme and the spin-offs benefiting the civil sector in public health. In other cases the defensive programme was briefly

---

[70] The Moscow Joint Statement is discussed in chapter 1, section XI in this volume.

[71] DDA/4-92/BWIII (note 65), p. 78 (Canada); pp. 396–403 (USA); and pp. 246–47 (UK). A fourth and a fifth offensive R&D programme were declared in later returns from France, for 1946–73, and Russia. They fall outside the time limit of this analysis of initial declarations submitted on or not long after the due date of 15 Apr. 1992.

[72] DDA/4-92/BWIII (note 65), p. 78 (Canada); pp. 396–403 (USA); and pp. 246–47 (UK).

[73] DDA/4-92/BWIII (note 65), p. 78 (Canada).

[74] DDA/4-92/BWIII (note 65), pp. 21–23 (Australia); pp. 35–41, 78 (Canada); pp. 84–93, 99–101 (Czechoslovakia); pp. 109–17, 125 (Germany); pp. 129–36 (Mongolia); pp. 152–57, 168 (Norway); pp. 173–76, 182–84 (Sweden); pp. 223–37, 246–48 (UK); pp. 267–86, 395–405 (USA); Add.1 (note 68), pp. 47–49 (Finland); and pp. 81–86, 96 (the Netherlands).

summarized, as it was by Norway: 'The Norwegian Defence Microbiological Laboratory has maintained a low-key R&D program since the Laboratory's founding in 1970. The number of staff, organization and purpose has remained the same from 1970 until now. Activities have been basic research on pathogenicity and virulence, and development of diagnostic techniques and detection of B-agents, mainly bacteria and toxins.'[75]

Parties with no defensive programme to declare could either submit a negative declaration under CBM F or tick the 'nothing to declare' box on the cover sheet. Belarus, Hungary, South Korea and Switzerland chose the former option; Japan, New Zealand and Tunisia chose the latter.[76]

For most respondents the longest reports were filed under CBM A, listing high-containment facilities and giving more information on facilities involved in biological defence R&D programmes, and under CBM C on relevant publications. The USA, however, filed lengthy reports under every CBM including, under CBM F, a 'narrative of the Department of Defense offensive and defensive biological R&D program' organized into historical periods with significant end-dates (1941–46, 1946–49, 1950–53, 1954–58, 1959–62, 1963–68, 1969–72, 1973–77, 1977–) which will be invaluable to future historians of US policy and practice in this sector.[77]

Few conferences were reported under CBM D. Most returns under this confidence-building measure confined themselves to 'active promotion of contacts' on strictly scientific topics.

CBM B yielded several tables of background information on the incidence of reportable infectious diseases for each year from 1988 to 1991. In addition to reports of cases involving humans some countries also provided information on infectious diseases in animals where zoonotic information was thought to be of interest. Nine unusual outbreaks of disease were reported. Sweden reported two outbreaks of disease and South Korea one case that affected humans; all other cases (reported by the Netherlands, Switzerland and the UK) involved cattle, pigs or sheep.

Cholera was the gravest human disease reported. South Korea declared 113 cases of cholera in 1991, an unusually high number for that country. Its report noted that it also had provided the details of the outbreak to the WHO. Sweden declared outbreaks of legionnaires' disease in Värnamo hospital in early 1991 and of salmonella food poisoning which persisted from July to the end of 1991 on a ferry sailing between Helsingborg in Sweden and Helsingør in Denmark.[78]

Two of the animal disease outbreaks reported involved *Bacillus anthracis*, a potential agent of bacteriological warfare. The Netherlands declared an outbreak of anthrax in Groningen which killed 10 cattle, and the UK reported on an outbreak on a single intensive breeding-and-fattening pig farm in Wales which had persisted (unusually) over three months on the affected unit. At least 19 pigs had died of anthrax. The outbreak was reported under this CBM because of the persistence of a disease which is usually sporadic. The Nether-

[75] DDA/4-92/BWIII (note 65), pp. 152–57, 168 (Norway).
[76] DDA/4-92/BWIII (note 65), p. 127 (Japan); p. 143 (New Zealand); pp. 194, 211 (Switzerland); Add.1 (note 68), pp. 5, 24–25 (Belarus); p. 66 (Hungary); p. 97 (South Korea); and pp. 98, 116 (Tunisia).
[77] DDA/4-92/BWIII (note 65), pp. 395–405.
[78] DDA/4-92/BWIII (note 65), pp. 178–79 (Sweden); and Add.1 (note 68), p. 97 (South Korea).

lands and the UK also declared two outbreaks of other diseases—hog cholera from infected pigswill in South Holland and newly introduced blue-eared pig disease on Humberside in England—which were thought to have resulted from illegal acts. In addition, Switzerland reported its first case since 1982 of scrapie in sheep and its first case ever of bovine spongiform encephalopathy (BSE).[79]

IX. CBMs in the regime of compliance

Although few CBM reports were submitted in the first five months of 1992 some governments did prepare full declarations in accordance with the politically binding commitments agreed the previous September. The agreement reached at the Third Review Conference on enhancing and expanding the CBM programme had stipulated more precise reporting requirements and had also emphasized their mandatory character under the authority of the states parties acting collectively. Governments had had six months in which to prepare their CBM declarations, and the procedure for recording nil returns had been simplified. As noted above, these factors led to expectations that a higher response rate and greater transparency would be achieved on 15 April 1992 than was the case.

The regime of compliance in Mode B—with CBMs but without verification—will command only limited confidence until more parties honour their commitments under its subsidiary regime of CBMs. CBM requirements are not constraints on action but declarations of openness. A failure to honour commitments under this programme indicates either a lack of interest in openness or a lack of belief in the regime of compliance. Measures which are ignored may reduce rather than build confidence among parties, and, ultimately, the concept of CBMs will be weakened.

The parties to the BTWC have given CBMs a central role in the regime of compliance which may be transitory (until superseded by verification) or which may perform useful functions in strengthening the safeguards against BTW on a more lasting basis. For the moment, CBMs are the most fully articulated elements of the convention's regime of compliance. The sincerity of the commitment by governments to make the BTWC work more effectively is being tested by the thoroughness with which they discharge their commitment to exchange CBM information on time, accurately and comprehensively.

By 1 June 1992 much remained to be done since barely 10 per cent of the parties had submitted reports. By 1994 the reporting rate was still only 30 per cent. By 31 December 1993, 133 states were parties to the BTWC, although only a minority took part in the CBM programme. On 15 May 1994, the Centre for Disarmament Affairs in the UN Secretariat issued the 32 CBM returns submitted on or around the due date of 15 April 1994 for the year 1993.[80] Eight more returns were issued as late submissions on 5 August 1994.[81] The 40 returns represented 30 per cent of the 133 states which were parties to the BTWC during all or part of the reporting period. However, 32 submissions which were

[79] DDA/4-92/BWIII (note 65), p. 198 (Switzerland); pp. 240–43 (UK); and Add.1 (note 68), pp. 89–92 (the Netherlands).
[80] UN document CDA/16-94/BWIII, 15 May 1994.
[81] UN document CDA/16-94/BWIII/Add.1, 5 Aug. 1994.

received on time compared well with the 23 reports that were submitted on or around 15 April 1993 for the year 1992.[82]

In both 1993 and 1994, 17 parties submitted their reports on time. They were: Australia, Austria, China, Ecuador, France, Germany, Hungary, Iceland, Italy, the Netherlands, Norway, Romania, the Russian Federation, Sweden, Turkey, the UK and the USA. In either 1993 or 1994, but not both, 21 parties were on time: Argentina, Belarus, Brazil, Bulgaria, Canada, the Czech Republic, Estonia, Fiji, Finland, Greece, Iraq, Ireland, South Korea, Mexico, Nicaragua, Portugal, Seychelles, Slovakia, Slovenia, Switzerland and Ukraine. As in the past, Europe was the most strongly represented, followed by North, South and Central America. Nonetheless, some European parties (e.g., Belgium, Denmark, Poland and Spain) did not report on their activities in either 1992 or 1993 by the due date.[83] Few parties in Africa and Asia submitted reports.

Expert commentators differed in their assessment of the enhanced CBM arrangements. Graham Pearson compared CBM participation one year after the second and third review conferences, respectively. By September 1992, 35 of a possible 120 reports had been made; the figures for 1987 were 13 out of 110 reports. Pearson noted: 'Although small in comparison to the total number of states parties . . . this figure is far more encouraging than that of 1987.'[84]

Thomas Dashiell, however, judged that: 'the response to the [CBMs] has not been good (only 30 responses as of fall 1992). Understanding that these measures are not legally binding but only politically binding does not change the situation dramatically. If a country wants to make the BWC work, it will participate under any circumstances, with or without effective verification.'[85]

Whether there is reason for pessimism or optimism remains a pertinent question. It will remain so when, if ever, the proportion of parties engaging consistently in the CBM programme has risen to 50 per cent of the total number of parties. The parties to the BTWC might be given an incentive to participate if an annual review of CBM returns and additional compliance reports were held that was open only to CBM-participating states. Such a review could also encourage prompt submission of the CBM returns due on 15 April each year if those parties whose submissions were late lost the chance to attend the review that year, thereby forfeiting the chance to evaluate the quality and quantity of the data provided by others.[86]

Unfortunately, nothing is likely to be done until a unit of the UN Secretariat is given the resources and the mandate to seek CBM returns more actively and to process them more usefully. Currently, the United Nations confines itself to issuing the minimum number of copies (untranslated) of reports 'in the forms received'[87] and repeating a general call for increased participation: 'The General

[82] UN document ODA/9-93/BWIII, 15 May 1993.

[83] CBM reports from Denmark, Poland and Spain were issued on 5 Aug. 1994 (together with those of Bolivia, Cuba, Luxembourg, Malta and Sri Lanka). CDA/16-94/BWIII/Add.1 (note 81).

[84] Pearson, G. S., 'Prospects for chemical and biological arms control: the web of deterrence', *Washington Quarterly*, vol. 16, no. 2 (spring 1993), p. 156.

[85] Dashiell, T., 'A review of US biological warfare policies', ed. B. Roberts, *Biological Weapons: Weapons of the Future?* (CSIS: Washington, DC, 1993), p. 6.

[86] Sims, N. A., 'Strengthening compliance systems for disarmament treaties: the biological and chemical weapons conventions', eds Canadian Council on International Law and The Markland Group, *Treaty Compliance: Some Concerns and Remedies* (Kluwer Law International: London, The Hague and Boston, 1998), p. 136.

[87] Note by the Secretariat, CDA/16-94/BWIII (note 80).

Assembly . . . welcomes the information and data provided to date and reiterates its call upon all States Parties to the Convention to participate in the exchange of information and data agreed to in the Final Declaration of [1991]'.[88]

The future of the CBM programme has effectively been put on 'hold' by the strengthening process pursued through VEREX (1992–93),[89] the Special Conference (1994) and the Ad Hoc Group (1995–).[90] This reflects the continuing uncertainty over the relationship between a CBM programme and any verification system which might be agreed in future to strengthen compliance with the convention, for example, as part of the BTWC protocol being negotiated by the Ad Hoc Group.

X. CBMs at the Fourth Review Conference, 1996

Confidence-building measures were not expanded at the Fourth Review Conference in 1996 because the conference did not want to complicate matters for the Ad Hoc Group, whose work it was hoping to accelerate. However, the conference was presented with an analysis by Iris Hunger[91] which showed that:

CBMs have not worked as satisfactorily as had been hoped as it has taken nine years of participation to reach the stage at which over half of the States Parties to the BTWC [75 out of 138] have made at least one annual declaration. . . . It is disappointing to note that although 63 States participated in the Second Review Conference and 78 in the Third Review Conference which agreed the CBMs, most of these States have yet to provide an *annual* CBM return as they agreed to undertake to do in the Final Report of the Review Conferences. Only about one-third of the States Parties to the BTWC takes part in the information exchange under the CBMs per year. The number has grown over the years but is still far from satisfactory.[92]

The most encouraging trend was found in the number of states that had participated without interruption since their first year of participation. Although only 11 states had reported every year since 1987, 20 had reported every year since 1991, 23 every year since 1992, 28 every year since 1993, and 35 every year since 1994.[93]

The Fourth Review Conference was a time for consolidation, not expansion, as Dando and Pearson noted:

Consequently, at the Fourth Review Conference the importance of the existing confidence-building measures needed to be re-emphasised to avoid the risk that, through paying little attention to the existing CBMs—and because the Ad Hoc Group is addressing which CBMs are appropriate for incorporation into a legally binding instrument—States Parties might mistakenly draw the conclusion that providing annual

[88] UN document A/49/711, 28 Nov. 1994. Operative para. 3 of draft resolution A/C.1/49/L.13 was adopted without a vote by the First Committee of the General Assembly on 14 Nov. 1994.
[89] The Ad Hoc Group of Governmental Experts to Identify and Examine Potential Verification Measures from a Scientific and Technical Standpoint (VEREX) was established after the 1991 Review Conference.
[90] The Ad Hoc Group was established by the 1994 Special Conference of the BTWC and is open to all states parties.
[91] Hunger, I., 'Article V: confidence-building measures', eds G. S. Pearson and M. R. Dando, *Strengthening the Biological Weapons Convention: Key Points for the Fourth Review Conference* (Quaker United Nations Office: Geneva, 1996), pp. 77–92.
[92] Hunger (note 91), p. 78, emphasis in the original.
[93] Hunger (note 91), p. 80.

information as agreed upon at the Second and Third Review Conference is no longer important.[94]

The conference left the CBMs unchanged. In paragraph 5 of the Article V section of its Final Declaration it welcomed the exchange of information which had taken place and noted that it had contributed to enhancing transparency and building confidence. It also recognized that participation in CBMs had 'not been universal, and that not all responses have been prompt or complete'. While accepting that preparing CBM reports presented some parties with technical difficulties, the conference urged all parties 'to complete full and timely declarations in future'.[95] The Ad Hoc Group reserved draft Article VIII of its protocol for provisions on CBMs, but until mid-2000 no text for this article had been proposed.[96] Draft text was introduced by South Africa during the twentieth session (10 July–4 August 2000) of the Ad Hoc Group but not discussed.

XI. Conclusions

In a major survey of the subject, Marie Chevrier concluded: 'CBMs ought to be drafted with care and tailored to activities likely to yield the most relevant information [but] cannot be a substitute for a legally binding framework to enhance treaty compliance.'[97]

When the Ad Hoc Group finishes its work the role of CBMs in the treaty regime of compliance should be clearer. CBM status may still be needed for information which is not covered by the verification provisions included in a new, legally binding protocol. A system of declarations verified by inspection might be inappropriate for such information, but the application of CBMs might still generate some degree of compliance reassurance.

Reassurance is the key issue, and states parties should consider what information ought to be exchanged so that they are mutually reassured about one another's compliance with the convention. Patterns of normal behaviour should be established in order to enable identification of deviations from the norm, and information should be provided to demonstrate compliance to the satisfaction of those parties most likely to question it. Declarations should be made so that transparency is enhanced.

Although an item of information may have acquired CBM status, this does not establish its usefulness for all time, and some transparency may be irrelevant. It is important to limit the number of actual or potential CBMs to those which truly generate compliance reassurance. This is all the more important if, in the absence of verification, CBMs have to continue to support the regime of compliance as it evolves.

---

[94] Dando, M. R. and Pearson, G.S., 'The Fourth Review Conference of the Biological and Toxin Weapons Convention: issues, outcomes, and unfinished business', *Politics and the Life Sciences*, vol. 16, no. 1 (Mar. 1997), p. 121.

[95] Fourth Review Conference document BWC/CONF.IV/9, 6 Dec. 1996, p. 19.

[96] Procedural Report of the Ad Hoc Group, Twentieth Session, BWC/AD HOC GROUP/52, 11 Aug. 2000, part I, p. 112.

[97] Chevrier, M. I., 'Doubts about confidence: the potential and limits of confidence-building measures for the Biological Weapons Convention', ed. A. E. Smithson, *Biological Weapons Proliferation: Reasons for Concern, Courses of Action*, Report no. 24 (Henry L. Stimson Center: Washington, DC, Jan. 1998), pp. 53–75.

4. The regime of compliance: the addition of verification measures

I. Introduction

Chapter 2 described, analysed and assessed the original elements of the regime of compliance (national implementation, consultation and cooperation, complaint and assistance) and their gradual evolution—Mode A of the regime. It focused on specific articles of the 1972 Biological and Toxin Weapons Convention. Chapter 3 examined Mode B: the regime of compliance with the addition of confidence-building measures. The CBMs, which function within the limits set by the BTWC, are the most concrete element of the regime of compliance as it currently operates.

The regime-building process has been exclusively endogenous, developing the latent strength of the various articles of the convention at successive review conferences, in particular, through an accumulation of 'informal undertakings'.[1] Clarifications, definitions and procedural decisions support an increasingly articulated set of rules and expectations for 'strengthening the norm of the Convention'.[2]

This chapter examines the treatment of verification at the second and third review conferences and at the 19–30 September 1994 Special Conference and also traces the development of thinking about verification as it evolved after 1986. In addition, it addresses the 'strengthening' process which was institutionalized in the Ad Hoc Group of Governmental Experts to Identify and Examine Potential Verification Measures from a Scientific and Technical Standpoint (VEREX) in 1992–93 under its mandate from the 1991 Third Review Conference; in the Special Conference to which VEREX reported; and in the Ad Hoc Group (established by the Special Conference and open to all states parties). The Ad Hoc Group has met since 1995 to consider and, since 1997, to negotiate ways of strengthening the BTWC. Its mandate is to develop appropriate measures, including possible verification measures, and to draft proposals for a legally binding instrument (e.g., an additional or supplementary protocol).

The proponents of verification as a way to strengthen the convention argue that it is certain and reliable because of its exogenous character. Verification would have to be added formally and legally to the BTWC, and it is unclear whether it would wholly supplant the regime of compliance which has grown up endogenously or could complement the existing elements. The regime of compliance with verification added, Mode C, is not necessarily incompatible with modes A and B, but it may raise questions about their continued relevance.

---

[1] The term was introduced by Ambassador Rolf Ekéus at the Second Review Conference. Ekéus, R., Sweden, Second Review Conference document BWC/CONF.II/SR.7, 15 Sep. 1986, para. 16.

[2] Lowitz, D., Second Review Conference document BWC/CONF.II/SR.3, 9 Sep. 1986, para. 24; and Lowitz, D., USA, BWC/CONF.II/SR.10, 26 Sep. 1986, para. 25. A fuller discussion of this concept is presented in section III of chapter 6 in this volume.

II. Verification in perspective

It is a common misapprehension that proposals to strengthen the regime of compliance, in particular by adding a verification apparatus, originated in the mid-1990s. Although there was concern at that time in the West regarding compliance with the BTWC, Iraqi biological and toxin weapon activity and fear of BTW proliferation to states of concern and terrorists (both state-sponsored and sub-national groups) this view lacks historical perspective. Verification had been discussed as an element of the regime of compliance as early as 1986. (Its genealogy goes back to the identification of functional substitutes for verification of biological disarmament which had been agreed in 1971. However, these were later viewed by some as inadequate even with the addition of CBMs.) The essential components of a verification apparatus for the BTWC were already clear in 1986–91.

Verification has since become more politically acceptable and—especially for its proponents, although not yet for all parties—confidence has grown concerning its place in the evolving regime of compliance. It has moved from relative marginality to relative centrality, which was reflected in the intensity of the verification debates in the Ad Hoc Group and the prominence of verification proposals (under other names) in the rolling text being developed. Discussion of a verification protocol became commonplace in the mid-1990s, although it ran ahead of what had been agreed.

At that time concern about verification focused on three areas. The West raised questions about how the BTW programme of the Soviet Union affected the compliance of its successor, the Russian Federation, with the BTWC. Additionally, as mentioned above, Iraqi BTW activity and fear of BTW proliferation were also of concern.

The issues related to Iraq and Russia have, however, been addressed by measures that are independent of the BTWC and without waiting for it to be strengthened. The problem of Iraq's BTW capability, including plans for its dismantlement and prevention of its re-establishment, was addressed by the United Nations Security Council in resolutions 687 and 715 and by the UN Special Commission on Iraq.[3] Questions about Soviet BTW activities and concern regarding Russia's compliance with the BTWC were addressed by the trilateral process, which was inaugurated by the 11 September 1992 Moscow Joint Statement that gave Russia, the United Kingdom and the United States a framework within which to assure one another of their compliance.[4] The UK and the USA were also given the authority to assist Russia in eliminating any remnants of the Soviet BTW programme that were incompatible with the BTWC.

The Special Conference issued a mandate on 1 October 1994, which is discussed below in section XIII, that governs what the Ad Hoc Group is to consider and, since 1997, to negotiate (i.e., appropriate measures, including possible verification measures, and draft proposals to strengthen the convention). It reflected the view that effective verification could reinforce the BTWC, but the

---

[3] UN Security Council Resolution 687, 3 Apr. 1991; and UN Security Council Resolution 715, 11 Oct. 1991.

[4] Joint Statement on Biological Weapons by the Governments of the United Kingdom, the United States and the Russian Federation, cited in *Chemical Weapons Convention Bulletin*, no. 18 (Dec. 1992), pp. 12–13; it is discussed in chapter 1, section XI in this volume.

mandate was more inexact and tentative than the European Union (EU) and other proponents of verification wanted. Their attempts to revise it at the 1996 Fourth Review Conference were unsuccessful. The formal position thus remains the same: a verification protocol is an option, not a certainty.

III. Verification at the 1986 Second Review Conference

The last General Secretary of the Communist Party of the Soviet Union and last Soviet President, Mikhail Gorbachev, and his Foreign Minister, Eduard Shevardnadze (now President of Georgia), significantly affected the consideration of verification as a way to strengthen the BTWC's regime of compliance. The 'new political thinking' associated with Gorbachev and Shevardnadze transformed Soviet disarmament diplomacy in 1985–86. By September 1986 this transformation, which included a growing readiness to accept on-site inspection as a central feature of international verification systems, had considerably influenced several negotiating processes, including the multilateral chemical weapon disarmament negotiations at Geneva. At the 1984–86 Conference on Confidence- and Security-Building Measures (CSBMs) and Disarmament in Europe (the Stockholm Conference) it was also about to produce a breakthrough with respect to the new subsidiary regime of CBMs.[5]

At the Second Review Conference of the BTWC Ambassador Viktor Issraelyan announced, on 15 September 1986, that: 'the Soviet Union had initiated a formal proposal to work out and adopt a Supplementary Protocol to the Convention which would contain measures to strengthen the control machinery'.[6] As submitted in the Committee of the Whole, the text of the proposal made clear that the new political thinking had completely overturned the Soviet doctrine presented by Issraelyan at the 1980 First Review Conference and also by Vadim Perfiliev, speaking for the Soviet delegation in committee. The 1980 doctrine had stated that attending to 'points of detail' deemed unsatisfactory and asserting a need to strengthen the convention tended to weaken it by calling the effectiveness of the BTWC text into question.[7] The Soviet Union under the leadership of President Leonid Brezhnev and Foreign Minister Andrey Gromyko had been immovable on this point, and the word 'strengthen' had been unacceptable in 1980 ('clarification' was used instead). Even the word 'review' had been suspect because it might lead to 'revision' if it were not strictly confined to the operation of the convention, narrowly construed.

Issraelyan also noted that the assumption through a formal conference procedure of new, legally binding obligations to accept verification now occupied a central position in Soviet thinking about compliance. The full text read:

The Conference, taking into account the unanimity among the States participating in the Conference concerning the need to strengthen and effectively implement the provisions of the Convention on the Prohibition of Bacteriological (Biological) and Toxin Weapons and on their Destruction, as well as the need to specify ways of achieving this end, decides to prepare an Additional Protocol to the Convention providing for meas-

---

[5] The breakthrough at the Stockholm Conference is discussed in chapter 3, section II in this volume.

[6] Issraelyan, V., USSR, BWC/CONF.II/SR.7 (note 1), para. 61.

[7] Perfiliev, V., USSR, First Review Conference document BWC/CONF.I/C/SR.3, 12 Mar. 1980, paras 27–30. Similar concerns were expressed by Issraelyan in First Review Conference document BWC/CONF.I/C/SR.6, 14 Mar. 1980, paras 6, 14.

ures to strengthen the system of verification of compliance with the Convention. The required preparatory work will be carried out in the form acceptable to the States Parties to the Convention.

The Conference decides that, after the necessary preparations, a Conference of the States Parties should be held for the purpose of drafting and adopting an Additional Protocol to the Convention.[8]

On 9 September 1986 Issraelyan had foreshadowed the proposal when he drew attention to the new emphasis on 'the problem of control' and claimed that 'the Soviet Union was no less, indeed rather more, concerned about verification of over [*sic*] compliance with the Convention than other countries'.[9] From the Soviet point of view, it was no doubt disappointing that the proposal was not more enthusiastically embraced by delegations outside its immediate group. (The Federal Republic of Germany was also disappointed in 1986 when it proposed the creation of a verification regime and found it was 'not well received at that time'.[10]) Issraelyan declared in the final plenary session that: 'it was a matter of regret to him that States which claimed to be the champions of verification had not agreed that a special conference should be convened with a view to the adoption of a Protocol on' a verification mechanism combined with international legal obligations.[11]

One explanation of the failure to adopt a verification protocol is contextual: the President of the Third Review Conference remarked, five years later, that at the time of the 1986 review 'the international community was still virtually inarticulate in the language of the new détente'.[12] In 1986 the 'champions of verification' in the West, to whom Issraelyan had alluded, were not yet ready to accept the Gorbachev–Shevardnadze initiative at face value. Long experience of negotiating with their predecessors had bred scepticism with regard to Soviet disarmament initiatives, which would take time to dispel.

At the Stockholm Conference, in the CSCE context, the new Soviet openness *had* been taken seriously, and agreement on far-reaching verifiable CSBMs (the Stockholm Document) was imminent. The BTW context was different and complicated by unresolved compliance anxieties. In the case of BTW disarmament in September 1986 the Western governments which professed the greatest concern over alleged non-compliance with the BTWC were inclined to see this proposal for a supplementary or additional protocol as an attempt to distract international attention from the grave allegations still being levelled at the Soviet Union. On this view, instead of trying to 'seize the high ground' on verification of compliance with new proposals of vague import, the USSR ought rather to have concentrated on clarifying its own, much-questioned, compliance record by supplying hard information.

[8] Annex to the Report of the Committee of the Whole, Second Review Conference document BWC/CONF.II/9, 22 Sep. 1986, p. 24.

[9] Issraelyan, V., USSR, BWC/CONF.II/SR.3 (note 2), para. 37.

[10] Also under instructions from the Bundestag during its 1981 ratification debate the FRG delegation had worked actively for the creation of a verification regime. Beck, V. and Salber, H., 'The Third Review Conference of the Biological Weapons Convention: results and experiences', ed. O. Thränert, *The Verification of the Biological Weapons Convention: Problems and Perspectives* (Friedrich Ebert Stiftung: Bonn, 1992), pp. 26–27.

[11] Issraelyan, V., USSR, BWC/CONF.II/SR.10 (note 2), para. 19.

[12] Statement by Ambassador Roberto Garcia Moritán at the opening session of the Third Review Conference, 9 Sep. 1991, p. 2. Text supplied by the conference secretariat.

Issraelyan responded that his government had presented more information than ever before on the anthrax outbreak at Sverdlovsk in April 1979 in a special presentation for all delegations and that: 'Had the United States had any serious doubts as to compliance with the Convention, the United States delegation would have shown some interest in the Soviet Union's readiness to give appropriate explanations at the meeting held on 10 September 1986 with a Soviet expert.'[13]

The United States was not alone in continuing to express concern over the Soviet compliance record.[14] France, which had voiced its strong commitment to verification on acceding to the BTWC in 1984[15] and again on this occasion, declared bluntly that the major cause of erosion of confidence in the convention was 'political behaviour at variance with the spirit of the Convention rather than technical factors'. Ambassador Jacques Jessel stated that: 'France could not ignore allegations of the use of prohibited weapons in South East Asia, or for that matter in Afghanistan, any more than it could ignore certain ambiguous aspects of the outbreak of anthrax reported in 1979 at Sverdlovsk. In all those cases, the parties concerned did not seem to have done everything in their power to demonstrate their good faith.'[16]

France wanted verification machinery for the convention, but a review conference was not the place to amend the BTWC, so 'more limited and pragmatic solutions must be sought'.[17] The French preference was for CBMs: France advocated all of the CBMs which were eventually adopted in 1986, plus several more which were not (e.g., the reporting of vaccination campaigns, the addition of 'mass poisoning or accidents occurring in facilities and involving many casualties' to the CBM on unusual outbreaks of disease, and serological proof that the staff of high-containment facilities and military personnel were not vaccinated against presumed biological warfare agents).[18]

Another reason for the cool reception accorded the Soviet proposal of 15 September 1986 was the overcrowded agenda of the review conference and the emphasis on the CBM approach to strengthening the regime of compliance. The conference was already negotiating an array of CBMs and arguing about such points as whether the CBM on high-containment facilities ought to cover the P3—later known as biosafety level 3 (BL3)—category of facilities on as mandatory a basis as those in the highest category (P4 or BL4).[19] This was an

[13] Issraelyan, V., USSR, BWC/CONF.II/SR.7 (note 1), para. 57. There was uncertainty over whether the Soviet delegation thought that the US delegation had boycotted the presentation by Professor N. S. Antonov of the Soviet Ministry of Health (alternate representative of the USSR at both the first and second review conferences) or thought that US attendance on 10 Sep. had not been at a sufficiently official level.

[14] BWC/CONF.II/SR.3 (note 2), paras 12, 13, 17, 19, 21; and Lowitz, BWC/CONF.II/SR.10 (note 2), para. 24. Other states (e.g., Canada and the Netherlands) did not mention the USSR explicitly. Després, A., Canada, Second Review Conference document BWC/CONF.II/SR.4, 9 Sep. 1986, para. 7; and ter Haar, B., the Netherlands, Second Review Conference document BWC/CONF.II/SR.5, 10 Sep. 1986, para. 54.

[15] Relevant statements by French Foreign Minister Claude Cheysson and the French Government between 1982 and 1984 are reproduced (in translation) in Sims, N. A., *The Diplomacy of Biological Disarmament: Vicissitudes of a Treaty in Force, 1975–85* (Macmillan: London and St Martin's Press: New York, 1988), pp. 263–65.

[16] Jessel, J., France, Second Review Conference document BWC/CONF.II/SR.8, 15 Sep. 1986, para. 22.

[17] Jessel (note 16), para. 23.

[18] Jessel (note 16), para. 23.

[19] The unsatisfactory nature of biosafety levels as a basis for risk classification and the consequent difficulty in agreeing the appropriate reporting threshold are discussed in, e.g., Geissler, E. and Brunius, G.,

issue which opposed the USA ('4 only') to the Netherlands ('4 *and* 3').[20] Both France and other states (for example, Finland, Pakistan and Sweden) were having difficulty gaining acceptance of their CBM proposals. The Soviet initiative came too late to gain a prominent place on the agenda of the review conference. Its greatest impact occurred rather in the years following the Second Review Conference when the Gorbachev–Shevardnadze initiative came to shape the new, expanded agenda of the review process.

IV. The outcome of the Second Review Conference

The Second Review Conference did not ignore verification, but it did not initiate preparations for a special conference to adopt a verification protocol (advocated by the USSR) and limited the mandate of the 1987 Ad Hoc Meeting of Scientific and Technical Experts to CBMs.[21] A wider mandate, which could have included scientific advice leading to a verification protocol negotiation, had been proposed for the Meeting of Experts by the Soviet Union and two of its allies, the German Democratic Republic and Hungary.[22]

The Final Declaration of the Second Review Conference *did* include a section on verification under its Article XII heading. It elaborated on the decision to convene a further review, at the request of a majority, not later than 1991:

The Conference, noting the differing views with regard to verification, decides that the Third Review Conference shall consider, *inter alia*:

– the impact of scientific and technological developments relevant to the Convention,

– the relevance for effective implementation of the Convention of the results achieved in the negotiations on prohibition of chemical weapons,

– the effectiveness of the provisions in Article V for consultation and co-operation and of the co-operative measures [subsequently to be called CBMs] agreed in this Final Declaration, and

– in the light of these considerations and of the provisions of Article XI, whether or not further actions are called for to create further co-operative measures in the context of Article V, or legally binding improvements to the Convention, or a combination of both.[23]

Legally binding improvements to the BTWC would have to take the form either of amendments, in which case Article XI would apply, or of an additional

'Information on high-risk laboratories', ed. E. Geissler, *Strengthening the Biological Weapons Convention by Confidence-Building Measures*, SIPRI Chemical & Biological Warfare Studies no. 10 (Oxford University Press: Oxford, 1990), pp. 80–84.

[20] ter Haar, B., Center for Strategic and International Studies (CSIS), *The Future of Biological Weapons*, Washington Paper no. 151 (Praeger: New York, 1991), pp. 39–40.

[21] Recommended accounts of the Second Review Conference include: Lang, W., 'The Second Review Conference of the 1972 Biological Weapons Convention', ed. J. Kaufmann, United Nations Institute for Training and Research (UNITAR), *Effective Negotiation: Case Studies in Conference Diplomacy* (Martinus Nijhoff: Dordrecht, 1989), pp. 191–203; McFadden, E. J., 'The Second Review Conference of the Biological Weapons Convention: one step forward, many more to go', *Stanford Journal of International Law*, vol. 24, no. 1 (fall 1987), pp. 85–109; Rosenberg, B. H., 'Updating the biological weapons ban', *Bulletin of the Atomic Scientists*, vol. 43, no. 1 (Jan./Feb. 1987), pp. 40–43; Sims, N. A., 'The Second Review Conference on the Biological Weapons Convention', ed. S. Wright, *Preventing a Biological Arms Race* (MIT Press: Cambridge, Mass., 1990), pp. 267–88; and ter Haar (note 20), pp. 27–48. The Ad Hoc Meeting of Experts is discussed in chapter 3, section II in this volume.

[22] Second Review Conference document BWC/CONF.II/9/Add.1, 29 Sep. 1986, p. 4.

[23] Second Review Conference document BWC/CONF.II/13/II, 26 Sep. 1986, p. 10.

or supplementary protocol. In the latter case, the protocol would come into force only for those BTWC parties which accepted it and not for new parties to the convention unless they voluntarily adopted it. The free-standing text of the protocol would contain its own entry-into-force provisions, which might, for instance, specify a minimum number of ratifications. Debate on verification was thereby deferred to the Third Review Conference, and all options were left open.

In 1986 consideration of a verification protocol was postponed until not later than 1991, in part because the CW disarmament negotiations were expected to conclude successfully in 1987 or 1988. Various parties and the neutral and non-aligned countries, in particular, wanted to ensure that the changes which were made to strengthen the BTWC would take into account a newly concluded CW convention. Many parties expected the date of the Third Review Conference to be moved forward once a CW convention was concluded so that the two treaty regimes could be brought into conformity to the extent desirable without delay. One major determinant of the relationship between the conventions would be their respective verification provisions: the more closely these provisions resembled one another, the closer the relationship (and its eventual institutionalization) could be.

There was therefore reluctance in 1986 to engage in substantive discussion of BTW verification. Many delegations preferred to meet again after a CW convention had been finalized to decide what should be done to adapt the BTWC to the new situation.[24] The delegates were overly optimistic, however, since the Chemical Weapons Convention was not concluded until 1992 and was not opened for signature until 13 January 1993. In 1986 it appeared that negotiation of the CWC would soon conclude and that a 'chemical disarmament race' was imminent.[25] At that time it would have been hard to imagine that the CWC would not be finalized until 1992.

V. Follow-up to the Second Review Conference

The Soviet Union did not immediately follow up its initiative of 15 September 1986 with a detailed verification scheme. This absence of detail was unfortunate in so far as it enabled critics of the proposal to diminish its significance, dismiss it as a rhetorical flourish in the Russian and Soviet tradition of disarmament diplomacy and characterize it as vague and lacking in content.

Evidence was sought that the Soviet establishment had changed its mind on verification so radically as to welcome international supervision in place of national control. National guarantees had been considered sufficient in the past, and in 1986 Issraelyan had repeated the Soviet position that compliance with the provisions of the BTWC was 'guaranteed by the relevant State institutions in accordance with Soviet legislation and practice'.[26]

[24] Rosenberg, B. H. and Burck, G., 'Verification of compliance with the Biological Weapons Convention', ed. Wright (note 21), pp. 300–302.

[25] Findlay, T., *Peace Through Chemistry: The New Chemical Weapons Convention*, Peace Research Centre Monograph no. 14 (Australian National University: Canberra, 1993), p. 6.

[26] Issraelyan, V., USSR, BWC/CONF.II/SR.3 (note 2), para. 35.

On 16 August 1990 the Soviet Union revealed that its verification system was to be based on national biological registers (NBRs).[27] Certain facilities—including those which a state was obliged to report under the CBM on high-containment facilities and others involved in work on protection against BTW—would be listed on its NBR. Under an eventual verification protocol, these declared facilities would be subject to on-site inspection without right of refusal in order to ensure their full compliance with the convention.

In a working paper which the Soviet Union presented at the Third Review Conference the NBR concept was subsumed under a strengthening of the CBM programme which concentrated (as did proposals by Canada, France, Sweden and the UK) on sharpening the focus of confidence-building measure A so as to derive a more complete picture of each state's BTW defence programme. National biological registers were intended to contribute to this strengthening through a more indirect form of verification than the challenge inspection which Ambassador Sergey Batsanov had been understood as offering in his statement to the Conference on Disarmament on 16 August 1990:

On the basis of the submitted information a National Biological Register could be drawn up on each State Party to the Convention with [an] indication of all facilities declared by the State and a corresponding international data bank set up ... States Parties would provide annual information on their possibilities and terms for receiving scientists at their biological facilities included in National Biological Registers and on units of the facilities where scientists could work. Other States Parties could forward a request that their scientist(s) be received at the indicated facilities. A State Party having received such a request is expected to consider it favourably, *inter alia*, taking into account the principle of reciprocity and interests of non-proliferation of technologies which can be used for creating biological weapons. Other possible forms of the exchange of scientists, including holding joint research, could also be envisaged.[28]

The penultimate sentence reflects caution arising from the fear of BTW proliferation which was being expressed in 1991. That fear might have prevented the opening of research and development laboratories to inspection by all parties. However, it is unclear why a challenge inspection under a verification protocol was regarded as possibly promoting BTW proliferation.

An evident limitation of the NBR approach to verification is that it allows each party to determine the range of facilities open to inspection (or to an exchange of scientists) by deciding whether or not to include them in its register. A verification scheme without a provision for challenge inspection of undeclared facilities might not be worth having. The feasibility of the Russian proposal was questioned since, if BTW agents were developed and produced, this might occur on a small scale, and a wide range of undeclared facilities might come under suspicion as possible sites of development and production.

A significant body of policy-oriented literature on BTW verification was produced in the years following 1986 as a result of the Soviet initiative.[29] Some of

[27] *Chemical Weapons Convention Bulletin*, no. 9 (Sep. 1990), p. 19, reporting Ambassador Sergey Batsanov's statement in the Conference on Disarmament.

[28] Third Review Conference document BWC/CONF.III/17, 24 Sep. 1991, pp. 30–32.

[29] A bibliography for 1986–91 is presented in de Jonge Oudraat, C., 'Publications on biological weapons and disarmament', *Biological Weapons: Research Projects and Publications*, special issue of the *UNIDIR* [United Nations Institute for Disarmament Research] *Newsletter* (Geneva), vol. 4, no. 2 (June 1991), pp. 17–20.

this literature was prescriptive; much of it was speculative; and all of it derived encouragement from the new perspectives on reinforcement of the BTWC.

Although the Soviet Government did not follow up its initiative fully, the proposal encouraged individual 'friends of the Convention' and groups of scientists to suggest ways of verifying compliance with the BTWC, confident that such verification was henceforth 'practical politics'. Verification proposals could no longer be dismissed outright, but would have to be considered on their merits.

VI. Verification proposals, 1986–91

At the time of the Second Review Conference little had been published on BTW verification since the six-volume study by the Stockholm International Peace Research Institute, a comprehensive survey of the problems related to chemical and biological warfare.[30] In a SIPRI collection of scientific studies prepared for the Second Review Conference, Raymond A. Zilinskas revived the subject,[31] and the results of the conference were analysed by Eric J. McFadden.[32] Barbara Hatch Rosenberg and Gordon Burck formulated a detailed verification proposal which was published in mid-1990 in *Preventing a Biological Arms Race*.[33] The book was the product of several years' writing for the Council for Responsible Genetics (CRG), mainly by US scientists, under the direction of Susan Wright. Its importance lay not just in its numerous policy prescriptions, some of which were directed specifically to the US Government and others to the parties generally,[34] but also in the emphasis it placed on the ethical responsibility of scientists to see that their work did not directly or indirectly facilitate BTW or weaken the inhibitions against its use. This was the context in which the verification proposal by Rosenberg and Burck was designed to operate.

During 1990 the Federation of American Scientists (FAS), linked via Rosenberg with the CRG, launched a special study of BTW verification through a working group chaired by Robert A. Weinberg. It drew on the experience of two former US ambassadors closely associated with the BTWC—James F. Leonard, who had led the US delegation to the Conference of the Committee on Disarmament when the convention was under negotiation in 1971, and Charles C. Flowerree, who had led the US delegation to the First Review Conference in 1980. In addition, molecular biologists and other scientists were members of its Core Group; a larger review group ensured wide international scrutiny of the proposals emerging from the Core Group. This thorough method of proceeding produced a first set of proposals in September 1990[35] and a more detailed draft

[30] SIPRI, *The Problem of Chemical and Biological Warfare*, 6 vols (Almqvist & Wiksell: Stockholm, 1971–75). The series is available on a CD-ROM, which is described at URL <http://editors.sipri.se/cd.cbw.html>.

[31] Zilinskas, R. A., 'Verification of the Biological Weapons Convention', ed. E. Geissler, SIPRI, *Biological and Toxin Weapons Today* (Oxford University Press: Oxford, 1986), pp. 82–107.

[32] McFadden (note 21).

[33] Rosenberg and Burck (note 24).

[34] Falk, R. and Wright, S., 'Preventing a biological arms race: new initiatives', ed. Wright (note 21), pp. 330–51.

[35] Federation of American Scientists (FAS), *Proposals for the Third Review Conference of the Biological Weapons Convention*, 1990, and subsequent editions (FAS: Washington, DC, 1990–91). The Oct. 1990 edition (reporting the Sep. 1990 proposals) is also reproduced in *Arms Control*, vol. 12, no. 2 (Sep. 1991), pp. 240–54.

for a verification protocol in February 1991.[36] The FAS proposals were reissued in successive revisions for the Third Review Conference, and a third FAS report was prepared for the first VEREX session in March 1992.[37]

Meanwhile the CRG,[38] the Canadian Science for Peace group[39] and other non-governmental organizations (NGOs) drafted separate verification proposals for the Third Review Conference. Two significant books were published in 1991: *Views on Possible Verification Measures for the Biological Weapons Convention*, edited by S. Johan Lundin;[40] and *Prevention of a Biological and Toxin Arms Race and the Responsibility of Scientists*, edited by Erhard Geissler and Robert Haynes, which was the result of a September 1990 scientific colloquium at Kühlungsborn in the GDR.[41] The United Nations Institute for Disarmament Research brought together specialists in a Moscow seminar and assembled contributors to a special issue of its *UNIDIR Newsletter*, which contained an invaluable bibliography of work published in 1986–91.[42] Like the UNIDIR research paper by Jozef Goldblat and Thomas Bernauer,[43] these volumes went beyond verification to overall consideration of the convention and provided a reminder that verification was not the only way to strengthen the BTWC, a point which was emphasized in a discussion paper published by the London-based Council for Arms Control.[44] Some BTW disarmament specialists contributed to more than one of these publications; however, the cumulative range of expertise of the writers was impressive.

Governmental thinking was paralleled or preceded by non-governmental effort. Informal international networks of scientists and scholars offered ideas to all delegations to the Third Review Conference in the hope that some of the ideas would be included in the Final Declaration. The official UN periodical *Disarmament* featured articles by leading NGO advocates of stronger verification, such as Rosenberg and Geissler, together with the Netherlands diplomat Barend ter Haar (whose findings are discussed below) in preparation for the Third Review Conference.[45]

A common theme in many of these studies was the need to identify those technologies and capabilities which ought to make a facility liable to verifica-

---

[36] FAS, *Implementation of the Proposals for a Verification Protocol to the Biological Weapons Convention*, Feb. 1991, and subsequent editions (FAS: Washington, DC, 1991); and *Arms Control* (note 35), pp. 255–78.

[37] FAS, *A Legally-Binding Compliance Regime for the Biological Weapons Convention: Refinement of Proposed Measures through Trial Facility Visits* (FAS: Washington, DC, Mar. 1992).

[38] Council for Responsible Genetics (CRG), Committee on the Military Use of Biological Research, *Statement for the Third Review Conference of the Biological Weapons Convention* (CRG: Cambridge, Mass., Apr. 1991).

[39] Science for Peace, *Workshop on the Biological Weapons Convention*, co-sponsored by the Markland Group, Toronto, 19 June 1991.

[40] Lundin, S. J. (ed.), *Views on Possible Verification Measures for the Biological Weapons Convention*, SIPRI Chemical & Biological Warfare Studies no. 12 (Oxford University Press: Oxford, 1991).

[41] Geissler, E. and Haynes, R. H. (eds), *Prevention of a Biological and Toxin Arms Race and the Responsibility of Scientists* (Akademie Verlag: Berlin, 1991).

[42] de Jonge Oudraat (note 29).

[43] Goldblat, J. and Bernauer, T., *The Third Review of the Biological Weapons Convention: Issues and Proposals*, UNIDIR Research Paper no. 9 (United Nations: New York, 1991).

[44] Sims, N. A., *Reinforcing Biological Disarmament: Issues in the 1991 Review*, Faraday Discussion Paper no. 16 (Council for Arms Control: London, 1991), pp. 16, 19.

[45] Rosenberg, B. H., 'The next step: a biological verification regime'; Geissler, E., 'Strengthening the Biological Weapons Convention'; and ter Haar, B., 'The state of the Biological Weapons Convention', all in the special feature, *Towards the Biological Weapons Convention Review Conference*, of *Disarmament*, vol. 14, no. 2 (1991).

tion in order to provide compliance reassurance. Some authors favoured lists of agents and toxins, while others concentrated on the equipment for engineering, containment or other biotechnological processes. Most of the writers attempted to find the key indicators which would indicate a need for verification; general criteria that encompassed every laboratory and factory would be too cumbersome and expensive. The most far-reaching proposals for inspection were made by the FAS Working Group on BTW Verification; at the time of the first VEREX session in 1992 the FAS was able to present findings from trial inspections of a variety of US establishments.[46] However, it was difficult to distinguish permitted from prohibited activities, when the subjective concept of intent was deeply rooted in the convention. A need existed to determine whether quantitative criteria could be introduced.

One of the most interesting proposals for a verification protocol was drafted by ter Haar as an annexe to a paper for the Center for Strategic and International Studies. He had been involved in efforts to strengthen the ban on BTW since 1982, including leading the Netherlands delegation to the 1987 Ad Hoc Meeting of Experts; ter Haar had also held positions in the Netherlands Ministry of Foreign Affairs and had helped to shape NATO and European policy making on BTW. His study, *The Future of Biological Weapons*, concluded that:

confidence-building measures alone will not remove all doubts. A verification regime also is required. Such a regime should consist of routine inspections of declared facilities and the possibility of challenge inspections. In its present form the Biological Weapons Convention is unverifiable because all principal provisions are linked to a party's intentions. But introducing objective criteria would be relatively simple, and such criteria could form the basis of an effective verification regime.[47]

Such criteria 'could be found by subjecting relevant items to obligatory declaration and quantitative constraints'. A party would no longer be able to invoke subjective criteria like 'justification for prophylactic, protective or other peaceful purposes' and 'designed to use such agents or toxins for hostile purposes or in armed conflict'. 'Purpose criteria' would disappear altogether as potential loopholes, and every criterion would be strictly quantitative. This would have the advantage of making compliance or non-compliance a matter of objective measurement alone, since motives and purposes would not be considered. The veracity of declared data would determine whether a party was in compliance with its obligations or not.[48] The first article of the verification protocol thus would read:

Each State Party undertakes not to research, develop, produce, otherwise acquire, stockpile, transfer, or retain any of the biological agents and toxins listed in the annex to this Article for non-prohibited purposes in quantities larger than [x] grams.

Each State Party undertakes to limit the capacity of equipment for production, harvesting, and long-term conservation of biological agents or toxins of every facility that is involved in protection and prophylaxis against possible hostile use of such agents and toxins, and handles one or more of the agents and toxins listed in the annex to this Article, to a maximum of [to be defined].[49]

[46] FAS (note 37).
[47] ter Haar (note 20), p. 111.
[48] ter Haar (note 20), p. 108.
[49] ter Haar (note 20), p. 155.

According to ter Haar, later articles would provide for annual declarations of agents, toxins and facilities matching any one of seven key indicators. Each declared facility would be subject to routine on-site inspection to verify the accuracy of the annual declarations, but each party would additionally 'have the right to request inspection of any location or facility under the jurisdiction or control of another State Party, in order to clarify any matter which causes doubts about compliance with the Convention'.[50]

Barend ter Haar's seven indicators for a verification protocol, which were subject to further definition in an annexe, were: (a) has high-containment facilities; (b) researches, develops, produces or stockpiles any of the biological agents or toxins listed in the annexe; (c) has production equipment with a combined capacity of [to be defined] or more that is particularly suited for production of biological agents; (d) has advanced equipment for harvesting biological agents (e.g., continuous-flow centrifuges and filtration techniques); (e) has equipment for long-term storage of agents (e.g., freeze-drying equipment); (f) has equipment for micro-encapsulation; and (g) is involved in R&D for protection and prophylaxis against possible hostile use of biological agents or toxins.[51]

Like the FAS Working Group on BTW Verification and others who developed proposals for a verification protocol or similar arrangement, ter Haar found it necessary to pair research with development in order to make his scheme workable. By ratifying the verification protocol, parties would in effect extend the scope of the convention as among themselves to research, subjecting research to the same high level of constraint as other BTW activities. A similar effect would be achieved by an agreement to ban (in line with the British proposal of 1969) *activities aimed at developing* biological weapons, as proposed in 1992 by Lundin.[52]

The seven elements of verification proposed by ter Haar in 1991 were noteworthy for their economy and for the clarity of the concept. Yet they could only serve as the basis of a practical scheme the working out of which would test the sincerity of governments: 'A credible verification regime will entail costs, both literally and in terms of openness, but an effective ban is worth it.'[53]

Despite its merits, the emphasis on defined types and quantities rather than on purposes meant that care would have to be taken so that the comprehensiveness of the prohibition in Article I did not suffer. In addition, it was vital that controls be enforceable. Questions were raised about the effectiveness of such verification measures if a government were uncooperative and whether a government suspected of being in non-compliance with the convention would allow itself to become party to such a protocol in the first place.

VII. Verification at the 1991 Third Review Conference

When the Third Review Conference met in 1991 the most significant policy difference over verification was between France and the USA. There was concern that the USA would impose its view that the convention could not be effect-

[50] ter Haar (note 20), p. 157.
[51] ter Haar (note 20), p. 156.
[52] Lundin, S. J., 'Views on the verification possibilities for the Biological Weapons Convention', ed. Thränert (note 10), p. 76, emphasis added.
[53] ter Haar (note 20), pp. 111–12.

ively verified on the other parties so forcefully as to prevent them from agreeing on a procedure to investigate verification possibilities. Australia, Canada, Germany, Italy, the Netherlands and the UK sympathized with France to varying degrees.

The US position was that verification could not be made effective, and an ineffective verification system would engender false confidence and create an illusion of security. In the US view it was better to leave the convention unverified and strengthen the 'norm' of compliance through the 'greater international transparency and openness with regard to the Convention' which it had advocated at the closing session of the Second Review Conference.[54] In addition to the measures for strengthening Article V which it had welcomed in 1986 the USA suggested adding support for enhanced CBMs, establishing export control policies more sensitive to the dangers of BTW proliferation and putting pressure on governments to cease offensive R&D if they were suspected of such activity.

For 20 years France had held the position that the convention was gravely defective without verification and that this defect must be remedied.[55] This view had been reaffirmed by Foreign Minister Claude Cheysson at the time of France's accession to the convention in 1984, and by the leader of the French delegation, Jacques Jessel, at the Second Review Conference. Most important, in his statement of French arms control and disarmament policy on 3 June 1991, President François Mitterrand had also supported this view as his objective for a successful outcome of the Third Review Conference.[56]

At the start of the review conference both France and the USA revised their previous positions. France conceded that the conference would not be the occasion for *substantive* agreement on verification provisions. The USA conceded that *procedural* agreement could be reached on how the issue might be investigated and perhaps resolved between the third and fourth review conferences. The review conference therefore was able to concentrate on negotiating the procedural agreement. Both the Committee of the Whole and the Drafting Committee used a 'focal point' to coordinate consultations on verification.[57] Two issues had to be resolved by the review conference: first, the kind of group to be entrusted with advancing the conference's deliberately unfinished business on verification; and second, the mandate it should be given.

VIII. Negotiation of the VEREX group

The issue of the type of group to deal with verification was complicated by the fact that this was not the only topic which the Third Review Conference was unable to resolve regarding compliance. Sweden preferred that a single group,

[54] BWC/CONF.II/SR.10 (note 2).

[55] UN General Assembly Resolution 2826 (XXVI), 16 Dec. 1971. In 1971 France had abstained on the commendatory resolution adopted 110–0–1 in the General Assembly. France's was the only formal abstention, although 21 states were absent from the vote, including China; 3 of the 21 states, including Iraq, later advised the UN Secretariat that they had intended to vote in favour of the resolution.

[56] France, Plan for arms control and disarmament, Conference on Disarmament document CD/1079, 3 June 1991.

[57] Sylwin Gizowski, counsellor in Poland's delegation to the CD and deputy leader of the Polish delegation to the Third Review Conference, was 'focal point' for verification issues in both committees. Report of the Committee of the Whole, Third Review Conference document BWC/CONF.III/17 (note 28), para. 4; and Report of the Drafting Committee, Third Review Conference document BWC/CONF.III/22/Add.2, 27 Sep. 1991, para. 4.

an ad hoc group of governmental experts, tackle 'the implementation and further improvements of agreed confidence-building measures, complaints procedures, and the technical feasibility and possible modalities of a verification regime'.[58]

This synoptic approach was similar to earlier Swedish initiatives, in particular General Assembly Resolution 37/98C, co-sponsored by Austria, Colombia, Ecuador, the FRG, Ireland, Mexico, Pakistan, Uruguay and Yugoslavia. The resolution recommended that a special conference of parties to the BTWC be convened in order to establish a 'flexible, objective and non-discriminatory procedure to deal with issues concerning compliance with the Convention'.[59] Such a conference had not taken place. In these circumstances, an 'open-ended' ad hoc group might be able to prepare the way for a special conference if it took the whole compliance regime as its agenda, including the imperfect Article V provisions for a consultative meeting, which Sweden subsumed conceptually under the heading 'complaints procedures'.[60]

Brazil and Chile presented another approach and announced that they:

consider it fundamental to adopt a follow-up mechanism which would specifically address the elaboration of verification measures, which, due to their complexity, require a special study.

In this context, we consider that verification needs to be examined in an independent way, i.e. in a separate group, different from the group on confidence-building measures.[61]

This latter view prevailed in 1991, resulting in the creation of VEREX. No working group or other follow-up mechanism was created for CBMs, complaint procedures or any other element of the regime of compliance—except verification.

IX. Negotiation of the VEREX mandate

The US view on the issue of the mandate to be entrusted to VEREX was regarded as too restrictive by several other parties. Nigeria, for example, wanted the group: 'to study and elaborate, for consideration of the Fourth Review Conference, a verification regime, in an additional protocol to the Convention. The verification regime should be non-discriminatory, transparent and should not in any way jeopardize the economic and social developments [*sic*] of States Parties'.[62] Brazil listed four main tasks and a fifth: to 'propose verification techniques capable of serving the purposes of the BWC'.[63]

Canada, with much Western support, had as early as February 1991 called for such a group to draft a verification protocol. Foreign Minister Joe Clark had set 1993 as the year in which a special conference of the parties should adopt a

---

[58] The Swedish proposal of 16 Sep. 1991 is contained in BWC/CONF.III/17 (note 28), p. 51.

[59] UN General Assembly Resolution 37/98C, 13 Dec. 1982. The resolution and the diplomatic activity connected with it, up to 1985, are discussed in Sims (note 15), pp. 208–12.

[60] The proposal is discussed further in chapter 2, section VI in this volume.

[61] The joint proposal by Brazil and Chile of 16 Sep. 1991 is contained in BWC/CONF.III/17 (note 28), p. 43.

[62] Nigeria, Proposals for the Final Declaration, 16 Sep. 1991, BWC/CONF.III/17 (note 28), p. 34.

[63] The Brazilian proposal of 19 Sep. 1991 is contained in BWC/CONF.III/17 (note 28), p. 51.

verification protocol to strengthen the BTWC.[64] Other Western states favoured 1994 for a special conference both to fulfil and transcend the purposes of the special conference called for in the Swedish resolution.[65]

These proposals were unacceptable to the USA, which opposed holding a special conference in 1993 or 1994, or allowing VEREX to elaborate a draft verification protocol (the Nigerian proposal) or even to propose verification techniques (as proposed by Brazil). The USA held the view that VEREX could be allowed only: 'to identify and examine potential verification measures from a scientific and technical standpoint'. This became the central clause of the mandate eventually negotiated. The word 'evaluation' was also acceptable to the USA, which enabled the mandate to include the provision that: 'Specifically, the Group shall seek to evaluate potential verification measures, taking into account the broad range of types and quantities of microbial and other biological agents and toxins, whether naturally occurring or altered, which are capable of being used as a means of warfare.'[66]

The USA also accepted the proposition (in the preamble to the VEREX mandate) that effective verification *could* (not *would*) reinforce the BTWC because the USA itself had been exploring verification measures and found none effective. It would do no harm therefore if other parties to the BTWC were to find this out on their own. In the course of identifying, examining and evaluating potential measures VEREX could be expected to reach the same conclusions.

The first two stages of the VEREX mandate were the identification and examination of potential measures. Evaluation came to be considered a third stage. Identification was straightforward and served mainly to narrow the exercise to the prohibitions in Article I. No mention was made of the activities which are prohibited under Article III nor of research or use, neither of which is expressly prohibited in the convention. It was stated that:

The Group shall seek to identify measures which could determine:
– whether a State Party is developing, producing, stockpiling, acquiring or retaining microbial or other biological agents or toxins, of types and in quantities that have no justification for prophylactic, protective or peaceful purposes;
– whether a State Party is developing, producing, stockpiling, acquiring or retaining weapons, equipment or means of delivery designed to use such agents or toxins for hostile purposes or in armed conflict.[67]

Following the evaluation clause (above), six criteria were listed to govern the examination stage of the exercise:

To these ends the Group could examine potential verification measures in terms of the following main criteria:
– their strengths and weaknesses based on, but not limited to, the amount and quality of information they provide, and fail to provide;
– their ability to differentiate between prohibited and permitted activities;
– their ability to resolve ambiguities about compliance;

[64] External Affairs and International Trade Canada, *Disarmament Bulletin*, no. 16 (summer 1991). The proposal was first circulated in Canada's 'post-war planning' initiative of 8 Feb. 1991 on the control of weapons of mass destruction. Information supplied by the Canadian High Commission, London.
[65] UN General Assembly Resolution 37/98C (note 59).
[66] BWC/CONF.III/22/Add.2 (note 57), pp. 9–10.
[67] BWC/CONF.III/22/Add.2 (note 57), p. 9.

– their technology, material, manpower and equipment requirements;

– their financial, legal, safety and organizational implications;

– their impact on scientific research, scientific cooperation, industrial development and other permitted activities, and their implications for the confidentiality of commercial proprietary information.[68]

The sixth and last of these criteria had been proposed by Brazil, which also had recommended that VEREX should 'study the financial costs associated with the verification regime' and was therefore responsible for part of the fifth criterion.[69]

The above text combined the concerns of parties which favoured verification in both 'North' and 'South'. The North was most concerned with establishing the value of particular measures in regard to such criteria as the ability to resolve compliance ambiguities and differentiate between what is and is not banned. The South shared these concerns but was also anxious not to incur costs which it feared might fall disproportionately on developing countries. The South was also particularly sensitive to the possibility that the developing nations might suffer commercial disadvantage if their capacity for industrial development or scientific research were impaired or if proprietary information were lost through a breach of confidentiality. The states of the South were insistent that they not be denied access to advances in biotechnology on the pretext of counter-proliferation trade restrictions.

In 1992 Thomas Bernauer wrote that it was simplistic to portray the North as favouring verification and the South as opposed to verification at the Third Review Conference. The North was divided between the USA and most of the other developed states; the South included strong supporters of verification such as Nigeria, as noted above, but also critical voices:

The positions of developing countries with regard to the question of establishing a verification mechanism for the Convention, and the willingness to link the verification issue to tangible economic and technological benefits, vary to a considerable extent. Countries such as China, Cuba, India and Pakistan are very cautious with regard to verification, irrespective of economic benefits they could obtain in exchange for concessions in this field, and irrespective of the technical feasibility of effective verification.[70]

It became clear that the most influential Latin American parties would play a pivotal role in determining the attitude of the South to verification. In 1990–91 Argentina and Brazil had moved towards international controls (bilateral, regional and global) in the field of nuclear energy, and at the CWC negotiations (with Peru) they led the way in seeking a balance between verification and cost so that their civil industries would not suffer while military CW activities were effectively controlled. A similar preoccupation with equitable treatment could be expected to characterize their contribution to the BTW verification debate. In 1991 Argentina expressed the view 'that one should provide the Biological Weapons Convention with verification instruments definitely far bolder than a set of confidence-building measures' and that international trade precautions

[68] BWC/CONF.III/22/Add.2 (note 57), p. 10.

[69] Brazilian proposal (note 63).

[70] Bernauer, T., 'Verification of compliance with the Biological Weapons Convention: developing countries between passive participation and obstruction', ed. Thränert (note 10), p. 62.

against accidentally assisting BTW proliferation must 'avoid opaque and dis-criminatory regulations' which might disadvantage the South as unfairly as if it had to bear a disproportionate share of the costs of verification.[71]

The USA secured a mandate for VEREX which prevented it from making proposals or drawing up a verification protocol and sought to ensure that VEREX would not generate unstoppable momentum. The USA ensured that after the initial session, on 30 March–10 April 1992, the future of VEREX was left as vague as possible: 'The Group will hold additional meetings as appropri-ate to complete its work as soon as possible, preferably before the end of 1993.'[72] Its Chairman, Ambassador Tibor Tóth of Hungary, would be assisted by two Vice-Chairmen to be elected at the first meeting. The VEREX report was to be descriptive, not prescriptive: 'The Group shall adopt by consensus a report taking into account views expressed in the course of its work. The report of the Group shall be a description of its work on the identification and exam-ination of potential verification measures from a scientific and technical stand-point, according to this mandate.'[73]

The need for consensus meant that the USA could ensure that the mandate was construed as narrowly as it thought proper, even if many parties preferred a more liberal interpretation of what should be included in the report. The con-sensus rule could be used by the USA if it felt that the VEREX report was straying into prescription.

The decision of the Third Review Conference which contained the VEREX mandate also specified the next step: 'If a majority of States Parties ask for the convening of a conference to examine the report, by submitting a proposal to this effect to the Depositary Governments, such a conference will be convened. In such a case the conference shall decide on any further action. The conference shall be preceded by a preparatory committee.'[74]

Significantly, the United States had ensured that there would be no automatic progression from VEREX to the convening of a special conference. Canada and the other parties which in 1991 had sought to schedule a special conference in 1993 or 1994 had failed to secure their objective. On the other hand, the Third Review Conference had decided that such a conference must be convened if a majority requested it; the consensus rule could not be invoked to prevent its tak-ing place. If the USA remained determined to block the adoption of a verifica-tion protocol, it had opportunities to do so both at and after a special confer-ence. However it could not prevent a conference being convened once the VEREX report had been circulated and a majority of parties had submitted a proposal to this effect in London, Moscow and Washington.

X. The Western Group and US approaches to VEREX

In 1991–92, and to a lesser extent in 1993, there was a division within the Western Group[75] over the aim of VEREX. For France it was 'the elaboration of

[71] Statement by the Representative of Argentina, Rafael Mariano Grossi, 13 Sep. 1991, pp. 3, 5. Text supplied by the Argentine delegation to the Third Review Conference.
[72] BWC/CONF.III/22/Add.2 (note 57), p. 9.
[73] BWC/CONF.III/22/Add.2 (note 57), p. 9.
[74] BWC/CONF.III/22/Add.2 (note 57), p. 11.
[75] The Western Group consisted of those BTWC parties which comprised the Western Group in the CD (at that time 10 out of the CD's then 38 members: Australia, Belgium, Canada, France, Germany, Italy,

a set of measures resulting in the preparation of a Verification Protocol'.[76] Perhaps France defined the 'ultimate objective' of VEREX in such terms because of its history of insistence on the need to subject compliance with the BTWC to verification, as discussed above in section VII.

The USA objected that an ineffective verification procedure would be worse than none because: 'Ineffective verification regimes . . . are not acceptable. Nor are regimes that foster a false sense of confidence . . . . An ineffective verification regime force-fed into the BW convention could ultimately make cheating easier and more rewarding by creating a false sense of confidence.'[77]

Both France and the USA made concessions at the Third Review Conference. France conceded that nothing more than the mandate for a feasibility study could be decided at the review conference, and the USA allowed the mandate to be negotiated. However, their basic differences on verification of BTW disarmament persisted.

France continued to receive support from Germany, which expressed a 'long-standing desire' for 'an improvement in verification [as] of prime importance' in its attachment to the convention.[78] Australia, Canada, Italy, the Netherlands and the UK also agreed with the French position.

From the beginning of VEREX the UK took issue with the US proposition that imperfect verification was worse than none. In its first working paper the UK described verification as a deterrent which was valuable even if it fell short as a detector device: 'As the primary operational objective is to detect non-compliance, candidate regimes should be evaluated in terms of their ability to achieve a reasonable probability of detecting non-compliance in a reasonable proportion of evasion scenarios. However, a verification regime aimed at detecting evasion that even performs only moderately well is likely to have a significant deterrent effect on potential evaders.'[79]

Michael Moodie, Assistant Director for Multilateral Affairs of the US Arms Control and Disarmament Agency, took exception to the British stance, stating that: 'Verification is not a confidence-building exercise. . . . It is intended to increase the ability of others to see if violations are going on before they have a military impact.'[80]

The British working paper, however, made the point that: 'The wider the range of the national activities, whether research, industry, public and veterinary health, or military, that are subject to scrutiny by a BWC regime, the harder it is likely to be for an evader to conceal a BW programme, the higher the risk of discovery, and the greater the deterrence.'[81] The British paper portrayed the desired verification regime as generating a third benefit, in addition to detection of non-compliance and deterrence of evasion. The third benefit would be the

Japan, the Netherlands, the UK and the USA) together with such other BTWC parties as chose to associate themselves with the ten.

[76] France, Group of Experts on the verification of the Biological Weapons Convention, Third Review Conference document BWC/CONF.III/VEREX/WP.2, 30 Mar. 1992, p. 8.

[77] Statement by Ambassador Ronald F. Lehman II, 10 Sep. 1991, pp. 13–14. Text supplied by the US delegation to the Third Review Conference.

[78] Beck and Salber (note 10), pp. 26–27.

[79] UK, Verification of the BWC: possible directions, Third Review Conference document BWC/CONF.III/VEREX/WP.1, 30 Mar. 1992, para. 5. The paper, dated 18 Mar. 1992, had been made available prior to VEREX.

[80] Quoted in Webb, J., 'US sceptical over germ warfare controls', New Scientist, 28 Mar. 1992, p. 14.

[81] BWC/CONF.III/VEREX/WP.1 (note 79).

increased 'confidence in national intent to comply with the BWC' which would result from increased transparency in relevant scientific, industrial and military activities, thereby helping to reveal the motives behind these activities.[82]

The question of whether synthesis or complementarity should exist between CBMs and verification may determine the future shape of the regime of compliance. The British paper opposed developing baseline verification out of the data supplied in CBM declarations and argued that 'it would not be appropriate to use these declarations for a verification regime, since they were not designed for that purpose'. It did accept that 'some account should be taken of them in drawing up any new set of declarations for verification in order to avoid duplication'.[83]

France proposed: 'a suitable declaration system, avoiding duplication' between verification and CBM data (i.e., a degree of complementarity between verification and the existing CBM element of a regime of compliance). France cited CBMs as one of the foundations of its desired 'edifice' of verification.[84] The French paper advocated using 'a number of convergent indicators'[85] to establish compliance, while the UK recommended a 'systems approach':[86]

A raft of measures rather than a single solution is more likely to create the required climate of international confidence. Further study could be carried out on two verification elements:

a. The establishment of national profiles which would provide a framework against which information gained on subsequent inspections would be evaluated. The regime could include declarations of relevant facilities, of micro-organisms and toxins and relevant equipment acquired, imported or exported, and of unusual outbreaks of disease.

b. Inspections of facilities or locations of unusual outbreaks of disease to allow:

(i) Confirmation of compliance through consistency with previously declared national profile data;

(ii) Evaluation of compliance with the BWC.[87]

XI. The VEREX Final Report

The Expert Group met four times in 1992 and 1993. VEREX-1 (30 March–10 April 1992) identified possible verification measures. VEREX-2 (23 November–4 December 1992) concentrated on examination of the measures identified at VEREX-1, and VEREX-3 (24 May–4 June 1993) focused on evaluation. VEREX-4 (13–24 September 1993) adopted the report of the Expert Group. Malcolm Dando has given a detailed account of these meetings.[88] A full record with lists of documents is also attached to the VEREX Final Report, and the most important documents are reproduced.[89]

In 1992–93 the VEREX participants gradually accepted the concept of 'measures in combination' (i.e., a synergetic relationship to bolster the deterrent

[82] BWC/CONF.III/VEREX/WP.1 (note 79), para. 37.
[83] BWC/CONF.III/VEREX/WP.1 (note 79), para. 26.
[84] BWC/CONF.III/VEREX/WP.2 (note 76), p. 6.
[85] BWC/CONF.III/VEREX/WP.2 (note 76), p. 6.
[86] BWC/CONF.III/VEREX/WP.1 (note 79), paras 16–17.
[87] BWC/CONF.III/VEREX/WP.1 (note 79), para. 38.
[88] Dando, M., *Biological Warfare in the 21st Century* (Brassey's: London, 1994), pp. 157–79. Dando is Professor of International Security in the Bradford University Department of Peace Studies.
[89] Third Review Conference document BWC/CONF.III/VEREX/9, 24 Sep. 1993.

effect of verification on any government contemplating violation of the convention). The then Director-General (1984–95) of the British Ministry of Defence's Chemical and Biological Defence Establishment at Porton Down Graham Pearson proposed a 'web of deterrence' to describe the context within which VEREX could make a distinctive contribution. Export controls, effective protective measures and the expectation of a 'politically unacceptable' response (i.e., a penalty for violation of the convention) were also needed to make the web 'strong and seamless'.[90] Deterrence was central to Pearson's proposal. VEREX must aim at 'the development of a cost-effective verification regime that will deter States Parties from acquisition of BW capabilities'.[91] This required:

two key elements. The first is declarations of relevant activities within a state to provide a baseline of information. It is clear that any judgments of compliance must be made against an appreciation of what is the norm for the country concerned. That norm will be based on various sources of information but will depend primarily on declarations made by a State Party. The second element is on-site inspections of the sites and facilities that present the greatest risk to the BTWC. The on-site inspection regime needs a considerable degree of flexibility so that an appropriate degree of intrusion can be made as necessary to confirm compliance.[92]

Pearson continued:

A spectrum of potential measures to detect and deter violation of the BTWC has been devised, ranging from political declarations through the CBMs agreed at the review conferences to declarations of patterns of national activity and inspections of high-risk sites to intrusive inspections. As we move across the spectrum we find increased confidence, increased deterrence, and an increased number of compliant countries. It will be necessary to strike the right balance so as to maximise the benefits to global and national security deriving from confidence that would-be possessors are effectively deterred. It is important to recognize that the inspection regime will have a significant deterrent effect, and the chance that a state will be deterred from acquisition of a BW capability will be very much greater than the chance that noncompliance will be detected. Nevertheless, there has to be a finite probability of detection of noncompliance to achieve a deterrent effect. For this reason, there must be planned uncertainty in the precise activities of a verification regime so that a potential proliferator remains uncertain as to whether his activities will be detected. Over a period of time, as more and more declarations are made by states and a better pattern of activity or norm for the state is built up, so the deterrent effect of the regime will increase.[93]

Moodie took issue with two elements of Pearson's approach: 'two problems—mistaking detection for deterrence and the difference and confusion over the purposes of verification—are at the heart of the US concern about the current debate within the international community about verification of the BWC'.[94] Moodie was opposed to an on-site inspection system which would give a false impression of reliability of detection. The contribution of arms con-

[90] Pearson, G. S., 'Prospects for chemical and biological arms control: the web of deterrence', *Washington Quarterly*, vol. 16, no. 2 (spring 1993), pp. 158, 161.

[91] Pearson (note 90), p. 161.

[92] Pearson (note 90), p. 157.

[93] Pearson (note 90), pp. 157–58.

[94] Moodie, M., 'Arms control programs and biological weapons', ed. B. Roberts, *Biological Weapons: Weapons of the Future?* (CSIS: Washington, DC, 1993), p. 55.

trol to ameliorating the BW problem, he wrote: 'will be diminished if a clumsily designed inspection system is added to the regime that over time serves to encourage proliferators, weaken resolve among States Parties to deal with the political aspects of compliance and erodes confidence in the regime'.[95]

Not only US officials were sceptical of on-site inspection. Four Australians, who helped to conclude the CWC, wrote: 'Unfortunately, the ease with which evidence of BW production can be disposed of will ensure that verification of BW production will never be as reliable as that for CW production unless unacceptably intrusive verification measures are introduced.'[96]

Others expressed concern over intrusiveness. On 4 June 1993, the last day of VEREX-3, the Group of Non-Aligned and Other Developing Countries urged the VEREX participants to: 'spare no effort in trying to identify and examine potential verification measures from a scientific and technical standpoint *which, in our opinion, should be the least intrusive as possible*, while still reliable and capable of deterring any States Parties from engaging in or being involved with activities which run counter to the object and purpose of the convention'.[97] The group warned against a potential North–South collision if their interests were not taken sufficiently into account and emphasized the costs of compliance if an expensive verification system were grafted on to the convention. Their statement reflected the trend of certain parties to seek a quid pro quo for the adherence of developing countries to the convention. The statement ended:

[VEREX] should, first of all, take into account the existing conditions in all States Parties to the Convention, especially that of the developing countries, thereby avoiding any infringement of their legitimate interests in the field of bio-technological development for peaceful purposes, as well as their national sovereignties, as recognized by international law.

We regret to note that, so far, the exercise carried out in the Ad Hoc Group has concentrated on accommodating the interests of the developed countries. These countries have proven to possess resources, capabilities, expertise and technology enabling them to conduct the work of the Group without due regard to the legitimate interests and concerns expressed by developing countries.[98]

This warning presaged trouble at the 1994 Special Conference, but VEREX was able to agree a cautiously positive report in September 1993. Latin American countries as diverse as Brazil and Cuba played an important part in bridging the North–South gap at VEREX-4. Its conclusions were summarized by its chairman, Ambassador Tóth, in his letter of 24 September 1993 transmitting the VEREX Final Report to the foreign minister of each party:

As a result of its deliberations, the Group had identified in all 21 potential measures. Based on the examination and evaluation of the measures against the criteria given in the mandate, the Group considered, from a scientific and technical standpoint, that some of the verification measures would contribute to strengthening the effectiveness

---

[95] Moodie (note 94), p. 57.

[96] Letts, M. *et al.*, 'The conclusion of the Chemical Weapons Convention: an Australian perspective', *Arms Control*, vol. 14, no. 3 (Dec. 1993), p. 328.

[97] BWC/CONF.III/VEREX/WP.150, 4 June 1993, was reproduced as Attachment 4 in BWC/CONF.III/VEREX/9 (note 89), p. 327, emphasis added.

[98] BWC/CONF.III/VEREX/WP.150 (note 97). The 'quid pro quo trend' is traced through the review conferences in chapter 5 in this volume.

and improve the implementation of the Convention, also recognizing that appropriate and effective verification could reinforce the Convention.[99]

It was preceded by a fuller assessment:

The Ad Hoc Group of Governmental Experts concluded that potential verification measures as identified and evaluated could be useful to varying degrees in enhancing confidence, through increasing transparency, that States Parties were fulfilling their obligations under the BWC. While it was agreed that reliance could not be placed on any single measure to differentiate conclusively between prohibited and permitted activity and to resolve ambiguities about compliance, it was also agreed that the measures could provide information of varying utility in strengthening the BWC. It was recognized that there remain a number of further technical questions to be addressed such as identity of agent, types and quantities, in the context of any future work. Some measures in combination could provide enhanced capabilities by increasing, for example, the focus and improving the quality of information, thereby improving the possibility of differentiating between prohibited and permitted activities and of resolving ambiguities about compliance.[100]

Commercial proprietary information (CPI) received particular attention. A bilateral trial inspection in a large vaccine facility had been conducted by the Netherlands and Canada,[101] and a practice compliance inspection had been carried out at a British pharmaceutical pilot plant.[102] These governments reported 'that the access given had not compromised commercial confidentiality'.[103]

Matters on which concern had been expressed and further consideration would be needed included financial implications, technical difficulties in identifying biological agents, protection of sensitive CPI and national security needs.[104] The specific concerns of developing countries were not acknowledged except for a reference to the impact of the 21 measures on 'scientific research, scientific cooperation, industrial development and other permitted activities' having been evaluated, in accordance with the Brazilian part of the VEREX mandate.[105]

XII. The 1994 Special Conference

In 1991 it was agreed that a special conference would be convened to examine the VEREX Final Report if a majority of parties to the BTWC so requested. Approximately 67 requests would be needed (depending on the exact number of parties on the operative date).

Early in 1994 Zimbabwe's request triggered the necessary action by the depositary governments. A clear majority of parties (71) agreed on the need for

---

[99] BWC/CONF.III/VEREX/9 (note 89), p. ii. The second sentence of Tóth's letter reproduces the text of the final paragraph of Conclusions, BWC/CONF.III/VEREX/9 (note 89), p. 9, para. 32.

[100] Conclusions, BWC/CONF.III/VEREX/9 (note 89), p. 9, para. 31.

[101] The Netherlands and Canada, Bilateral trial inspection in a large vaccine production facility: a contribution to the evaluation of potential verification measures, Third Review Conference document BWC/CONF.III/VEREX/6/WP.112, 24 May 1993.

[102] UK, UK practice inspection: pharmaceutical pilot plant, Third Review Conference document BWC/CONF.III/VEREX/6/WP.141, 24 May 1993.

[103] Other aspects, BWC/CONF.III/VEREX/9 (note 89), p. 7, para. 18.

[104] Conclusions, BWC/CONF.III/VEREX/9 (note 89), p. 8, paras 24–25.

[105] Conclusions, BWC/CONF.III/VEREX/9 (note 89), p. 8, para. 23.

a special conference.[106] It was scheduled for 19–30 September 1994, and its Preparatory Committee was to meet in April. The timetable was similar to that of the second and third review conferences and their preparatory committees in 1986 and 1991, respectively, but the mandate was significantly narrower.

The Special Conference played a pivotal role in the evolution of biological disarmament in terms of conversion and propulsion. It converted the VEREX findings, which were exclusively scientific and technical, into the basis for diplomatic efforts. Following the Special Conference diverse political and economic considerations could be introduced in the context of a multilateral negotiating process. In addition, it propelled the question of strengthening the BTWC by a verification protocol or other legally binding instrument higher up on the international agenda. A procedure was set in motion to present the Fourth Review Conference with a set of well-considered proposals as a basis for decision, following thorough consideration in an open-ended multilateral forum.

The Special Conference did, however, experience difficulties. Before it convened there was uncertainty as to how far it could go beyond conversion and propulsion since the Third Review Conference had left its powers unclear. It was empowered to 'decide on any further action' but whether this was to be interpreted as substantive or procedural action had not been determined. In addition, the status of its final document had not been specified. On 15 April 1994 the Preparatory Committee decided to include an 'appropriate' Final Report item[107] on the provisional agenda of the Special Conference but attached a rider: 'on the understanding that the Preparatory Committee could not prejudge the end-results and the decisions to be taken by the Special Conference'.[108]

There was uncertainty regarding how much was to be negotiated in the Special Conference and how much referred to a follow-up body for subsequent negotiation. In particular, there were questions about whether the Special Conference could draft a binding instrument or a verification protocol. Ultimately, it could not, and it proved difficult enough to agree on a mandate for a follow-up body: the Ad Hoc Group of States Parties, which started its work in January 1995. The bearing of Article X issues on its mandate was particularly difficult for the Special Conference. Tensions among different groups of signatories to the CWC had a negative effect on this aspect of strengthening the BTWC.

Three months after the VEREX Final Report was agreed at Geneva, it was commended to all parties to the BTWC by the UN General Assembly in a resolution which was adopted without a vote.[109] However, the same session of the UN General Assembly was unable to adopt a resolution on the CWC because it was deadlocked over the largely North–South issue of unrestricted free trade in chemicals versus continuing controls on chemical exports through the coordinating machinery of the Australia Group for a time after entry into force of the CWC.[110] A Netherlands draft resolution welcoming the CWC was blocked in

[106] List of States Parties which requested the convening of the Special Conference, Preparatory Committee for the Special Conference document BWC/SPC/PC/6, 15 Apr. 1994, annex III.

[107] BWC/SPC/PC/6 (note 106), para. 25.

[108] BWC/SPC/PC/6 (note 106), para. 22.

[109] UN General Assembly Resolution 48/65, 16 Dec. 1993.

[110] The Australia Group is an informal group of states which meets to discuss issues related to chemical and biological weapon proliferation. It is discussed in Anthony, I. and Zanders, J. P., 'Multilateral

committee by a coalition of developing countries under the leadership of Iran. The Iranian draft amendment was unacceptable to the members of the Australia Group because they felt that it would rule out sooner than they thought prudent all export controls extraneous to the CWC among its parties. The General Assembly was unable to adopt a resolution on the CWC in 1993 or 1994 because the issue remained unresolved.

This deadlock aggravated the long-standing tension between Article III and Article X emphases in the BTWC and intensified the concern about avoiding economic disadvantage in the field of biotechnology which the Group of Non-Aligned and Other Developing Countries had expressed earlier.[111] Those states would only allow the Special Conference to create a follow-up body if its mandate gave adequate recognition to their concerns. On 1 October 1994 such a mandate was agreed. Pearson noted:

There was however a fair measure of agreement that States Parties should encourage the transfer of information relevant to the implementation of a verification regime of the BTWC and to improvement of biosafety standards as proposed by Brazil (BWC/SPCONF/WP.4 of 21 September 1994). The mandate requires consideration of specific measures designed to ensure effective and full implementation of Article X, which also avoid any restrictions incompatible with the obligations undertaken under the Convention.[112]

It was also of relevance that the mandate recognized the need to avoid any negative impact on scientific research, international cooperation and industrial development, as well as to protect sensitive CPI and legitimate national security information.

In addition to the above-mentioned paper presented by Brazil to the Special Conference a strong 'free trade' joint working paper was submitted by China, India and Iran. The effect of the acrimonious UN General Assembly debate on the future of the Australia Group once the CWC entered into force is reflected in the paper:

Full implementation of Article X of the Convention [shall be one of the main tasks of the Working Group established by the Special Conference]. All States Parties shall have an ensured access to materials, equipment and technology in the field of biology and biotechnology for peaceful purposes. There shall be no restrictions for the States Parties in this regard. All the existing restrictions against the States Parties must be removed. The development and promotion of cooperation in peaceful area[s] between States Parties as enshrined in Article X of the Convention shall by no means be hindered in formulation of elaborated verification mechanism. It shall be enhanced. The development of the future mechanism shall be combined with guarantees for full access to materials, technology for peaceful purposes.[113]

security-related export controls', *SIPRI Yearbook 1998: Armaments, Disarmament and International Security* (Oxford University Press: Oxford, 1998), pp. 386–94; and Anthony, I. and Zanders, J. P., 'Multilateral weapon and technology export controls', *SIPRI Yearbook 1999: Armaments, Disarmament and International Security* (Oxford University Press: Oxford, 1999), pp. 694–95.

[111] BWC/CONF.III/VEREX/WP.150 (note 97).

[112] Pearson, G. S., 'Strengthening the Biological and Toxin Weapons Convention: the outcome of the Special Conference', *Chemical Weapons Convention Bulletin*, no. 26 (Dec. 1994), pp. 5–6.

[113] Special Conference document BWC/SPCONF/WP.14, 23 Sep. 1994, para. 6(c).

The demand that 'All the existing restrictions against the States Parties must be removed' implies that the Australia Group should not coordinate export controls in the field of microbiology (as it had been doing since 1991) against parties to the BTWC. This contention was diluted in the Final Declaration of the Special Conference, but its influence is reflected in the document's negative references to restrictions.

Many national papers sought to steer the mandate of the follow-up body towards the drafting of a verification protocol. The paper submitted by Germany on behalf of the European Union (then about to expand from 12 to 15 states) was significant. It stated: 'that a verification protocol should now be concluded as expeditiously as possible',[114] and that the new body established by the Special Conference should be called the Ad Hoc Working Group on Verification.[115] The EU paper in its 'proposal for a mandate' suggested:

4. The objective of the Ad Hoc Working Group on Verification shall be to draft a verification protocol, drawing on the VEREX Final Report as appropriate, establishing a mandatory regime that provides or enhances openness and transparency of all activities relevant to the Biological and Toxin Weapons Convention.

Such a regime shall include the following basic elements:

– off-site measures, including national declarations covering a broad range of activities in States Parties, such as BW-defence programs, vaccines, relevant pharmaceutical and biotechnology activities, and facilities handling specific organisms and toxins;

– on-site measures such as information visits to declared facilities, short-notice inspections, and investigations of allegations of use.

The regime shall also include a provision for multilateral information sharing, on a voluntary basis, to contribute to the efficacy of verifying compliance with the Convention.

5. The regime should apply to commercial, academic and government facilities as legitimate potential objects of verification, bearing in mind that all activities must include appropriate means to protect proprietary rights and sensitive information not related to biological and toxin weapons activities.

6. The Ad Hoc Working Group on Verification shall consider how such a regime might best be implemented by an independent inspectorate, taking into account such factors as financial, legal, safety, technology, material, manpower, equipment and organizational implications; but these aspects shall not be construed in such a manner as to distract from the regime's core objectives and contents.[116]

The draft mandate was endorsed by Australia,[117] and similar proposals were put forward in national papers from Bulgaria,[118] New Zealand,[119] Switzerland[120] and—with some divergence, representing greater caution—Japan[121] and

[114] Special Conference document BWC/SPCONF/WP.1, 20 Sep. 1994, para. 2.

[115] BWC/SPCONF/WP.1 (note 114), para. 3.

[116] BWC/SPCONF/WP.1 (note 114), paras 4–6.

[117] Australia, Special Conference document BWC/SPCONF/WP.6, 21 Sep. 1994. Australian views on the form of future negotiations were further developed in Special Conference document BWC/SPCONF/WP.12, 22 Sep. 1994.

[118] Bulgaria, BWC/SPCONF/WP.14 (note 113).

[119] New Zealand, Special Conference document BWC/SPCONF/WP.8, 21 Sep. 1994.

[120] Switzerland, Special Conference document BWC/SPCONF/WP.3, 21 Sep. 1994.

[121] Japan, Special Conference document BWC/SPCONF/WP.9, 22 Sep. 1994.

Russia.[122] The Brazilian[123] and South African[124] contributions were two of the most comprehensive national papers; they favoured a similar verification protocol but stressed peaceful use (Article X) issues, which they saw as complementary.

In a joint paper China, India and Iran stated that: 'much more work is needed towards the strengthening of the convention before devising any effective verification mechanism'; they proposed that the mandate be 'wide enough to allow the coverage of all aspects, including confidence-building measures' in an 'indepth consideration and identification of appropriate and necessary further measures for comprehensive strengthening [of] the Convention including the proposals for a legal instrument'.[125] China separately proposed 'drafting a legally binding instrument' as part of the mandate; its national paper[126] seemed more sympathetic to a protocol-drafting role for the Ad Hoc Group than the paper with India and Iran.

China was careful to avoid the word 'verification' in its 'view on follow-up mechanism for strengthening the BWC'. The United States also did not refer to verification in its 'mandate to strengthen' the BTWC. Both countries suggested an Ad Hoc Group of Governmental Experts which would seek to strengthen implementation by means of 'transparency'. (The USA added 'openness'.)

The US draft mandate differed from China's in avoiding any reference to Article X or the listing of 'types and quantities' prohibited under Article I (which China advocated 'to provide the prerequisite for enhanced further measures for the strengthening of the Convention'). Instead it recommended as the objective of the Ad Hoc Group:

to draft a protocol that provides for a regime with the following basic elements:
– The regime should build on measures such as those contained in the VEREX Final Report, plus any additional new measures the Group believes necessary.
– The regime should be mandatory and legally binding.
– The regime should provide or enhance openness and transparency of activities relevant to the BWC for all stages of potential biological and toxin warfare activities, from research through production, stockpiling, and weaponization.
– The regime should include off-site and on-site measures, including short-notice on-site measures.
– Any on-site measures should be designed to, among other things, strengthen confidence in information exchanged among States Parties or provide a mechanism for pursuing specific activities of concern.[127]

In the Committee of the Whole the US representative to the Special Conference, Donald A. Mahley, restated his government's reluctance to use verification in this discourse:

Building confidence in compliance with a Convention is a task that we firmly believe must be tailored in each instance to the unique features of the weapons being prohib-

122 Russia, Special Conference document BWC/SPCONF/WP.7, 21 Sep. 1994.
123 Brazil, Special Conference document BWC/SPCONF/WP.4, 21 Sep. 1994; and Brazil, Special Conference document WP.5, 21 Sep. 1994.
124 South Africa, Special Conference document BWC/SPCONF/WP.11, 22 Sep. 1994.
125 China, India and Iran, Special Conference document BWC/SPCONF/WP.15, 23 Sep. 1994, paras 4, 6(a).
126 China, Special Conference document BWC/SPCONF/WP.13, 23 Sep. 1994, para. 2.
127 USA, Special Conference document BWC/SPCONF/WP.10, 22 Sep. 1994.

ited or controlled. Procedures or standards crafted for different conditions and different weapons would both ignore some of the unique characteristics of biological weapons and would provide a potentially damaging false confidence in compliance in that states would be claiming compliance on the basis of adherence to incomplete or misleading criteria that may not ensure such compliance.

The US believes that the term 'effective verification' in the specialized context of formal arms control, refers to a set of measures designed to verify compliance with the provisions of a treaty with sufficient confidence to detect any militarily significant violation in time for other state parties to take appropriate countermeasures. In addition, an effective verification regime should safeguard non-relevant national security and industrial proprietary information and provide a net benefit to state parties' national security. In the case of the BWC, it should further the non-proliferation goals set forth by the international community.

This definition further assumes that measures are developed with an ability to distinguish between treaty prohibited and permitted activities with a minimum of ambiguity. The VEREX Ad Hoc Group of Experts recognized the great difficulty in meeting this condition but 'concluded that potential measures as identified and evaluated could be useful to varying degrees in enhancing confidence, through increased transparency, that states parties were fulfilling their obligations under the BWC'. Further, 'The group considered, from the scientific and technical standpoint, that some of the verification measures would contribute to strengthening the effectiveness and improve the implementation of the Convention.'

Even under this relaxed definition of verification, i.e. compliance enhancement, it is an extremely complex task to define as well as distinguish between 'treaty prohibited' and 'permitted activities' with regard to the unique prohibition of the BWC with a reasonable level of confidence. Determination of whether a violation of the BWC has occurred is not a straightforward analytical task, and is dependent on intent as well as physical evidence. This statement does not imply that we are against strengthening the Biological Weapons Convention but the Protocol must reflect what is both technically and politically feasible.[128]

This US statement illustrates what had and had not changed in the US position since 1991. At the Third Review Conference the US conviction had been that the convention could not be effectively verified.[129] In 1993 a Clinton Administration policy review had moved the USA towards favouring a legally binding protocol, the position of the other members of the Western Group, which enabled consensus on convening the Special Conference. However, the USA did not abandon its doctrine altogether; it still was not inclined to support far-reaching change in the BTWC and continued to consider the convention as incapable of effective verification.[130] Progress at the Special Conference therefore depended upon the USA accepting as transparency measures what others in the Western Group were espousing as verification, which is what happened.

Under the chairmanship of Ambassador Christopher Westdal of Canada, the Committee of the Whole held seven meetings between 20 and 23 September 1994, as well as informal consultations,[131] which resulted in 'general support for

---

[128] USA, Special Conference document BWC/SPCONF/WP.16, 23 Sep. 1994.

[129] Statement by Ambassador Ronald F Lehman II (note 77); and Quoted in Webb (note 80).

[130] Dando (note 88), p. 178. Milton Leitenberg discusses the evolution of US policy in the VEREX–Special Conference–early Ad Hoc Group period. Leitenberg, M., *Biological Weapons Arms Control*, PRAC [Project on Rethinking Arms Control] Paper no. 16 (University of Maryland Center for International and Security Studies: College Park, Md, May 1996), pp. 60–69, and references cited therein.

[131] Report of the Committee of the Whole, Special Conference document BWC/SPCONF/WP.19, 26 Sep. 1994.

a legally-binding instrument which would apply to all activities and facilities relevant to the BWC'. A number of VEREX measures and CBMs were cited, but the word 'verification' was avoided. There was also 'general support for the establishment of a follow-up mechanism, which should take the form of an Ad Hoc Working Group open to all States Parties and consist of governmental representatives supported by experts'.[132]

The EU countries and like-minded states still wanted the word 'verification' to be included in the title and mandate of the Ad Hoc Working Group: 'A commonly supported view was that the title should reflect the Group's objectives. Several proposals were made.'[133] A resource paper for the chairman of the Drafting Committee showed six alternative titles using 'verification', 'compliance' or neither word.[134]

Under the chairmanship of Ambassador Jorge Berguño of Chile the Drafting Committee held further rounds of negotiation, and before the mandate of the Ad Hoc Group was finalized the word 'working' was deleted from its name. Verification was mentioned in the mandate, but it was given less prominence than in the EU proposal and was absent from the name of the group.[135]

XIII. The outcome of the Special Conference

On 1 October 1994 the Special Conference agreed paragraphs 35 and 36, the last two paragraphs of its Final Declaration, which were drastically recast from an earlier version. Paragraph 35 categorized verification as one potential element of a coherent regime which would be the product of a gradual approach. This was far from the German/EU concept, in which a verification protocol was central, and it reflected the lack of consensus on anything but a tentative step forward:

35. The Conference also recognized that the complex nature of the issues pertaining to the strengthening of the Biological Weapons Convention underlined the need for a gradual approach towards the establishment of a coherent regime to enhance the effectiveness of and improve compliance with the Convention. This regime would include, *inter alia*, potential verification measures, as well as agreed procedures and mechanisms for their efficient implementation and measures for the investigation of alleged use.

Paragraph 36 contained the mandate for the Ad Hoc Group. Measures to promote compliance and implement Article X were given equal status with Article I lists and CBM/transparency measures. This mandate may point the way forward, if the treaty regime can be steered into a sectorally balanced pattern of evolution. Paragraph 36 read:

[132] Non-Paper of the Chairman of the Committee of the Whole, Special Conference document BWC/SPCONF/WP.17/Rev.1, 23 Sep. 1994; it was originally issued as Paper of the Chairman of the Committee of the Whole, Special Conference document BWC/SPCONF/WP.17, 23 Sep. 1994.

[133] Note 132.

[134] Special Conference document BWC/SPCONF/DC/WP.1, 27 Sep. 1994, section III.

[135] BWC/SPCONF/WP.17/Rev.1 (note 132). In the Drafting Committee chairman's rolling text the reference was to 'an Ad Hoc Working Group, whose objective shall be the consideration of appropriate measures to strengthen the Convention, including drafting a legally binding instrument to that effect'. Special Conference document BWC/SPCONF/DC/WP.2, 28 Sep. 1994. The words 'including possible verification measures' were added subsequently to compensate for the deletion of more explicit references to a verification system in the detailed mandate which had been in the chairman's rolling text.

36. In pursuance of the second part of its mandate under Item 9 [decision on any further action with a view to strengthening the Convention] the Conference, determined to strengthen the effectiveness and improve the implementation of the Convention and recognizing that effective verification could reinforce the Convention, decides to establish an Ad Hoc Group, open to all States Parties. The objective of this Ad Hoc Group shall be to consider appropriate measures, including possible verification measures, and draft proposals to strengthen the Convention, to be included, as appropriate, in a legally binding instrument, to be submitted for the consideration of the States Parties. In this context, the Ad Hoc Group shall, *inter alia*, consider:

– Definitions of terms and objective criteria, such as lists of bacteriological (biological) agents and toxins, their threshold quantities, as well as equipment and types of activities, where relevant for specific measures designed to strengthen the Convention;

– The incorporation of existing and further enhanced confidence-building and transparency measures, as appropriate, into the regime;

– A system of measures to promote compliance with the Convention, including, as appropriate, measures identified, examined and evaluated in the VEREX Report. Such measures should apply to all relevant facilities and activities, be reliable, cost-effective, non-discriminatory and as non-intrusive as possible, consistent with the effective implementation of the system and should not lead to abuse;

– Specific measures designed to ensure effective and full implementation of Article X, which also avoid any restrictions incompatible with the obligations undertaken under the Convention, noting that the provisions of the Convention should not be used to impose restrictions and/or limitations on the transfer for purposes consistent with the objectives and the provisions of the Convention of scientific knowledge, technology, equipment and materials.

Measures should be formulated and implemented in a manner designed to protect sensitive commercial proprietary information and legitimate national security needs.

Measures shall be formulated and implemented in a manner designed to avoid any negative impact on scientific research, international cooperation and industrial development.[136]

Like VEREX and the Special Conference, the Ad Hoc Group was to be chaired by Ambassador Tóth. It was to 'complete its work as soon as possible and submit its report, which shall be adopted by consensus, to the States Parties, to be considered at the Fourth Review Conference or later at a [second] Special Conference'. This timescale followed the advice of Australia. After urging 'a more time-intensive process than the VEREX process' for consideration of a legally binding protocol (which it hoped would turn into negotiation), and intersessional work to minimize travel to plenary sessions, Australia stated:

We do not believe it would be wise for the Special Conference mandate rigidly to stipulate that a protocol be ready for signature by the time of the 1996 Fourth Review Conference, although it would be appropriate for the negotiating process firmly to *aim* for that objective. Some allowance should be made for extending negotiation for a protocol beyond the Fourth Review Conference if that proves necessary to achieve a protocol.[137]

The mandate had not specified the nature of the 'legally binding instrument' in which measures were to be included 'as appropriate' only. There were therefore questions about the nature of the protocol; it might be a verification proto-

136 Special Conference document BWC/SPCONF/1, 1 Oct. 1994.
137 BWC/SPCONF/WP.12 (note 117), para. 4, emphasis in the original.

col or it might be something different. Pearson, who had been a leading British Government player both at the Special Conference and at VEREX, was confident that it would be the former, and advised that:

In developing a verification protocol it is necessary to select measures that strengthen both the assurance that States are compliant and the deterrent effect against non-compliance. The essential measures needed for a protocol include mandatory declarations and on-site inspections allowing both for visits to validate declarations and short notice inspections of both declared and undeclared facilities and activities including sites of alleged use.[138]

XIV. Proposals for verification institutions

At the Special Conference several national papers recognized a potential need for institutions to implement a verification protocol. South Africa wanted 'an international appeal mechanism' to which a party challenged to accept 'inspections incorporating more intrusive measures' could have recourse. This mechanism would determine whether adequate cause had been shown why illegitimate activities should be suspected at a particular site.[139] As noted above, the German/EU proposal had envisaged consideration of 'how such a regime might best be implemented by an independent inspectorate'.[140] Australia, which had been one of the leading proponents of addressing institutional questions, deliberately abstained on this occasion from making other than procedural proposals because 'it would be counterproductive here to reopen debate on the substance of any specific measures. Debate on the substance of specific measures ought to be left to the future working group'.[141] Switzerland proposed, as part of a fact-finding or transparency regime to be established under the eventual protocol, a commission open to all parties:

This Commission should meet periodically or at short notice upon request of a state party. The Commission should hold substantial discussions on the results of the transparency measures and fact-finding missions; lead consultations on diverging standpoints with regard to violation or compliance under the BWC; consider and, if possible, agree on specific measures to dispel doubts about compliance with the BWC; and address other matters with regard to compliance under the BWC.[142]

Brazil envisaged a set of institutions—a Conference of States Parties, an Executive Council and a Technical Secretariat incorporating an inspectorate—copied from the prospective Organisation for the Prohibition of Chemical Weapons of the CWC, although the size of the BTWC organization or the scale of its 'verification system' (a phrase which Brazil used frequently in its paper) relative to those to be set up under the CWC was not addressed.[143] It may have been in reaction to this proposal that China, India and Iran in their joint paper urged: 'Establishment of a cost-effective mechanism. We should try to make

[138] Pearson (note 112), p. 6.
[139] BWC/SPCONF/WP.11 (note 124).
[140] FRG on behalf of the European Union, BWC/SPCONF/WP.1 (note 114), para. 6.
[141] BWC/SPCONF/WP.6 (note 117).
[142] BWC/SPCONF/WP.3 (note 120), para. 3.
[143] BWC/SPCONF/WP.4 (note 123). The OPCW was provided for by Article VIII of the CWC, which did not enter into force until 29 Apr. 1997.

better use of existing facilities in order to prevent the creation of a large bureau-cracy.'[144] However, there had never been any prospect of 'a large bureaucracy' for the BTWC. On the contrary, the parties had refrained from creating even modest supportive institutions on a limited-duration intersessional basis.

XV. Establishment of the Ad Hoc Group in 1995

In accordance with the decision of the Special Conference, an organizational meeting of the newly established Ad Hoc Group was held in Geneva on 4–8 January 1995. It was agreed that two substantive meetings would be held on 10–21 July and on 27 November–8 December 1995, both in Geneva. By 8 December 1995 agreement was to be reached on the number and dates of meetings to be scheduled for 1996. In 1996, 1997, 1998, 1999 and 2000 the same cumbersome scheduling procedure was used.

Australia had expressed the hope that 'at some stage in the process of negoti-ating a protocol' there would be 'a meeting dedicated to allowing national dele-gations to exchange views with industry representatives'. The best time, it sug-gested, would be 'at a stage where ideas on what would be required in a veri-fication regime were well-formed with respect to each basic element, but where detailed agreement had not yet been reached'.[145]

Approximately 50 of the nearly 140 parties in 1995 took part in the Ad Hoc Group, including all the parties which had been active in VEREX and the Special Conference. In 1995–2000 Australia, Chile (later succeeded by Brazil), France, Germany, Hungary, India, Iran, Japan, Pakistan, South Africa and the UK were allocated particular items or issue areas, mostly as Friends of the Chair. The caucuses of the Western and the Non-Aligned and Other Developing Countries groups organized the proceedings, as they had done in VEREX, but there were significant tensions and differences within and between groups, as is discussed below.

The aim was to produce a report for submission to the Fourth Review Confer-ence, but the Ad Hoc Group was not given a timetable. It could, if necessary, continue its deliberations beyond the review conference and report instead to a second Special Conference. One-half of the time available was to be spent on 'measures to promote compliance' with the convention, including VEREX measures, a decision welcomed by proponents of a verification protocol.

XVI. The United States and verification

The outcome of any proposal will inevitably be affected by the willingness of the USA to accept it. The slow progress of policy formation through the inter-agency process made it hard for the US delegation at Geneva to express a US view with authority. This has hampered the development of a common Western position and has slowed the pace of the work of the Ad Hoc Group.

By March 1995 the USA was ready to discuss, first with its close allies and then with the Western Group as a whole, a draft protocol with a technical annexe containing lists of measures proposed to enhance compliance with the

---

[144] BWC/SPCONF/WP.15 (note 125).
[145] BWC/SPCONF/WP.12 (note 117), para. 5.

convention. Although the USA avoided the word 'verification', its interpretation of 'transparency' was close to what the other Western states meant by verification. Protection of CPI against confidentiality breaches, however, remained a major US concern. The USA could perhaps be reassured about a verification provision by the practice compliance inspections of its allies,[146] the 1996 Brazilian–British joint non-challenge visit at the Instituto Butantan in São Paulo,[147] and the impressively detailed proposals of the FAS.[148] However, there were also factors working against US approval of a verification protocol, including bureaucratic reorganization, inter-agency tensions, disappointment over Russian use of the trilateral process and its effect on US government–industry relations in respect of verifying the non-production of biological and toxin weapons.[149]

The United States may be so confident of its intelligence, deterrence or intervention capabilities that it perceives no advantage in a multilateral apparatus for detecting and identifying breaches of the convention. Such an apparatus would also have to be 'sold' to the US pharmaceutical industry and other interest groups affected which are suspicious of international scrutiny and vocal in defence of their CPI against foreign inspectors.[150] Unilateral US action would enable it to avoid making the political effort necessary to persuade industry of the value of a verification protocol. It could also continue to discriminate between one alleged BTW-possessor and another in its efforts to combine worldwide vigilance to combat BTW proliferation with the pursuit of wider US interests, taking into account bilateral relationships and regional considerations. Dando is one of the experts on verification of the convention who find this explanation plausible.[151] Whether unilateralism is in the long-term interests of the USA is questionable.

The United States may become more amenable to persuasion that the BTWC should be explicitly verified now that the CWC has entered into force. It would be wrong to suppose, however, that a verification scheme tailor-made for the CWC could simply be translated into a verification protocol for the BTWC. As early as 1992 Brad Roberts warned against this 'quick fix' temptation, which should be resisted because 'precedent suggests that monitoring and compliance methodologies cannot easily be imported from one to another treaty'.[152] Jonathan Tucker has compared the verification requirements of chemical and

[146] Examples of allied governments' reports demonstrating the compatibility of inspection with protection of CPI are: the Netherlands and Canada, BWC/CONF.III/VEREX/6/WP.112 (note 101); United Kingdom, BWC/CONF.III/VEREX/6/WP.141 (note 102); Walker, J. R., Phillips, A. P. and Miller, L., 'Verification of the Biological and Toxin Weapons Convention and the UK's Practice Compliance Inspection Programme: Final Report', eds J. B. Poole and R. Guthrie, *Verification 1996: The VERTIC Yearbook* (Westview Press: Boulder, Colo. and Oxford, 1996), pp. 171–91.

[147] Walker, J. R. *et al.*, 'The Biological and Toxin Weapons Convention: report of a joint UK–Brazil practice non-challenge visit', ed. R. Guthrie, *Verification 1997: The VERTIC Yearbook* (Westview Press: Boulder, Colo. and Oxford, 1997), pp. 121–30.

[148] Chevrier M. I. *et al.*, *Beyond VEREX: A Legally Binding Compliance Regime for the Biological and Toxin Weapons Convention* (FAS: Washington, DC, July 1994, and subsequent revisions).

[149] Smithson, A. E., 'Man versus microbe: the negotiations to strengthen the Biological Weapons Convention', ed. A. E. Smithson, *Biological Weapons Proliferation: Reasons for Concern, Courses of Action*, Report no. 24 (Henry L. Stimson Center: Washington, DC, Jan. 1998), pp. 107–28.

[150] Woollett, G. R., 'Industry's role, concerns and interests in the negotiation of a BWC compliance protocol', ed. Smithson (note 149), pp. 39–52.

[151] Dando (note 88), p. 179.

[152] Roberts, B., 'Implementing the Biological Weapons Convention: looking beyond the verification issue', ed. Thränert (note 10), p. 101.

biological disarmament and concluded that: 'Taken together, the various elements of the CWC verification regime provide a useful model for a workable BWC compliance protocol. Depending on the specific issue, however, the CWC model is sometimes readily adaptable, sometimes in need of adjustment for the BWC context, and sometimes incapable of meeting the unique challenges of monitoring biological weapons activities.'[153]

BTW disarmament has to be verified on the basis of procedures specially devised for it, if it is to be verified by systematic, multilateral methods. It remains an open question whether the United States will ratify any protocol which embodies such methods of verification.

XVII. Verification issues in the Ad Hoc Group

Since 1995 the Ad Hoc Group has been considering (and since 1997 negotiating) ways to strengthen the convention. Verification is mentioned in the mandate which the Ad Hoc Group received from the 1994 Special Conference, but not exclusively. Its place has been correspondingly open to disagreement.

In the category 'Measures to promote compliance', for which the United Kingdom has provided successive Friends of the Chair, the negotiation of a verification protocol is the clear objective, with the UK as its leading proponent. That objective is resisted to a varying extent by other parties.

The dominant groups within the Ad Hoc Group remain the Western and the Non-Aligned and Other Developing Countries groups, although attitudes to verification cut across groups. As noted above, unlike other Western Group members, the USA prefers the terms 'transparency' or 'compliance measures'. However, in his 27 January 1998 State of the Union message President Bill Clinton seemed to indicate that the USA was preparing to move closer to the mainstream Western position. Brazil and South Africa, members of the Group of Non-Aligned and Other Developing Countries, favour verification, but other non-aligned participants in the Ad Hoc Group are suspicious of verification and view it as a potentially discriminatory intrusion into the privacy of sovereign states. Russia has expressed doubts over the verification institutions and there has been uncertainty over the Chinese and Japanese positions on transparency and access.

For the parties which favour a verification protocol the pace of the Ad Hoc Group has been too slow. In 1997 and 1998 Australia and the EU states attempted to speed up negotiations but achieved only limited success, as they had done at the Fourth Review Conference. The Ad Hoc Group had reported to the review conference that it had met four times in 1995–96 and had 'made significant progress towards fulfilling the mandate given by the Special Conference, including by identifying a preliminary framework and elaborating potential basic elements of a legally-binding instrument to strengthen the Convention'.[154]

The Fourth Review Conference welcomed the promised intensification of the group's work and encouraged it 'to review its method of work and to move to a

---

[153] Tucker, J. B., 'Verification provisions of the Chemical Weapons Convention and their relevance to the Biological Weapons Convention', ed. Smithson (note 149), p. 77.
[154] Ad Hoc Group document BWC/AD HOC GROUP/32, 27 Sep. 1996.

negotiating format in order to fulfil its mandate'.[155] However, it refrained both from endorsing a South African proposal for specifying the negotiating agenda of the Ad Hoc Group more precisely and also from setting 1998 as a target date for completion of the negotiations, as had been hoped by the parties that favour a verification protocol.[156] Instead, it asked for completion 'as soon as possible' before the next review,[157] and left the mandate unchanged.

Under the 1994 mandate, because the Ad Hoc Group did not complete its task in time for the Fourth Review Conference, a second Special Conference is to be held to culminate the 'strengthening' process. It could take place immediately before the Fifth Review Conference in 2001 if a legally binding instrument is not ready earlier. This would be later than the target date suggested by the UK and other parties, but as in other negotiations (e.g., the CWC) drafting often proceeds slowly. Minor procedural issues create problems and numerous issues are not resolved until the 'endgame'—whenever that may occur. Two expert scientific advisers to the Australian delegation suggested that: 'The inability of the AHG [Ad Hoc Group] to conclude a Verification Protocol by the end of 1996 should not be interpreted as a lack of will or interest, but more a reflection on the complexity of the issues involved.'[158]

Under the heading 'Measures to promote compliance' the Ad Hoc Group confronts numerous verification issues including: disagreement over which categories of civilian facility (vaccine production plants, high-containment units in the biotechnology and pharmaceutical industries, etc.) should be added to the list of military facilities to be declared for verification purposes and possible international inspection; the procedures for triggering an investigation; the 'red light or green light' argument (whether a qualified majority vote of the Executive Council should be required for the initiation or cancellation of an investigation); whether other types of visit (regular, clarification, non-challenge, etc.) should be allowed in addition to challenge investigations; the modalities of the conduct of challenge investigations; the role of the Security Council; and how to preserve the full prohibitory scope of Article I unimpaired.

Verification measures must still be considered and compared with other ways of strengthening the treaty regime, within an Ad Hoc Group mandated to consider 'appropriate measures, including possible verification measures, and draft proposals to strengthen the Convention'.[159] Many obstacles must be overcome before a legally binding instrument emerges from the Ad Hoc Group. When it is ready, it will not necessarily contain the word 'verification' or provisions which amount to de facto verification. If it does, it must still be adopted by a second Special Conference before it can be opened for signature, and even if they sign the new instrument not all parties to the convention will necessarily take the next step—ratification.

[155] Fourth Review Conference document BWC/CONF.IV/9, 6 Dec. 1996, p. 29.

[156] Dando, M. R. and Pearson, G. S., 'The Fourth Review Conference of the Biological and Toxin Weapons Convention: issues, outcomes, and unfinished business', *Politics and the Life Sciences*, vol. 16, no. 1 (Mar. 1997), pp. 119–20.

[157] BWC/CONF.IV/9 (note 155).

[158] Duncan, A. and Mathews, R. J., 'Development of a verification protocol for the Biological and Toxin Weapons Convention: progress in 1996', ed. R. Guthrie, *Verification 1997: The VERTIC Yearbook* (note 147), p. 117.

[159] BWC/SPCONF/1 (note 136), p. 10.

For these reasons, even assuming the most positive outcome of the Ad Hoc Group, it would be premature to take verification for granted as replacing, or even complementing, the earlier (original and CBM) elements of the regime of compliance. Mode B has been added to Mode A; but whether Mode C will ever join or supersede them remains to be seen.

XVIII. Conclusions

There is both interest and the opportunity to reinforce BTW disarmament by strengthening its regime of compliance. A procedure has been defined to enable the parties to shift the BTW regime of compliance into Mode C—the regime of compliance with verification added—or to add Mode C to modes A and B if their relationship is seen to be complementary.

Views on the convention range from those which rate it as ineffectual, with verification all that matters, to those which attribute the greatest value to its endogenous evolution. The latter view questions whether the emphasis placed on verification in the 1990s is not too exclusive of other elements of the regime of compliance.

Some regard verification as indispensable for reinforcement of the BTWC, and the only meaningful way to strengthen the convention. Events of the 1990s on this view rendered verification increasingly necessary and opportune. Dando noted in 1997 that: 'There is a sense that this job has to be done *now*. There is a window of opportunity because concerns about the proliferation of biological weapons are evident at high political levels, and because the technical work required to [draft in] detail much of the additional instrument has been done since 1991.'[160] He argued that the failure of the Ad Hoc Group to produce a verification protocol would leave the convention in a worse state than before: 'These negotiations to strengthen the BWC may fail in the face of the evident difficulties, but, should this happen, there will be profound consequences. Without a strengthened BWC the international community will have less legal and institutional legitimacy in dealing with potential proliferators.'[161]

'Potential proliferators' which are parties to the convention would be unlikely to favour a verification protocol or assume new obligations under it. The BTWC retains its importance as a prohibitory treaty. Parties which implement it in good faith will have to continue to use its provisions, as clarified and elaborated into procedures, to cope with those parties whose good faith may be more questionable. The endogenous evolution of the treaty regime is more necessary for that reason.

The endogenous process is valuable as it exists, but it could be strengthened by a system of verification, especially if the parties heed Gordon Vachon's warning that they face an 'important challenge . . . to confront the resource/performance interface'.[162] They cannot hope to establish a stronger regime unless they allocate resources to the task. As Vachon has noted:

---

[160] Dando, M. R., 'Consolidating the arms control regimes for biological and chemical weapons', *Disarmament*, vol. 20, nos 2–3 (1997), p. 44, emphasis in the original.

[161] Dando (note 160), p. 45.

[162] Vachon, G. K., 'Post-1995 verification challenges: chemical and biological weapons', eds J. M. Beier and S. Mataija, *Proliferation in All Its Aspects Post-1995: The Verification Challenge and Response* (York University Centre for International and Strategic Studies: Toronto, 1995), p. 47.

Those calling for strengthening the Convention will have to confront the reality that arms control verification is not a cost-free undertaking. All would agree, however, that costs need to be kept commensurate with the achievable objective. The difficulty is that there is no easy or direct way to quantify the value that derives from a shared determination to demonstrate compliance with international obligations, and a shared determination to ensure that those obligations are observed by others.[163]

Questions arise that are even more fundamental to a conceptual analysis than the question of resources. Some of the questions are:

1. If verification is added (Mode C), what happens to CBMs (Mode B), consultative mechanisms and other original elements (Mode A) in the regime of compliance as it has evolved?

2. Is verification a further point along a continuum of elements constituting such a regime?

3. Can verification be achieved by introducing a challenge inspection procedure or by formalizing the degree of obligation which attaches to the existing reporting requirements under the CBM sub-regime?[164] (This would be accomplished by converting their status from politically to legally binding and then subjecting governments to checks on the veracity of the declared data.)

4. Should verification be perceived as an adjunct to the convention which may, when brought into effect, render redundant the less powerful machinery of the pre-existing regime of compliance?

The main elements of the pre-existing regime belonged originally to the category 'functional substitutes for verification'. In the course of the regime-building process these elements have achieved a certain momentum and acquired their own *raison d'être*. It would be premature to write off those elements of the regime which have transcended their original role as mere functional substitutes for verification.

If verification is feasible, it ought logically to supersede the functional substitutes for verification (which could be regarded as having served their purpose as stopgaps until verification became feasible). However, if such elements as national implementation, consultation and cooperation, complaint, assistance and confidence-building measures have succeeded in transcending their origins, they should continue to be utilized: 'Verification in its "anytime, anywhere" form, or in a more restricted mode, may or may not prove acceptable. But in any event verification should not be expected to carry the entire weight of the world's hopes for the future of the BWC. For verification is not a panacea for the Convention, which needs a more rounded evolution of all aspects of its treaty regime to keep it in good health.'[165]

Verification is not the sole determinant of compliance. The social bases of compliance are many. At the international level, governments comply with their

[163] Vachon, G. K., 'Verifying the Biological Weapons Convention: the role of inspections and visits', ed. O. Thränert, *Enhancing the Biological Weapons Convention* (Dietz: Bonn, 1996), p. 152.

[164] Major surveys of the CBM sub-regime in theory and practice are those by Hunger, I., 'Article V: confidence-building measures', eds G. S. Pearson and M. R. Dando, *Strengthening the Biological Weapons Convention: Key Points for the Fourth Review Conference* (Quaker United Nations Office: Geneva, 1996), pp. 77–92; and Chevrier, M. I., 'Doubts about confidence: the potential and limits of confidence-building measures for the Biological Weapons Convention', ed. Smithson (note 149), pp. 53–75.

[165] Sims (note 44), p. 16.

obligations for a variety of reasons, including habit, convenience and perceptions of interest. In international society obligations are assumed more voluntarily than in many other social contexts through the consensual basis of treaty-making in particular. This means that treaties are more likely than not to be honoured. If states did not intend to comply with their obligations they need not have entered into them. Other than Iraq, which uniquely was required to ratify the BTWC by the UN Security Council in 1991,[166] no state has been forced to join.

The entrenchment of expectations of compliance and rules of conduct and procedures for compliance reassurance creates strong incentives to comply. The complex of norms, expectations, rules and procedures known as a regime may generate its own 'indirect verification' effect. This does not mean that verification would add nothing to the BTWC, but it should be combined carefully with the existing elements of the regime of compliance. It may be that some forms of 'indirect verification', like the concept of a regime of compliance, can bridge the gap between endogenous evolution and added verification.

Prudence dictates that the regime-building process should proceed so that the Mode A original elements of the compliance regime are strengthened and the Mode B programme of CBMs maintained—at least until an effective verification scheme takes it into Mode C. The elements in that regime may be able to coexist even then. Abandoning interest in the regime-building process as it has evolved in the absence of verification would be unwise. That process has strengthened the BTWC and with careful steering could do more.

Perhaps what is most needed is an evolution of expectations so that parties expect to *demonstrate their compliance*. It is impossible to prove a negative, but something not dissimilar is what both the CWC and the BTWC require of their parties.

Biological disarmament must be valued as a public good, and an integrated treaty regime will steer the regime of development towards the promotion of safe practice in the peaceful application of microbiology. This, in turn, enables the parties to demonstrate that (taking their cue from the 1992 Moscow Joint Statement[167]) they possess no equipment or excess capacity inconsistent with the stated purpose of their facilities. In that and other ways the regime of compliance can be enhanced. Regimes of permanence and probably of research are also vital to the achievement of this integrated whole. Without supportive institutions and the legal and diplomatic elements which commit parties to biological disarmament in perpetuity—combined with the openness and demonstrable inoffensiveness of research—the convergence of the regimes of compliance and development will remain fragile, if attained. This theme is addressed again in the final chapter of this volume.

---

[166] UN Security Council Resolution 687 (note 3), para. 7.
[167] The Moscow Joint Statement is discussed in section XI of chapter 1 in this volume.

5. The regime of development

I. Introduction

It has not been common ground among the states parties to the 1972 Biological and Toxin Weapons Convention that the BTWC should have a development orientation. In this context 'development' means what the 1980 Final Declaration of the First Review Conference called 'economic and social development, particularly in the developing countries'.[1]

This chapter discusses the regime of development, a concept which is considerably less clear and whose content is less firmly established than the regime of compliance examined in chapters 2–4. It has little basis in the BTWC and is derived more from subsequent interpretation of the convention at the first four review conferences than from the treaty text.

The BTWC focuses on the politico-military problem of biological and toxin weapons and to a lesser extent on the prevention of disease. However, it is only indirectly concerned with economics, and it makes no mention of industry. The obligations which the BTWC proclaims as incumbent upon states parties are primarily disarmament obligations that barely extend into the realm of development. In short, the BTWC is a disarmament not a development treaty.

This chapter explores the manner in which the development orientation of the BTWC has come to be the principal criterion, or one of the key criteria, by which many of its parties judge its success. Article X is the starting point for tracing the emergence of the regime of development.

II. Article X

The development obligation in Article X of the BTWC is expressed in negative terms. In its second paragraph Article X provides that:

This Convention shall be implemented in a manner designed to avoid hampering the economic or technological development of States Parties to the Convention or international cooperation in the field of peaceful bacteriological (biological) activities, including the international exchange of bacteriological (biological) agents and toxins and equipment for the processing, use or production of bacteriological (biological) agents and toxins for peaceful purposes in accordance with the provisions of the Convention.[2]

The phrase 'to avoid hampering' is a negative obligation. The first paragraph of Article X contains a positive obligation, but development is not mentioned in that paragraph save in the narrow context of 'the further development and application of scientific discoveries'. Instead it is 'exchange' and scientific, particularly health, 'cooperation' that receive positive commendation—with no

---

[1] First Review Conference document BWC/CONF.I/10, 21 Mar. 1980, Article X section, p. 9.

[2] The text of the Convention on the Prohibition of the Development, Production and Stockpiling of Bacteriological (Biological) and Toxin Weapons and on their Destruction is available at the SIPRI Chemical and Biological Warfare Project Internet site, URL <http://projects.sipri.se/cbw/cbw-mainpage.html>. It is reproduced as annexe A in this volume.

mention of economic, social or technological development. Paragraph 1 of Article X reads:

The States Parties to this Convention undertake to facilitate, and have the right to participate in, the fullest possible exchange of equipment, materials and scientific and technological information for the use of bacteriological (biological) agents and toxins for peaceful purposes. Parties to the Convention in a position to do so shall also cooperate in contributing individually or together with other States or international organizations to the further development and application of scientific discoveries in the field of bacteriology (biology) for prevention of disease, or for other peaceful purposes.[3]

There is much that can be criticized in the drafting of both paragraphs. They are so loosely constructed as to mean almost anything that a government or individual invoking them wants them to mean. Phrases like 'the field of peaceful bacteriological (biological) activities' and 'facilitate . . . the fullest possible exchange' leave the extent of Article X unclear. It is therefore not surprising that the advent of genetic modification techniques and the growth of industrial biotechnology have led to an expectation that obligations can be read into Article X which are not there. The negative and positive obligations, which are in separate paragraphs, tend to be conflated into a single unwarranted obligation to promote development.

Two contexts: the NIEO and the NPT

The NIEO context

One of the contexts in which Article X has been interpreted is the climate of raised expectations arising from the concept of the New International Economic Order (NIEO). On 2 May 1974 the United Nations General Assembly adopted a Declaration of Principles and a Programme of Action supporting the NIEO.[4] That outcome of the Sixth Special Session of the General Assembly was followed by the adoption of a Charter of Economic Rights and Duties of States in December 1974 when the General Assembly met in regular session,[5] and by the achievement of a fuller consensus at its Seventh Special Session in September 1975.[6] In retrospect these events were less decisive than they seemed to be at the time, and the appearance of consensus was deceptive. By the end of the 1970s the NIEO was in deep trouble. The 'global economic negotiations' were unsuccessful, and the institutions of the UN system failed to meet the expectations of the NIEO's proponents in the South. The NIEO was more openly opposed following the shift to the political right in the United Kingdom, the United States and the Federal Republic of Germany associated with Prime Minister Margaret Thatcher, President Ronald Reagan and Chancellor Helmut Kohl, respectively. These leading governments in the North no longer felt it necessary to pay lip service even to a qualified acceptance of NIEO thinking.

[3] BTWC (note 2).

[4] UN General Assembly Resolution 3201 (S-VI), 2 May 1974; and UN General Assembly Resolution 3202 (S-VI), 2 May 1974.

[5] UN General Assembly Resolution 3281 (XXIX), 12 Dec. 1974.

[6] UN General Assembly Resolution 3362 (S-VII), 16 Sep. 1975.

Ironically, it was in the 1980s that the NIEO idea came to permeate the discussion of Article X. While the free play of market forces was applauded in the North and the United Nations became less redistributive in its ineffectually interventionist development policies, the conviction grew in the South that the advantages of biotechnology would not reach their industries unless deliberate action was taken to accelerate the transfer of that technology. Intervention in the market could best be promoted by linking the development orientation of Article X with the advocacy of technology transfer, which was one of the main planks of the NIEO programme designed to narrow the economic gulf between North and South.

The survival of NIEO thinking into the 1980s with regard to discussion of Article X is probably explained by two factors. First, the delay in popularizing industrial applications of gene splicing meant that biotechnology was much more salient in the 1980s than in the 1970s. Second, despite its uncertain status, the NIEO programme was never formally abandoned, and it could still be drawn on contextually by parties to the BTWC after its central policy impetus in the UN system was much diminished.

As expressed in the original NIEO Declaration of Principles, technology transfer was the sixteenth of 20 principles. (The NIEO was 'to be founded on full respect for' these principles.) It read: 'To give to the developing countries access to the achievements of modern science and technology, to promote the transfer of technology and the creation of indigenous technology for the benefit of the developing countries in forms and in accordance with procedures which are suited to their economies'.[7]

Section IV of the Programme of Action was devoted to the transfer of technology. It specified *inter alia* that access 'on improved terms' should be given and that commercial practices governing technology transfer should be adapted to the requirements of the developing countries, and that all efforts be made 'to prevent abuse of the rights of sellers'.[8]

Adapted to the circumstances of the convention, an obligation to transfer technology became seen as a quid pro quo. This was the principal obligation read, retrospectively (and questionably), into Article X. If countries in the South had taken on a self-denying ordinance with regard to BTW, it was argued, they should be compensated with easier access to the peaceful applications of industrial biotechnology. So long as the regime of compliance remained elementary this was a particularly weak argument because there were no obvious costs of compliance and hence no direct financial expenditure for which to be compensated. Countries in the South were in the same position as countries in the North since the same self-denying ordinance applied to all and cost no one anything. As the regime of compliance began to take shape, however, it became possible to argue that there would be compliance costs, if only in the amassing of information for regular declarations to be made in accordance with an agreed programme of confidence-building measures, and that these bore more heavily on poor countries.

At the current stage of evolution of the regime of compliance this is not a particularly strong argument. There *may* be a case for extending technical assist-

[7] UN General Assembly Resolution 3201 (note 4), para. 4 (p).
[8] UN General Assembly Resolution 3202 (note 4), section IV (b), (d).

ance to the governments of parties in order to help them gather the required data, but this has little to do with Article X.

The NPT context

If the argument for compensation for compliance costs is considered insufficient the second context acquires relevance. Although it is a self-contained treaty, with no juridical relationship to the 1968 Treaty on the Non-Proliferation of Nuclear Weapons (Non-Proliferation Treaty, NPT), the BTWC is strongly influenced in its form and drafting by the NPT precedent. The political–psychological overlay is strong, and even though it is less tangible than the textual similarities—which have been analysed elsewhere[9]—it may ultimately be of greater significance.

Within this context Article X can be seen to echo two provisions of the NPT: the promotion of nuclear energy for peaceful purposes, and positive discrimination in favour of non-nuclear weapon states which are parties to the NPT. However, there was no obvious equivalent in the BTW field, except perhaps as regards the promotion of public health, and public health was seldom discussed in the negotiations and is mentioned only once in Article X. Accordingly, it seems not to have been elevated to a status equal to that of nuclear energy in the NPT. Indeed, one of the problems of Article X is that it is not more like the NPT, as Erhard Geissler, Iris Hunger and Ernst Buder have noted:

In comparison with the BWC the advantage of the NPT is that the term *nuclear energy* and hence the goal of its Article IV are well defined . . . . The basic problem of the proper implementation of Article X of the BWC is that this Convention lacks definitions, including definitions of the areas dealt with in Article X, in contrast to both the CWC and the NPT. Cooperation is requested by Article X of the BWC in the use of bacteriological (biological) agents and toxins for peaceful purposes. Cooperation in *which* use of *which* agents and toxins?[10]

The NPT sources are articles IV.2 and III.3, which correspond to the first and second paragraphs of Article X, respectively.[11] In Article X there is, however, no provision corresponding to the positive discrimination in favour of non-nuclear weapon states which are parties to the NPT in 'the developing areas of the world' which was added to Article IV.2 in the final (New York) phase of the NPT negotiations, at the instigation of Chile and Nigeria. This is notable

---

[9] Sims, N. A., *The Diplomacy of Biological Disarmament: Vicissitudes of a Treaty in Force, 1975-85* (Macmillan: London and St Martin's Press: New York, 1988), pp. 21–29, 34–36.

[10] Geissler, E., Hunger, I. and Buder, E., 'Implementing Article X of the Biological Weapons Convention', ed. O. Thränert, *Enhancing the Biological Weapons Convention* (Dietz: Bonn, 1996), p. 160.

[11] Article IV.2 of the NPT states: 'All the Parties to the Treaty undertake to facilitate, and have the right to participate in, the fullest possible exchange of equipment, materials and scientific and technological information for the peaceful uses of nuclear energy. Parties to the Treaty in a position to do so shall also co-operate in contributing alone or together with other States or international organizations to the further development of the applications of nuclear energy for peaceful purposes, especially in the territories of non-nuclear-weapon States Party to the Treaty, with due consideration for the needs of the developing areas of the world.'

Article III.3 of the NPT reads: 'The safeguards required by this Article shall be implemented in a manner designed to comply with Article IV of this Treaty, and to avoid hampering the economic or technological development of the Parties or international co-operation in the field of peaceful nuclear activities, including the international exchange of nuclear material and equipment for the processing, use or production of nuclear material for peaceful purposes in accordance with the provisions of this Article and the principle of safeguarding set forth in the Preamble of the Treaty.'

since discussion of the regime deriving from Article X has often appeared to proceed on the erroneous assumption that positive discrimination in favour of developing countries is written into the BTWC.[12]

There is also a more fundamental difference: unlike the NPT, the BTWC is not a non-proliferation treaty. It does have an anti-proliferation clause (Article III), but that is not the basic prohibition contained in the convention. All its provisions apply to all parties without distinction, except for Article II. The point of Article II is to transform BTW-possessor states into non-possessor states as soon as possible by obliging them to disarm within nine months of the entry into force of the convention for them.

The NPT, on the other hand, is thoroughly discriminatory. It classifies states into two categories by their ostensible nuclear weapon status (as of 1 January 1967 in respect of the 'manufactured and exploded' definition of that status in Article IX.3). The NPT is a carefully constructed assemblage of quid pro quo provisions balancing the reciprocal obligations of states which possess nuclear weapons and those which do not possess them. It could hardly have been otherwise since the main criterion to be satisfied by a non-proliferation treaty had already been set out by the UN General Assembly on 23 November 1965, when it declared that the eventual NPT 'should embody an acceptable balance of mutual responsibilities and obligations' as between nuclear weapon and non-nuclear weapon states.[13]

The problem with such an approach to the construction of Article X of the BTWC is that it assumes a similarity to the NPT which does not exist. The NPT imposed safeguards obligations *only* on its non-nuclear weapon parties and balanced these with easier access to the peaceful applications of nuclear energy. There is no parallel to this in the BTWC because there is no equivalent to the categories of nuclear weapon states and non-nuclear weapon states which are found in the NPT.

The BTWC makes no distinction between 'haves' and 'have-nots' in respect of weapons. All are (or must become) have-nots in terms of BTW possession. Article II requires that all the prohibited objects must be destroyed, or diverted to peaceful purposes, 'as soon as possible but not later than nine months after the entry into force of the Convention'. The BTWC does not require or even encourage positive discrimination in favour of 'the developing areas of the world', not does it apply safeguards. It includes only the ill-defined idea that cooperation should benefit parties to the convention rather than non-parties. In neither the NPT nor the BTWC, however, is it laid down that non-parties are to be excluded from commercial or other cooperative relations. There is no equivalent to Article VI of the Chemical Weapons Convention.[14] It is natural

---

[12] It may be argued from the *travaux* (preparatory material) that there was an intent to prioritize the interests of the developing countries, but in the NPT the Chilean–Nigerian addendum at the end of Article IV integrates that status into the text. It provides for 'due consideration for the developing areas of the world'. Such a phrase was not included in the draft text which became Article X of the BTWC or even in the first text in which the future Article X is discernible: the socialist states' revised draft CBW convention. UN document A/8136, 23 Oct. 1970. It is reproduced in SIPRI, *The Problem of Chemical and Biological Warfare*, vol. 4, *CB Disarmament Negotiations, 1920–1970* (Almqvist & Wiksell: Stockholm, 1971), pp. 326–30. The series is available on a CD-ROM, which is described at URL <http://editors.sipri.se/cd.cbw.html>.

[13] UN General Assembly Resolution 2028 (XX), 23 Nov. 1965, para. 2(b).

[14] The CWC grants its parties the right of access to certain dual-use chemical compounds and technologies for purposes it does not prohibit. Article VI.2 provides that the chemicals listed in the 3 CWC sched-

that the notion of a preferential regime for those inside the convention (at the expense of those who choose to stay outside it) has emerged, but it has less warrant in the BTWC than in the NPT (and even there it has not been conspicuously well observed in practice).

The NPT context impelled the most vocal European advocates in the 1970s of egalitarian globalism or 'democratic international relations' (Romania and Yugoslavia), together with the economically disadvantaged South, to search for a microbiological equivalent of nuclear energy for peaceful purposes, if not for disarmament-related savings, which could be diverted to development.[15] It was mistakenly assumed that there must be something, however elusive, which could constitute a material quid pro quo, a countervailing element to the arms ban in the overall balance of treaty obligations.

At the First Review Conference, the idea of balance was invoked by Ambassador Constantin Ene of Romania in his plenary statement on Article X:

[Article X] occupied a special place in the structure of the Convention. Its purpose was to ensure the necessary balance between the obligations into which States Parties entered and to encourage international co-operation in the peaceful use of bacteriological (biological) agents and toxins. The significance of the latter objective derived form the ever-growing importance of the biological sciences in various fields ranging from diagnosis, disease prevention and cell research in the health field to the use of bacteria to obtain products necessary for economic development, particularly in the developing countries. The Conference should therefore remind all States Parties of their legal commitments in that area. . . . .

The experience gained from the disarmament negotiations, and particularly from the Review Conference on the Non-Proliferation Treaty [meaning the First Review Conference, held in 1975], proved that the effectiveness of a treaty depended both on strict compliance with its substantive provisions and on the extent to which it reflected trends in the international situation and the concerns and interests of States.[16]

The medical dimension in implementation of Article X: 1979

It was not until 1979 that the parties to the BTWC began to compare notes on how they had implemented Article X. In July 1979 the Preparatory Committee for the First Review Conference invited them to provide information on compli-

ules can only be transferred to other states in accordance with the relevant provisions of the CWC's Verification Annex. The CWC categorizes chemical compounds of particular concern in 3 schedules depending on their importance for the production of chemical warfare agents or for legitimate civilian manufacturing processes. Each list has different reporting requirements. Schedule 1 chemicals can only be transferred between 2 parties and cannot be retransferred to a third state. Since 29 Apr. 2000, the third anniversary of entry into force of the CWC, Schedule 2 chemicals may only be transferred among states parties. The transfer of Schedule 3 chemicals is only addressed in relation to non-parties. There are no quantitative limits on such transfers, but the exporting state party must ensure that the chemicals will not be used for purposes prohibited by the CWC. An end-use certificate is also required. Five years after entry into force of the CWC the Conference of the States Parties will consider the need for additional measures regarding the transfer of Schedule 3 chemicals to non-parties. The Convention on the Prohibition of the Development, Production, Stockpiling and Use of Chemical Weapons and on their Destruction (corrected version), 8 Aug. 1994, is reproduced on the SIPRI Chemical and Biological Warfare Project Internet site at URL <http://www.sipri.se/cbw/docs/cw-cwc-texts.html>. The proposed 31 Oct. 1999 amendment to Part VI of the CWC is reproduced at URL <http://projects.sipri.se/cbw/docs/cw-cwc-verannex5bis.html>.

[15] Conference of the Committee on Disarmament document CCD/341, 17 Aug. 1971.

[16] Ene, C., Romania, First Review Conference document BWC/CONF.I/SR.5, 6 Mar. 1980, paras 37, 40.

ance with six specified articles of the BTWC.[17] In their replies, collated by the UN Secretariat and published on 20 February 1980,[18] information regarding compliance with Article X was supplied by only nine parties: the Byelorussian Soviet Socialist Republic, Canada, the German Democratic Republic, Kuwait, Norway and Poland; and the three depositaries—the Soviet Union, the UK and the USA. Kuwait alone expressed interest in being helped: 'Though Kuwait has no expertise in this field, yet it would like to benefit from the experience of countries or international organizations to [*sic*] the further development and application of scientific discoveries in the field of bacteriology for prevention of disease, or for other peaceful purposes (Article X).'[19]

The Byelorussian, East German and Polish replies confined themselves to generalizations about contributing to the international exchange of views and opinion and participating in various forms of international cooperation for peaceful purposes—without specifying whether medical, industrial or other applications were involved.[20]

Norway reported: 'All research in micro-organisms and toxins, carried out in both civilian and military establishments, is directed solely towards problems related to medical treatment and prophylaxis. In accordance with the substance and spirit of Article X the research is unclassified, and the results are published in scientific literature.'[21]

The longest replies (from Canada, the UK, the USA and the USSR) placed particular emphasis on the 'prevention of disease' reference in choosing what to report as evidence of their compliance with Article X.

Canada reported under the Article X section of its reply:

Most of Canada's work has not been directly in biological defence but rather in related areas applied to peaceful purposes. Expertise gained by conducting a biological defence research and development programme (e.g. expertise in aerobiology of micro-organisms, and with special techniques and equipment) has been applied to studies of diseases of special concern to the military. These have included studies of the transmission of meningococcal meningitis and studies of the virulence of its causative agent, *Neisseria meningetidis*, and studies of the aetiology of various respiratory disease-causing micro-organisms including *Mycoplasma pneumoniae*. Since these diseases also are of immediate public health concern, most of the work has been reported in open scientific literature, or has been presented at open scientific conferences. The remaining work which relates solely to biological defence, in general, is exchanged only with countries with which Canada has formal defence agreements.[22]

It is interesting to note that neither Canada nor Norway laid claim to any particular form of international 'peaceful purposes' cooperation with other parties to the convention per se. They also did not point to implementation of Article X through their (by 1979) long-established programmes of development cooper-

[17] First Review Conference document BWC/CONF.I/3, 18 July 1979, para. 10. The 6 articles specified were articles I, II, III, IV, V and X.
[18] Compliance with obligations concerning the prohibition of bacteriological (biological) weapons, background paper relating to the convention, First Review Conference document BWC/CONF.I/4, 20 Feb. 1980, section II.
[19] First Review Conference document BWC/CONF.I/4, section II (note 18), item 42 (Kuwait).
[20] BWC/CONF.I/4, section II (note 18), item 32 (Byelorussian SSR), item 38 (GDR), and item 46 (Poland).
[21] BWC/CONF.I/4, section II (note 18), item 45 (Norway).
[22] BWC/CONF.I/4, section II (note 18), item 33 (Canada).

ation and technical assistance through bilateral and multilateral aid pro-grammes. Instead they evidently relied upon open publication policies and the accessibility of the relevant scientific literature to fulfil the international aspect of their Article X obligations.

In the individual reports of the depositaries, however, the international aspect was more strongly emphasized, albeit in different ways. For all three of them, as for Canada, the medical dimension was clearly essential to their conception of responsibility for the implementation of Article X. In 1979 this was how they perceived their international cooperation obligations, and they gave no sign of extending their scope beyond the field of medicine and public health.

The United Kingdom briefly mentioned 'its contribution to international organizations such as the World Health Organization' but chose to highlight its bilateral health agreements with the USSR (1975), Czechoslovakia (1976), the GDR (1977), Hungary (1978) and Finland (1978). All had been concluded since the entry into force of the BTWC; all provided for bilateral cooperation 'in the field of medicine and public health'; and all were 'designed to provide the fullest possible exchanges of information' including 'where appropriate, provisions for exchange on the use of bacteriological (biological) agents and toxins for peaceful purposes'.[23]

Another party which highlighted bilateral cooperation was the Ukrainian Soviet Socialist Republic. In its plenary statement, rather than in the prepara-tory document, cooperation was cited between the Institute of Microbiology and Virology of the Ukrainian SSR's Academy of Sciences and scientific insti-tutes in Czechoslovakia and the GDR.[24]

In the Soviet Union's 1979 reply, as in that of the UK, Article X received most attention:

In implementation of Article X of the Convention, the Soviet Union engages in co-operation in peaceful bacteriological (biological) activities with many countries which are Parties to the Convention and takes part in bilateral scientific programmes aimed at solving urgent problems of virology and bacteriology and questions relating to the prevention and cure of infectious diseases. A broad exchange of specialists takes place for this purpose.

As a Party to the Convention, the USSR is promoting the fullest possible exchange of information about the use of bacteriological (biological) agents and toxins for peace-ful purposes. Research materials are widely publicized in scientific publications.

Soviet scientists participate in international congresses and conferences and present reports at them about the latest advances. Foreign specialists are invited to attend con-gresses, conventions and conferences of microbiologists, epidemiologists and special-ists in infectious diseases held in the Soviet Union.

The last two paragraphs addressed the needs of developing countries:

The USSR provides assistance to many countries in the form of supplies of a variety of vaccines, serums and antibiotics. In particular, 94 million doses of smallpox vaccine have been provided to the World Health Organization in recent years. Smallpox vac-cine has also been supplied to Afghanistan, Laos and Liberia. Countries in South

---

[23] BWC/CONF.I/4, section II (note 18), item 52 (UK).
[24] Kochubey, Y. N., Ukrainian SSR, First Review Conference document BWC/CONF.I/SR.4, 6 Mar. 1980, para. 9.

America, Africa and Asia have been provided with vaccines against cholera, polio-myelitis and other diseases.

Together with specialists from other countries, Soviet specialists also actively participate in the implementation of WHO programmes for the prevention and cure of infectious diseases, in particular in the programme proposed by the Soviet Union for the elimination of smallpox under natural conditions.[25]

The United States provided an interesting parallel in its reply:

The United States has undertaken a number of activities in accordance with the provisions of Article X to facilitate the fullest possible exchange of equipment, materials and scientific and technological information for the use of bacteriological (biological) agents and toxins for peaceful purposes. These activities include bilateral co-operative efforts as well as participation in international organizations concerned with the further development and application of scientific discoveries in the field of bacteriology (biology) for prevention of disease, or for other purposes.

The National Institute of Allergy and Infectious Diseases (NIAID), a component of the National Institutes of Health (NIH), supports international research in the field of bacteriological and other infectious diseases and this effort amounted to 19 million dollars in fiscal year 1978, the most recent period for which full data is available. Programmes included 215 extramural and intramural grants and contracts to support research in United States and foreign institutions to develop new knowledge applicable to the diagnosis, prevention and treatment of tropical and parasitic diseases such as malaria, schistosomiasis, cholera and leprosy, as well as parasitology, medical entomology and arbovirology.

An important example of the United States' commitment to further bacteriological and other infectious disease research is the support, 1.4 million dollars in fiscal year 1978, given the Gorgas Memorial Laboratory in Panama through the Fogarty International Center of NIH. This private institution, created in 1928, also promotes bilateral co-operation between the United States and the Republic of Panama in training scientists and physicians (United States, Panamanian and other Latin American nationals) in the diagnosis and management of tropical diseases.

The United States currently has in force 29 bilateral agreements at either the government-to-government or institute-to-institute level, many of which are designed to promote biomedical research. In addition, United States multilateral involvement in biomedical [research] and health encompasses virtually the whole range of health and health-related activities from epidemiological surveillance of disease to the most sophisticated research involving recombinant DNA techniques.

The United States currently contributes 25 per cent of the assessment budget for the World Health Organization (WHO), which amounts to approximately 114 million dollars for the 1980–1981 biennium. This total does not include voluntary extrabudgetary donations made in support of various WHO programmes. The United States played a major supportive role in the WHO successful programme to eradicate smallpox. The United States also provides substantial extrabudgetary support for WHO programmes directed toward research and training in several tropical diseases and increased immunization of children, especially in the developing world.

The regional office for WHO in the Americas, the Pan American Health Organization (PAHO), has extensive programmes in tropical diseases and has been especially active in attempting to combat zoonosis which poses a continuing threat in the Western hemisphere. For the biennium 1980–1981, the United States share of the PAHO budget amounts to 49.9 million dollars.

[25] BWC/CONF.I/4, section II (note 18), item 51 (USSR).

The United States also participates in the International Agency for Research on Cancer, whose major thrust is international epidemiological studies on cancer.[26]

Credit for medical assistance to the developing world was claimed in somewhat different terms by Cuba in a plenary statement by Ambassador Luis Solá Vila:

True to its policy of international co-operation and solidarity, Cuba had come to the assistance of countries and peoples, not only of the Latin American continent but also in Africa and Asia, by sending them physicians, medical personnel and medicaments. That utilization for peaceful purposes of scientific and technological developments in the field of bacteriology was something which the international community, and in particular the developing countries, were entitled to demand.[27]

This invocation of developing countries 'entitled to demand' action under Article X was not unique to Cuba, as the following discussion demonstrates.

Dissatisfaction with the implementation of Article X: 1980

The first signs of dissatisfaction with the implementation of Article X were revealed in ambassadorial statements in 1980 during the early plenary sessions of the First Review Conference. Most of the ambassadors who spoke in this vein represented members of the Group of Twelve (i.e., the Neutral and Non-Aligned states caucus in the Conference of the Committee on Disarmament before its 1975 expansion) which had endeavoured without success to strengthen the 'disarmament–development link' while the BTWC was still being negotiated at Geneva in 1971. Ambassador Celso Antonio de Souza e Silva of Brazil noted that his country had co-sponsored the Group of Twelve's proposal[28] that the BTWC preamble should affirm the principle that disarmament-related savings should be devoted to promoting economic and social development, particularly in the developing countries. He expressed regret 'that the final text of the Convention had not taken account of that issue, which had since acquired greater relevance'.[29]

Ambassador Oluyemi Adeniji said that Nigeria 'had taken note of the efforts being made by the developed countries' but that it would, 'however, urge the need for greater efforts in view of the developing countries' pressing health problems, particularly in regard to debilitating diseases such as malaria and

[26] BWC/CONF.I/4, section II (note 18), item 53 (USA).

[27] Solá Vila, L., Cuba, First Review Conference document BWC/CONF.I/SR.8, 10 Mar. 1980, para. 24.

[28] CCD/341 (note 15). Strictly speaking it was a working paper in the names of 11 delegations only, because 1 member of the Group of Twelve (neutral and non-aligned states members of the CCD) was missing: Argentina. The 11 co-sponsors were Brazil, Burma, Ethiopia, India, Mexico, Morocco, Nigeria, Pakistan, Sweden, the United Arab Republic (UAR) and Yugoslavia. (This was one of the last acts of the UAR, created in 1958, which had effectively been coterminous with Egypt since Syria left the union in 1961. Egypt changed its official title from UAR to Arab Republic of Egypt on 2 Sep. 1971.) Only 2 of the textual proposals in CCD/341 concerned the provisions which became Article X. The 11 delegations succeeded in having added to the text of the BTWC the sentence which now concludes ('for the prevention of disease, or for other peaceful purposes') the first paragraph of Article X. This was their eleventh proposal. Where they failed was in their eighth proposal: 'Insert a new [preambular] paragraph twelve which would read as follows: "*Affirming* the principle that a substantial portion of the savings derived from measures in the field of disarmament should be devoted to promoting economic and social development, particularly in the developing countries".'

[29] de Souza e Silva, C. A., Brazil, First Review Conference document BWC/CONF.I/SR.7, 7 Mar. 1980, para. 4.

cholera. That would also open up an avenue for the transfer of resources from military to civilian needs.'[30]

For Pakistan, Ambassador Jamsheed Marker stated that: 'international co-operation in this area had remained restricted and ad hoc in nature, and was not consonant with the letter and spirit of Article X of the Convention'.[31]

The fullest statement in the plenary session on 7 March 1980 concerning Article X was made by Ambassador Marko Vrhunec of Yugoslavia:

Since the Convention's entry into force, considerable efforts had been made to promote co-operation in accordance with Article X and certain results had been achieved. Unfortunately, however, the situation with regard to international co-operation in the use of available knowledge and expertise was as yet far from satisfactory. There was an urgent need for more tangible and direct co-operation and assistance in the application of scientific achievements and the transfer and exchange of information, equipment, material and technological know-how to developing countries. Such co-operation between the developed and developing countries should be of a long-term nature and should proceed on a footing of equality without monopolistic or protectionist restrictions by the developed countries. The most immediate form of such co-operation was the training of personnel from developing countries and their active engagement in the execution of national programmes agreed on with United Nations agencies and implemented under their supervision and guidance. Projects devised for that purpose were already in existence, but they by no means satisfied the developing countries' needs.[32]

When the draft report of the Committee of the Whole was under consideration at its eighth meeting, on 17 March 1980, the delegates of Brazil, Nigeria and Yugoslavia, together with Romania, proposed strengthening the paragraph dealing with the review of Article X.[33] Their proposal for draft paragraph 23 (renumbered 21) was accepted:

In the context of Article X, many participants *urged an increased exchange of information* amongst states, and *technical assistance to the developing countries* for the use of toxins and microbial agents for peaceful purposes, and the *promotion of the fullest possible international co-operation* in this field. Parties to the Convention, in a position to do so, should co-operate in contributing, individually or collectively, with other States and international organizations, to the further development of these applications, *with due consideration for the needs of the developing countries*. In this connexion, one participant noted that since the entry into force of the Convention the international community had devoted *increased attention to the relationship between disarmament and development*, and proposed, with the support of other participants, that for future reviews of the Convention a document, for the information of States Parties, should be prepared on the implementation of the provisions of Article X, *particularly with a view to promoting economic and social development*. The developed countries, it was suggested, *should share their knowledge in this field to a greater extent and in a more systematic manner*.[34]

[30] Adeniji, O., Nigeria, BWC/CONF.I/SR.7 (note 29), para. 16.

[31] Marker, J., Pakistan, BWC/CONF.I/SR.7 (note 29), para. 40.

[32] Vrhunec, M., Yugoslavia, BWC/CONF.I/SR.7 (note 29), para. 27.

[33] First Review Conference document BWC/CONF.I/C/SR.8, 17 Mar. 1980, paras 20–23.

[34] First Review Conference document BWC/CONF.I/7, 18 Mar. 1980, para. 21. The phrases which represent the first hints of a regime of development are emphasized to distinguish them from the language of Article X.

The obligation 'to avoid hampering' development had been converted into the idea that the implementation of Article X should positively promote it. The middle section of the above text, inserted on the initiative of Brazil and Romania, added another context to Article X: the disarmament–development link. By reviving this proposal from CCD/341,[35] Brazil and Romania sought to legitimize such a contextual reference nine years after it had been unsuccessfully proposed for insertion into the preamble to the BTWC. The concept of a disarmament–development link had been legitimized in the 1970s, which the United Nations had proclaimed the Decade of Disarmament[36] as well as the Second Development Decade. By 1980 it had become the theme of a major UN study (launched in 1978[37]) chaired by Swedish Under-Secretary of State for Disarmament Inga Thorsson. The concept proved attractive in theory but difficult to put into practice, and as an organizing theme of UN activity its influence declined in the late 1980s following a US boycott of the 1987 UN Conference on Disarmament and Development.

The subsequent evolution of the 1980 Final Declaration, through a Draft Elements group and revision in the Drafting Committee, has been recounted in an earlier book.[38] Article X was the subject of a compromise text negotiated principally between the Brazilian and British delegations in the Draft Elements group which, after consideration in the Drafting Committee (open to all delegations), was referred to an informal discussion on 20 March 1980 in which the Argentine and Nigerian delegations were notably active. The Article X section of the 1980 Final Declaration was finalized at that meeting. Its first paragraph contained all the new emphases from the Committee of the Whole except the request for a special report to the Second Review Conference, which was included in its third paragraph.

The Article X section of the 1980 Final Declaration read:

The Conference notes that, since the entry into force of the Convention, increasing importance has been attached by the international community to the principle that the disarmament process should help promote economic and social development, particularly in the developing countries. Accordingly, the Conference calls upon States Parties, especially developed countries, to increase, individually or together with other States or international organizations, their scientific and technological co-operation, particularly with developing countries, in the peaceful uses of bacteriological (biological) agents and toxins. Such co-operation should include, *inter alia*, the transfer and exchange of information, training of personnel and transfer of materials and equipment on a more systematic and long-term basis.

Furthermore, the Conference notes with satisfaction that the implementation of the Convention has not hampered the economic or technological development of States Parties.

The Conference requests the United Nations Secretariat to include in the background materials prepared for the Second Review Conference of the Parties to the Convention on the Prohibition of the Development, Production and Stockpiling of Bacteriological

[35] CCD/341 (note 15).

[36] UN General Assembly Resolution 2602 E (XXIV), 16 Dec. 1969.

[37] UN General Assembly Resolution 32/88 A, 12 Dec. 1977. Paras 94–95 of the Final Document of the First Special Session on Disarmament, adopted by UN General Assembly Resolution S-10/2, 30 June 1978.

[38] Sims (note 9), pp. 145–48.

(Biological) and Toxin Weapons and on their Destruction, information on the implementation of Article X by States Parties.[39]

Two other points of the text are of particular interest. First, it did not refer to the 'prevention of disease', although it built on every other element of Article X. Such a reference had been included in the Brazilian–British draft that did not survive the final week's negotiation.[40] Second, it suggested by omission that the cooperation of one developed country with another was not the kind of implementation in which the conference was interested.

In both these respects the conference was implicitly seeking to steer developed countries away from the concept of Article X which they had revealed in their preparatory documents into one which located its implementation within a North–South context and one in which the prevention of disease was no longer stressed. In effect, this treated Article X as the basis for an increasingly articulated (and not specifically medical) regime of development.

The contrast with 1979 was not as much remarked upon at the time as, with the benefit of hindsight, it deserved. Effectively, it determined the lines along which the nascent regime of development was to evolve, with more rhetoric than substance, over the next two decades.

Organizing the implementation of Article X: 1986

The 1986 Second Review Conference focused on the implementation of Article X. It could do so confident that Article X was now oriented towards development and that its implementation consisted essentially of actions by parties in the North to benefit those in the South. By 1986 the question of machinery to articulate the regime of development occupied centre stage.

In 1980 Pakistan had proposed 'the creation of institutional structures to ensure a regular flow of information on technical progress in the implementation of the Convention' along with three other kinds of machinery: a UN seminar 'to promote greater participation in the economic and medical uses of biological agents and toxins, particularly by the developing countries'; UN responsibility 'for the dissemination of information about technical and other progress in the implementation of the Convention'; and 'machinery for more frequent monitoring of the implementation of the Convention'.[41]

However, even after 1986 the parties to the BTWC were no nearer to realizing the aspirations which were now read into Article X. It was one thing to proclaim that a regime of development ought to flow from the BTWC and quite another to enable that to occur.

On 9 September 1986 Ambassador Mansur Ahmad of Pakistan noted: 'Unfortunately co-operation remained insignificant and the background papers produced for the Conference contained scanty information on the subject.'[42]

Some developed countries now emphasized their technical assistance to developing countries: 'In New Zealand, Government research institutions,

[39] BWC/CONF.I/10 (note 1).

[40] Sims (note 9), p. 145.

[41] Bashir, S., Pakistan, First Review Conference document BWC/CONF.I/C/SR.5, 13 Mar. 1980, para. 19.

[42] Ahmad, M., Pakistan, Second Review Conference document BWC/CONF.II/SR.4, 9 Sep. 1986, para. 43.

semi-governmental institutions, universities and the private sector regularly made services available to other countries, particularly developing countries of South Pacific, and exchanged information on materials and technology with them.'[43] Other developed countries attached at least equal importance to their cooperation across the East–West divide, as the United Kingdom had done in 1979 with its list of bilateral health agreements. Ambassador Harald Rose of the GDR stressed the importance of relations with other developed countries: 'In recent years, conferences, seminars, and training courses had been organized in the German Democratic Republic and contacts had been promoted between research institutions in the Republic and their counterparts in Sweden, Finland, India, the United States of America, France, the United Kingdom and other countries. His country also co-operated closely with the other members of the Council for Mutual Economic Assistance.'[44]

The Council for Mutual Economic Assistance (CMEA) at that time included several developing countries (Cuba, Mongolia and Viet Nam) as full members and others as associates. The key countries, however, remained the USSR and its Warsaw Pact allies in the developed world region of Central and Eastern Europe.

Rose also emphasized the value of global cooperation noting that: 'In the medical field, his country was working together with other countries, primarily under WHO programmes, on the use of bacterial and viral strains for vaccination purposes, and the development of immune toxins for tumour therapy.'[45]

In addition, there was increasing recognition of the importance of non-medical applications of microbiology because of the perception that a wide range of such applications of the biological sciences ought to be promoted under Article X, an idea which Ambassador Ene of Romania had expressed in 1980.[46] This point of view was now infused with NIEO-inspired references to issues of economic justice.

In his plenary statement, Ambassador Stanislaw Turbanski of Poland exemplified the stage this conceptual development had reached by 1986:

International co-operation in the field of the biological sciences was still far from satisfactory. The exchange of information amongst States Parties should be facilitated, there should be more tangible and direct co-operation, free from any political or protectionist restrictions, and technical assistance should be expanded, especially to developing countries. It would then be seen that, in addition to its undeniable positive impact on international security, the Convention could also serve to promote development and contribute to the increase of agricultural production as well as improved health protection and nutrition in many parts of the world.[47]

Poland also wanted action under the BTWC to include safeguards against accidents and agreement in advance on international cooperation in the event of

[43] Lineham, B. T., New Zealand, Second Review Conference document BWC/CONF.II/SR.5, 10 Sep. 1986, para. 11.

[44] Rose, H., GDR, BWC/CONF.II/SR.4 (note 42), para. 32.

[45] Rose, H., GDR, BWC/CONF.II/SR.4 (note 42), para. 32.

[46] BWC/CONF.I/SR.5 (note 16), para. 37.

[47] Turbanski, S., Poland, Second Review Conference document BWC/CONF.II/SR.6, 10 Sep. 1986, para. 33.

an accident, in view of 'the risks inherent in the current stage of development of the biological sciences'.[48]

The GDR delegation was highly qualified and active and took the lead in various initiatives at the Second Review Conference. Together with the Polish and Ukrainian delegations in one document, and with the Czechoslovak and Soviet delegations in another, it presented the fullest attempt to list, in broad terms, relevant areas of scientific endeavour to which the international cooperation obligation under Article X should apply. The first document read:

The principal objectives of co-operation in the field of biotechnology:
   – prevention and effective curing of grave diseases of the population;
   – sharp increase of food resources;
   – improvement in the utilization of the natural resources;
   – the mastering of the new easily renewable energy sources;
   – the development of low-waste production;
   – the reduction of the harmful effects on the environment;
   – the development of fundamental research in the whole complex of biological sciences and other fields of natural sciences directly connected with the study of physical and chemical foundations of biophenomena.[49]

The second document, co-authored by Czechoslovakia, the GDR and the USSR, listed 'specific directions and areas for the co-ordination of efforts' under Article X:

1. New biologically active substances and medicinal preparations for drugs (interferon, insulin, human growth hormones, monoclonal antibodies, etc.);
   2. Microbiological means of plant protection against diseases and pests, bacterial fertilizers, plant growth regulators, new highly productive varieties and hybrids of agricultural plants that are resistant to the adverse factors of the environment and are obtained by genetic and cellular engineering methods;
   3. Valuable feed additives and biologically active substances (feed protein, amino acids, enzymes, vitamins, veterinary preparations, etc.) for raising the productivity of cattle-breeding; new methods of bioengineering for the effective treatment, diagnosis and therapy of the main diseases of agricultural animals;
   4. New biotechnologies for obtaining economically valuable products for use in the food, chemical, microbiological and other branches of industry;
   5. Biotechnologies for intensive and effective processing of agricultural, industrial and urban waste, utilization of sewage and gas discharges for the production of biogas and high-quality fertilizers.[50]

On behalf of the group of socialist states, Hungary presented the 'Accelerated development of biotechnology' chapter of the Comprehensive Programme for Scientific and Technological Progress of CMEA Member States up to the Year 2000, which the CMEA had adopted in December 1985.[51]

Biotechnology was presented in expansive terms, and preoccupation with its apparently limitless promise—for those with access to it—infused the debate over implementation of Article X with a note of impatience and sharpened the NIEO-influenced insistence on technology transfer. For the first time, the non-

[48] BWC/CONF.II/SR.6 (note 47), para. 32.
[49] Second Review Conference document BWC/CONF.II/9, 22 Sep. 1986, annex, pp. 32–33.
[50] BWC/CONF.II/9 (note 49), annex, p. 29.
[51] Second Review Conference document BWC/CONF.II/7, 15 Sep. 1986.

proliferation clause (Article III) was perceived as a possible obstacle to such transfer if 'the possibility of military applications'[52] were used as a pretext for the imposition of trade barriers or other restrictions. Another new and potentially significant element was the implication of a balance between verification and the implementation of Article X. This view gained prominence at the Third Review Conference in 1991 and in the Ad Hoc Group negotiations on a legally binding instrument from 1997, but it was introduced already in 1986. Ambassador Mario Cámpora's plenary statement for Argentina is representative of this view:

it would not be enough simply to develop detailed verification and control procedures. Efforts must also be made to facilitate the widest possible exchange of scientific and technical equipment, raw materials and information. The best means of building international confidence in that field, as in others relating to high technology, would be to set up a dynamic and non-discriminatory system of exchanges of scientific and technological information and to promote international co-operation. In the field of biotechnology which, by its very nature, influenced all the other sectors, increasingly rapid scientific and technological advances made it necessary to have wider access to the results of research. States would not otherwise be able to strengthen their technological capacity and answer the needs arising in the fields of health and food production, both of which were priority areas for the developing countries.

   Bacteriology and microbiology had both peaceful and military applications, a duality inherent in any technology. The possibility of military applications must not be allowed to serve as a pretext for restrictions that would hamper the transfer of technology and international co-operation in that field. It would be inappropriate to place obstacles in the way of using a technology that was capable of promoting economic and social development in accordance with the needs, priorities and interests of each State.

Ambassador Cámpora also noted that Argentina, accordingly:

hoped that, in its Final Declaration, the Second Review Conference would recognize the urgent need to set up a system of co-operation that would enable all States to profit from the application of scientific progress, on an equal footing and with no monopolistic or protectionist restrictions, and that would facilitate the transfer of information, equipment, raw materials and knowledge to the benefit of the developing countries.[53]

This was broadly the position also espoused by India,[54] Pakistan[55] and Venezuela.[56] India and Venezuela attached particular importance to the contribution which the International Centre for Genetic Engineering and Biotechnology (ICGEB) could make in training the scientists of developing countries. Other states, such as Cyprus, advocated 'more tangible co-operation', understood as a duty under Article X,[57] although not all went as far as Peru to state explicitly that 'the developing countries should enjoy preferential treatment in such broad exchanges'.[58]

---

[52] Cámpora , M., Argentina, BWC/CONF.II/SR.6 (note 47), para. 24.

[53] BWC/CONF.II/SR.6 (note 47), paras 23–24.

[54] Teja, J. S., India, Second Review Conference document BWC/CONF.II/SR.7, 15 Sep. 1986, para. 54.

[55] Ahmad, M., Pakistan, BWC/CONF.II/SR.4 (note 42), para. 43.

[56] ter Horst, E., Venezuela, BWC/CONF.II/SR.7 (note 54), para. 73.

[57] Nicolaides, A. A., Cyprus, Second Review Conference document BWC/CONF.II/SR.8, 15 Sep. 1986, para. 28.

[58] Morelli Pando, J., Peru, BWC/CONF.II/SR.8 (note 57), para. 7.

With the 'have-nots' demanding their fair share from the 'haves', the question was whether this confrontation would be repeated at each review conference, or whether the demand for a 'system of co-operation' could be institutionalized in the BTWC. The basic demand was for 'some kind of institutionalization of co-operation and technical assistance in the peaceful uses of biotechnology within the United Nations system'.[59]

Several organizations of the UN system were already involved in such efforts. Ambassador Fan Guoxiang of China reported: 'remarkable successes . . . in co-operation and exchanges with international organizations such as WHO and UNICEF [United Nations Children's Fund] and with other countries in the fields of medicine and public health'.[60] The Ukrainian representative pointed out that since 1981 his country had organized seminars on the peaceful application of biology for foreign students under programmes sponsored by the United Nations Development Programme (UNDP), the Food and Agriculture Organization (FAO) and the WHO.[61] However, this was not what the states which wanted a system of cooperation had in mind.

Ambassador Ahmad of Pakistan urged the review conference to 'take concrete steps towards the establishment of *adequate* institutional means within the United Nations system to facilitate the exchange of scientific and technological information for peaceful purposes', which suggested that Pakistan considered the existing institutions inadequate.[62]

The clearest call for institutional change came in the plenary statement of Ambassador J. S. Teja of India, who:

stressed that the gap between the developed and developing countries in the availability of information on the use of biotechnology and genetic engineering for peaceful purposes had widened since 1980. A routine call for the free flow of information and transfer of technology would not result in any improvement of the implementation of Article X. Most of the scientific and technological information in the area was in private hands and would be transferred only for profit, if at all. Ongoing researches in those areas were highly classified industrial secrets. Institutional ways and means should therefore be sought of assuring co-operation between the developed and developing countries through the intervention of the States Parties to the Convention.[63]

India, Pakistan and Peru put forward institutional proposals in the Committee of the Whole.[64] Argentina concentrated its efforts on ensuring that 'the need for broad and non-discriminatory access to research results . . . to respond adequately to economic and social development needs' would be expressed in the Final Declaration.[65]

India did not propose a new organization as such but rather 'an institutional mechanism' and 'the transfer of equipment and material in a more systematic or institutionalized manner, the transfer and exchange of information, training of

[59] Bassoy, U., Turkey, BWC/CONF.II/SR.7 (note 54), para. 65.
[60] Fan Guoxiang, China, BWC/CONF.II/SR.5 (note 43), para. 48.
[61] Kochubey, Y. N., Ukrainian SSR, BWC/CONF.II/SR.6 (note 47), para. 46.
[62] Ahmad, M., Pakistan, BWC/CONF.II/SR.4 (note 42), para. 43, emphasis added.
[63] Teja, J. S., India, BWC/CONF.II/SR.7 (note 54), para. 54.
[64] BWC/CONF.II/9 (note 49), annex, pp. 30–32.
[65] BWC/CONF.II/9 (note 49), annex, p. 28.

personnel and co-operation with international organizations such as the WHO and the International Centre for Genetic Engineering and Biotechnology'.[66]

Peru proposed that: 'the Conference should establish machinery to promote and implement international co-operation in the peaceful uses envisaged by the Convention'.[67]

Pakistan wanted the Final Declaration to recommend: 'that a conference of States Parties and relevant specialized agencies be convened by the United Nations to propose measures for the establishment of adequate institutional means within the United Nations system in order to facilitate and promote such co-operation'.[68]

The rivalry between India and Pakistan was intensified at the Second Review Conference by strains within the NNA group of states parties. The Indian delegation, by virtue of India's triennial presidency of the Non-Aligned Movement (NAM), was the official coordinator of the group (corresponding to Hungary and Norway as coordinating delegations for the socialist and Western groups). However, Pakistan expressed impatience with India's allegedly ineffectual performance of the coordinator role and worked closely with the Irish, Swedish and other delegations in an informal coalition crossing NNA and other group boundaries.

Consequently, the Committee of the Whole failed to resolve the institutional question. It merely reported that 'various proposals were made' for 'the establishment of adequate institutional means within the United Nations system and the full utilization of the possibilities of the specialized agencies and other international organizations'.[69]

It was left to the Drafting Committee to resolve this issue—along with many others—in the final week of the Second Review Conference. The Chairman of the Drafting Committee, Australian Ambassador Richard Butler, made particular use of the Bulgarian, East German, Norwegian and Swedish delegations in conducting 'arduous negotiations' over the Final Declaration through 'detailed and exhaustive consultations'.[70]

China welcomed the Article X section as among the most outstanding achievements of the conference.[71] However, this view was not shared by the UK, which did not include that section in its list of the four most positive aspects of the conference.[72] A retrospective judgement by Jozef Goldblat and Thomas Bernauer appeared in their 1991 study:

This subject was often addressed during the Second Review Conference, especially by developing countries. However, efforts led by India, Pakistan and several other States to set up a specialized institution for international co-operation in the peaceful uses of biological agents and toxins did not yield results. The discussion led to the inclusion of a lengthy but vague paragraph in the Final Declaration. It was stated that, in order to

[66] BWC/CONF.II/9 (note 49), annex, pp. 30–31.
[67] BWC/CONF.II/9 (note 49), annex, p. 32.
[68] BWC/CONF.II/9 (note 49), annex, p. 31.
[69] BWC/CONF.II/9 (note 49), para. 30.
[70] Second Review Conference document BWC/CONF.II/SR.10, 26 Sep. 1986, para. 7. Ambassador Butler introduced the 'major achievement' of an agreed report of the Drafting Committee, 'the outcome of detailed and exhaustive consultations'. Second Review Conference document BWC/CONF.II/11, 26 Sep. 1986. The reference to 'arduous negotiations' was made by the President of the Second Review Conference, Ambassador Winfried Lang of Austria, in BWC/CONF.II/SR.10, para. 11.
[71] Fan Guoxiang, China, BWC/CONF.II/SR.10 (note 70), para. 22.
[72] Edis, R., UK, BWC/CONF.II/SR.10 (note 70), para. 29.

foster the exchange of relevant equipment, material and information among States, and to increase technical assistance, adequate institutional means within the United Nations and other existing international organizations should be used.[73]

The medical dimension, which was omitted in 1980, was restored in a single sentence: 'The Conference calls for greater co-operation in international public health and disease control.'[74] As noted above, the Brazilian–British language had been lost in the final drafting week of the First Review Conference.

Progress in biotechnology was now significant, and almost the whole of the Article X section of the 1986 declaration concerned its dissemination 'to help promote economic and social development, and scientific and technological progress, particularly in the developing countries, in conformity with their interests, needs and priorities'. Three references to the developing countries in this section accentuated the development orientation of Article X as now interpreted. Contextualization is a feature of disarmament treaty regimes, and the third reference referred back to paragraph 35 of the Final Document of 1978 (adopted by the First UN Special Session on Disarmament) and forward to the UN Conference on the Relationship between Disarmament and Development which was scheduled for 1987.

However, the majority could not achieve a clear-cut statement of obligation to transfer technology as a restitutive measure of economic justice in the NIEO tradition. The 1986 Final Declaration instead stated that the conference: 'urges States Parties to provide wider access to and share their scientific and technological knowledge in this field, on an equal and non-discriminatory basis, in particular with the developing countries, for the benefit of all mankind'.[75]

The issue of institutional adequacy proved difficult to resolve. In the end a compromise was negotiated which took account both of Pakistan's desire for a special Article X conference and of India's call for 'an institutional mechanism'. There was to be a 'discussion and examination of the means for improving institutional mechanisms'. It is unlikely that the leading Western governments would have allowed anything more concrete (and costly) to be authorized. In so far as they influenced the Article X outcome in 1986, it was in the direction of resistance and restraint.[76]

The part of the Article X section which addressed the creation of an institution started with a sentence inspired by a Hungarian proposal[77] in the Committee of the Whole that was introduced on behalf of 'a group of Socialist States': 'The Conference urges that co-operation under Article X should be actively pursued both within the bilateral and the multilateral framework and further urges the use of existing institutional means within the United Nations

[73] Goldblat, J. and Bernauer, T., *The Third Review Conference of the Biological Weapons Convention: Issues and Proposals*, UNIDIR Research Paper no. 9 (United Nations: New York, 1991), p. 19. The 'lengthy but vague paragraph' in fact ran to 2 pages (of a total of 9 pages for the whole Final Declaration). BWC/CONF.II/13/II, 26 Sep. 1986, pp. 8–9.

[74] BWC/CONF.II/13/II (note 73), p. 8.

[75] BWC/CONF.II/13/II (note 73), pp. 8–9.

[76] Lang, W., 'The Second Review Conference of the 1972 Biological Weapons Convention', ed. J. Kaufmann, UNITAR, *Effective Negotiation: Case Studies in Conference Diplomacy* (Martinus Nijhoff: Dordrecht, 1989), p. 194.

[77] BWC/CONF.II/9 (note 49), annex, p. 30.

system and the full utilization of the possibilities provided by the specialized agencies and other international organizations.'[78]

A passage followed in which proposals by India, Pakistan and Peru were reduced to a compromise text:

The Conference, noting that co-operation would be best initiated by improved institutionalized direction and co-ordination, recommends that measures to ensure co-operation on such a basis be pursued within the existing means of the United Nations system. Accordingly, the Conference requests the Secretary-General of the United Nations to propose for inclusion on the agenda of a relevant United Nations body a discussion and examination of the means for improving institutional mechanisms in order to facilitate the fullest possible exchange of equipment, materials and scientific and technological information for the use of bacteriological (biological) agents and toxins for peaceful purposes. The Conference recommends that invitations to participate in this discussion and examination should be extended to all States Parties, whether or not they are members of the United Nations, and concerned specialized agencies.

The Conference requests the States Parties and the United Nations Secretariat to include in the document materials prepared for the above-mentioned discussion of States Parties, information and suggestions on the implementation of Article X, taking into account the preceding paragraphs. Furthermore, it urges the specialized agencies, *inter alia*, FAO, WHO, UNESCO [United Nations Educational, Scientific and Cultural Organization], WIPO [World Intellectual Property Organization] and UNIDO [United Nations Industrial Development Organization], to participate in this discussion and fully co-operate with the Secretary-General of the United Nations and requests the Secretary-General to send all relevant information of this Conference to these agencies.[79]

The five specialized agencies mentioned above could be supposed to have a functional interest in the implementation of Article X: the WHO most obviously, because it has to do with health, and the others because implementation of Article X has a bearing on food and agriculture, education and science, intellectual property and industrial development. UNIDO's interest lies particularly in the ICGEB, located in New Delhi and Trieste (spanning the developing and developed worlds).

The UN failure to organize implementation of Article X: 1986–91

The proposals made at the Second Review Conference failed to be implemented. The intended 'discussion and examination of the means for improving institutional mechanisms' was not placed on the agenda of a relevant UN body. Following the First Review Conference the UN Secretariat could have used the provisions of the 1980 Final Declaration (under articles X and XII)[80] to compile a substantive report on Article X implementation as a background document for the Second Review Conference. Instead, individual parties addressed the issue in their respective general reports on compliance. The request by Pakistan that the UN Secretariat should prepare a report was weakened, which enabled the Secretariat to interpret the request as requiring it to do no more than collate

[78] BWC/CONF.II/9 (note 49), annex, p. 30.
[79] BWC/CONF.II/9 (note 49), annex, p. 30.
[80] BWC/CONF.I/10 (note 1), pp. 9–10.

national information on Article X implementation supplied by states parties on a single occasion before the Second Review Conference. The Secretariat could have used the article X and XII sections of the 1980 Final Declaration as authority for a more active role, and it probably needed firmer guidance in 1986 to prevent recurrence of the same inaction.

In 1986 it would have been prudent for the Final Declaration to have identified the relevant UN organ, on the agenda of which the follow-up was to be proposed for inclusion, and to have set a time limit. Alternatively, this aspect of the implementation of Article X might have been referred to an appendix meeting a few months later, as was done in respect of CBMs under Article V (the April 1987 Ad Hoc Meeting of Scientific and Technical Experts).

When the Third Review Conference met in 1991 there was no improvement of the situation in 1986. Such information as was provided on implementation of Article X was still to be found only in the national compliance reports of those parties which felt they had something relevant to report. As in 1986, there was no report on the implementation of Article X from the UN Secretariat.

The United Nations, however, is not just its Secretariat. Despite the amount of space that they had devoted to Article X in the Final Declaration of 26 September 1986, its member states apparently also had lapsed into inactivity. (Out of 159 members of the United Nations at that time, 61 states had participated in the Second Review Conference as states parties to the BTWC.[81])

It appears that even vocal advocates of more effective institutional mechanisms and implementation of Article X, such as Argentina, India, Pakistan and Peru, were not sufficiently interested after September 1986 to maintain pressure on the UN Secretary-General. In 1991 part of the blame for the UN's failure to act as requested in 1986 surely lay with those governments which did not ensure that their initiative was followed through. The implication was that Article X was not as important to them as the rhetoric of their review conference statements had suggested.

National compliance reports on the implementation of Article X: 1991

The UN's failure was overlooked by the Preparatory Committee which met in April 1991. It devoted three paragraphs of its report to decisions on background documentation to be supplied in advance of the Third Review Conference, but neither the UN report due in 1986 nor information on the UN follow-up to the first two review conferences on Article X was requested from the UN Secretary-General.[82]

National compliance reports added little. The first seven such reports (from Bulgaria, Canada, Czechoslovakia, Denmark, the Republic of Korea (South Korea), Sweden and Thailand) were issued together on 26 August 1991, the date imposed on the Secretariat by the Preparatory Committee. Nine more reports were issued in addenda while the conference was in session (those from Australia, China, Italy, Norway and the USSR on 10 September; France and the

---

[81] Five other UN member states attended the 1986 review conference (4 signatories only and 1 non-signatory observer) in addition to the 61 full participants which were UN members and the two (San Marino and Switzerland) which were not.

[82] Third Review Conference document BWC/CONF.III/1, 15 Apr. 1991, paras 21–23.

UK on 12 September; and Austria and Finland on 18 September).[83] The omissions are remarkable, including as they do such major participants in the Third Review Conference as Argentina, Hungary, India, the Netherlands, Pakistan, Peru, Poland and the USA.

Bulgaria, China, Finland, France and South Korea referred to their international cooperation under Article X in general terms. Italy reiterated its support for a regime of 'open laboratories' to facilitate scientific exchanges and sharing of knowledge. Sweden made a more substantial contribution:

With regard to Article X of the Convention, Sweden has, during the period of review, participated in various international efforts to facilitate the free exchange of information on the peaceful uses of biotechnology.

A number of industrial countries support, as part of their foreign aid programmes, projects to further knowledge and applications of biotechnology. Through the Swedish Agency for Research Co-operation with Developing Countries (SAREC), Sweden is supporting biotechnological research and co-operation in several developing countries, *inter alia* Kenya, Sri Lanka and Bangladesh. This research focuses on efforts to improve agricultural production and health care with the help of biotechnology. SAREC is also a sponsor of the International Board for Plant Genetic Resources in Rome, through FAO. Through international organizations such as WHO, FAO, UNESCO and IBRD [International Bank for Reconstruction and Development], Sweden also takes part in international programmes in this area. Sweden has participated in a number of international conferences with the aim of identifying problems of developing countries and of providing solutions based on biotechnology.

There exists a potential conflict of interest between growing commercial interests in the area of biotechnology and genetic engineering on the one hand, and the interests of a free exchange of information on the other. This too deserves to be stressed in the present context.[84]

The United Kingdom reported that it:

plays its full part in fulfilling the provisions of this Article by its funding of reference collections of micro-organisms such as the National Collection of Type Cultures, the National Collection of Yeast Cultures, the National Collection of Food Bacteria and the World Reference Laboratory for Foot-and-Mouth Disease. The United Kingdom also contributes to international bodies such as the World Health Organisation and the European Molecular Biology Organization.[85]

It added examples of bilateral agreements on cooperation in the field of medicine and public health, starting with the UK's 1975 agreement with the Soviet Union,[86] which by 1991 had been reactivated. The agreements with Czechoslovakia (1976), Hungary (1978), Egypt (1981) and Romania (1991) were also cited, as was the Memorandum of Understanding on Health Co-operation concluded in 1984 with China, under the Sino-British Agreement on Scientific and Technological Co-operation.[87]

---

[83] Background document on compliance by states parties with all their obligations under the convention . . . prepared by the Secretariat, Third Review Conference document BWC/CONF.III/3, 26 Aug. 1991; BWC/CONF.III/3/Add.1, 10 Sep. 1991, BWC/CONF.III/3/Add.2, 12 Sep. 1991; and BWC/CONF.III/3/Add.3, 18 Sep. 1991.

[84] BWC/CONF.III/3 (note 83).

[85] BWC/CONF.III/3/Add.2 (note 83).

[86] BWC/CONF.III/3/Add.2 (note 83).

[87] BWC/CONF.III/3/Add.2 (note 83).

The fullest report on Article X implementation (two and one-half pages) came from the Soviet Union. It included much detail on the cooperation of particular institutes with their counterparts and companies in developed countries of Europe and North America; on Soviet participation in congresses, conferences and seminars; and on contracts and research programmes ranging from the Pharmacia Corporation of Sweden to the Human Genome Project.

In the long Soviet report the paragraphs of greatest relevance to the development orientation of Article X were the following:

The Soviet Union has 32 centres collaborating with the World Health Organization in all the most topical areas of infectious disease prevention; 17 belong to the system of scientific institutes operated by the USSR Academy of Medical Sciences, and 11 to the USSR Ministry of Health.

They include centres working on viral hepatitis, poliomyelitis, arboviral infections, brucellosis, leptospyrosis, hydrophobia, chlamydia infections, mycoplasmatales, malaria, plague and other zoonoses.

The USSR Ministry of Health's Central Institute of Epidemiology is a leader in research into the aetiology, clinical treatment and prevention of infectious diseases. In connection with its research on HIV infection, improvements in immunology and especially dangerous infections, it has extensive scientific contacts with countries in Eastern and Western Europe, South-East Asia and Mongolia, and trains foreign specialists. The USSR Ministry of Health's Institute of Medical Parasitology and Tropical Medicine is engaged in a programme of scientific collaboration with Thailand, China, Cuba and the United Kingdom. It regularly holds seminars on the epidemiology and treatment of malaria and how to control the vectors of malaria. The most recent was held in 1990.

A programme of scientific and technological assistance under the Treaty of Friendship and Co-operation between the USSR and India to help India produce polio vaccine is nearing completion.

The Epidemiology and Microbiology Research Institute of the USSR Academy of Medical Sciences is the country's largest institute studying bacterial and other infectious diseases. Besides basic research, it engages in extensive international scientific contacts. It includes seven centres collaborating with WHO on subjects including rhinitis and chlamydia, vectors and how to control them, and natural outbreaks of disease.[88]

Bilateral cooperation with a developing country (India) was also cited in the case of organizing the manufacture of a vaccine against hepatitis B, and studying the aetiology and epidemiology of viral hepatitis as a whole, which would involve Soviet–Indian collaboration.

Of the 118 states parties to the BTWC at the time the Third Review Conference assembled, over 100 had submitted no compliance report. Although some could point to their CBM declarations[89] as having covered the most important aspects of compliance, that seems a poor response given the wider scope of the compliance reports invited by the Preparatory Committee through the UN Secretariat. The request was for 'States Parties to provide information regarding compliance with all the provisions of the Convention'.[90]

---

[88] BWC/CONF.III/3/Add.1 (note 83).

[89] Third Review Conference document BWC/CONF.III/2 and Add.1, 2 and 3 converted these CBM declarations into background documentation for the Third Review Conference.

[90] BWC/CONF.III/1 (note 82), para. 23.

Of the 16 reports which were submitted in 1991, 7 made no reference to Article X at all and 5 reports referred to it only in general terms. Only 4 substantial contributions were submitted. The different approaches taken by Italy, Sweden, the UK and the Soviet Union served to emphasize the wide variety of ways in which these parties saw implementation of Article X taking place. There was no point of convergence to lend clarity.

The Third Review Conference was thus given no lead on how it might hope to steer the implementation of Article X into a regime of development.

Dangers of fragmentation: 1991

There was little chance of organizing a coherent regime of development at the Third Review Conference, and the dangers of fragmentation were evident. Its best hope for success lay in entrusting the coordination of Article X implementation to new, supportive institutions serving the parties between reviews. There was, however, little support for an interim committee or intersessional machinery with responsibilities extending beyond the processing of CBMs within the regime of compliance. Even that proved impossible to agree within the three weeks of the conference.

The proposal for a Secretariat Unit, dedicated to the convention and consisting of just two specially-funded posts within the UN Department for Disarmament Affairs, was unacceptable to the delegations. Had it been set up, as seemed likely until the closing hours of the conference, Yugoslavia would have wanted it to 'include in its activities supervision and support of all international cooperation in this field', namely, research in medicine 'and other disciplines' where it is difficult to differentiate between offensive and defensive programmes.[91]

Individual delegations, or pairs of delegations, sought to adapt the implementation of Article X to their own concerns, which were widely disparate. Ukraine and Byelorussia (both had recently dropped the title 'Soviet Socialist Republic' upon declaring their independence, but Byelorussia had not yet changed its name to Belarus) wanted research on the influence of enhanced radioactivity on micro-organisms to be undertaken within the programme of minimization of the consequences of the 1986 Chernobyl nuclear reactor accident.[92] India wanted a commitment to active association with institutions such as the ICGEB in New Delhi.[93] Thailand requested that training courses be provided 'both in the field of verification and confidence-building measures as well as in the use of bacteriological agents and toxins for peaceful purposes', as part of the technical assistance programmes of the UN and parties with advanced technologies.[94]

There were also three proposals for major new areas of implementation of Article X on a global scale.

Under a French proposal 'The Conference calls upon States Parties to cooperate in providing information on their national epidemiological surveillance and

---

[91] Third Review Conference document BWC/CONF.III/17, 24 Sep. 1991, p. 68, reproducing a Yugoslav proposal of 17 Sep. 1991.

[92] BWC/CONF.III/17 (note 91), p. 69, reproducing a Ukrainian–Byelorussian proposal of 17 Sep. 1991, which superseded Ukraine's proposal of 16 Sep. 1991.

[93] BWC/CONF.III/17 (note 91), p. 71, reproducing an Indian proposal of 17 Sep. 1991.

[94] BWC/CONF.III/17 (note 91), p. 70, reproducing a Thai proposal of 17 Sep. 1991.

data reporting systems, and in providing assistance, on a bilateral level, regarding epidemiological surveillance, with a view to improvements in the identification and timely reporting of significant outbreaks of human and animal diseases.'[95] Iran suggested 'that the establishment of a world data bank under the supervision of the United Nations is a suitable way for smoothing the flow of information in the field of genetic engineering, biotechnology and other scientific developments'.[96] Peru put forward[97] the imaginative scheme, initiated by Professor Erhard Geissler and promoted by the Federation of American Scientists, for an international programme of vaccine development, which is discussed below.[98]

The French, Indian, Iranian, Peruvian and Ukrainian–Byelorussian proposals were all accepted for incorporation into the 1991 Final Declaration, which also carried forward most of the 1986 language. The possibility of cooperating with the WHO was added to the French proposal, and in the text of the Iranian proposal for a world data bank the word 'facilitating' replaced 'smoothing'.[99]

The problem of fragmentation remained. There was little coherence in the list of suggestions for action—some medical, some industrial and some with a stronger development orientation than others—which followed the introduction to the Article X section. There was a hiatus between the grand introduction and the assorted specific items which followed. The items did not appear to add up to a coherent regime of development, distinctly identified with the convention and with the political commitment of its parties, which flowed clearly from the understanding of their Article X obligations as set out in the introduction.

Attached to the report of the Committee of the Whole were 106 proposals (twice the 1986 total). India had failed in its efforts to get a reference to the 1987 UN Conference on Disarmament and Development (which the USA had boycotted) into the Final Declaration, and there was also no reference to the 1978 Special Session of the UN General Assembly in this section, or to the NIEO.[100] There was, however, one move in the direction of NIEO thinking: China succeeded in inserting 'technological transfer' into an opening passage otherwise left largely unchanged from 1986. This passage, the nucleus of any regime of development, now introduced the Article X section of the Final Declaration as follows:

The Conference emphasizes the increasing importance of the provisions of Article X, especially in the light of recent scientific and technological developments in the field of biotechnology, bacteriological (biological) agents and toxins with peaceful applications, which have vastly increased the potential for cooperation between States to help promote economic and social development, and scientific and technological progress, particularly in the developing countries, in conformity with their interests, needs and priorities.

[95] BWC/CONF.III/17 (note 91), p. 71, reproducing a French proposal of 17 Sep. 1991.

[96] BWC/CONF.III/17 (note 91), p. 70, reproducing an Iranian proposal of 17 Sep. 1991.

[97] Letter of 7 Feb. 1992 to the author from Dr Félix Calderón, Alternate Representative of Peru and Minister-Counsellor at Geneva, Special Delegation of Peru to the Conference on Disarmament.

[98] Geissler, E. and Woodall, J. P. (eds), *Control of Dual-Threat Agents: The Vaccines for Peace Programme*, SIPRI Chemical & Biological Warfare Studies no. 15 (Oxford University Press: Oxford, 1994).

[99] Draft Final Declaration, Article X section, Third Review Conference document BWC/CONF.III/22/Add.2, 27 Sep. 1991, p. 16.

[100] BWC/CONF.III/17 (note 91), p. 71, reproducing para. 4 of an Indian proposal of 17 Sep. 1991.

The Conference, while acknowledging what has already been done towards this end, notes with concern the increasing gap between the developed and the developing countries in the field of biotechnology, genetic engineering, microbiology and other related areas. The Conference urges all States Parties *actively to promote international cooperation and exchange with States Parties in the peaceful uses of biotechnology, and urges the developed countries possessing advanced biotechnology to adopt positive measures to promote technological transfer and international cooperation* on an equal and non-discriminatory basis, in particular with the developing countries, for the benefit of all mankind.

The Conference urges *the United Nations and* States Parties to take specific measures within their competence for the promotion of the fullest possible international cooperation in this field through their active intervention.[101]

The 1986 wording, which was now superseded, had been: 'to provide wider access to and share their scientific and technological knowledge in this field'.[102] The 1991 text uses the word 'urges' three times in odd contrast with the lack of urgency which had characterized the follow-up to the Article X sections of the 1980 and 1986 final declarations.

Nigeria openly accepted that implementation had been poor and proposed, unsuccessfully, the insertion of the words 'notes with grave concern that due to poor implementation of this Article the gap between the developed and the developing countries has continued to widen' at the beginning of the second paragraph.[103] It was more successful with its proposal that the 1986 request to the UN Secretary-General should be reiterated, since the Second Review Conference had already identified 'improved institutionalized direction and co-ordination' as the best means of implementing Article X. Nigeria also succeeded in adding a further request from the Third Review Conference: 'that the Secretary-General collate on an annual basis, and for the information of States Parties, reports on how this Article is being implemented'.[104]

Lastly, a time frame was proposed within which the UN Secretary-General would be expected to meet the original request to include 'a discussion and examination of the means for improving institutional mechanisms' on the agenda of a relevant UN body. In a joint proposal issued on 13 September 1991 Chile, Panama, Peru and Venezuela put forward the time limit 'not later than 1992'.[105] This formula was included in the chairman's summary of the Committee of the Whole discussion,[106] but it was subsequently modified to 'not later than 1993'.[107] Except for the addition of the time limit and the new request for annual reports on Article X implementation, the 1991 text retained the terms of the 1986 request and reiterated it.

No action was taken in 1992 or 1993. At the Fourth Review Conference in 1996, the requests to the UN Secretary-General were repeated, but this time without a date earlier than the Fifth Review Conference being specified. Presumably, the expectation of any action being taken was so low by 1996 that the

---

[101] BWC/CONF.III/17 (note 91), p. 70, reproducing a Chinese proposal of 16 Sep. 1991. Language which was new in 1991 is emphasized.

[102] BWC/CONF.II/13/II (note 73), p. 8.

[103] BWC/CONF.III/17 (note 91), p. 69, reproducing a Nigerian proposal of 17 Sep. 1991.

[104] BWC/CONF.III/22/Add.2 (note 99), p. 17, drawing on language in the Nigerian proposal (note 103).

[105] BWC/CONF.III/17 (note 91), p. 69.

[106] BWC/CONF.III/17 (note 91), p. 104.

[107] BWC/CONF.III/22/Add.2 (note 99), p. 17.

requests made were for form's sake. In 1996 they were expressed in the 17-paragraph Article X section of the Final Declaration as follows:

6. The Conference reiterates its call upon the Secretary-General of the United Nations to propose for inclusion on the agenda of a relevant United Nations body, before the next Review Conference, a discussion and examination of the means of improving institutional mechanisms in order to facilitate the fullest possible exchange of equipment, materials and scientific and technological information regarding the use of bacteriological (biological) agents and toxins for peaceful purposes.

7. The Conference recommends that invitations to participate in this discussion and examination should be extended to all States Parties, whether or not they are members of the United Nations or concerned specialized agencies.[108]

. . . .

14. The Conference requests the Secretary-General to collate on an annual basis, and for the information of States Parties, reports on how this article [Article X] is being implemented.[109]

This time neither Nigeria nor the Latin American states proposed specific dates to the Committee of the Whole, and Australia's proposed language, which would have placed on the record the *non-fulfilment* of the 1991 requests to the Secretary-General,[110] did not survive into the Final Declaration.

In 1991 and 1996 there was a continued descent into fragmentation, away from a coherent regime of development.

The Vaccines for Peace proposal: an example of a possible Article X programme

If progress is to be made on an Article X programme, states parties may be well advised to concentrate their efforts on a selected project which provides a sharper focus for cooperative efforts and can therefore be the nucleus of an evolving regime of development.

The proposal for an international programme of vaccine development is an example of such a project. The Vaccines for Peace (VFP) programme, which aroused considerable interest at the third and fourth review conferences, has been particularly associated since 1989 with Professor Erhard Geissler.[111] The parties to the BTWC are also indebted to him for doing what the United Nations failed to do: interpreting and arranging in intelligible form the mass of data from the CBM rounds of 1987–89.[112]

[108] Fourth Review Conference document BWC/CONF.IV/9, 6 Dec. 1996, p. 24.
[109] BWC/CONF.IV/9 (note 108), p. 26.
[110] BWC/CONF.IV/9 (note 108), p. 55.
[111] Geissler has been a major scientific figure in the recuperation of the BTW disarmament regime. He was a member of the GDR delegation at the Second Review Conference. He was Professor of Genetics at the Institute of Molecular Biology of the GDR Academy of Sciences until 1990 and Head of the Bioethical Research Group at the Max Delbrück Centre for Molecular Medicine in Berlin until his retirement in 1999. Geissler, E. (ed.), SIPRI, *Biological and Toxin Weapons Today* (Oxford University Press: Oxford, 1986); Geissler, E. (ed.), *Strengthening the Biological Weapons Convention by Confidence-Building Measures*, SIPRI Chemical & Biological Warfare Studies no. 10 (Oxford University Press: Oxford, 1990); Geissler, E. and Haynes, R. H. (eds), *Prevention of a Biological and Toxin Arms Race and the Responsibility of Scientists* (Akademie Verlag: Berlin, 1991); Geissler, E., 'Vaccines for Peace: an international program of development and use of vaccines against dual-threat agents', *Politics and the Life Sciences*, vol. 11, no. 2 (1992) pp. 231–43; and Geissler and Woodall (note 98).
[112] Geissler, *Strengthening the Biological Weapons Convention by Confidence-Building Measures* (note 111).

Geissler pointed out that since many bacteria, viruses and toxins are natural causes of disease—especially in developing countries—but are also regarded as putative warfare agents, research on vaccines and their development is necessary for both civilian and military use. However, research and development on vaccines in military BTW defence programmes sometimes raises suspicion of possible offensive intent. It is therefore desirable to bring the process under WHO supervision, following the model of the WHO's Intensified Smallpox Eradication Programme. The WHO should convene an expert committee to run the programme, whose members—drawn from governmental and non-governmental backgrounds—would have expertise in *inter alia* epidemiology, biotechnology, molecular microbiology and BTW defence. The committee should elaborate a list of putative BTW agents against which vaccination is necessary for both civilian and military purposes. This criterion would exclude, for example, the AIDS virus HIV because it is militarily useless, which would keep the list manageably short.

The list should be subdivided into those agents against which the production and use of vaccines is technically possible and should be initiated or maintained, and those agents against which vaccines are urgently needed but require further research. National and international research centres and production facilities should thereafter be encouraged to undertake R&D or production as appropriate, under WHO supervision. Each participating facility should be obliged to involve scientific and technical staff from developing countries which are parties to the BTWC, and the resulting vaccines should be made available to states parties, under WHO supervision, for civilian use and permitted (i.e., prophylactic and protective) military purposes.

The Third Review Conference responded warmly to the VFP proposal, and text welcoming it was added to the Article X section of the 1991 Final Declaration:

The Conference welcomes efforts to elaborate an international programme of vaccine development for the prevention of diseases which would involve scientific and technical personnel from developing countries which are States Parties to the Convention. The Conference recognizes that such a programme might not only enhance peaceful international cooperation in biotechnology but also will contribute to improving health care in developing countries and provide transparency in accordance with the Convention.[113]

This initiative was taken near the close of the conference by Peru. Another Peruvian initiative, linked to the VFP proposal,[114] addressed the problem of so-called 'scientific mercenaries' through an appeal to the ethical and social responsibility of scientists. Accordingly, the following paragraph was added at the end of the Article I section of the Final Declaration: 'Based on the principle that sciences should support quality of life, the Conference appeals through the States Parties to their scientific communities to continue to support only activities that have justification under the Biological and Toxin Weapons Conven-

---

[113] The text was added after the Committee of the Whole stage, which is why it does not appear as a proposal annexed to the committee's report. BWC/CONF.III/22/Add.2 (note 99), p. 17, as editorially corrected (from 'involving' to 'which would involve' in the third line, to reduce ambiguity) in Third Review Conference document BWC/CONF.III/23, 1992, p. 23.

[114] Letter . . . (note 97).

tion for prophylactic, protective or other peaceful purposes, and refrain from activities which are in breach of obligations deriving from the provisions of the Convention.'[115]

This approach seeks to revitalize the idea that the world must unite its scientific and material resources in making war on germs, not utilizing them. That conviction had been one of the driving forces among scientists favouring a biological disarmament treaty in the 1960s. It corresponds to the view that scientists have a high calling and must take personal as well as collective responsibility for the uses to which science is put.

A VFP programme could put this conviction into practice. Since 1991 vaccine production facilities have been subject to a CBM reporting requirement. Vaccine R&D may be close to the borderline between offence and defence in its implications for national security if not placed beyond suspicion by internationalization.

After the Third Review Conference the VFP programme was developed with the help of a grant from the Volkswagen Foundation and active interest from quarters as disparate as the Stockholm International Peace Research Institute and the United States Army Medical Research Institute on Infectious Diseases. A workshop was held at Biesenthal, Germany in September 1992, which resulted in a subsequent SIPRI publication.[116]

One prospective difficulty with the VFP programme is the criterion for inclusion. If only those developing countries which are parties to the BTWC can participate in the programme and benefit from its preferential access to new vaccines that would constitute an incentive to ratify or accede to the convention. However, it would conflict with the principle of universality among members of the United Nations and the WHO, and non-parties might prefer to uphold non-discrimination in WHO programmes rather than join the VFP programme. Vulnerable citizens prey to infectious diseases, not their governments, would suffer if the universality principle were to be discarded. There is, however, an understandable inclination on the part of some to restrict Article X cooperation to states parties, as for example in the recommendation formulated by Goldblat and Bernauer in an article evaluating the Third Review Conference: 'All cooperation in the field of biology and related technology with non-parties should cease. This would help avoid possible misuse of such cooperation for purposes prohibited by the BW Convention.'[117]

Even if the parties to the BTWC are not willing to go that far, it is not inconceivable that in order to strengthen articles III and X they might discriminate in favour of other parties if convinced of the danger in dealing with non-parties in certain technologies. This remains to be seen. There are 50 states which are not parties to the BTWC. It might be possible to exclude them from the benefits of protective R&D, which is primarily military-oriented, but it is harder to see the benefits of prophylactic R&D (leading to better vaccines for soldiers and civilians alike) being withheld from some WHO member states by others, especially as the BTWC—unlike the WHO—does not possess financial resources which it can allocate.

---

[115] BWC/CONF.III/22/Add.2 (note 99), p. 3.
[116] Geissler and Woodall (note 98).
[117] Goldblat, J. and Bernauer, T., 'Towards a more effective ban on biological weapons', *Bulletin of Peace Proposals*, vol. 23, no. 1 (Mar. 1992), p. 40.

The Fourth Review Conference: 1996

At the second and third review conferences little progress was made on sharpening the definition of the regime of development concept or remedying the UN's failure to take it forward through the agenda of an appropriate United Nations organ. The Fourth Review Conference in 1996 also made limited progress.

The Final Declaration of the Fourth Review Conference expressed support for most of the projects and programmes favoured in 1991 and added several others. This was done in order to take account of the 1992 United Nations Conference on Environment and Development (UNCED) at Rio de Janeiro, including the adoption of Agenda 21 and the Rio Declaration; of the new Convention on Biological Diversity and its biosafety provisions; and of the establishment within the WHO, following a resolution of the 1995 World Health Assembly, of a Division of Emerging and Other Communicable Diseases Surveillance and Control. Malcolm R. Dando and Graham S. Pearson have provided a useful discussion of these new contexts.[118] In a long text on Article X, largely derived from a Non-Aligned Group proposal in the Committee of the Whole,[119] the Fourth Review Conference failed to differentiate what should be made to happen within the context of the BTWC from what should be encouraged to take place outside its confines.

Paragraphs 5, 10 and 13 of the Article X section are examples of this failure. Paragraph 5 states: 'The Conference notes that existing institutional ways and means of ensuring multilateral cooperation between the developed and developing countries would need to be developed further in order to promote international cooperation in peaceful activities in such areas as medicine, public health and agriculture.'[120]

However, in order to give more concrete expression to the regime of development parties need to focus on a particular project within medicine, public health or agriculture, which lends itself to promotion under the auspices of the BTWC rather than under any other institutional framework. Paragraph 5 does not narrow the focus or make a deliberate choice among alternatives. Paragraphs 10 and 13 have similar deficiencies:

10. The Conference shares the worldwide concern about new, emerging and re-emerging infectious diseases and considers that the international response to them offers opportunities for increased cooperation in the context of Article X application and of strengthening the Convention. The Conference welcomes the efforts to establish a system of global monitoring of disease and encourages States Parties to support the World Health Organization, including its relevant newly established division, the FAO and the OIE [Office International des Epizooties], in these efforts directed at assisting Member States to strengthen national and local programmes of surveillance for infectious diseases and improve early notification, surveillance, control and response capabilities.

. . .

---

[118] Dando, M. R. and Pearson, G. S., 'The Fourth Review Conference of the Biological and Toxin Weapons Convention: issues, outcomes and unfinished business', *Politics and the Life Sciences*, vol. 16, no. 1 (Mar. 1997), pp. 121–23.
[119] Proposal by non-aligned countries, BWC/CONF.IV/9 (note 108), pp. 55–58.
[120] BWC/CONF.IV/9 (note 108), p. 24.

13. The Conference considers that a worldwide data bank might be a suitable way of facilitating the flow of information in the field of genetic engineering, biotechnology and other scientific developments. In this context, the Conference underlines the importance of monitoring all relevant developments in the field of frontier science and high technology in the areas relevant to the Convention.[121]

With its continuing institutional deficit, the BTWC was unable to steer 'the international response' to new infectious diseases, let alone monitor 'all relevant developments in the field of frontier science and high technology' in relevant areas. There may be value in the United Nations discourse of exhortation and contextualization, but Article X needs greater precision and a sharper focus on acceptable projects or programmes, with institutional support to match.

The Fourth Review Conference achieved little in this regard; the Ad Hoc Group may, however, be more successful.

The Ad Hoc Group

Since 1995 the Group of Non-Aligned and Other States in the Ad Hoc Group has focused its efforts on Article X. In 1997, as the talks moved into the negotiating mode, it appeared that Article VII in the rolling text of an eventual legally binding instrument or protocol would be devoted to Article X issues. Since 1997 Article VII has continued to take shape. Like Article X, the emerging protocol text is in two parts: promotional and regulatory. Promotional paragraphs list the categories of desirable modes of international cooperation familiar from the final declarations of review conferences; the regulatory part addresses export controls and is the more contentious of the two parts. What is still sought is an acceptable balance of promotion of trade under Article X and safeguards against proliferation under Article III. The key may lie in the emergence of a non-discriminatory system of trade controls among states parties:

A way to avoid unilateral disadvantages resulting from export controls without promoting proliferation could be to establish a trade control system where all member states have to fulfil the same obligations concerning transfer of relevant agents and equipment. Transparent cooperation in the field of export control would be more efficient than the existing export control regulations. Such a cooperation would not only eliminate the contradiction between Article III and X, but improve them both synergistically.[122]

Whatever is negotiated as Article VII of the eventual protocol to the BTWC will have a strong influence on the evolution of the regime of development under Article X of the BTWC. There is now the prospect of a cooperation committee within the future organization, which would be responsible for devising a framework for the promotion of Article X measures. For the first time there will be an institutional focus specific to Article X. This structural innovation is intended to ensure continuous attention to the regime of development as it evolves among parties to the BTWC protocol, to which the cooperation committee will belong. The Fifth Review Conference may need to consider this prospect together with the relevant experience of the CWC's Organisation for

[121] BWC/CONF.IV/9 (note 108), pp. 25–26.
[122] Geissler, Hunger and Buder (note 10), p. 165.

the Prohibition of Chemical Weapons[123] in order to progress beyond the 'wish lists' which threatened to fragment the regime of development in 1991 and 1996.

III. Conclusions

A system of trade controls that is non-discriminatory and sensitive to proliferation concerns is one promising approach to strengthening the BTWC. Another is cooperation in good manufacturing practice for safety in biotechnology industries. A third approach is the continued search for global programmes—of epidemiological surveillance, of vaccine development and production, or for countering newly emerging infectious diseases—which take up the 'prevention of disease' element of Article X. The parties to the BTWC need to determine which of such projects is appropriate to the convention, as distinct from other contexts and institutions, and then to choose one or more programmes for implementation by the parties under the auspices of Article X.[124]

The regime of development needs to move beyond the NIEO and NPT contexts which shaped it in the 1970s and at the first two review conferences. It must emerge in its own right as part of an overall treaty regime for biological disarmament, authentically derived from Article X of the convention and strengthened by Article VII of the BTWC protocol.

A regime of development is currently more an aspiration than an achievement because so little has been done to give effect to the many statements made in support of Article X. It may remain a problem area that will never emerge in as well-articulated and fully evolved a form as the many-layered regime of compliance seems likely to do. As Goldblat and Bernauer warned: 'In any event, the BW Convention is primarily a disarmament measure, and one should not expect too much from it as regards redressing the existing inequalities among States in the field of science and technology or the furtherance of economic development.'[125]

The paradox is that, the higher the expectations of the regime of development, the harder it may prove to give concrete expression to Article X because any practical programme of implementation will fall short of those unrealistic expectations.

---

[123] The Technical Secretariat of the OPCW is involved in the concrete implementation of Article XI of the CWC. As the OPCW bodies meet frequently, the debate on international cooperation and technology exchange has become permanent and institutionalized. As a result, the countries with the greatest interest in receiving technology are required to move from general policy statements and statements of principle to a formulation of concrete needs and expectations.

[124] This theme is taken up in section VIII of chapter 7 in this volume.

[125] Goldblat and Bernauer (note 117), p. 39.

6. The regime of permanence

I. Introduction

How can a treaty regime be rendered more permanent? Whatever a treaty says in law about its own duration it cannot in practice guarantee its durability. It is vulnerable to the vicissitudes of time, and, if governments are determined to disregard their treaty obligations, the law cannot deter them. Nevertheless, prudent measures can be taken to strengthen the permanence of a treaty regime in order to make it more difficult to disregard. There may be value in giving greater salience to the elements of the biological and toxin weapons disarmament regime which emphasize its permanence. They must not be overlooked or taken for granted but instead should play their part in the evolution of biological disarmament.

The elements which comprise the emergent regime of permanence which is derived from the 1972 Biological and Toxin Weapons Convention should be identified, and ways of strengthening those elements and integrating them into the convention should be sought.

The textual sources for the concept of a regime of permanence are the ninth paragraph of the preamble of the BTWC, which states that the convention is based on a determination 'to *exclude completely* the possibility of bacteriological (biological) agents and toxins being used as weapons'; the first line of Article I: 'Each State Party to this Convention undertakes *never in any circumstances* to develop, produce, stockpile or otherwise acquire or retain' any of the prohibited objects; and the first paragraph of Article XIII: 'This Convention shall be of *unlimited duration*'.[1]

These passages provide clues to the intentions of the negotiators who concluded the convention and indicators that a regime of permanence was being deliberately inaugurated. The provisions of the text cannot guarantee permanence. However, they establish expectations and incorporate an amalgam of legal, diplomatic and political elements into the structure of international society, which will be increasingly difficult to dismantle, ignore or override.

Perceptions and signals are important in international relations, and it would be a mistake to underrate the significance of psychology in keeping a treaty regime strong. Attitudes, expectations, confidence and reinforcement are essential to promoting the health of biological and toxin disarmament and other international treaty regimes.

This chapter explores three contributions which developments in international law and diplomacy have begun to make to the process of creating expectations of permanence. Each plays a role in regime reinforcement, particularly as regards the perceived durability of the treaty regime. States which choose to emphasize the permanence of the treaty regime can act to enhance its durability.

Three propositions regarding a regime of permanence are examined in this chapter. First, the regime is strengthened by the withdrawal of those reserva-

---

[1] Emphasis added. The significance of the second paragraph of Article XIII, under which a state party may withdraw from the BTWC if extraordinary events jeopardize its supreme interests, is discussed in Sims, N. A., 'Withdrawal clauses in disarmament treaties: a questionable logic?', *Disarmament Diplomacy*, no. 42 (Dec. 1999), pp. 15–19.

tions to the 1925 Geneva Protocol which reserve a right of retaliation as regards BTW. Second, although this argument is more equivocal, under certain conditions the regime may be fortified by the emergence of a norm of customary international law identical or coextensive with the prohibitions embodied in the BTWC. Third, the quinquennial review conferences provide a coherent pattern of diplomacy, with cumulative authority in the absence of a continuous administration, and by their perpetuation contribute significantly to a regime of permanence.

II. Withdrawal of Geneva Protocol reservations

The Geneva Protocol is a law of war. Unlike the BTWC, it is not a disarmament treaty or an arms control agreement, and its scope is narrower. Essentially, it is a contract engaging only the High Contracting Parties of 1925 and those states which have subsequently chosen to join the protocol. It applies only 'as among themselves' and does not, of itself, constrain its parties in their use of chemical or bacteriological methods of warfare against non-parties (although a norm of customary international law may extend such constraints more widely).

The BTWC, on the contrary, applies *erga omnes*[2] in the sense that each party is individually committed to respect its renunciation of BTW. This is not so much a contract as a disarmament imperative. As such, it continues in force even if a party is threatened or attacked with BTW by another party or by a non-party. Article I stipulates that never in any circumstances may it develop, produce, stockpile or otherwise acquire or retain any of the objects prohibited by the convention. Only after invoking the withdrawal procedure contained in Article XIII, paragraph 2 and awaiting the expiry of three-months' notice can a party be relieved of its obligations, and then only by withdrawing from the BTWC. However, Article VII is designed to render withdrawal unnecessary by mandating the provision of international assistance if the United Nations Security Council decides that a party to the BTWC has been exposed to danger because of a violation.

The negotiators of the BTWC held the Geneva Protocol in high regard and Article VIII of the convention reflects this view: 'Nothing in this Convention shall be interpreted as in any way limiting or detracting from the obligations assumed by any State under the Protocol for the Prohibition of the Use in War of Asphyxiating, Poisonous or Other Gases, and of Bacteriological Methods of Warfare, signed at Geneva on June 17, 1925.'

In addition, the BTWC in its final form omitted the prohibition on use of BTW which had been included in the proposed Article I of the 1969 British draft convention. It was argued that such a provision would detract from the authority of the Geneva Protocol as regards chemical warfare if the ban on use of bacteriological methods of warfare were repeated and extended *erga omnes* without doing the same simultaneously with regard to chemical warfare. This weak argument was criticized at the time and the apprehension deemed groundless. However, the argument was repeated in the 1971 negotiations by those delegates to the Conference of the Committee on Disarmament—notably Minister without Portfolio (Disarmament) Alva Myrdal of Sweden and

---

[2] The term *erga omnes* indicates that non-parties as well as states parties are included.

Ambassador Kroum Christov of Bulgaria—who regretted the failure of the conference to pursue a single treaty that would embrace both biological weapons and chemical weapons. That approach had been promoted in 1969–71 as an alternative to the British draft convention. When the Soviet Union abandoned the single-treaty approach in March 1971, those who had favoured it instead concentrated their efforts on preventing inclusion of a prohibition on use in the convention. They were successful and the British proposal was not accepted.

In 1996 the Fourth Review Conference spelled out the implicit ban on use which flowed from the prohibitions in Article I of the BTWC. The Final Declaration of the Fourth Review Conference contained repeated affirmations that any use of BTW would involve a breach of the convention. The inclusion of this language averted the amendment of the BTWC to add the prohibition of use to Article I and to the title of the convention, as proposed by Iran.

Certain reservations which states had attached to their ratification of the Geneva Protocol created problems for the BTWC after it was finalized in 1972. The reservations which caused concern were those by states that reserved the right of retaliation against a party which engaged in chemical or bacteriological warfare. Some reservations extended their scope to allies; others invoked a 'condition of reciprocity'. The relationship of the reservations to the potential invocation of belligerent reprisals was unclear. Moreover, although commonly regarded as enabling the parties to engage in 'retaliation in kind', this description confers on the reservations a limiting character which few deserved. Most of the reservations permitted retaliatory use of bacteriological warfare against prior chemical warfare, and of chemical warfare against prior bacteriological warfare, but did not distinguish between the two categories. They thereby went beyond the strict understanding of retaliation in kind.

Such reservations created problems because they could be used to legitimize the stockpiling of weapons for deterrent purposes and, if deterrence were to fail, for retaliation. The reservations also complicated the nature of the Geneva Protocol treaty regime and raised the issue of non-use or no-first-use. This, in turn, affected the BTWC treaty regime for the states which were parties to both treaties.

By legalizing the use of BTW in certain circumstances—even against fellow parties to the Geneva Protocol—the reservations cast doubt on the renunciation of BTW *erga omnes* which states had undertaken by becoming parties to the BTWC. Conversely, that renunciation raised questions about the continued relevance of the reservations to the Geneva Protocol, because if states complied with the BTWC it was unclear how the means of retaliation were to be procured. In other words, the problem was one of asymmetry of obligations. The Geneva Protocol and the BTWC were different kinds of treaty, prohibiting different things, and belonging to different bodies of international law. However, these two treaties alone sought to regulate or prohibit BTW activities on a worldwide basis. It follows that the entry of most states into obligations under both treaties made it imperative that there should be internal consistency within that overall structure of obligations.

An asymmetry of obligations would result for a state, party both to the Geneva Protocol and to the BTWC, if it were to reserve a right of retaliation in respect of BTW use in war, while being bound 'never in any circumstances' to develop, produce, stockpile, acquire or retain BTW. The right of retaliation with BTW could only be exercised by a state which had first violated the latter obligation. This asymmetry had to be resolved.[3]

This view had been argued for 20 years before it was accepted at the Third Review Conference whose Final Declaration included the following words in its Article VIII section: 'The Conference stresses the importance of the withdrawal of all reservations to the 1925 Geneva Protocol related to the Biological and Toxin Weapons Convention.'[4]

The maintenance of a purported right of retaliation with weapons whose development, production, stockpiling, acquisition and retention have all been renounced brings the structure of international law built on treaty commitments into disrepute. If it is meant to be taken seriously as a deterrent threat it undermines the permanence of the BTWC and calls into question the obligations assumed under it. This latter consideration motivated the Irish Government to act to resolve the asymmetry of obligations. Its actions prevented the asymmetry from arising for the Republic of Ireland by anticipating Irish adherence to the BTWC.

In February 1972 the Republic of Ireland withdrew the reservation which the Irish Free State had attached to its instrument of accession to the Geneva Protocol on 29 August 1930.[5] It conflated the prohibitions of acquisition and retention into a single prohibition of possession: 'Ireland considers that the Convention could be undermined if reservations made by the parties to the 1925 Geneva Protocol were allowed to stand, as the prohibition of possession is incompatible with the right to retaliate, and that there should be an absolute and universal prohibition of the use of the weapons in question.'

When the BTWC was opened for signature on 10 April 1972 Ireland attached this note to its signature. It thereby emphasized as strongly as possible the direct connection between the Geneva Protocol and the BTWC, and the need to ensure full compatibility of the obligations under the two instruments.[6]

The same point was made by academic commentators. Jozef Goldblat of the Stockholm International Peace Research Institute, and a former disarmament negotiator at Geneva, wrote in 1972:

According to Article VIII of the convention, nothing shall be interpreted as in any way limiting or detracting from the obligations assumed by any state under the Geneva Protocol. This may imply that the reservations—part and parcel of the obligations—will continue to subsist. Legally, they can be nullified only through a direct act of withdrawal.

To avoid misunderstandings and incompatibility with the new commitments, the countries which have attached reservations to the Geneva Protocol should declare them

---

[3] The fullest treatment of this issue up to 1985 is 'Resolving the asymmetry of obligations', Sims, N. A., *The Diplomacy of Biological Disarmament: Vicissitudes of a Treaty in Force, 1975–85* (Macmillan: London, and St Martin's Press: New York, 1988), pp. 273–87, and, up to 1992, Sims, N. A., 'Commonwealth reservations to the 1925 Geneva Protocol, 1930–1992: treaty constraints on chemical and biological warfare and the right of retaliation in kind', *The Round Table: the Commonwealth Journal of International Affairs*, no. 324 (Oct. 1992), pp. 477–99.

[4] Third Review Conference document BWC/CONF.III/22/Add.2, 27 Sep. 1991, p. 14.

[5] Republic of Ireland, Note of 7 February 1972 to the Depositary, Paris, 10 Feb. 1972.

[6] SIPRI, *World Armaments and Disarmament: SIPRI Yearbook 1976* (Almqvist & Wiksell International: Stockholm, and MIT Press: Cambridge, Mass. and London, 1976), p. 468.

null and void, at least with regard to biological and toxin weapons, at the time of ratification or accession to the biological disarmament convention.[7]

The present author urged that in order to avoid legal and logical anomalies
the 'reserving' states should examine their Geneva Protocol reservations to
determine whether they were still justifiable in the light of their subsequent
adherence to the BTWC.[8] Canada had opened the way to such an examination
with its declaration in 1970 that it would not use biological or toxin weapons at
any time in the future.[9] It announced that it was retaining a right of retaliation in
respect of chemical warfare. This 1970 declaration was given legal effect in
1991 as described below, when Canada modified its reservations to the Geneva
Protocol. Belgium announced in 1971, when the definitive draft convention was
under scrutiny in the First Committee of the General Assembly, that after the
entry into force of the BTWC it would study the possibility of a similar
modification: of abandoning its reservation pertaining to retaliation as far as
biological and toxin weapons were concerned.[10] In the event, as described
below, it did not make a modification but proceeded to full withdrawal of its
reservations to the Geneva Protocol in 1997.

In 1971 Morocco had also warned that 'failure to cancel' those reservations
would limit the BTWC in its intended function of 'completely and finally prohibiting bacteriological and toxin weapons'. Morocco had added that if the
reservations were not withdrawn they would also be likely 'to give rise to
erroneous interpretations of Article VII'. This was because, if a right of retaliation under the Geneva Protocol were retained, the Article VII provision enjoin-
ing assistance to victims of BTW attack could conceivably be envisaged in
terms of retaliation in kind. This was a misinterpretation of the Article VII provision for medical and other humanitarian assistance.

Morocco contended that the BTWC required 'that all states parties shall be
absolutely certain in law that the reservations . . . have been declared null and
void with regard to the use of bacteriological and toxin weapons.'[11] The United
Kingdom left matters uncertain: 'We trust therefore that, even though the reservations to the Geneva Protocol may legally remain in force, for all practical purposes the risk of biological weapons or toxins actually being used for hostile
purposes will be reduced to negligible proportions.'[12]

Phrases such as 'for all practical purposes' and 'reduced to negligible proportions' do not belong in treaties, and the British approach did not serve the convention well. However, this view dominated the next two decades. Whether or
not they agreed with the UK, few of the 'reserving' states which adhered to the
BTWC from 1972 followed the Irish example until the late 1980s.

[7] Goldblat, J., 'Chemical and biological disarmament', SIPRI, *World Armaments and Disarmament: SIPRI Yearbook 1972* (Almqvist & Wiksell: Stockholm, Humanities Press: New York, and Paul Elek: London, 1972), p. 509.

[8] Sims, N. A., 'Etat actuel des négociations multilatérales pour une réduction des armements' [Current state of the multilateral negotiations on arms reduction], *Politique Etrangère* (Paris), vol. 35 (Dec. 1972), p. 689.

[9] Ignatieff, G., Canada, UN document A/C.1/PV.1765, 19 Nov. 1970, para. 59.

[10] Van Ussel, M., Belgium, UN document A/C.1/PV.1841, 1 Dec. 1971, para. 35.

[11] Conference of the Committee on Disarmament document CCD/347, 24 Aug. 1971, para. 4.

[12] Hainworth, H. C., UK, Conference of the Committee on Disarmament document CCD/PV.542, 28 Sep. 1971, para. 70.

Many states had not reserved a right of retaliation when they ratified or acceded to the Geneva Protocol. They included, among others, Egypt, Germany, Hungary, Italy, Japan, Persia (Iran), Poland, Turkey, all the Nordic countries and almost all the Latin American countries.

There was no problem for the Netherlands in terms of compatibility with the convention. Since its ratification in 1930 it alone of the parties to the Geneva Protocol had restricted its reservation to chemical warfare and thereby rendered its renunciation of BTW as unconditional as that of the 'non-reserving' parties to the Geneva Protocol.

This had not been the Netherlands' original intention. The initial proposal of its Defence, Foreign Affairs and Colonies ministers had envisaged a reservation covering both chemical and bacteriological warfare. However, after elaborate discussions in parliament the government decided to limit the right of retaliation to chemical warfare only. In its official explanation accompanying the final text of the law governing the Netherlands' ratification the government declared that 'some methods of warfare are so reprehensible that their use is under no circumstances permissible'. It had decided to draw the line explicitly between chemical warfare (permissible in retaliation) and bacteriological warfare (never permissible even in retaliation). This consideration arose in the parliamentary debate. The debate was shaped by the idea, absent from the government's official explanation, that bacteriological weapons were uncontrollable and therefore practically of no use in war, whereas chemical weapons could be contained to a certain degree.[13]

This position, adopted 45 years earlier by the Netherlands, was taken up by the United States on 10 April 1975, when it ratified the Geneva Protocol which it had signed in 1925. The USA had been preparing its ratification since 1970. The decision to reserve a right of retaliation only in respect of chemical warfare had been transmitted to the US Senate as early as 19 August 1970 with President Richard M. Nixon's formal request for its advice and consent to US ratification of the Geneva Protocol.[14] The US renunciation of biological warfare, even in retaliation, as a future party to the Geneva Protocol fitted in with the decision in favour of unilateral destruction of its BW stockpile, which Nixon had announced on 25 November 1969. It was a logical consequence of that historic act of disarmament (to which toxins had subsequently been added). Moreover, it meant that there would be no asymmetry of obligation for the USA as a party to the BTWC and the Geneva Protocol. This was made easier by the parallel consideration of both treaties in the ratification hearings conducted by the US Senate, which led to its advice and consent to US ratification of both instruments being given to President Gerald Ford on 16 December 1974.

Barbados took similar action to the Republic of Ireland, on 22 June 1976, when it addressed a Note to France as depositary declaring that it considered the Geneva Protocol to be in force for Barbados by virtue of its extension to Barbados by the UK, but that the reservation made on 9 April 1930 was with-

[13] Letter of 24 Feb. 1992 to the author from Baron M. R. O. Bentinck, Head of Non-Nuclear Arms Control and Disarmament Department, Ministry of Foreign Affairs, The Hague, based on research by J. T. Versteeg of that Department.

[14] Goldblat, J., SIPRI, *The Problem of Chemical and Biological Warfare,* vol. 4, *CB Disarmament Negotiations, 1920–1970* (Almqvist & Wiksell: Stockholm, and Humanities Press: New York, 1971), pp. 283–84. The series is available on a CD-ROM, which is described at URL <http://editors.sipri.se/cd.cbw.html>. The text is reproduced in USA, *Department of State Bulletin*, 7 Sep. 1970, 63:273 ff.

drawn.[15] Barbados did not, however, relate this action directly to the BTWC, which it had ratified on 16 February 1973.

The problem of asymmetry of obligations had been noted by Belgium at the UN in 1971, and New Zealand drew attention to it during the First Review Conference in 1980.[16] However, neither country took action at that time on its Geneva Protocol reservation.

In fact, nothing more was done to address the problem until states began to withdraw their reservations in the late 1980s. Between the second and third review conferences reservations were withdrawn by Australia (1986), New Zealand (1989), Mongolia (1990), Czechoslovakia (1990), Romania (1991) and Bulgaria (1991).[17] Their reservations dated from 1930, 1930, 1968, 1938, 1929 and 1934, respectively. Moreover, at the summer 1991 session of the Conference on Disarmament Chile announced that it was introducing the necessary parliamentary procedures for withdrawal,[18] and Spain that it was studying the possibility of withdrawal.[19] Their reservations dated from 1935 and 1929, respectively. Their motivation had as much, and probably more, to do with the prospect of chemical disarmament as with the (by then) long-established regime of BTW disarmament. All the states which withdrew their reservations were keen to demonstrate their support for the 1993 Chemical Weapons Convention under negotiation in the CD and to emphasize, in the words of New Zealand, that there were no circumstances conceivable in which they would wish to use CW.[20]

On 26 November 1986, Australia was the first of this group to withdraw. It did not mention BTW disarmament but confined its statement to chemical weapons, perhaps because it assumed that the BTW option had already been foreclosed by its 1977 ratification of the BTWC. Australian Foreign Minister Bill Hayden stated simply that 'the government rejected the assumption that Australia would be prepared, under certain circumstances, to use chemical weapons'; that, on 16 March 1986, 'in condemning Iraq's use of chemical weapons in the [First] Gulf War, he had made clear that the Australian government did not consider the use of chemical weapons justified under any circumstances'; that Australia's action 'was consistent with the government's view and with general international opinion that chemical warfare was an abhorrent activity'; and that 'it also reflected the Australian government's strong commitment to the early conclusion' of a CWC. Hayden concluded that 'by withdrawing its own reservation and by its active pursuit of the Convention, Australia aimed to strengthen the international norms against chemical warfare'.[21]

[15] SIPRI, 'International agreements related to arms control and disarmament, as of 31 December 1976', *World Armaments and Disarmament: SIPRI Yearbook 1977* (Almqvist & Wiksell: Stockholm, and MIT Press: Cambridge, Mass. and London, 1977), p. 374.

[16] Farnon, E., New Zealand, First Review Conference document BWC/CONF.I/SR.6, 7 Mar. 1980, para. 14.

[17] Information supplied by Jozef Goldblat in 1989–91 and the London embassies of Czechoslovakia, Romania and Bulgaria.

[18] González, R., Chile, Conference on Disarmament document CD/PV.605, 4 Sep. 1991, p. 12.

[19] Pérez-Villanueva, J., Spain, Conference on Disarmament document CD/PV.597, 25 June 1991, p. 6.

[20] New Zealand statement at the Paris Conference on the Interdiction of Chemical Weapons, 7–11 Jan. 1989, text supplied by Jozef Goldblat.

[21] Australian Minister for Foreign Affairs, 'Australian action on chemical weapons', News Release M189, 26 Nov. 1986. Text supplied by the Chemical and Biological Disarmament Section, Department of Foreign Affairs and Trade, Canberra.

The Third Review Conference

The Third Review Conference took place in September 1991. Since June the CD had been officially committed to a timetable which envisaged completion of its work on the CWC in 1992. There was general agreement that at some point all reservations of the right of retaliation in respect of chemical weapons under the Geneva Protocol would have to be withdrawn, but the point at which this would occur had not been determined. Austria wanted a special conference to be held for this withdrawal of reservations, while Egypt advocated making such withdrawal a specific requirement of the CWC, but one which would apply at the time of signature. Other states, however, were reluctant to act before the USA. In May 1991 the USA agreed to withdraw its reservation at the time of entry into force (rather than 8 or 10 years later on satisfaction of additional conditions relating to CWC universality and progress in the destruction of stockpiles, as it had earlier suggested).

It was not surprising therefore that the states parties to the BTWC failed to issue an unqualified call for the withdrawal of all Geneva Protocol reservations (in respect of chemical warfare as well as biological and toxin warfare). Instead they stressed the importance of the withdrawal of 'all reservations to the 1925 Geneva Protocol related to the Biological and Toxin Weapons Convention'.[22] This could be interpreted either as meaning modification of existing reservations, assimilating them to the intermediate position occupied by the Netherlands since 1930 and by the USA since 1975, or as going further in the spirit of the 1972 Irish statement on withdrawal. The withdrawal of 'all reservations to the 1925 Geneva Protocol related to the Biological and Toxin Weapons Convention' accommodated both possibilities, and it was included in the 1991 Final Declaration as representing a consensus within the Third Review Conference.[23]

During the Third Review Conference no further withdrawals of reservations were announced, but there were two announcements of modification: by Canada on 10 September and the UK on 27 September. Both adopted the intermediate position, choosing to retain the reservation pertaining to chemical retaliation for the time being, but removing the asymmetry of obligation between the Geneva Protocol and the BTWC.

Ambassador Peggy Mason, leader of the Canadian delegation, announced:

that Canada has recently modified its reservations to the 1925 Geneva Protocol which prohibits the use in war of chemical weapons and of bacteriological methods of warfare, by removing the reservations insofar as they relate to bacteriological methods of warfare.

. . .

As long ago as 1970, the Canadian Government unilaterally declared that it would not use biological or toxin weapons at any time in the future. The more recent formal action taken with regard to the 1925 Geneva Protocol is meant simply to ensure that

---

[22] BWC/CONF.III/22/Add.2 (note 4).
[23] The provision was negotiated by interested delegations under the informal chairmanship of Ambassador Winfried Lang of Austria, a veteran of all three review conferences and president of the Second Review Conference.

there can be no suggestion of uncertainty anywhere as to the extent of Canada's abhorrence of biological warfare and the means of conducting it.[24]

For the United Kingdom, Ambassador Tessa Solesby stated that:

Her Majesty's Government has now decided to withdraw that part of its reservation to the Protocol . . . which maintained our right to retaliate in kind if biological weapons were used against the United Kingdom. This decision reflects the continued determination of the British Government to exclude the possibility of the use of biological agents and toxins as weapons. It also demonstrates HMG's commitment to the two key international instruments for this purpose, the 1925 Geneva Protocol and the Biological Weapons Convention.[25]

The Fourth Review Conference

A call for withdrawal of reservations was made at the 1996 Fourth Review Conference. The Article VIII section of its Final Declaration retained and slightly rearranged the 1991 text up to and including (as paragraph 5 in 1996) the Austrian-negotiated compromise language[26] of 1991: 'The Conference stresses the importance of the withdrawal of all reservations to the 1925 Geneva Protocol related to the Biological and Toxin Weapons Convention.' On the initiative of France and the Netherlands the Fourth Review Conference added the following text: '6. The Conference welcomes the actions which States Parties have taken to withdraw their reservations to the 1925 Geneva Protocol related to the Biological and Toxin Weapons Convention, and calls upon those States Parties that continue to maintain pertinent reservations to the 1925 Geneva Protocol to withdraw those reservations, and to notify the Depositary of the 1925 Geneva Protocol of their withdrawals without delay.'[27] The adjective 'pertinent' had been added to the original proposal.

A new paragraph, which was slightly abridged from a proposal by Chile, Mexico and Peru, was also added: '7. The Conference notes that reservations concerning retaliation, through the use of any of the objects prohibited by the Biological and Toxin Weapons Convention, even conditional, are totally incompatible with the absolute and universal prohibition of the development, production, stockpiling, acquisition and retention of bacteriological (biological) and toxin weapons, with the aim to exclude completely and forever the possibility of their use.'[28]

In their proposal Chile, Mexico and Peru had referred to 'the reservation of a purported right to retaliation' and had suggested a qualifying clause 'notwithstanding and without prejudice to the legal positions of all States Parties'. In all other substantive respects, their proposed paragraph was accepted.[29]

[24] Text supplied by the Canadian Delegation to the Third Review Conference, Geneva.
[25] Text supplied by the Arms Control and Disarmament Department, Foreign and Commonwealth Office, London.
[26] BWC/CONF.III/22/Add.2 (note 4).
[27] Fourth Review Conference document BWC/CONF.IV/9, 6 Dec. 1996, p. 22; the original proposal of France and the Netherlands is at p. 52.
[28] BWC/CONF.IV/9 (note 27), pp. 22–23.
[29] BWC/CONF.IV/9 (note 27), pp. 51–52.

This was a much stronger statement than could have been agreed in 1991. It reflected the evolution of biological disarmament. The persuasive efforts which had begun in 1971 bore fruit in 1996.

In addition to the passage of time, which had added further withdrawals of reservations since the Third Review Conference to reinforce the momentum built up in the years 1986–91, three factors contributed to the adoption of a stronger statement in 1996.

One factor was the Iranian proposal for a formal amendment under the Article XI procedure to add prohibition of use to Article I and to the title of the BTWC. The 1996 Final Declaration weakened support for the Iranian proposal by implying that such an amendment was unnecessary. It pointed out, more emphatically than previous final declarations had done, that any use of BTW would involve a breach of the BTWC. The comments of the Fourth Review Conference on Article VIII supported other affirmations to this effect in its Final Declaration. An unequivocal statement was included at the end of paragraph 7 of the section on Article VIII: the 'aim' of all the prohibitions regarding BTW already contained in Article I was 'to exclude completely and forever the possibility of their use'.[30]

A second factor was the availability of suitable language for this expanded commentary on Article VIII. Draft paragraphs had been circulated to all delegations in a 'briefing book'.[31] The substance of the 1996 paragraphs 6 and 7 of the Article VIII section of the Final Declaration, including the key phrase 'incompatible with the absolute and universal prohibition', had been proposed in 1988,[32] but it was not until its reappearance in the 1996 briefing book that it was added to the final text.

The third factor was the occurrence of the Fourth Review Conference within the 180 days preceding entry into force of the CWC. On 31 October 1996, deposit of the 65th instrument of ratification triggered the process which culminated in the entry into force of the CWC on 29 April 1997. The certainty of the CWC's imminent entry into force gave those many parties to the BTWC which had ratified or were about to ratify the CWC further reason to review their Geneva Protocol position. As of 29 April 1997 there would be no longer any reason to cling to reservations of a right of retaliation in respect of either BW or CW. (The CWC explicitly prohibits the use of chemical weapons.) Instead, there would be every reason to bring their Geneva Protocol treaty status into conformity with the obligations incumbent on them in complying with the BTWC and CWC.

By the late 1990s withdrawal of Geneva Protocol reservations had become almost 'normal' practice.

Chile and Spain, as noted earlier, had announced their interest in withdrawal in the CD before the Third Review Conference. Chile's withdrawal of its 1935 reservation took effect on 15 October 1991, and Spain's withdrawal of its 1929

[30] BWC/CONF.IV/9 (note 27), p. 23. The Iranian amendment proposal is further discussed in section VI of chapter 7 in this volume.

[31] Sims, N. A., 'Article VIII: Geneva Protocol obligations', eds G. S. Pearson and M. R. Dando, *Strengthening the Biological Weapons Convention: Key Points for the Fourth Review Conference* (Quaker United Nations Office: Geneva, 1996), pp. 106–107. The volume was an early part of the now long-established project to strengthen the BTWC which was funded by the Joseph Rowntree Charitable Trust and based at the Department of Peace Studies at the University of Bradford.

[32] Sims, *The Diplomacy of Biological Disarmament* (note 3), p. 284.

reservation on 28 December 1992. South Africa followed in time for the Fourth Review Conference: the withdrawal of its 1930 reservations took effect on 20 October 1996. Most significantly of all, France, the depositary government for the Geneva Protocol, which had also been the first to ratify it (on 10 May 1926), took action during the Fourth Review Conference: France announced withdrawal of its reservations on 25 November 1996, taking effect on 12 December 1996.

The process continued after the Fourth Review Conference. Belgium withdrew its 1928 reservations with effect from 27 February 1997 and Estonia its 1931 reservation with effect from 29 July 1999.[33] Belgium might have been expected to opt for modification first, as the USA had done in 1975 and Canada and the UK in 1991, when they had adjusted their Geneva Protocol status in respect of the scope of their potential retaliation to the position occupied by the Netherlands since 1930. In 1971 Belgium had stated: 'The Belgian authorities intend to study, after the entry into force of the new convention, the possibility, as far as biological and toxin weapons are concerned, of abandoning the reservation.'[34] However, Belgium never adopted the intermediate position foreshadowed in its 1971 statement. Instead it waited until 1997 when it withdrew its reservations in full.

The process is not yet complete. Although exact numbers are difficult to establish,[35] it is certain that at least three non-parties to the BTWC (Algeria, Angola and Israel) and, of greater significance for the BTWC treaty regime, 18 parties to the BTWC (Bahrain, Bangladesh, China, Fiji, India, Iraq, Jordan, Korea (North), Korea (South), Kuwait, Libya, Nigeria, Papua New Guinea, Portugal, Russia, Solomon Islands, Viet Nam and Yugoslavia) retain reservations which have not been modified to exclude BTW from the scope of their potential retaliation.

It is possible that some reservations have been retained, unmodified, through inattention to Geneva Protocol status, but it seems unlikely that all have been retained by default. Although several of these states, parties both to the Geneva Protocol and to the BTWC, showed some interest during the 1990s in withdrawing or modifying their protocol reservations, or declared their intention to do so, none had officially notified the depositary by 31 December 1999. As of that date, their reservations accordingly remained in force.[36]

The most intriguing of these unfulfilled declarations of intent came from the newly post-Soviet government of the Russian Federation, as recorded by Adam Roberts and Richard Guelff in their latest account of the status of the Geneva Protocol: 'President Yeltsin, in a statement on 29 January 1992, declared Russian withdrawal of the USSR's reservation to the 1925 Protocol "concerning the possibility of using biological weapons as a response".[37] However,

[33] Information supplied by the Embassy of France, Stockholm, 10 May 2000.

[34] Van Ussel (note 10).

[35] Sims, *The Diplomacy of Biological Disarmament* (note 3), pp. 280–83, on legal uncertainties arising from succession to obligations (and, more controversially, to reservations) upon decolonization. This accounts for the largest part, but not the whole, of the difficulty of compiling an authoritative list of states parties to the Geneva Protocol with reservations and establishing the extent of such reservations.

[36] Information supplied by the Embassy of France, Stockholm, 10 May 2000.

[37] Letter dated 30 January 1992 from the Representative of the Russian Federation addressed to the President of the Conference on Disarmament transmitting the text of the statement made on 29 January 1992 by B. N. Yeltsin, the President of the Russian Federation, on Russia's policy in the field of arms limitation and reduction, Conference on Disarmament document CD/1123, 31 Jan. 1992, p. 7, quoted in

Yeltsin said nothing in the statement about the possibility of using chemical weapons as a response; and in any case Russia has not officially informed the Depositary of this partial withdrawal of reservations.'[38]

The Yeltsin statement of 29 January 1992 suggested that Russia would follow the examples of Canada, the UK and the USA in using the Geneva Protocol to make absolute their renunciation of biological and toxin weapons. Even though it has not yet been translated into a legally effective act through notification to the depositary, it demonstrates nevertheless the growing acceptability of with-drawal or modification of reservations as the 'normal' response to the problem of asymmetry of obligations for a minority of states parties to both the protocol and the BTWC. (Only for that minority does the problem arise.)

Withdrawal of reservations had to start somewhere, however normal it had become by 1996, and credit is due to those governments which acted before there was any certainty that a CWC would be concluded and to those which made explicit their commitment to the regime of biological disarmament. They followed the example of the 1972 Irish decision[39] and laid the foundation for the regime of permanence.

III. Emergence of an international legal norm

An international norm implies the existence of a legal obligation independently of treaty status. The notion of an international norm against the use of bacterio-logical methods of warfare goes back at least to the Geneva Protocol which first gave expression to the prohibition in treaty form. How firmly this norm had established itself in customary international law by 1972 was explored most fully by Anders Boserup and Henri Meyrowitz.[40] Both authors were confident that BW of all kinds, not only the bacterial category, had become subject to a customary prohibition of use.

However, this does not address the issue of a norm of customary international law applicable to BTW activities falling short of actual use. It is those activities, not use, that are explicitly prohibited by the BTWC. During the Second Review Conference in 1986 several Western delegations invoked a norm closely related to the BTWC. This might imply the universal applicability of a legal rule that 'never in any circumstances' may BTW be developed, produced, stockpiled, acquired or retained.[41]

It is not clear that this was the intention of the norm language employed in 1986. Although not all norm references appeared in the Summary Record of the Second Review Conference, advance texts supplied by delegations show a con-vergence in Western statements around the four such references made by

Roberts, A. and Guelff, R. (eds), *Documents on the Laws of War*, 3rd edn (Oxford University Press: Oxford, 2000), p. 165.

[38] Roberts and Guelff (note 37).

[39] Republic of Ireland (note 5).

[40] Boserup, A., 'The Geneva Protocol', SIPRI, *The Problem of Chemical and Biological Warfare*, vol. 3, *CBW and the Laws of War* (Almqvist & Wiksell: Stockholm, 1973); and Meyrowitz, H., *Les armes biologiques et le droit international (droit de la guerre et désarmement)* [Biological arms and international law: the law of war and disarmament] (Pedone: Paris, 1968). *The Problem of Chemical and Biological Warfare* series is available on a CD-ROM, that is described at URL <http://editors.sipri.se/cd.cbw.html>.

[41] Sims, N. A., 'Morality and biological warfare', *Arms Control,* vol. 8 (May 1987), pp. 13–19.

Ambassador Donald Lowitz of the USA on 9 September 1986.[42] Three times in that plenary session he asserted a US commitment to maintain, support and strengthen 'the international norm against biological and toxin weapons established by this Convention'. He concluded with a fourth such reference, saying of the convention 'all States Parties have a solemn legal obligation to uphold its provisions and the norm which it establishes'.

Ambassador Richard Butler of Australia declared on 15 September 1986 that: 'Together with the 1925 Protocol . . . the Convention establishes an important norm of international behaviour, namely that States shall not possess or use biological agents or toxins as weapons.'[43]

On 9 September 1986, Arsène Després, for Canada, stated the relationship differently when he noted 'the need for universality of adherence to the Convention and the norms which it embodies'.[44]

On the same day, speaking on behalf of the 12 member states of the European Communities (EC) in European political cooperation, British Ambassador Dr Ian Cromartie implied that the treaty obligation was the only source of law by urging wider adherence to 'increase confidence in, and enhance the authority of, the Convention as the international norm against biological weapons'. He appeared to suggest another similar source of legal obligation when he changed the definite article to the indefinite: 'The Twelve . . . reaffirm their support for the Convention as an international norm against biological and toxin weapons, and one which provides a political and indeed moral standard by which the conduct of states in this area should be judged.'[45]

The BTWC had 'established' the norm (Australia and the USA), or 'embodied' the norm (Canada), or *was itself* either 'the' international norm or 'an' international norm (the UK, on behalf of the Twelve). The nuances of these different expressions of the relationship may have to do partly with differing traditions of international legal doctrine as regards the identity or parallelism of customary norms with treaty obligations. The language differences may also be related to the political implications of asserting or denying the possibility of an autonomous existence for the customary norm independently of the convention. (This assumes that the phraseology was carefully chosen in each instance, which may not have been the case.)

When the Second Review Conference went into committee, the United States said it was 'interested in enhancing the norm of the Convention with strengthening/supporting measures'.[46] It is unclear what was meant by 'the norm of the Convention'. In another of the proposals annexed to the Report of the Committee of the Whole, the Federal Republic of Germany and the UK embraced the US/Australian formula and jointly asserted 'the need for strengthening the verification of compliance with *the norm established by this Convention*'.[47] That

---

[42] Text supplied by the US Delegation. One of the 4 norm references survived into the Summary Record, Second Review Conference document BWC/CONF.II/SR.3, 9 Sep. 1986, para. 24.

[43] Text supplied by the Australian Delegation. In the Summary Record at Second Review Conference document BWC/CONF.II/SR.8, 15 Sep. 1986, para. 8.

[44] Text supplied by the Canadian Delegation.

[45] Text supplied by the British Delegation. Only the second 'norm' reference survived into the Summary Record, BWC/CONF.II/SR.3 (note 42), para. 2. The Twelve, the 1986 EC member states, were Belgium, Denmark, France, the FRG, Greece, Ireland, Italy, Luxembourg, the Netherlands, Portugal, Spain and the UK.

[46] Second Review Conference document BWC/CONF.II/9, 22 Sep. 1986, p. 15.

[47] BWC/CONF.II/9 (note 46), p. 23, emphasis added.

was as far as norm language went at the 1986 review conference. It was absent both from the Report of the Committee of the Whole and from the Final Declaration.

It is difficult to prove the existence of a norm of customary international law. By its nature it develops over time and emerges in a form often less precise than that of a treaty obligation, and its status is more likely to be disputed. A high participation rate for treaties containing coextensive or identical obligations (e.g., the 102 states parties to the BTWC at the time of the Second Review Conference) does not prove the existence of a norm, but it does support the proposition that such a norm exists. Other vital elements are the practice of states and their voting record on relevant UN resolutions. If states in sufficient numbers refrain from the possession of BTW, ratify or accede to the BTWC, and vote to express their abhorrence of BTW strong evidence for the 'material' element of the norm exists. The 'psychological' element, the sense of legal obligation, is another factor to be considered, as is the question of a 'sufficient' number of states. Thought must be given to whether such arguments lead to majoritarianism in international legislation to the detriment of states' separate sovereignties, of their sovereign right to decide to enter into some treaty obligations but not others, and of the principle of consent to be bound.

Apart from the difficulty inherent in proving its existence, elucidation of the norm is necessary. It is unlikely that the 15 Western delegations responsible (11 of them via association with the EC statement presented by the UK) for norm references in 1986 shared an understanding of the implications of the norm language that they were using or had defined the legal autonomy of the norm from the BTWC which had established it.

International initiatives often have domestic origins, and initiatives in the diplomacy of BTW disarmament have been no exception. The idea of a norm was established by the BTWC, yet it was in some sense additional to the convention (i.e., not wholly and exclusively embodied in it). The idea may have been accepted in the USA in the summer of 1986 less for its legal significance than as a way to assuage inter-agency tensions. It was well known that conflicting attitudes towards the BTWC—and differing assessments of its capacity for recuperation or survival—were complicating the preparation of US policy for the Third Review Conference. US officials were divided regarding the convention's value, and the US Government was unable to give it more than lukewarm support. In this context, norm language performed a useful bridging role in the US policy process and one that was more urgently needed in 1986 than it would be in 1991. By 1991 US confidence in the BTWC as 'the world's principal bulwark'[48] against BTW was unequivocal and the USA was willing (as it had not been in 1986) to join in making diplomatic approaches to non-parties to persuade them of the convention's continuing value.

Perhaps in consequence of this, at the Third Review Conference, norm language was rare. Not only was it absent (as in 1986) from both the Report of the Committee of the Whole and the subsequent Final Declaration; in 1991 (unlike 1986) it did not appear in any of the 106 proposals (double the 1986 total) which were attached to the Report of the Committee of the Whole.[49] Exhaustive

[48] Plenary statement by Ronald F. Lehman, Director of the US Arms Control and Disarmament Agency, to the Third Review Conference on 9 Sep. 1991. Text supplied by the US Delegation.
[49] Third Review Conference document BWC/CONF.III/17, 24 Sep. 1991.

search of the texts of statements delivered in plenary session, as supplied in advance by delegations, shows norm references only in two: those delivered on 10 September 1991 by Director of the US Arms Control and Disarmament Agency Ambassador Ronald Lehman and Ambassador Hendrik Wagenmakers of the Netherlands.

Lehman stated: 'Our strategy [on compliance] supports the international norm against biological and toxin weapons by (i) continuing to draw attention to violations of the BW Convention and the lack of international response to those violations as a threat to the norm.'[50] Wagenmakers, speaking for the 12 EC members, repeated almost verbatim the norm reference made by the British Presidency for the Twelve at the Second Review Conference, as noted above. He stated: 'The Twelve believe that further accessions will reinforce international confidence in the authority of the Convention as the international norm against biological and toxin weapons.'[51]

In view of its 1986 origins, norm language as a means of strengthening the BTW disarmament treaty regime will only command support if it can be sufficiently separated from the argument between those US officials espousing relatively optimistic and those adopting relatively pessimistic attitudes towards the BTWC. This should now be easier. However, the sponsors of norm language will have to demonstrate their support for the BTWC as a permanent international structure and persuade sceptics that by drawing attention to a norm of customary international law they seek to strengthen the BTWC rather than to insure against the contingency of its eventual collapse.

The way in which norm language contributes to confidence in a regime of permanence depends in part on its scope. A norm which was coextensive with the BTWC would logically include the notion of withdrawal, but the only norm which would be of any use would be one confined to prohibitions and corresponding to the prohibitions contained in the convention. Such a norm would therefore render any party which chose to withdraw from the convention still liable to find itself in breach of an international legal obligation if it then went ahead with the development, production, stockpiling, acquisition, retention or transfer of BTW.

If a new norm of customary international law has emerged, identical or coextensive with the prohibitions embodied in the BTWC, the net effect on the treaty regime is not immediately clear. On the one hand, the independent existence of such a norm, equally binding on all states regardless of their treaty status under the convention, suggests that the BTWC has become logically redundant. States' obligations would remain the same if it did not exist. On the other hand, the existence of such a norm renders it futile for parties to try and diminish the constraints on their freedom of action by withdrawing from the convention. Article 43 of the 1969 Vienna Convention on the Law of Treaties is explicit on this point:

43. Obligations imposed by international law independently of a treaty

The invalidity, termination or denunciation of a treaty, *the withdrawal of a party from it*, or the suspension of its operation, as a result of the application of the present Convention or of the provisions of the treaty, shall not in any way impair the duty of any

---

[50] Plenary statement . . . (note 48).
[51] Text supplied by the Delegation of The Netherlands.

State to fulfil any obligation embodied in the treaty to which it would be subject under international law independently of the treaty.[52]

Withdrawal from the BTWC is possible within its provisions (Article XIII, second paragraph). This is not obviously the case with termination, denunciation or suspension, where recourse would have to be had to the Vienna Convention instead. That would be the case in the event that any treaty was alleged to be invalid if these acts were to have legal standing.

The value of norm language consists, first, in persuading parties that there is nothing to be gained from exercising the right of withdrawal from the convention. There is no point in withdrawing because they would still be bound by the obligations imposed on them by international law.

They would, however, free themselves of subordinate and more detailed requirements, such as the confidence-building data exchanges which are only politically and not legally binding because their authority resides solely in the consensual declarations of review conferences. It must therefore remain a high priority for the parties to the BTWC to organize themselves so that participation in the treaty regime brings them sufficient benefits to outweigh the burden (if they perceive it as burdensome) of providing the data required under the confidence-building measures they have agreed.

The value of norm language consists, second, in persuading non-parties that they have nothing to lose from ratifying or acceding to the convention. They are already subject to its prohibitions but do not have the standing to realize its benefits. This argument perceives the treaty regime as producing utility for its participants, whether as beneficiaries of enhanced security alone or potentially of medical, industrial or scientific cooperation as well.

So far norm language has not been a prominent factor in the reinforcement of the regime of permanence. Such language is found in the national statements and proposals of some Western governments and in the committee papers of the 1986 review, but it has not yet been utilized in a final declaration. Its contribution to regime reinforcement is latent and has yet to become substantial.

The best place for a statement of the customary norm as identical or coextensive with the prohibitions embodied in the BTWC may be in the final declaration of a review conference, subsequently repeated in the corresponding follow-up resolution of the UN General Assembly to enhance its authority. However, careful preparation would be necessary in order to secure a text which was both legally correct and politically influential in reinforcing the regime of permanence.

IV. Perpetuation of quinquennial review conferences

One key diplomatic element of the regime of permanence has almost been put into place: the perpetuation of a sequence of quinquennial review conferences stretching into the future without limit, as befits a treaty of unlimited duration.

Article XII of the BTWC only required one review conference to be held. In March 1980 when the delegations of the parties to the BTWC met in Geneva it was by no means certain that they would meet again. At that time the Soviet

[52] The text of the convention is reproduced at URL <http://www.unog.ch/archives/vienna/vien_69.htm>, emphasis added.

Union and its closest allies (Bulgaria was the most vocal on this issue) did not want a commitment to a further review to be included in the Final Declaration. Canada led the delegations which favoured a firm commitment to further review within five years. These positions were far apart, and the issue was closely tied to the central question of clarifying compliance dispute procedures under Article V. Consequently, this issue and articles V and VI were reserved for negotiation after proposals had been completed on all other sections of the Final Declaration by the Draft Elements Group at the working (sub-ambassadorial) level. Negotiation of the remaining issues was entrusted to British Ambassador David Summerhayes, Soviet Ambassador Viktor Issraelyan and Swedish Ambassador Curt Lidgard.[53] Their compromise reflected the opening positions on Article XII but did not unconditionally endorse either of them.

The First Review Conference decided that a further review should take place, at the request of a majority of the parties, not earlier than 1985 nor later than 1990. As late as May 1984 diplomatic discussions in conjunction with a session of the UN Disarmament Commission failed to produce agreement on a date. The United States considered 1986 too late and the Soviet Union considered that date too early. Subsequently, US officials who had favoured 1985 were persuaded of the advantages of delay, and Soviet objections to 1986 diminished. By the end of 1984 Norway (which held the presidency of the First Review Conference and coordinated the difficult 1984 discussions) was able to report that a majority of the parties to the BTWC had decided on 1986 for the holding of the Second Review Conference.[54]

The Second Review Conference left the convening of a subsequent review conference to the decision of a majority of the parties but with a stronger presumption in favour of a five-year interval. At Sweden's instance the words 'not later than 1991' were inserted into the Final Declaration of 1986.[55] Austria, the new president, coordinated simpler consultations than those of 1984, and these led to the decision in favour of 1991.[56]

It was not until the Third Review Conference that the quinquennial principle was adopted on a permanent basis. The Final Declaration of 1991 committed the parties to a fourth review conference, to be held at the request of a majority of the parties to the BTWC no later than 1996. On the initiative of Chile, Panama, Peru and Venezuela[57] the Final Declaration recommended the holding of review conferences at least every five years thereafter, giving them, in the words of the Committee of the Whole, 'the status of regularity'.[58]

The qualifying condition of a majority request is almost meaningless. Like much else in the 1991 Final Declaration, it was copied from the 1986 Final Declaration, which was in turn copied from the 1980 Final Declaration, with insufficient thought apparently being given to its contemporary relevance. The First Review Conference had inserted a qualifying condition in order to secure Soviet acceptance of the possibility of a review date as early as 1985. The situ-

[53] Sims, *The Diplomacy of Biological Disarmament* (note 3), pp. 150–51.
[54] Sims, *The Diplomacy of Biological Disarmament* (note 3), p. 319. The decision was recorded in UN General Assembly Resolution 39/65D, 12 Dec. 1984.
[55] BWC/CONF.II/9 (note 46), p. 33.
[56] The decision was recorded in UN General Assembly Resolution 45/57B, 4 Dec. 1990.
[57] BWC/CONF.III/17 (note 49), p. 72.
[58] BWC/CONF.III/17 (note 49), p. 6.

ation had changed and the condition ought to have been deleted, but it was retained in the Final Declaration of 1996.[59]

The Fifth Review Conference in 2001 should remove the qualifying condition and turn the 1991 recommendation (repeated in 1996) into a firm decision which would place the pattern of reviews on a permanent basis. This would give quinquennial reviews 'the status of regularity' without ambiguity or the need for laborious diplomatic consultation on each occasion in order to agree a date before the appropriate UN General Assembly resolution is introduced.

This new element of the regime of permanence has implications for the relationship between the BTWC and its eventual protocol as regards review. The protocol under negotiation in the Ad Hoc Group envisages a review procedure closer to that of the CWC, while favouring the principle of quinquennial reviews. The organization to be established by the protocol would be governed by a conference of states parties to the protocol, and it would meet in review mode every five years in addition to its annual session and other sessions provided for in Article IX of the protocol.

However, in negotiating Article XIII on review of the protocol the Ad Hoc Group has also recognized the desirability of synchronizing the two sets of review conferences, since all parties to the protocol will by definition be parties to the BTWC. If, for example, the protocol were to enter into force in the year 2006, its first review conference (i.e., the Conference of States Parties of the new organization, meeting in review mode) might well coincide with the Seventh Review Conference of the BTWC in 2011. It might immediately precede or follow the Seventh Review Conference. The word 'coincide', currently favoured for inclusion in the protocol, has the advantage of leaving flexible the precise order of events (on which the Ad Hoc Group is not agreed) while indicating that there should be some systematic relationship between the two sets of reviews, and as great a proximity as possible between the conferences.[60]

The assumption is made here that the roster of parties to the protocol will approximate increasingly over time to that of the BTWC, favouring greater cooperation between the institutions of the two instruments. It would, however, be premature to assume an early and total convergence of the two sets of review conferences, especially if the protocol enters into force significantly earlier or later than a BTWC review conference year. Scheduling reviews for maximum convenience may be more realistic in the short term. An established schedule of sixth, seventh and subsequent review conferences of the BTWC—desirable in any case as an element of the regime of permanence—has the additional advantage of providing fixed points in time which the Conference of States Parties to the protocol can use in planning its review conference sessions.

The perpetuation of quinquennial reviews does not, of itself, solve all problems for a treaty. This is evident from the history of the 1968 Treaty on the Non-Proliferation of Nuclear Weapons (Non-Proliferation Treaty, NPT), but it does add to the emergent regime of permanence. This is especially important

[59] However, it was retained in a form ('at the request of the majority of States Parties, or in any case not later than 2001') which could be construed as a requisition clause additional to the 2001 commitment through the use of the disjunctive 'or'. BWC/CONF.IV/9 (note 27), p. 27.
[60] Pearson, G. S. and Sims, N. A., 'Article XIII: review of the protocol', eds G. S. Pearson and M. R. Dando, *The BTWC Protocol: Evaluation Papers*, Evaluation Paper no. 11 (Department of Peace Studies, University of Bradford: Bradford, Nov. 1999), pp. 6–7.

given the tenuous position of the review process and its uncertain periodicity in the earlier history of the BTWC, notably in 1980 and 1984.

The uses made of review conferences, once their periodicity has been established, depend on diplomatic determination. Drafting skills can be deployed to support elements that favour the regime of permanence, which can then be negotiated through to the final declaration of each conference.

V. Conclusions

This chapter examines the concept of a regime of permanence through developments in international law and diplomacy.

The withdrawal of Geneva Protocol reservations pertaining to a purported right of retaliation removes an asymmetry of obligations with the renunciation of BTW under the BTWC. It sends a clear signal that biological and toxin warfare has been completely renounced under two different categories of international law. The emergent norm of customary international law, identical or coextensive with the prohibitions of the BTWC, is more equivocal in its effect. It remains latent rather than actualized, but in the right circumstances the norm may make a positive contribution to reinforcing expectations of durability for the convention.

Both these developments are extrinsic to the BTWC in the sense that they arise from actions taken by states in other legal capacities than that of parties to the convention. Nevertheless their relevance to the BTWC is clearly established through the history of the review process as traced in this chapter.

The third contribution to a regime of permanence examined here is, on the other hand, intrinsic to the convention. The evolution of the review conference has been made possible by creative use of Article XII. It has been the deliberate choice of the parties to the BTWC to hold more than the one review conference which Article XII required. The review conferences have evolved into a regular pattern of diplomacy, capable of being established on a permanent basis. They have provided the BTWC, from its own resources, with a durable institution of cumulative authority at the level of politically binding commitments agreed by consensus.

In the absence of a continuous administration these are the elements of a regime of permanence—for want of a better alternative. The regime would be strengthened by the establishment of a permanent organization to give the BTWC a continuous administration in the service of its parties: an organization dedicated to BTW disarmament.

The parties may eventually arrive at this point. Article IX of the draft protocol being negotiated in the Ad Hoc Group provides for an Organization for the Prohibition of Bacteriological (Biological) and Toxin Weapons. It is likely to be governed by a conference of states parties with an executive council, a technical secretariat led by a director-general, a scientific advisory board, a confidentiality commission (all copied from the CWC and its Organisation for the Prohibition of Chemical Weapons) and a cooperation committee to give effect to a framework for promotion of international cooperation under Article X of the BTWC (Article VII of the draft protocol). Although not yet agreed its outline has begun to take shape, and in 1999 there was already competition for the seat of the organization between Geneva, Switzerland, and The Hague, the Netherlands.

The eventual organization will belong solely to the parties to the protocol which brings it into being. If only a minority of the parties to the BTWC accept the protocol, its membership will remain small. If, on the other hand, most of the parties to the BTWC also become parties to the protocol the membership of the organization will embrace most states with obligations under the BTWC. Such an organization may indirectly provide a functional substitute for the permanent organization which the convention has never had. However, it will be a long process, and legally it will be difficult to confer functions on the protocol organization which derive from the BTWC rather than the protocol. In particular, care will have to be taken to avoid conferring either rights or responsibilities on those parties to the BTWC which remain outside the protocol and, consequently, outside its organization.

There is still therefore a problem of institutional deficit for the BTWC which has yet to be addressed. That issue is discussed in section IV of the final chapter in this volume. The tentative nature of the regime of permanence examined in this chapter reflects the institutional deficit. It may also be the case that the institutional deficit has persisted over a quarter of a century in part because expectations of durability have taken shape only gradually and uncertainly among the parties to the BTWC.

7. Towards convergence: the treaty regime and its future

I. The evolution of the treaty regime and its sectoral regimes

This book examines the elements of the treaty regime flowing from the 1972 Biological and Toxin Weapons Convention sector by sector. This chapter assesses the conclusions which can be drawn about the evolution of the treaty regime in each sector and overall. It begins by recapitulating the principal themes explored in the preceding chapters.

The regime of compliance

The regime of compliance has evolved the furthest. Its original elements embrace requirements for national implementation of the central obligations of the BTWC, a consultative procedure including the foundations of a contingency mechanism for handling compliance disputes, and provisions for complaint and assistance. Since 1986–87 a sub-regime of confidence-building measures has been added. In varying degrees, according to the original element in question, the regime of compliance has progressively elaborated norms, rules and expectations of behaviour, and it has gradually added procedures over and above those specified in the convention to give effect to those norms, rules and expectations. However, full (as distinct from occasional) participation in the CBM programme has remained limited to a minority of states parties, even since its enhancement in 1991. The Third Review Conference attempted to improve the quality and quantity of the CBM declarations from 15 April 1992[1] but with little success. The experience of Cuba's invocation of the Article V contingency mechanism in 1997 showed that multilateral consultation regarding compliance concerns could be handled successfully, although the episode was also used as an argument for new procedures. Every element in the regime of compliance remains underdeveloped, and each can be strengthened. The process of investing the convention with elements of a working system which ought to have been integral to its regime of compliance from the beginning is far from complete.[2]

One of the most pressing issues which the parties to the BTWC confront in this sector is the prospect of grafting verification provisions on to the convention. If a scheme of verification, whether wholly or only partly intrusive, were to be introduced, it would either augment the existing elements analysed in chapters 2 and 3 in this volume or supersede them. In the latter case it would transform the regime of compliance into a different one from the regime which has evolved through successive reviews. The path to that eventuality has proved tortuous. First, the prospective measures of verification under study had to be collectively identified, classified and assessed by the scientific and technical

---

[1] The Third Review Conference stated that, from 15 Apr. 1992, parties to the BTWC under CBM E: 'shall be prepared to submit copies of the legislation or regulations or written details of other measures on request to the UN Department for Disarmament Affairs or to an individual State Party'. Third Review Conference document BWC/CONF.III/22/Add.3, 27 Sep. 1991, pp. 18–19.

[2] See chapters 2 and 3 in this volume.

experts of governments. This VEREX exercise,[3] initiated by the Third Review Conference, was completed in 1992–93 and its report was considered by the Special Conference in 1994. It, in turn, mandated a new Ad Hoc Group to consider measures to strengthen the BTWC, including possible verification measures. Verification has now reached the stage of active political consideration in the Ad Hoc Group, convened in 1995, which has been meeting in negotiating mode since 1997. However, it is by no means certain that, even if agreement is found on the practice of verification, there will be a smooth or easy transition from the negotiation of verification measures by the Ad Hoc Group to their adoption by a second Special Conference and then to the ratification of the protocol containing them by all parties to the BTWC.[4]

The regime of development

The regime of development is still contentious, much reviewed but with little substance. Aspiration far outstrips achievement. One reason is the absence of consensus among the parties as to the nature and extent of their obligations under Article X of the BTWC. There is a widening gap between the original content of Article X and its reinterpretation by successive review conferences. This raises the question of how far a disarmament treaty can bear reinterpretation as an instrument for the promotion of technology transfer and other economic development policies. Repeated, unproductive rhetorical clashes between North and South tempt some developed country parties to discard the development orientation of the convention altogether. However, that would alienate developing countries in those parts of the world where biological and toxin weapons present little military threat. For those countries Article X provides the main incentive to join the BTWC. A more constructive response is to examine the potential of the convention as a framework for international cooperation in the prevention of disease. Within this framework it may be possible to identify and promote cooperative programmes, perhaps for vaccine development and distribution or for epidemiological surveillance. What is most important is that such programmes should, as a matter of deliberate policy, confer disproportionate benefits on the neediest people living in the less-developed countries of the world. In addition, they should simultaneously relate closely to the focus of the BTWC, reinforcing the regime of compliance and thereby encompassing additional safeguards against BTW.[5]

The regime of permanence

The regime of permanence is a new concept. It groups together a number of ways in which parties can emphasize the unlimited duration of the convention. Its importance lies in the political–psychological reinforcement which the treaty regime as a whole derives from perceptions of permanence. Already some actions have been taken, in withdrawing or modifying Geneva Protocol reservations, which accentuate the absolute renunciation of BTW. This is one method

[3] The Ad Hoc Group of Governmental Experts to Identify and Examine Potential Verification Measures from a Scientific and Technical Standpoint (VEREX) is discussed at length in chapter 4, sections VIII–XI.
[4] See chapter 4 in this volume.
[5] See chapter 5 in this volume.

of enhancing the credibility of the convention which is readily available, costs nothing and was successfully pioneered by 12 parties between 1972 and 1992. Since then 4 other parties have followed their example. Beyond that method there is the possibility of reinforcing the treaty regime through agreement on the definition of a corresponding norm of customary international law. These measures have in common the removal of legal asymmetries or inconsistencies. They aim to clarify and give greater salience to those parts of the BTWC that already emphasize its irreversibility. The pattern of review conferences has also been important in giving expression to this expectation of permanence.[6]

II. Towards convergence

The three sectors of the overall treaty regime defined here are: a multilayered regime of compliance, a regime of development and a regime of permanence. Within each sector progress has been uncertain, and there has been uneven growth within and between sectors.

The regime of compliance has evolved the furthest, but even within that sector it is far from clear that the efforts of the parties to promote compliance with the BTWC have been sufficient to safeguard biological disarmament. Only with difficulty have the parties reached agreement on which additional measures are the most necessary to negotiate in order to strengthen the convention by reinforcing its regime of compliance.

The regime of development and the regime of permanence have evolved less far than the regime of compliance. Each has its own problems. Their importance lies in their potential evolution, without which the regime of compliance is unlikely to prosper on its own.

This chapter continues to examine the evolution of the overall treaty regime. A central argument is that in order for the regime to be steered into a constructive evolution greater efforts have to be made to identify and encourage a convergence of interests among different groups of parties to the BTWC. In the absence of a global trade-off—which (as argued in section VII) is not available—such convergence will only be realized by a series of separate solutions which together emphasize the superordinate goal of a BTW-free world. Only consciousness of a shared superordinate goal can overcome differences by pointing out to the parties what it is that unites them.

A well-balanced treaty regime requires a certain convergence in the lines of evolution followed in each of its sectors. This chapter emphasizes the need for the parties to maximize cross-sectoral equilibrium in the overall regime. It also draws attention to two further gaps in the treaty regime which must be filled.

One gap is institutional. It is necessary to remedy the institutional deficit of the BTWC through interim arrangements pending the eventual integration of the convention and its strengthening protocol, with the latter contributing its organization to the whole regime.[7]

The other gap concerns the regulation of research, which the BTWC does not mention. Without such regulation the convention is vulnerable to undermining. A regime of research is needed, at least as urgently now as when originally

---

[6] See chapter 6 in this volume.
[7] See section IV below.

envisaged in 1968–69, in order to complement and reinforce the existing sectoral regimes and to complete the construction of an overall regime which promotes the goal of a world free of BTW.[8]

III. An evolutionary approach for a fragile organism

This study favours an evolutionary approach in analysis and prescription that takes into account the vulnerable nature of the treaty regime of biological disarmament.

Emphasis on evolution in making the BTWC work better does not exclude the negotiation of a strengthening protocol, although it does preclude uncritical acceptance. This approach focuses on maximizing the benefits which can be derived concurrently from what already exists. It draws attention to the possibilities, latent in the text of the BTWC, for reinforcing the treaty regime by clarification of provisions and elaboration of procedures. It also favours exploration of those possibilities and deprecates the tendency to dismiss the convention as irremediably feeble or fatally flawed. This view affirms the continuing value of the convention but without complacency, for it accepts that its treaty regime is a fragile organism.

This approach has certain policy implications. It implies a continuing interest in improving the review process and in endowing the treaty regime with supportive institutions to enable it to work better between reviews. It also implies an openness to advancing on all fronts so that the evolution of all sectors proceeds towards convergence and at a rate which does not unbalance the overall regime. This requires oversight and steering. The institutional deficit cannot safely be prolonged.

The evolution of the convention regime may usefully be complemented by the negotiation of a strengthening protocol. If sensitively handled, this complementarity should produce a more robust and fully integrated disarmament regime as both the BTWC and the protocol attract the widest possible participation. Skill will be needed to maximize the value that can be derived from the continued evolution of the convention regime and the entry into force of the protocol while steering the two processes towards eventual integration. This may be exemplified by consideration of how to remedy the institutional deficit of the BTWC.

IV. Remedying the institutional deficit of the BTWC

Institutional improvements may hold the key to further, balanced evolution of the treaty regime. Conversely, perpetuation of the BTWC's long-standing institutional deficit threatens to delay progress in steering that evolution in a constructive direction to the benefit of all parties.

The Third Review Conference considered but did not approve the creation of a small 'secretariat unit' dedicated to helping the parties honour their newly agreed CBM commitments. This failure disappointed those governments and non-governmental organizations which held the view that a secretariat unit

---

[8] See sections V and VI below.

within the United Nations was the minimal acceptable outcome of their efforts in 1990–91 to secure intersessional machinery for the BTWC.

The Fourth Review Conference gave unprecedented space to NGO contributions, but no advance was made on the institutional front. There is still no secretariat dedicated to the support of the convention or of its CBM programme. There is also no intersessional committee to give the convention the continuous support and oversight it has always needed. This institutional deficit remains a major weakness of the BTWC.

The issue has declined in salience since 1990–91. The institutional deficit has been masked by the existence of the two successive ad hoc groups: VEREX in 1992–93 and the new group created by the 1994 Special Conference. Since 1995 the current Ad Hoc Group has met several times each year, more intensively since it moved into negotiating mode in 1997, and some 40–50 parties have maintained a high level of interest in its activities. However, like VEREX, the group has a specific and limited mandate which would preclude it from overseeing the operation of the BTWC on a continuing basis, even if it were not preoccupied with bringing the negotiation of its draft protocol to a successful conclusion by the year 2001.

After 2001 the underlying institutional deficit of the convention will become evident again. It never went away: the 'strengthening' process of 1992–2001 merely, regrettably, obscured the urgency of the institutional imperative. It will soon re-emerge.

Even if the protocol negotiations are successful, the new organization to be created by Article IX of the protocol (as currently drafted[9]) will be open only to those parties to the BTWC which also join the protocol. It is hoped that, ultimately, the two rosters of parties will be coterminous. In the short term, this seems unlikely. There will therefore be a continuing need for the parties to the BTWC to have their own institutional machinery for some years after the entry into force of the protocol. This machinery may be designed to consist of supportive institutions for an interim period pending eventual integration of the convention and the protocol.

Supportive institutions are needed to sustain the BTWC during the interim period after the entry into force of the protocol (and even more so pending that event) so long as any significant disparity exists between the rosters of parties to the convention and to the protocol. However, it is important to emphasize the interim character of these arrangements.

Supportive institutions can be put in place by the Fifth Review Conference on a temporary basis to bridge the gap between the fifth and sixth review conferences, and probably also the sixth and seventh conferences. It will be clearly understood that these arrangements are to lapse when there is a sufficient degree of identity between the two rosters of parties and when there is sufficient capacity in the organization set up under the protocol to care for the needs of the convention as well. Synchrony of reviews in 2011 might provide the occasion for this to happen.

The Fifth Review Conference should appoint an interim or intersessional oversight committee which is entrusted with maintenance of the convention and

---

[9] Procedural Report of the Ad Hoc Group, Twentieth Session, Ad Hoc Group document BWC/AD HOC GROUP/52, 11 Aug. 2000, part I, pp. 113–26.

its effective operation until the Sixth Review Conference. The oversight committee might be elected ad hoc in 2001 or it might consist of the bureau of the Fifth Review Conference[10] with continuing responsibility after the conference ends. In 2006 the Sixth Review Conference could renew or amend the mandate of the committee and change its membership as necessary. If, by that time, the new protocol has entered into force there will be a need to ensure that the oversight committee of the BTWC works closely with the organization of the protocol. If by 2011 the two rosters are approximately identical the interim machinery and the permanent machinery can be combined into one organization to serve both the protocol and the BTWC.

The prospect of eventual integration of the two instruments with a single organization should not be allowed to obscure the need for interim arrangements. Supportive institutions would give the convention the continuity of attention and the collective identity it has lacked. Such institutions would serve all the parties to the BTWC equally, irrespective of their status with regard to the protocol.

The full set of supportive institutions earlier proposed—committee of oversight, legal advisory panel, scientific advisory panel and secretariat[11]—may be considered excessive as interim machinery. However, a small secretariat in support of the oversight committee will be indispensable. There is no danger of governments creating a cumbersome bureaucracy; they are more likely to spend too little on the infrastructure of biological disarmament than too much.

What institutions cannot guarantee is the convergence of the regime of compliance, the regime of development and the regime of permanence which the overall equilibrium of the treaty regime requires. However, they can at least monitor the pace and direction of regime evolution in each sector, as well as steering cross-sectoral evolution. The institutions can also encourage the parties to the BTWC to seize opportunities to steer its sectors along convergent lines for the benefit of the overall regime and the eventual integration of the BTWC and the protocol.

V. Comparison of two regimes

In approaching the issue of regulating research it is useful to compare the current state of the regime flowing from the BTWC with that envisaged by the United Kingdom when it promoted its Microbiological Warfare Convention in 1968–69.[12]

---

[10] This would revive an idea of the late Ambassador Charles C. Flowerree, who led the US delegation to the First Review Conference. Flowerree, C. C., 'On tending arms control agreements', *Washington Quarterly*, vol. 13, no. 1 (winter 1990), pp. 199–214.

[11] Sims, N. A., 'Organizational aspects with regard to possible verification tasks under the Biological Weapons Convention', ed. S. J. Lundin, *Views on Possible Verification Measures for the Biological Weapons Convention*, SIPRI Chemical & Biological Warfare Studies, no. 12 (Oxford University Press: Oxford, 1991), pp. 45–48.

[12] Eighteen-Nation Disarmament Committee document ENDC/231, 6 Aug. 1968; Eighteen-Nation Disarmament Committee document ENDC/255, 10 July 1969; and Eighteen-Nation Disarmament Committee document ENDC/255/Rev.1, 26 Aug. 1969. The expansion of the 18-member body to 26 members took place in 2 stages: Japan and Mongolia were admitted in July 1969, and Argentina, Hungary, Morocco, the Netherlands, Pakistan and Yugoslavia were admitted in August. The change of name was also delayed. In retrospect, for purposes of revision, the British draft convention came to be referred to as Conference of the Committee on Disarmament document CCD/255.

The Microbiological (later Biological) Warfare Convention first advocated by the British Government in 1968 was submitted as a draft treaty in 1969 and, slightly revised to encompass toxins, resubmitted in 1970.[13] This draft remained the official British preference until September 1971 when—together with Canada, Italy and the Netherlands—the UK co-sponsored the text which was to become the BTWC together with the United States, the Soviet Union and its Warsaw Pact allies.[14] The BTWC lacked the explicit ban on BTW use which was to have comprised Article I of the convention envisaged by the UK.

The British initiative had targeted warfare first and weapons second so a strict comparison of like with like is not possible. Nevertheless, an attempt at comparison was made by Matthew Meselson, Martin M. Kaplan and Mark A. Mokulsky. Treating the concept of verification more broadly than some commentators, they compared 'the verification regime created by the BWC and enhanced by the agreements achieved at the Review Conferences and at the UN with the verification provisions of the first draft treaty for biological weapons disarmament, that proposed by Great Britain in July 1969'.[15] Writing between the second and third review conferences, they concluded that the regime flowing from the BTWC, as augmented by UN decisions, already represented an advance on that envisaged in the draft treaty of 1969. They made the following specific comparisons:

The British proposal would have given the UN Secretary-General authority to investigate allegations of the use of biological weapons, an authority he now indeed possesses, not from the BWC itself, but rather from the more recent actions of the General Assembly. In the 1969 proposal, as now, UN investigations of other allegations of non-compliance, such as production or stockpiling of biological weapons, cannot be undertaken solely on the authority of the Secretary-General, but require a request from the Security Council. The annual data exchanges agreed to by the Second BWC Review Conference, however, go well beyond the provisions of the original British proposal, which had no such reporting provisions. Thus, although the verification of biological and toxin weapons disarmament can certainly be strengthened further . . . there has been considerable progress beyond the British draft treaty of 1969 and beyond the BWC itself.[16]

In making this comparison Meselson, Kaplan and Mokulsky did not comment on the far-reaching constraint on research which the UK was proposing. The obligation 'not to conduct, assist or permit research aimed at production of the kind prohibited' under the British draft convention (i.e., production of 'microbial or other biological agents or toxins of types and in quantities that have no justification for prophylactic or other peaceful purposes' and of 'ancillary equipment and vectors the purpose of which is to facilitate the use of such agents or toxins for hostile purposes'[17]) would have entailed a regime of correspondingly enhanced openness. This had been recognized by the UK:

---

[13] Conference of the Committee on Disarmament document CCD/255/Rev.2, 8 Aug. 1970.

[14] Conference of the Committee on Disarmament document CCD/353, 28 Sep. 1971.

[15] Meselson, M., Kaplan, M. M. and Mokulsky, M. A., 'Verification of biological and toxin weapons disarmament', eds F. Calogero, M. L. Goldberger and S. P. Kapitza, *Verification, Monitoring Disarmament* (Westview Press: Boulder, Colo., London, 1990), p. 157.

[16] Meselson, Kaplan and Mokulsky (note 15).

[17] Draft Article II of CCD/255/Rev.2 (note 13). 'Protective purposes' was added later.

[The convention] should also provide for the appropriate civil medical or health authorities to have access to all research work which might give rise to allegations that the obligations imposed by the Convention were not being fulfilled. Such research work should be open to international investigation if so required and should also be open to public scrutiny to the maximum extent compatible with national security and the protection of industrial and commercial processes.[18]

The failure of the BTWC to mention research, let alone constrain it, was only slightly ameliorated by the addition of 'development' to the list of activities prohibited in respect of biological warfare agents, toxins, weapons, equipment and means of delivery. The constraints on research that were envisaged in 1968 would have entailed such openness that much of the CBM sub-regime of 1986–87, even as enhanced and extended in 1991,[19] would have been largely anticipated from the outset of the convention's existence.

Whether this regime of openness would have been legally binding is less clear. In 1968 the UK had tentatively proposed 'a competent body of experts, established under the auspices of the United Nations'[20] to investigate allegations of non-compliance, but it did not specifically include this proposal in its 1969 draft convention. However, even after 1991 the CBMs have only the status of political commitments voluntarily assumed by the parties to the convention. They are arguably weaker than the corresponding regime of openness under the British draft convention would have been. The latter would have been a corollary to a legally binding obligation, integral to the treaty text, 'not to conduct, assist or permit research'.

Meselson, Kaplan and Mokulsky are correct in their comparison of the investigative powers given to the UN Secretary-General and the Security Council, respectively, and also in their statement that there were no 'reporting provisions' in the British proposal.[21] The UK, however, had seen openness in research as one of several functional substitutes for verification, arguing that: 'verification, in the sense in which the term is normally used in disarmament negotiations, is not possible . . . because the organisms which would be used are required for medical and veterinary uses and could be produced quickly, cheaply and without special facilities either in established laboratories or in makeshift facilities'.[22]

Indirect means of demonstrating compliance thus must be found instead. A similar interest in openness as the best means of demonstrating compliance with the BTWC, sometimes called 'indirect verification', was also a component of schemes proposed by Barend ter Haar and the Federation of American Scientists in 1991.[23]

All such plans suffered from the disadvantage that they could not be attached to a legally binding constraint on research, because there is no such constraint

---

[18] UK, Working paper on microbiological warfare, ENDC/231 (note 12), para. 7.
[19] See chapter 3 in this volume.
[20] ENDC/231 (note 12), para. 8.
[21] Meselson, Kaplan and Mokulsky (note 15), p. 157.
[22] ENDC/231 (note 12), para. 3.
[23] ter Haar, B., Center for Strategic and International Studies (CSIS), *The Future of Biological Weapons*, Washington Paper no. 151 (Praeger: New York, 1991), pp. 107–110, 155–158; Federation of American Scientists (FAS), 'Implementation of the proposals for a verification protocol to the Biological Weapons Convention', reprinted in *Arms Control*, vol. 12, no. 2 (Sep. 1991), pp. 255–78; and FAS, 'Proposals for the Third Review Conference of the Biological Weapons Convention', *Arms Control*, vol. 12, no. 2 (Sep. 1991), pp. 240–54. The schemes are also discussed in section VI of chapter 4 in this volume.

in the BTWC. Adherence to the British proposal would have ensured that there was. Section VI explores how, given that failure, a regime of research can still be integrated into the BTWC treaty regime.

VI. The BTWC and a regime of research

Research and use are among the major lacunae of the convention. In considering how to integrate a regime of research into the BTWC treaty regime, the experience of dealing with the gap over use is a convenient starting point.

In 1996 the parties to the BTWC utilized the Final Declaration of the Fourth Review Conference to make explicit what was previously implicit: namely, that any use of BTW by a party to the convention would involve a prior violation of the BTWC. Logically, any use of BTW must have been preceded by at least one of the activities—development, production, stockpiling, acquisition or retention—which are prohibited by Article I.

The Final Declaration of the Fourth Review Conference stressed this point in three places. First, in the ninth paragraph of the 'solemn declaration' which opens the Final Declaration, the parties 'solemnly declare. . . . their recognition that purposes of this Convention include the prohibition of the use of biological weapons as contrary to the purpose of the Convention'. Second, in the third paragraph of the Article I section of the Final Declaration, 'The Conference reaffirms that the use by the States Parties, in any way and under any circumstances, of microbial or other biological agents or toxins, that is not consistent with prophylactic, protective or other peaceful purposes, is effectively a violation of Article I of the Convention.' Third, in the seventh paragraph of the Article IV section of the Final Declaration, 'The Conference reaffirms that under all circumstances the use of bacteriological (biological) and toxin weapons is effectively prohibited by the Convention.'[24]

By making this logic explicit and by giving it prominence at three points in the 1996 Final Declaration the parties to the BTWC went as far as they could towards incorporating a ban on use within the treaty regime. They thereby minimized the need for formal amendment of the convention to be undertaken through the procedures of Article XI and diminished the support which Iran might otherwise have attracted for its proposal to invoke Article XI in order to add 'use' to the title of the convention and to Article I.[25] The 'solemn declaration' reference to 'purposes' also ensured that any use of BTW by one of the 18 signatories which had not ratified the convention would be in breach of its obligation, under Article 18 of the 1969 Vienna Convention on the Law of Treaties, 'to refrain from acts which would defeat the object and purpose of a treaty when: (*a*) it has signed the treaty . . . until it shall have made its intention clear not to become a party to the treaty'.[26]

---

[24] Fourth Review Conference document BWC/CONF.IV/9, 6 Dec. 1996, pp. 15, 19.

[25] Islamic Republic of Iran, Fourth Review Conference document BWC/CONF.IV/COW/WP.2, 1996; and Zanders, J. P. and Eckstein, S., 'The prohibition of "use" under the BTWC: backgrounder on relevant development during the negotiations, 1969–1972', reproduced at URL <http://www.sipri.se/cbw/research/btwc-use.pdf>, Dec. 1996.

[26] The Vienna Convention on the Law of Treaties is reproduced at URL <http://www.unog.ch/archives/vienna/vien_69.htm.

Research, however, cannot so easily be incorporated within the BTWC treaty regime. There are three reasons for this.

First, there are problems of definition of the nature and purpose of research which make a ban on BTW research less meaningful and less unambiguous than a ban on BTW use. It is not immediately clear at what point a line of research crosses the threshold of BTW-relevance into the area of prohibition. However, as is shown below, the parties to the BTWC have already begun to define this threshold.

Second, a ban on research does not flow as logically from the Article I prohibitions as does a ban on the use on BTW. This is largely because use follows the commission of one or more of the prohibited acts, but research necessarily precedes it.

Third, there is no existing constraint on BTW-relevant research in treaty or customary law comparable to the constraints on use which antedated the BTWC. Use of BTW was already subject to certain restrictions (albeit incomplete, and imperfectly applied) under both the treaty law of the 1925 Geneva Protocol and the relevant norm of international customary law.

It is arguable that, in respect of research on toxins, as distinct from biological weapons, there is a constraint upon parties to the 1993 Chemical Weapons Convention. Although research is not listed among the activities prohibited by Article I of the CWC, commentators on the CWC have interpreted the ban on 'development' of chemical weapons in paragraph 1(a) of Article I as encompassing research which is not permitted. Walter Krutzsch and Ralf Trapp observed:

As far as the prohibited activities under subparagraph (a) are concerned: '*develop*' is by virtue of its purpose, the preparation of the production of chemical weapons *as distinct from permitted research*. This prohibited objective might also materialize and become obvious through specific equipment used and methods applied. The difference between research for purposes not prohibited and development of chemical weapons is also important for Article III, subparagraph 1(d), which stipulates declarations of facilities designed, constructed or used since January 1946 primarily for development of chemical weapons.[27]

Krutzsch and Trapp also noted that in Article XI, paragraph 2(a), of the CWC 'the general right of all States Parties to develop, produce, acquire, retain, transfer, use and conduct research with chemicals is repeated'[28] from Article VI, paragraph 1. However, the words 'and conduct research with', which occur in Article XI, paragraph 2(a), are not found in Article VI, paragraph 1. The implication may still be drawn from Article XI, paragraph 2(a) that the general right to conduct research with chemicals is constrained to the same extent (i.e., by Article I) as the general right to develop, produce, acquire, retain, transfer or use chemicals.

The CWC covers toxins, and most parties to the BTWC are also parties to the CWC. If the interpretation of the CWC set out above is accepted, there is a treaty law constraint on research that is relevant to one part of the BTWC which already applies to most parties. Apart from that possibility, however, which

[27] Krutzsch, W. and Trapp, R., *A Commentary on the Chemical Weapons Convention* (Martinus Nijhoff: Dordrecht, 1994), p. 13, emphasis added.
[28] Krutzsch and Trapp (note 27), p. 215.

only applies to research on toxins, the incorporation of research into the BTWC treaty regime has to proceed without the advantages of the pre-existing restrictions which attended the incorporation of a ban on use.

Incorporation of research within the BTWC treaty regime can proceed by the endogenous route through the final declarations of successive review conferences. It began in 1991 when the Article I section of the Final Declaration of the Third Review Conference included, as its fourth and seventh paragraphs:

The Conference notes that experimentation involving open-air release of pathogens or toxins harmful to man, animals or plants that has no justification for prophylactic, protective or other peaceful purposes is inconsistent with the undertakings contained in Article I.

. . .

On the basis of the principle that sciences should support quality of life, the Conference appeals through the States Parties to their scientific communities to continue to support only activities that have justification under the Biological and Toxin Weapons Convention for prophylactic, protective or other peaceful purposes, and refrain from activities which are in breach of obligations deriving from provisions of the Convention.[29]

In 1996 the Fourth Review Conference repeated the statement on experimentation involving open-air release of pathogens or toxins. It became paragraph 7 of the Article I section of its Final Declaration. The seventh paragraph of the Article I section from 1991 was repeated as the eighth paragraph of the Article I section in 1996 with several changes.[30] Among these, the 'quality of life' subordinate clause was omitted, and 'to continue to support' was changed to 'to lend their support'.

Building on these repeated statements on 'experimentation' and 'activities', the Fifth Review Conference in 2001 could expand the relevant content of its Final Declaration. It might, for example, return to the language of the British draft conventions of 1969 and 1970 and state that the parties recognize an obligation 'not to conduct, assist or permit research aimed at production of the kind prohibited'[31] under Article I of the BTWC.

It might also declare that research and development are so intricately related to each other that, in order for the ban on BTW development to be upheld, it is necessary for research to be constrained by the same condition. Research would then require 'justification for prophylactic, protective or other peaceful purposes':[32] the same set of criteria by which development and production are already governed. The general purpose criterion would be understood as also encompassing research.

As noted above, it is not immediately clear at what point a line of research crosses the threshold of BTW-relevance into the area of prohibition. That practical problem would remain, but the burden of proof would be shifted to the

[29] Third Review Conference document BWC/CONF.III/22/Add.2, 27 Sep. 1991, p. 3.
[30] BWC/CONF.IV/9 (note 24), p. 16. The text reads: 'The Conference appeals through the States Parties to their scientific communities to lend their support only to activities that have justification for prophylactic, protective and other peaceful purposes, and refrain from undertaking or supporting activities which are in breach of the obligations deriving from provisions of the Convention.'
[31] United Kingdom, ENDC/255 (note 12); ENDC/255/Rev.1 (note 12); and CCD/255/Rev.2 (note 13).
[32] Article I of the BTWC. The text of the BTWC is available at the SIPRI Chemical and Biological Warfare Project Internet site, URL <http://projects.sipri.se/cbw/cbw-mainpage.html>. It is reproduced as annexe A in this volume.

practitioner of research once it was agreed that research was encompassed by the general purpose criterion of the BTWC.

Acceptance of that principle is the point from which the search for practical solutions with more precise definitions can proceed. In the context of the obligation continuously to demonstrate compliance, groups of experts might be commissioned to advise the parties collectively on areas of research which should be avoided or more carefully regulated. This could be accomplished through the interim institutional arrangements recommended in section IV of this chapter and eventually through the new organization.

If the Fifth Review Conference were to record acceptance of the principle, it would also recognize the desirability of closing a tempting avenue that is currently open to a government intent upon starting, or retaining, an offensive R&D capability with regard to BTW. It would achieve this goal 'by bringing offensive BW research explicitly within the remit of the Convention so that arguments cannot be made that a piece of work is offensive research and not offensive development'.[33]

The unsuccessful attempt by Iran to amend the BTWC in respect of use[34] makes it even less likely that the convention will be formally amended in respect of research. As noted above, in 1996 the Fourth Review Conference opted for a different method of emphasizing the ban on BTW use. Alan P. Zelicoff has reported that: 'Privately, many delegations expressed concern about convening an amendment conference. There has never been such a proceeding in the BWC, and there was considerable concern that the entirety of the BWC could be opened to amendment in such a process, which could undermine the Convention's success.'[35] States parties chose the Final Declaration route instead of formal amendment of the convention. This is also the most promising way of bringing research within the ambit of the BTWC treaty regime.

An evolving regime of research may eventually come to play a part in achieving the convergence of interests on which the future survival of the BTWC depends. This is the subject of section VII.

VII. Convergence of interests

The future condition of the treaty regime depends not only on a propitious climate in the wider international political environment, but also on the demonstrated interest of the parties to the BTWC in nurturing it. That consistent theme of this volume bears repetition with a closer examination of the concept of interest.

It might be supposed that the impetus for steering the treaty regime into a constructive and well-balanced evolution could be provided by a perceived identity of interest. At the most fundamental level, there is a universal interest in not being attacked with biological or toxin weapons. Adhering to the BTWC as a security policy and working to strengthen its treaty regime might be

---

[33] Pearson, G. S., 'Verification of the Biological Weapons Convention', ed. O. Thränert, *The Verification of the Biological Weapons Convention: Problems and Perspectives* (Friedrich Ebert Stiftung: Bonn, 1992), p. 90.

[34] Islamic Republic of Iran (note 25).

[35] Zelicoff, A. P., 'BWC Fourth Review Conference', *APLS* [Association for Politics and the Life Sciences] *News*, vol. 1, nos 1–2 (Dec. 1996), p. 8.

thought to constitute a minimal expression of this universal interest. However, evidently, this is not how all governments perceive the situation. The credibility of the BTWC as a security guarantee is questioned, and even those governments which do see the convention as an important defence against the threat of BTW attack do not share a common view of how its treaty regime can best be strengthened.

A more practical approach may be the search for a convergence of interests in a consensual process of regime reinforcement. Even if there is general agreement, in principle, on an identity of interest, there is little that can be done about it in practice beyond continuing to appeal for universal participation. Convergent interests, on the other hand, may generate substantive programmes of activity. In such programmes policy prescriptions for the treaty regime can be tailored to the range of possible trade-offs so as to favour a sectorally balanced process of reinforcement, thereby maximizing the benefits to be derived from each sector.

The third and fourth review conferences, the 1994 Special Conference and the Ad Hoc Group since 1995 have left little doubt as regards the need for trade-offs between developed and developing countries. There might be more progress in negotiating such trade-offs if it were clearer what constituted an acceptable quid pro quo. In biotechnology, as in other fields, properly equitable relationships are harder to define in practical terms than to advocate in principle. Yet some way may eventually have to be found of giving practical expression to the pressure for technology transfer in order to narrow the gap between the industrial capacities of developed and developing countries. This must occur if the South is not to become ever more alienated from the convention in which, however mistakenly, it has invested its hope of securing such benefits.

A convergence of interests may be identifiable. Some parties stress the Article III prohibition of transfer, assistance, encouragement and inducement because they perceive the BTWC as being, among other things, an instrument in the continuing campaign against the proliferation of BTW capabilities in unstable regions of the South. Other parties want to emphasize Article X's encouragement of international cooperation in the peaceful applications of microbiology. They interpret this as implying as free a flow as possible of relevant knowledge and materials across national frontiers and from North to South, in particular.

These distinct and apparently divergent interests, in fact, converge on a common interest in regulating the trade in such knowledge and materials (from genetic modification to fermentation technology). As Amy E. Smithson has pointed out, export controls may benefit the South in terms of security; they are not merely of advantage to economic and security interests in the North.[36] The tension between Article III's prohibitions and Article X's encouragement of cooperation is not an inevitable feature of the treaty regime. It can be attenuated and ultimately removed by trading the interest in a freer flow of knowledge and materials for peaceful purposes against the interest in ensuring that no diversion to other ends takes place. This might be achieved by tightening export controls and end-use certification, while expanding trade on mutually acceptable terms

[36] Smithson, A. E., *Separating Fact from Fiction: The Australia Group and the Chemical Weapons Convention*, Occasional Paper no. 34 (Henry L. Stimson Center: Washington, DC, Mar. 1997), p. 25.

between groups of parties which recognize the need for such precautions and demonstrate the necessary openness (and governmental vigilance) to provide reliable reassurance.

Once the first trade-offs have been concluded parties may be encouraged to search for other convergent interests and even for areas of identical interest. An emphasis on the integral relationship with the prevention of disease may be the most promising means of realizing a perception of a shared interest. This approach was envisaged for the convention by some of its early advocates. It is discussed in section VIII below.

A necessary condition for the realization of convergent interests is the balanced evolution of the three sectors: the regimes of compliance, development and permanence, and the addition of a regime of research. This is also necessary for any subsequent transition from convergence of interests to identity of interest. Such evolution requires a supportive institutional framework to balance it. One sector must not outstrip the others in the process of regime reinforcement or the scope for trade-offs between convergent interests will be diminished. Should that occur, the likelihood that an identity of interests will come to be recognized at any level other than the rhetorical will be correspondingly reduced.

If a global trade-off were easily achieved it would already have been realized. The best that can be hoped for is a series of separate solutions to different problems. In their totality these solutions must be to the advantage of the BTWC as a whole and must enhance the strength of its internal structure by steering it towards a stronger cross-sectoral equilibrium and a more durable and integrated regime. That is the challenge of the current stage of the evolution of biological disarmament.

In order to recover the normative context in which the BTWC regime can hope to prosper, the British initiative from which the convention emerged in 1968–71 should be revisited.

The British draft convention envisaged a clearer line of reasoning in its proposed preamble than that of the current preamble to the BTWC. The British draft preamble read in part:

Believing that chemical and biological discoveries should be used only for the betterment of human life,
Recognising nevertheless that the development of scientific knowledge throughout the world will increase the risk of eventual use of biological methods of warfare,
Convinced that such use would be repugnant to the conscience of mankind and that no effort should be spared to minimise this risk,
Desiring therefore to reinforce the Geneva Protocol by the conclusion of a Convention making special provision in this field,
Declaring their belief that, in particular, provision should be made for the prohibition of recourse to biological methods of warfare in any circumstances.[37]

The above wording was not included in the final text of the convention's preamble. The idea 'that chemical and biological discoveries should be used only for the betterment of human life' is a concise statement (echoed in 'the principle

---

[37] The quoted text begins at paragraph 4 of the draft preamble. CCD/255/Rev.2 (note 13).

that sciences should support quality of life' in the 1991 Final Declaration[38]) of the wider normative context essential to chemical and biological disarmament.

VIII. Prevention of disease proposals

It is, however, not simple to apply a 'betterment of human life' criterion. There have been proposals for the regime of biological disarmament to combine the strongest possible safeguards against BTW with other desirable public policies. These have included biological safety (including good practice in the biotechnology industry and elsewhere), the promotion of public health, and the identification and prevention of outbreaks of disease.

The pioneering survey of chemical and biological warfare by John Cookson and Judith Nottingham envisaged an international centre which would be entrusted with the rapid identification of pathogens implicated in outbreaks of disease among human populations, whether such outbreaks were the consequence of a natural occurrence, an accident or biological warfare. The prime objective would be to speed up identification and so help the public health authorities to take countermeasures at an earlier stage of an outbreak. In so doing, the international centre would help to verify the ban on biological warfare by identifying breaches of the ban which might otherwise have been successfully disguised under the cover of a natural occurrence (e.g., if they involved the spreading of diseases already endemic to the target population).[39]

In the context of reinforcing the prevention of biological warfare, some 20 years later Herbert Marcovich of the Institut Pasteur in Paris proposed an International Biological Monitoring Agency.[40] Its concern would be with the safety and security of high-containment facilities. It would aim to respond at an international level to the problems raised by the safety requirements of laboratories at the highest biosafety level (BL4), by promoting a standard model requiring certain specifications and subjecting BL4 facilities to inspection.[41] The agency's responsibilities would include: examining installations and equipment to ascertain that they conformed with health and safety standards; requiring records to be kept of all genetic manipulation; ensuring non-diversion of biological products; taking the necessary measures to ascertain that biological products were not used for prohibited military purposes; guaranteeing confidentiality in respect of the peaceful uses of agents and techniques; and informing the UN Secretary-General of any violation noted by its inspectors. Marcovich also envisaged health monitoring of personnel, which would include the performance of 'immunological analyses permitting the detection of possible immunity against agents being utilized overtly or illicitly. It might thus detect the presence of antibodies directed against agents of which the Agency were

[38] BWC/CONF.III/22/Add.2 (note 29), p. 3.

[39] Cookson, J. and Nottingham, J., *A Survey of Chemical and Biological Warfare* (Sheed and Ward: London, Sydney, 1969), pp. 349–52. The study was compiled while the authors were students at the University of Newcastle upon Tyne in 1968.

[40] Marcovich, H., 'Proposal for an International Biological Monitoring Agency', ed. E. Geissler, *Strengthening the Biological Weapons Convention by Confidence-Building Measures*, SIPRI Chemical & Biological Warfare Studies, no. 10 (Oxford University Press: Oxford, 1990), pp. 198–201.

[41] Biosafety levels 1–4 are 'a series of four increasingly stringent designs developed by organizations and institutions such as WHO [the World Health Organization], NIH [the National Institutes of Health], US Centers for Disease Control (CDC), etc., for work with biological agents and/or for genetic engineering'. 'Glossary', ed. Geissler (note 40), p. 202.

[*sic*] not aware as, for example, those which might facilitate clandestine or covert military research'.[42]

Incentives for cooperation with the agency would be the practical help it could offer in designing BL4 laboratories, advising on health and safety, arranging scientific exchanges and specialist training, and even product supply (assuming that it had been entrusted with 'the management, storage and surveillance of agents so as to prevent diversion of those which might be used for non-pacific purposes'), with a deliberate bias towards the needs of developing countries in peaceful applications of biology.[43]

In the 1990s the Vaccines for Peace (VFP) and Programme for Countering Emerging Infectious Diseases (ProCEID), initiatives of Erhard Geissler and others,[44] attracted support as another way of linking the BTW disarmament regime with programmes of health promotion and disease prevention. These proposals suggested removing vaccine production and use from the sphere of market forces and reducing the scope for evasion of the BTW ban through clandestine diversion of vaccine production facilities. ('Key objectives of ProCEID include, inter alia, the enhancement of peaceful international cooperation in molecular medicine and biotechnology and an increase of world capacity to produce and make available prophylactic, diagnostic, and therapeutic measures.'[45]) The Fourth Review Conference expressed support for the efforts to elaborate an international programme of vaccine development[46] and emphasized the importance of the Article X provisions in the light of international concern over new, emerging and re-emerging infectious diseases and the opportunities for increased cooperation in the international response to that situation.[47]

All these proposals emphasize the prevention of disease and Article X is relevant to each of them. This is also true of the proposals for a Global Epidemiological Surveillance System and a Program for Monitoring Emerging Diseases (ProMED)—further possible outcomes of a resolve to return to the fundamental purpose of Article X. These proposals also have a bearing on Article V because they seek to promote compliance by enhancing transparency (as noted by the Fourth Review Conference in 1996) and to make it easier to fulfil the obligation of the parties to cooperate and consult over compliance issues by diminishing suspicions, ambiguities and opportunities for evasion. They resemble in that respect the CBMs which were devised in 1986 and enhanced in 1991 to effect a linkage between Article V and Article X.

IX. Transparency and accountability

The idea of international accountability applied to control and cooperation in anti-BTW research could also contribute to the realization of greater open-

[42] Marcovich (note 40), p. 200.

[43] Marcovich (note 40).

[44] Geissler, E. and Woodall, J. P. (eds), *Control of Dual-Threat Agents: The Vaccines for Peace Programme*, SIPRI Chemical & Biological Warfare Studies, no. 15 (Oxford University Press: Oxford, 1994).

[45] Geissler, E., Hunger, I. and Buder, E., 'Implementing Article X of the Biological Weapons Convention', ed. O. Thränert, *Enhancing the Biological Weapons Convention* (Dietz: Bonn, 1996), pp. 170.

[46] Final Declaration, BWC/CONF.IV/9 (note 24), 16th para. of the Article X section, p. 26.

[47] Final Declaration, BWC/CONF.IV/9 (note 24), 10th para. of the Article X section, p. 25.

ness.[48] So too could the concept of 'open laboratories' which was promoted by the Italian delegation, in particular, at the Third Review Conference: 'In our view "open laboratories", i.e. an international scientific community closely interconnected, where scientists would be the first, vigilant witnesses to the peaceful objectives of biological research, are yet an additional answer to the risk represented by covert research and clandestine development of these as well as any other weapons of mass destruction.'[49]

This recalls the origins of the convention when microbiologists who wanted to prevent biological warfare met under the auspices of the Pugwash Conferences on Science and World Affairs and launched a pioneering project of cooperation between the Karolinska Institute, Stockholm, and microbiological laboratories in Austria, Czechoslovakia and Denmark. An authoritative account of this Pugwash project, its antecedents back to 1959 and later Pugwash activity has been published.[50] It is interesting, however, to recall how it was perceived at the time. R. W. Reid, a science journalist and broadcaster, wrote of this project in 1969:

Some of those biologists concerned with the Pugwash movement, for example, believe that control over biological weapon development can now only be achieved by international collaboration and that this can only be approached if open research and publication are reinstituted. In 1964 a group of scientists of the movement began to study and test the feasibility of a system of voluntary inspection of laboratories engaged in microbiological research and manufacture. With cooperation from the countries concerned, institutions in Austria, Czechoslovakia, Denmark and Sweden were visited and investigated, the long-term aim being to expand the scheme on a world-wide basis. If all laboratories could be thrown open to inspection of this kind and a viable open research agreement reached, and if the internationalism amongst scientists were to become so powerful that infringements of agreements could easily be detected, then the fear of some massive mistake leading to a biological holocaust could be removed.[51]

Perhaps the optimism of 1969 can be retrieved. 'Open skies'[52] was first proposed in the 1950s and finally gained acceptance in the 1990s among the governments of the North Atlantic Treaty Organization (NATO) and the former Warsaw Treaty Organization (WTO). The time may be ripe for 'open laboratories' as the cornerstone of a new regime of research favouring health and transparency: one loosely attached to, but extending beyond, the BTWC.

The inter-laboratory project which the Pugwash biologists launched in 1963–65 eventually resulted in a six-volume study by the Stockholm Inter-

[48] Sims, N. A., 'Control and cooperation in biological defence research: national programmes and international accountability', eds Geissler and Woodall (note 44), pp. 56–66.

[49] Statement by Ambassador Andrea Negrotto Cambiaso, 12 Sep. 1991, p. 4. Text supplied by the Italian Delegation to the Third Review Conference.

[50] Perry Robinson, J. P., 'The impact of Pugwash on the debates over chemical and biological weapons', *Scientific Cooperation, State Conflict: The Roles of Scientists in Mitigating International Discord*, Annals of the New York Academy of Sciences, vol. 866 (30 Dec. 1998), pp. 224–52.

[51] Reid, R. W., *Tongues of Conscience: War and the Scientist's Dilemma* (Constable: London, 1969), pp. 331–32.

[52] The Open Skies Treaty was signed in Helsinki, Finland on 24 Mar. 1992. It seeks to build an international regime of mutual trust and confidence as regards military activities by establishing a regime of unarmed aerial observation flights. A history of the treaty is presented in Clear, K. W. and Block, S. E., Defense Threat Reduction Agency, US Department of Defense, *The Treaty on Open Skies*, URL <http://www.dtra.mil/news/his_mat/books/openskies/nw_tabcon.html>.

national Peace Research Institute of which the final volume investigated the capability for early warning and rapid detection of biological warfare agents.[53]

Julian Perry Robinson has drawn attention to openness as an idea which Pugwash scientists have continuously emphasized not only in their work on chemical and biological warfare, but also in that of governments. This emphasis on:

the fundamental importance of openness in national CBW-related activities . . . recognizes the way in which secrecies, however justifiable each one may be in commercial or national-security terms, can together engender suspicion and mistrust, which will debilitate any collective international endeavor, especially where dual-use technologies are concerned. The greater part of the practical work that Pugwash has done on CBW issues has involved searching for ways of reconciling the principle of openness with imperatives of state and commercial behavior that necessarily incorporate secrecy.[54]

A special responsibility is incumbent on government scientists who are engaged in programmes of detection, protection and prophylaxis against BTW in order to find more effective ways both of demonstrating the non-offensive character of such programmes and of dissipating non-compliance anxieties while promoting international cooperation within the BTWC framework.[55]

Constant reaffirmation of the normative context outlined in section VII above is necessary along with the superordinate goal of safeguarding humanity from the threat of BTW. It is necessary if health and security are to be seen as in the common interest and if the vision of openness in international cooperation is to be recaptured. Such a vision might well take as its watchword the 5 August 1970 statement to the Conference of the Committee on Disarmament by Dr Joshua Lederberg, one of the founders of the science of molecular biology and recipient of the Nobel Prize for Medicine in 1958.[56] According to George Ignatieff, head of the Canadian delegation in Geneva, the warnings of Lederberg and other distinguished biologists had a positive effect on the conference.[57]

Lederberg warned the CCD that: 'On the one hand molecular biology could increase man's knowledge about himself and lead to revolutionary changes in

[53] Perry Robinson (note 50), pp. 237–38; and SIPRI, *The Problem of Chemical and Biological Warfare,* vol. 6, *Technical Aspects of Early Warning and Verification* (Almqvist & Wiksell: Stockholm, 1975). The series is available on a CD-ROM, which is described at URL <http://editors.sipri.se/cd.cbw.html>.
[54] Perry Robinson (note 50), p. 245.
[55] Sims (note 48), pp. 63–66.
[56] US working paper on remarks by Dr Joshua Lederberg at informal meeting of CCD, 5 Aug. 1970, Conference of the Committee on Disarmament document CCD/312, 27 Aug. 1970.
[57] Ignatieff, G., *The Making of a Peacemonger: The Memoirs of George Ignatieff* (Toronto University Press: Toronto, 1985), p. 252. Ignatieff credited the cumulative effect of their efforts on US policy as contributing to the achievement of the BTWC. Moreover, the Parliamentary Under-Secretary of State for Foreign and Commonwealth Affairs, the Marquess of Lothian, representing the UK in the First Committee of the UN General Assembly, testified to Lederberg's influence on the CCD's deliberations when he stated: 'I feel it necessary solemnly to warn the Committee that the biological weapon may not be as remote as many of us think. Further delay could be dangerous. This year [1970] saw the first synthesis of a gene and in the Conference of the Committee on Disarmament we heard an eminent Nobel Prize Laureate in the field of microbiology, Dr Lederberg, describe how it was already possible for men to manipulate the cross-breeding of different bacterial strains and thus "invent" new diseases which might not carry the risks for the user of the unreliability of current biological weapons and against which there might be absolutely no known defence. For the present, mercifully, this is not the case, and a treaty banning biological weapons before their further development is, I believe, within our grasp now. . . . Every month we delay may bring further discoveries.' UN document A/C.1/PV.1750, 4 Nov. 1970, para. 55.

medicine in such fields as cancer, ageing, congenital disease, and virus infections. It might also play a vital role in industry and in agriculture. On the other side it might be exploited for military purposes and eventuate in a biological weapons race whose aim could well become the most efficient means for removing man from the planet.'[58]

He argued that great biological dangers to the human race still existed and that there were immense gaps in the defences against them. The need to fight that menace and the requirements of the convention being negotiated led, in his view, to a common institutional requirement:

The promulgation of an international agreement to control biological warfare in a negative sense should, therefore, be accompanied by steps urgently needed to build positive efforts at international co-operation, a kind of defensive biological research against natural enemies of the human species.

One of the best assurances that any country might have that the microbiological research of its neighbours was directed towards human purposes would be constantly expanding participation in international health programmes. . . . Therefore, besides the obvious direct health benefits of expanded international co-operation we would also be rewarded by a higher level of mutual assurance that every party was indeed living up to the spirit of its obligations under a BW Convention.[59]

X. Ethical challenge and moral choice

Joshua Lederberg, Martin M. Kaplan, Matthew Meselson, John Humphrey and other biologists worked actively in the 1960s and later to bring the BTWC into being.[60] They shared a sense of the moral choice to be made by scientists in working for life or death, to disseminate health or disease. This conviction was sustained by NGOs like the Committee (later the Council) for Responsible Genetics in the 1980s with pledges by scientific personnel not to engage in work for BTW and campaigns to raise awareness of the moral gravity of both personal as well as governmental choices.[61]

Recently, national and international organizations of the medical profession have expressed similar views. The World Medical Association at its 48th General Assembly in Somerset West, South Africa, on 20–26 October 1996, stated that it 'recognises that modern medicine depends upon the continuous development of technology and insists that this technology must not be abused or diverted into weapons development'.[62] This statement followed closely upon the International Committee of the Red Cross (ICRC) Montreux Symposium on

[58] CCD/312 (note 56), p. 1.

[59] CCD/312 (note 56), pp. 7–8.

[60] Kaplan, M. M., 'The efforts of WHO and Pugwash to eliminate chemical and biological weapons—a memoir', *Bulletin of the World Health Organization*, vol. 77, no. 2 (1999), pp. 150–51; and Perry Robinson (note 50), pp. 236–40.

[61] There is an extensive literature on the moral responsibility of scientists in relation to war and weapons, e.g. Reid (note 51). A particularly thoughtful analysis is found in Lappé, M., 'Ethics in biological warfare research', ed. S. Wright, *Preventing a Biological Arms Race* (MIT Press: Cambridge, Mass., 1990), pp. 78–99. The same volume reproduces the Pledge Against the Military Use of Biological Research circulated from 1984 onwards by the Committee (now the Council) for Responsible Genetics and the Coalition of Universities in the Public Interest. Wright (note 61), p. 412.

[62] World Medical Association, *Statement on Weapons and their Relation to Life and Health*, adopted by the 48th General Assembly, Somerset West, Republic of South Africa, Oct. 1996 (World Health Association: Ferney-Voltaire, France, 1996), p. 2.

The Medical Profession and the Effects of Weapons, at which a future weapons working group 'concentrated particularly on biotechnology and the potential use of genetic research, which seems to be very much in the weapons threshold category'.[63] At the national level, a report commissioned by the British Medical Association (BMA) includes the following among its recommendations addressed to 'the scientific and medical community':

1. Professional scientists and physicians have an ethical responsibility to reinforce the central norm that biological and genetic weapons are unacceptable. This should be explicitly stated in codes of professional conduct in order to safeguard the public interest in matters of health and safety.

2. The potential for malign use of biotechnology places an ethical responsibility on the medical and scientific community to protect the integrity of their work.[64]

The same BMA report aims, through what John Humphrey long ago identified as the high standing of the medical profession in the public eye,[65] 'to stimulate debate and raise civic awareness of the potential abuse of biotechnology and the important steps that we can take to minimise the risk of development of biological weapons'.[66] These steps include notably, for the BMA, the strengthening of the BTWC[67] to counter 'the prospect of disease being deliberately applied for military or terrorist purposes through biological warfare'.[68] Meanwhile, medical researchers 'will face extraordinary ethical challenges as their work could be used by those who pay no regard to international law or accepted standards'.[69]

The parties to the BTWC endorsed this conviction at the Third Review Conference; the Article I section of its Final Declaration stated: 'On the basis of the principle that sciences should support quality of life, the Conference appeals through the States Parties to their scientific communities to continue to support only activities that have justification under the Biological and Toxin Weapons Convention for prophylactic, protective or other peaceful purposes, and refrain from activities which are in breach of obligations deriving from provisions of the Convention.'[70]

The appeal, slightly abbreviated, was repeated by the Fourth Review Conference: '8. The Conference appeals through the States Parties to their scientific communities to lend their support only to activities that have justification for prophylactic, protective and other peaceful purposes, and refrain from undertaking or supporting activities which are in breach of the obligations deriving from

[63] International Committee of the Red Cross, *The Medical Profession and the Effect of Weapons: Report of the Symposium, Montreux, March, 1996* (ICRC: Geneva, 1996).

[64] Dando, M. R., Nathanson, V. and Darvell, M., British Medical Association, *Biotechnology, Weapons and Humanity* (Harwood Academic Publishers: Amsterdam, 1999), p. 101.

[65] Humphrey, J., 'The development of the physicians' peace movements', *Medicine and War*, vol. 1, no. 2 (1985), pp. 87–99. 'When a substantial proportion of doctors are moved to make common cause over some issue their views are newsworthy, and indeed the media have given wider publicity to the activities of the physicians' organisations than to other groups of comparable size.' Cited in Lewer, N., *Physicians and the Peace Movement* (Frank Cass: London, 1992), pp. 79–80.

[66] Dando, Nathanson and Darvell (note 64), p. 1.

[67] Dando, Nathanson and Darvell (note 64), pp. 75–87, 91–94, 102.

[68] Pullinger, S., 'Fighting biological warfare', *British Medical Journal*, vol. 320 (22 Apr. 2000), p. 1089.

[69] World Medical Association (note 62), p. 1.

[70] BWC/CONF.III/22/Add.2 (note 29), p. 3 In Final Document, BWC/CONF.III/23, 1992, p. 11, 'Based on the principle' is changed to 'On the basis of the principle' in the opening line.

provisions of the Convention.'[71] Scientific communities may reasonably look to governments, not for a moral lead, but for good faith and a reasonable partnership in this historic enterprise. British Minister of State for Foreign and Commonwealth Affairs Lord Chalfont underestimated the problem of abolishing biological weapons when he told the UN First Committee in 1969: 'We think they can be eliminated at once, in a single blow.'[72] On the contrary, the abolition of biological weapons requires a long-sustained effort on many fronts, by governments and scientists in partnership.

The BTWC is a pioneering disarmament regime, and its parties must act, individually and collectively, to consolidate stronger safeguards against the threat of biological and toxin warfare. Convergence of sectors and interests and investment in supportive institutions, however modest, are needed to ensure the health of the BTWC. Statements of support at quinquennial review conferences are not enough. Sustained care and attention are necessary if the regime is to survive and flourish.

Governments should act to give practical effect to their intentions and substance to their sentiments. Friends of the Convention should encourage governments and one another to demonstrate persistence and ingenuity in steering the treaty regime through the remaining stages in its constructive evolution, until it can realize its potential in rendering biological and toxin warfare as remote a contingency as it can ever be amid the vicissitudes of international relations.

[71] BWC/CONF.IV/9 (note 24), p. 16.
[72] UN document A/C.1/PV.1694, 19 Nov. 1969, para. 58.

Annexe A. The 1972 Biological and Toxin Weapons Convention

CONVENTION ON THE PROHIBITION OF THE DEVELOPMENT, PRODUCTION AND STOCKPILING OF BACTERIOLOGICAL (BIOLOGICAL) AND TOXIN WEAPONS AND ON THEIR DESTRUCTION

Signed at London, Moscow and Washington on 10 April 1972
Entered into force on 26 March 1975
Depositaries: UK, US and Soviet governments

The States Parties to this Convention,

Determined to act with a view to achieving effective progress towards general and complete disarmament, including the prohibition and elimination of all types of weapons of mass destruction, and convinced that the prohibition of the development, production and stockpiling of chemical and bacteriological (biological) weapons and their elimination, through effective measures, will facilitate the achievement of general and complete disarmament under strict and effective international control,

Recognizing the important significance of the Protocol for the Prohibition of the Use in War of Asphyxiating, Poisonous or Other Gases, and of Bacteriological Methods of Warfare, signed at Geneva on June 17, 1925, and conscious also of the contribution which the said Protocol has already made, and continues to make, to mitigating the horrors of war,

Reaffirming their adherence to the principles and objectives of that Protocol and calling upon all States to comply strictly with them,

Recalling that the General Assembly of the United Nations has repeatedly condemned all actions contrary to the principles and objectives of the Geneva Protocol of June 17, 1925,

Desiring to contribute to the strengthening of confidence between peoples and the general improvement of the international atmosphere,

Desiring also to contribute to the realization of the purposes and principles of the Charter of the United Nations,

Convinced of the importance and urgency of eliminating from the arsenals of States, through effective measures, such dangerous weapons of mass destruction as those using chemical or bacteriological (biological) agents,

Recognizing that an agreement on the prohibition of bacteriological (biological) and toxin weapons represents a first possible step towards the achievement of agreement on effective measures also for the problem of the development, production and stockpiling of chemical weapons, and determined to continue negotiations to that end,

Determined, for the sake of all mankind, to exclude completely the possibility of bacteriological (biological) agents and toxins being used as weapons,

Convinced that such use would be repugnant to the conscience of mankind and that no effort should be spared to minimize this risk,

Have agreed as follows:

Article I

Each State Party to this Convention undertakes never in any circumstances to develop, produce, stockpile or otherwise acquire or retain:

1. Microbial or other biological agents, or toxins whatever their origin or method of production, of types and in quantities that have no justification for prophylactic, protective or other peaceful purposes;

2. Weapons, equipment or means of delivery designed to use such agents or toxins for hostile purposes or in armed conflict.

Article II

Each State Party to this Convention undertakes to destroy, or to divert to peaceful purposes, as soon as possible but not later than nine months after the entry into force of the Convention, all agents, toxins, weapons, equipment and means of delivery specified in article I of the Convention, which are in its possession or under its jurisdiction or control. In implementing the provisions of this article all necessary safety precautions shall be observed to protect populations and the environment.

Article III

Each State Party to this Convention undertakes not to transfer to any recipient whatsoever, directly or indirectly, and not in any way to assist, encourage, or induce any State, group of States or international organizations to manufacture or otherwise acquire any of the agents, toxins, weapons, equipment or means of delivery specified in article I of the Convention.

Article IV

Each State Party to this Convention shall, in accordance with its constitutional processes, take any necessary measures to prohibit and prevent the development, production, stockpiling, acquisition or retention of the agents, toxins, weapons, equipment and means of delivery specified in article I of the Convention, within the territory of such State, under its jurisdiction or under its control anywhere.

Article V

The States Parties to this Convention undertake to consult one another and to cooperate in solving any problems which may arise in relation to the objective of, or in the application of the provisions of, the Convention. Consultation and cooperation pursuant to this article may also be undertaken through appropriate international procedures within the framework of the United Nations and in accordance with its Charter.

Article VI

1. Any State Party to this Convention which finds that any other State Party is acting in breach of obligations deriving from the provisions of the Convention may lodge a complaint with the Security Council of the United Nations. Such a complaint should include all possible evidence confirming its validity, as well as a request for its consideration by the Security Council.

2. Each State Party to this Convention undertakes to cooperate in carrying out any investigation which the Security Council may initiate, in accordance with the provisions of the Charter of the United Nations, on the basis of the complaint received by the Council. The Security Council shall inform the States Parties to the Convention of the results of the investigation.

Article VII

Each State Party to this Convention undertakes to provide or support assistance, in accordance with the United Nations Charter, to any Party to the Convention which so requests, if the Security Council decides that such Party has been exposed to danger as a result of violation of the Convention.

Article VIII

Nothing in this Convention shall be interpreted as in any way limiting or detracting from the obligations assumed by any State under the Protocol for the Prohibition of the Use in War of Asphyxiating, Poisonous or Other Gases, and of Bacteriological Methods of Warfare, signed at Geneva on June 17, 1925.

Article IX

Each State Party to this Convention affirms the recognized objective of effective prohibition of chemical weapons and, to this end, undertakes to continue negotiations in good faith with a view to reaching early agreement on effective measures for the prohibition of their development, production and stockpiling and for their destruction, and on appropriate measures concerning equipment and means of delivery specifically designed for the production or use of chemical agents for weapons purposes.

Article X

1. The States Parties to this Convention undertake to facilitate, and have the right to participate in, the fullest possible exchange of equipment, materials and scientific and technological information for the use of bacteriological (biological) agents and toxins for peaceful purposes. Parties to the Convention in a position to do so shall also cooperate in contributing individually or together with other States or international organizations to the further development and application of scientific discoveries in the field of bacteriology (biology) for prevention of disease, or for other peaceful purposes.

2. This Convention shall be implemented in a manner designed to avoid hampering the economic or technological development of States Parties to the Convention or international cooperation in the field of peaceful bacteriological (biological) activities, including the international exchange of bacteriological (biological) agents and toxins and equipment for the processing, use or production of bacteriological (biological) agents and toxins for peaceful purposes in accordance with the provisions of the Convention.

Article XI

Any State Party may propose amendments to this Convention. Amendments shall enter into force for each State Party accepting the amendments upon their acceptance by a majority of the States Parties to the Convention and thereafter for each remaining State Party on the date of acceptance by it.

Article XII

Five years after the entry into force of this Convention, or earlier if it is requested by a majority of Parties to the Convention by submitting a proposal to this effect to the Depositary Governments, a conference of States Parties to the Convention shall be held at Geneva, Switzerland, to review the operation of the Convention, with a view to assuring that the purposes of the preamble and the provisions of the Convention, including the provisions concerning negotiations on chemical weapons, are being realized. Such review shall take into account any new scientific and technological developments relevant to the Convention.

Article XIII

1. This Convention shall be of unlimited duration.

2. Each State Party to this Convention shall in exercising its national sovereignty have the right to withdraw from the Convention if it decides that extraordinary events, related to the subject matter of the Convention, have jeopardized the supreme interests of its country. It shall give notice of such withdrawal to all other States Parties to the Convention and to the United Nations Security Council three months in advance. Such notice shall include a statement of the extraordinary events it regards as having jeopardized its supreme interests.

Article XIV

1. This Convention shall be open to all States for signature. Any State which does not sign the Convention before its entry into force in accordance with paragraph (3) of this Article may accede to it at any time.

2. This Convention shall be subject to ratification by signatory States. Instruments of ratification and instruments of accession shall be deposited with the Governments of the United States of America, the United Kingdom of Great Britain and Northern Ireland and the Union of Soviet Socialist Republics, which are hereby designated the Depositary Governments.

3. This Convention shall enter into force after the deposit of instruments of ratification by twenty-two Governments, including the Governments designated as Depositaries of the Convention.

4. For States whose instruments of ratification or accession are deposited subsequent to the entry into force of this Convention, it shall enter into force on the date of the deposit of their instruments of ratification or accession.

5. The Depositary Governments shall promptly inform all signatory and acceding States of the date of each signature, the date of deposit of each instrument of ratification or of accession and the date of the entry into force of this Convention, and of the receipt of other notices.

6. This Convention shall be registered by the Depositary Governments pursuant to Article 102 of the Charter of the United Nations.

Article XV

This Convention, the English, Russian, French, Spanish and Chinese texts of which are equally authentic, shall be deposited in the archives of the Depositary Governments. Duly certified copies of the Convention shall be transmitted by the Depositary Governments to the Governments of the signatory and acceding States.

Source: *Treaties and Other International Acts, Series 8062* (US Department of State: Washington, DC, 1975).

Annexe B. The 1925 Geneva Protocol

PROTOCOL FOR THE PROHIBITION OF THE USE IN WAR OF ASPHYXIATING, POISONOUS OR OTHER GASES, AND OF BACTERIOLOGICAL METHODS OF WARFARE (1925 GENEVA PROTOCOL)

Signed at Geneva on 17 June 1925
Entered into force on 8 February 1928
Depositary: French Government

The Undersigned Plenipotentiaries, in the name of their respective Governments:

Whereas the use in war of asphyxiating, poisonous or other gases, and of all analogous liquids, materials or devices, has been justly condemned by the general opinion of the civilised world; and

Whereas the prohibition of such use has been declared in Treaties to which the majority of Powers of the world are Parties; and

To the end that this prohibition shall be universally accepted as a part of International Law, binding alike the conscience and the practice of nations;

Declare:

That the High Contracting Parties, so far as they are not already Parties to Treaties prohibiting such use, accept this prohibition, agree to extend this prohibition to the use of bacteriological methods of warfare and agree to be bound as between themselves according to the terms of this declaration.

The High Contracting Parties will exert every effort to induce other States to accede to the present Protocol. Such accession will be notified to the Government of the French Republic, and by the latter to all signatory and acceding Powers, and will take effect on the date of the notification by the Government of the French Republic.

The present Protocol, of which the English and French texts are both authentic, shall be ratified as soon as possible. It shall bear to-day's date.

The ratifications of the present Protocol shall be addressed to the Government of the French Republic, which will at once notify the deposit of such ratification to each of the signatory and acceding Powers.

The instruments of ratification of and accession to the present Protocol will remain deposited in the archives of the Government of the French Republic.

The present Protocol will come into force for each signatory Power as from the date of deposit of its ratification, and, from that moment, each Power will be bound as regards other Powers which have already deposited their ratifications.

In witness whereof the Plenipotentiaries have signed the present Protocol.

Done at Geneva in a single copy, the seventeenth day of June, One Thousand Nine Hundred and Twenty-Five.

————

Source: *League of Nations Treaty Series*, vol. 94.

Annexe C. Signatories to the 1972 Biological and Toxin Weapons Convention

SIGNATURES TO THE BTWC

The Biological and Toxin Weapons Convention was signed at London, Moscow and Washington, DC, on 10 April 1972. It entered into force on 26 March 1975. Total number of signatories: 162[1]

Afghanistan signed 10 Apr. 1972
Albania signed 3 June 1992
Argentina signed 1 Aug. 1972
Armenia signed 7 June 1994
Australia signed 10 Apr. 1972
Austria signed 10 Apr. 1972

Bahamas signed 26 Nov. 1986
Bahrain signed 28 Oct. 1988
Bangladesh signed 11 Mar. 1985
Barbados signed 16 Feb.1973
Belarus signed 10 Apr. 1972
Belgium signed 10 Apr. 1972
Belize signed 20 Oct. 1986
Benin signed 10 Apr. 1972
Bhutan signed 8 June 1978
Bolivia signed 10 Apr. 1972
Bosnia and Herzegovina signed 15 Aug. 1994
Botswana signed 10 Apr. 1972
Brazil signed 10 Apr. 1972
Brunei Darussalam signed 31 Jan. 1991
Bulgaria signed 10 Apr. 1972
Burkina Faso signed 17 Apr. 1991
Burundi signed 10 Apr. 1972

Cambodia signed 10 Apr. 1972
Canada signed 10 Apr. 1972
Cape Verde signed 20 Oct. 1977
Central African Republic signed 10 Apr. 1972
Chile signed 10 Apr. 1972
China signed 15 Nov. 1984
Colombia signed 10 Apr. 1972
Congo, Republic of signed 23 Oct. 1978
Congo (Democratic Republic of the, formerly Zaire) signed 10 Apr. 1972
Costa Rica signed 10 Apr. 1972
Côte d'Ivoire signed 23 May 1972
Croatia signed 28 Apr. 1993
Cuba signed 10 Apr. 1972
Cyprus signed 10 Apr. 1972
Czech Republic signed 5 Apr. 1993

Denmark signed 10 Apr. 1972
Dominica signed 8 Nov. 1978
Dominican Republic signed 10 Apr. 1972

Ecuador signed 14 June 1972
Egypt signed 10 Apr. 1972
El Salvador signed 10 Apr. 1972
Equatorial Guinea signed 16 Jan. 1989
Estonia signed 21 June 1993
Ethiopia signed 10 Apr. 1972

Fiji signed 22 Feb. 1973
Finland signed 10 Apr. 1972
France signed 27 Sep. 1984

Gabon signed 10 Apr. 1972
Gambia signed 2 June 1972
Georgia signed 22 May 1996
Germany signed 10 Apr. 1972
Ghana signed 10 Apr. 1972
Greece signed 10 Apr. 1972
Grenada signed 22 Oct. 1986
Guatemala signed 9 May 1972
Guinea-Bissau signed 20 Aug. 1976
Guyana signed 3 Jan. 1973

Haiti signed 10 Apr. 1972
Honduras signed 10 Apr. 1972
Hungary signed 10 Apr. 1972

Iceland signed 10 Apr. 1972
India signed 15 Jan. 1973
Indonesia signed 20 June 1972
Iran signed 10 Apr. 1972
Iraq signed 11 May 1972
Ireland signed 10 Apr. 1972
Italy signed 10 Apr. 1972

Jamaica signed 13 Aug. 1975
Japan signed 10 Apr. 1972
Jordan signed 10 Apr. 1972

Kenya signed 7 Jan. 1976
Korea, Democratic People's Republic of (North Korea) signed 13 Mar. 1987
Korea, Republic of (South Korea) signed 10 Apr. 1972
Kuwait signed 14 Apr. 1972

Lao People's Democratic Republic (Laos) signed 10 Apr. 1972
Latvia signed 6 Feb. 1997
Lebanon signed 10 Apr. 1972
Lesotho signed 10 Apr. 1972
Liberia signed 10 Apr. 1972
Libya signed 19 Jan. 1982
Liechtenstein signed 30 May 1991
Lithuania signed 10 Feb. 1998
Luxembourg signed 10 Apr. 1972

[1] The United Nations' lists of parties and signatory-only states exclude Taiwan, which signed in 1972 and ratified in 1973 as the 'Republic of China' in Washington, DC. UN document BWC/AD HOC GROUP/INF.20, 20 July 1999.

Macedonia (Former Yugoslav Republic of)
  signed 24 Dec. 1996
Madagascar signed 13 Oct. 1972
Malawi signed 10 Apr. 1972
Malaysia signed 10 Apr. 1972
Maldives signed 2 Aug. 1993
Mali signed 10 Apr. 1972
Malta signed 11 Sep. 1972
Mauritius signed 10 Apr. 1972
Mexico signed 10 Apr. 1972
Monaco signed 30 Apr. 1999
Mongolia signed 10 Apr. 1972
Morocco signed 2 May 1972
Myanmar (Burma) signed 10 Apr. 1972

Nepal signed 10 Apr. 1972
Netherlands signed 10 Apr. 1972
New Zealand signed 10 Apr. 1972
Nicaragua signed 10 Apr. 1972
Niger signed 21 Apr. 1972
Nigeria signed 3 July 1972
Norway signed 10 Apr. 1972

Oman signed 31 Mar. 1992

Pakistan signed 10 Apr. 1972
Panama signed 2 May 1972
Papua New Guinea signed 27 Oct. 1980
Paraguay signed 9 June 1976
Peru signed 10 Apr. 1972
Philippines signed 10 Apr. 1972
Poland signed 10 Apr. 1972
Portugal signed 29 June 1972

Qatar signed 14 Nov. 1972

Romania signed 10 Apr. 1972
Russian Federation[2] signed 10 Apr. 1972
Rwanda signed 10 Apr. 1972

Saint Kitts and Nevis signed 2 Apr. 1991
Saint Lucia signed 26 Nov. 1986
Saint Vincent and the Grenadines signed
  13 May 1999
San Marino signed 12 Sep. 1972
Sao Tome and Principe signed 24 Aug. 1979
Saudi Arabia signed 12 Apr. 1972
Senegal signed 10 Apr. 1972
Seychelles signed 11 Oct. 1979
Sierra Leone signed 7 Nov. 1972
Singapore signed 19 June 1972
Slovakia signed 17 May 1993
Slovenia signed 7 Apr. 1992
Solomon Islands signed 17 June 1981
Somalia signed 3 July 1972
South Africa signed 10 Apr. 1972
Spain signed 10 Apr. 1972
Sri Lanka signed 10 Apr. 1972
Suriname signed 6 Jan. 1993
Swaziland signed 18 June 1991

Sweden signed 27 Feb. 1975
Switzerland signed 10 Apr. 1972
Syria signed 14 Apr. 1972

Taiwan[3] signed 10 Apr. 1972
Tanzania signed 16 Aug. 1972
Thailand signed 17 Jan. 1973
Togo signed 10 Apr. 1972
Tonga signed 28 Sep. 1976
Tunisia signed 10 Apr. 1972
Turkey signed 10 Apr. 1972
Turkmenistan signed 11 Jan. 1996

Uganda signed 12 May 1992
Ukraine signed 10 Apr. 1972
United Arab Emirates signed 28 Sep. 1972
United Kingdom of Great Britain and
  Northern Ireland signed 10 Apr. 1972
United States of America signed
  10 Apr. 1972
Uruguay signed 6 Apr. 1981
Uzbekistan signed 11 Jan. 1996

Vanuatu signed 12 Oct. 1990
Venezuela signed 10 Apr. 1972
Viet Nam signed 10 Apr. 1972

Yemen signed 26 Apr. 1972
Yugoslavia signed 10 Apr. 1972

Zimbabwe signed 5 Nov. 1990

_____

Source: Based on SIPRI Chemical and Biological Warfare Project, URL <http://projects.sipri.se/cbw/docs/bw-btwc-sig.html>.

[2] The Russian Federation succeeded on 26 Dec. 1991 to the international obligations of the Soviet Union, which had signed and ratified the convention.

[3] See note 1.

Annexe D. Parties to the 1972 Biological and Toxin Weapons Convention

RATIFICATIONS OF AND ACCESSIONS TO THE BTWC

Total number of ratifications and accessions: 144.[1] There are 18 signatories which have yet to ratify the convention. Information on declarations and reservations is available at SIPRI Chemical and Biological Warfare Project, 'Declarations and reservations to the BTWC', URL <http://projects.sipri.se/cbw/docs/bw-btwc-decres.html>.

Afghanistan signed 10 Apr. 1972 and ratified 26 Mar. 1975
Albania acceded 3 June 1992
Argentina signed 1 Aug. 1972 and ratified 27 Nov. 1979
Armenia acceded 7 June 1994
Australia signed 10 Apr. 1972 and ratified 5 Oct. 1977
Austria signed 10 Apr. 1972 and ratified 10 Aug. 1973

Bahamas acceded 26 Nov. 1986
Bahrain acceded 28 Oct. 1988
Bangladesh acceded 11 Mar. 1985
Barbados signed 16 Feb. 1973 and ratified 16 Feb. 1973
Belarus signed 10 Apr. 1972 and ratified 26 Mar. 1975
Belgium signed 10 Apr. 1972 and ratified 15 Mar. 1979
Belize acceded 20 Oct. 1986
Benin signed 10 Apr. 1972 and ratified 25 Apr. 1975
Bhutan acceded 8 June 1978
Bolivia signed 10 Apr. 1972 and ratified 30 Oct. 1975
Bosnia and Herzegovina acceded 15 Aug. 1994
Botswana signed 10 Apr. 1972 and ratified 5 Feb. 1992
Brazil signed 10 Apr. 1972 and ratified 27 Feb. 1973
Brunei Darussalam acceded 31 Jan. 1991
Bulgaria signed 10 Apr. 1972 and ratified 2 Aug. 1972
Burkina Faso acceded 17 Apr. 1991

Cambodia signed 10 Apr. 1972 and ratified 9 Mar. 1983
Canada signed 10 Apr. 1972 and ratified 18 Sep. 1972
Cape Verde acceded 20 Oct. 1977
Chile signed 10 Apr. 1972 and ratified 22 Apr. 1980
China acceded 15 Nov. 1984
Colombia signed 10 Apr. 1972 and ratified 19 Dec. 1983
Congo, Republic of acceded 23 Oct. 1978
Congo (Democratic Republic of the, formerly Zaire) signed 10 Apr. 1972 and ratified 16 Sep. 1975
Costa Rica signed 10 Apr. 1972 and ratified 17 Dec. 1973
Croatia acceded 28 Apr. 1993
Cuba signed 10 Apr. 1972 and ratified 21 Apr. 1976
Cyprus signed 10 Apr. 1972 and ratified 6 Nov. 1973
Czech Republic acceded 5 Apr. 1993

Denmark signed 10 Apr. 1972 and ratified 1 Mar. 1973
Dominica acceded 8 Nov. 1978
Dominican Republic signed 10 Apr. 1972 and ratified 23 Feb. 1973

Ecuador signed 14 June 1972 and ratified 21 Mar. 1975
El Salvador signed 10 Apr. 1972 and ratified 31 Dec. 1991
Equatorial Guinea acceded 16 Jan. 1989
Estonia acceded 21 June 1993
Ethiopia signed 10 Apr. 1972 and ratified 26 May 1975

Fiji signed 22 Feb. 1973 and ratified 4 Sep. 1973
Finland signed 10 Apr. 1972 and ratified 4 Feb. 1974
France acceded 27 Sep. 1984

Gambia signed 2 June 1972 and ratified 21 Nov. 1991
Georgia acceded 22 May 1996
Germany signed 10 Apr. 1972 and ratified 28 Nov. 1972
Ghana signed 10 Apr. 1972 and ratified 6 June 1975
Greece signed 10 Apr. 1972 and ratified 10 Dec. 1975
Grenada acceded 22 Oct. 1986
Guatemala signed 9 May 1972 and ratified 19 Sep. 1973
Guinea-Bissau acceded 20 Aug. 1976

---

[1] The United Nations' lists of parties and signatory-only states exclude Taiwan, which signed in 1972 and ratified in 1973 as the 'Republic of China' in Washington, DC. UN document BWC/AD HOC GROUP/INF.20, 20 July 1999.

Honduras signed 10 Apr. 1972 and ratified
14 Mar. 1979
Hungary signed 10 Apr. 1972 and ratified
27 Dec. 1972

Iceland signed 10 Apr. 1972 and ratified
15 Feb. 1973
India signed 15 Jan. 1973 and ratified
15 July 1974
Indonesia signed 20 June 1972 and ratified
19 Feb. 1992
Iran signed 10 Apr. 1972 and ratified
22 Aug. 1973
Iraq signed 11 May 1972 and ratified
19 June 1991
Ireland signed 10 Apr. 1972 and ratified
27 Oct. 1972
Italy signed 10 Apr. 1972 and ratified
30 May 1975

Jamaica acceded 13 Aug. 1975
Japan signed 10 Apr. 1972 and ratified
8 June 1982
Jordan signed 10 Apr. 1972 and ratified
30 May 1975

Kenya acceded 7 Jan. 1976
Korea, Democratic People's Republic of
(North Korea) acceded 13 Mar. 1987
Korea, Republic of (South Korea) signed
10 Apr. 1972 and ratified 25 June 1987
Kuwait signed 14 Apr.1972 and ratified
18 July 1972

Lao People's Democratic Republic (Laos)
signed 10 Apr. 1972 and ratified
20 Mar. 1973
Latvia acceded 6 Feb. 1997
Lebanon signed 10 Apr. 1972 and ratified
26 Mar. 1975
Lesotho signed 10 Apr. 1972 and ratified
6 Sep. 1977
Libya acceded 19 Jan. 1982
Liechtenstein acceded 30 May 1991
Lithuania acceded 10 Feb. 1998
Luxembourg signed 10 Apr. 1972 and ratified
23 Mar. 1976

Macedonia (Former Yugoslav Republic of)
acceded 24 Dec. 1996
Malaysia signed 10 Apr. 1972 and ratified
6 Sep. 1991
Maldives acceded 2 Aug. 1993
Malta signed 11 Sep. 1972 and ratified
7 Apr. 1975
Mauritius signed 10 Apr. 1972 and ratified
7 Aug. 1972
Mexico signed 10 Apr. 1972 and ratified
8 Apr. 1974
Monaco acceded 30 Apr. 1999
Mongolia signed 10 Apr. 1972 and ratified
5 Sep. 1972

Netherlands signed 10 Apr. 1972 and ratified
22 June 1981
New Zealand signed 10 Apr. 1972 and
ratified 13 Dec. 1972
Nicaragua signed 10 Apr. 1972 and ratified
7 Aug. 1975
Niger signed 21 Apr. 1972 and ratified
23 June 1972
Nigeria signed 3 July 1972 and ratified
3 July 1973
Norway signed 10 Apr. 1972 and ratified
1 Aug. 1973

Oman acceded 31 Mar. 1992

Pakistan signed 10 Apr. 1972 and ratified
25 Sep. 1974
Panama signed 2 May 1972 and ratified
20 Mar. 1974
Papua New Guinea acceded 27 Oct. 1980
Paraguay acceded 9 June 1976
Peru signed 10 Apr. 1972 and ratified 5 June
1985
Philippines signed 10 Apr. 1972 and ratified
21 May 1973
Poland signed 10 Apr. 1972 and ratified
25 Jan. 1973
Portugal signed 29 June 1972 and ratified
15 May 1975

Qatar signed 14 Nov. 1972 and ratified
17 Apr. 1975

Romania signed 10 Apr. 1972 and ratified
25 July 1979
Russian Federation[2] signed 10 Apr. 1972 and
ratified 26 Mar. 1975
Rwanda signed 10 Apr. 1972 and ratified
20 May 1975

Saint Kitts and Nevis acceded 2 Apr. 1991
Saint Lucia acceded 26 Nov. 1986
Saint Vincent and the Grenadines acceded
13 May 1999
San Marino signed 12 Sep. 1972 and ratified
11 Mar. 1975
Sao Tome and Principe acceded
24 Aug. 1979
Saudi Arabia signed 12 Apr. 1972 and ratified
24 May 1972
Senegal signed 10 Apr. 1972 and ratified
26 Mar. 1975
Seychelles acceded 11 Oct. 1979
Sierra Leone signed 7 Nov. 1972 and ratified
29 June 1976
Singapore signed 19 June 1972 and ratified
2 Dec. 1975
Slovakia acceded 17 May 1993
Slovenia acceded 7 Apr. 1992

[2] The Russian Federation succeeded on 26 Dec.
1991 to the international obligations of the Soviet
Union, which had signed and ratified the convention.

Solomon Islands acceded 17 June 1981
South Africa signed 10 Apr. 1972 and ratified
   3 Nov. 1975
Spain signed 10 Apr. 1972 and ratified
   20 June 1979
Sri Lanka signed 10 Apr. 1972 and ratified
   18 Nov. 1986
Suriname acceded 6 Jan. 1993
Swaziland acceded 18 June 1991
Sweden signed 27 Feb. 1975 and ratified
   5 Feb. 1976
Switzerland signed 10 Apr. 1972 and ratified
   4 May 1976

Taiwan[3] signed 10 Apr. 1972 and ratified
   9 Feb. 1973
Thailand signed 17 Jan. 1973 and ratified
   28 May 1975
Togo signed 10 Apr. 1972 and ratified
   10 Nov. 1976
Tonga acceded 28 Sep. 1976
Tunisia signed 10 Apr. 1972 and ratified
   18 May 1973
Turkey signed 10 Apr. 1972 and ratified
   25 Oct. 1974
Turkmenistan acceded 11 Jan. 1996

Uganda acceded 12 May 1992
Ukraine signed 10 Apr. 1972 and ratified
   26 Mar. 1975
United Kingdom of Great Britain and
   Northern Ireland signed 10 Apr. 1972 and
   ratified 26 Mar. 1975
United States of America signed
   10 Apr. 1972 and ratified 26 Mar. 1975
Uruguay acceded 6 Apr. 1981
Uzbekistan acceded 11 Jan. 1996

Vanuatu acceded 12 Oct. 1990
Venezuela signed 10 Apr. 1972 and ratified
   18 Oct. 1978
Viet Nam acceded 20 June 1980

Yemen signed 26 Apr. 1972 and ratified
   1 June 1979
Yugoslavia signed 10 Apr. 1972 and
   ratified 25 Oct. 1973

Zimbabwe acceded 5 Nov. 1990

Source: Based on SIPRI Chemical and Biological Warfare Project, URL <http://projects.
sipri.se/cbw/docs/bw-btwc-rat.html>.

[3] See note 1.

SIPRI publications on CBW

- The Problem of Chemical and Biological Warfare, 6 volumes

  1. The Rise of CB Weapons. 1971. ISBN 91–85114–10–3.
  2. CB Weapons Today. 1973. 91–85114–16–2.
  3. CBW and the Law of War. 1973. 91–85114–17–0.
  4. CB Disarmament Negotiations, 1920–1970. 1971. 91–85114–11–1.
  5. The Prevention of CBW. 1971. 91–85114–13–8.
  6. Technical Aspects of Early Warning and Verification. 1975. 91–85114–18–9.

  The series is available on a CD-ROM, which is described at URL <http://editors.sipri.se/cd.cbw.html>.

- Chapters in the SIPRI Yearbooks

  SIPRI Yearbook of World Armaments and Disarmament, 1968/69. 1969. 91–85114–03–0.
  pp. 112–34. Development in chemical and biological warfare.

  SIPRI Yearbook of World Armaments and Disarmament, 1969/70. 1970. 91–85114–07–3.
  pp. 185–206. The CBW debate and other disarmament measures.

  World Armaments and Disarmament: SIPRI Yearbook 1972. 1972. 91–85114–12–X.
  pp. 501–22. Chemical and biological disarmament.

  World Armaments and Disarmament: SIPRI Yearbook 1973. 1973. 91–85114–19–7.
  pp. 383–91. Chemical disarmament.

  World Armaments and Disarmament: SIPRI Yearbook 1974. 1974. 0–262–19129–6.
  pp. 370–84. Chemical disarmament.

  World Armaments and Disarmament: SIPRI Yearbook 1975. 1975. 0–262–19140–7.
  pp. 426–32. Chemical disarmament.

  World Armaments and Disarmament: SIPRI Yearbook 1977. 1977. 91–22–00116–6.
  pp. 86–102. Dioxin: a potential chemical-warfare agent; and
  pp. 364–67. Prohibition of biological and chemical weapons.

  World Armaments and Disarmament: SIPRI Yearbook 1978. 1978. 0–85066–134–X.
  pp. 360–76. The destruction of chemical warfare agents.

  World Armaments and Disarmament: SIPRI Yearbook 1979. 1979. 0–85066–181–1.
  pp. 470–89. Stockpiles of chemical weapons and their destruction.

  World Armaments and Disarmament: SIPRI Yearbook 1980. 1980. 0–85066–201–X.
  pp. 365–79. Chemical disarmament.

  World Armaments and Disarmament: SIPRI Yearbook 1982. 1982. 0–85066–230–3.
  pp. 317–61. The changing status of chemical and biological warfare: recent technical, military and political developments; and
  pp. 456–57. Chemical weapons.

  World Armaments and Disarmament: SIPRI Yearbook 1983. 1983. 0–85066–247–8.
  pp. 391–426. Chemical and biological warfare: developments in 1982; and
  pp. 563–67. Chemical disarmament.

  World Armaments and Disarmament: SIPRI Yearbook 1984. 1984. 0–85066–263–X.
  pp. 319–49. Chemical and biological warfare: developments in 1983; and
  pp. 421–54. Implications of genetic engineering for chemical and biological warfare.

  World Armaments and Disarmament: SIPRI Yearbook 1985. 1985. 0–85066–297–4.
  pp. 159–205. Chemical and biological warfare: developments in 1984; and
  pp. 206–19. An analysis of the reports of Iraqi chemical warfare against Iran, 1980–84.

  World Armaments and Disarmament: SIPRI Yearbook 1986. 1986. 0–19–829100–0.
  pp. 159–79. Chemical and biological warfare: developments in 1985.

  SIPRI Yearbook 1987: World Armaments and Disarmament. 1987. 0–19–829114–0.
  pp. 97–115. Chemical and biological warfare: developments in 1986.

SIPRI Yearbook 1988: World Armaments and Disarmament. 1988. 0–19–829126–4.
  pp. 101–25. Chemical and biological warfare: developments in 1987.

SIPRI Yearbook 1989: World Armaments and Disarmament. 1989. 0–19–827751–2.
  pp. 99–130. Chemical and biological warfare: developments in 1988.

SIPRI Yearbook 1990: World Armaments and Disarmament. 1990. 0–19–827862–4.
  pp. 107–40. Chemical and biological warfare: developments in 1989; and
  pp. 521–44. Multilateral and bilateral talks on chemical and biological weapons.

SIPRI Yearbook 1991: World Armaments and Disarmament. 1991. 0–19–829145–0.
  pp. 85–112. Chemical and biological warfare: developments in 1990; and
  pp. 513–39. Multilateral and bilateral talks on chemical and biological weapons.

SIPRI Yearbook 1992: World Armaments and Disarmament. 1992. 0–19–829159–0.
  pp. 147–86. Chemical and biological warfare and arms control developments in 1991; and
  pp. 509–30. The United Nations Special Commission on Iraq.

SIPRI Yearbook 1993: World Armaments and Disarmament. 1993. 0–19–829166–3.
  pp. 259–92. Chemical and biological weapons: developments and proliferation;
  pp. 293–305. Benefits and threats of developments in biotechnology and genetic engineering;
  pp. 691–703. The United Nations Special Commission on Iraq: activities in 1992;
  pp. 705–34. The Chemical Weapons Convention: the success of chemical disarmament negotiations; and
  pp. 735–56. The Convention on the Prohibition of the Development, Production, Stockpiling and Use of Chemical Weapons and on their Destruction.

SIPRI Yearbook 1994. 1994. 0–19–829182–5.
  pp. 315–42. Chemical weapon developments;
  pp. 685–711. The Chemical Weapons Convention: institutionalization and preparation for entry into force;
  pp. 713–38. Biological weapon and arms control developments; and
  pp. 739–58. UNSCOM: activities in 1993.

SIPRI Yearbook 1995: Armaments, Disarmament and International Security. 1995.
0–19–829193–0.
  pp. 337–57. Chemical and biological weapons: developments and destruction;
  pp. 597–633. Multilateral weapon-related export control measures; and
  pp. 725–60. Chemical and biological arms control.

SIPRI Yearbook 1996: Armaments, Disarmament and International Security. 1996.
0–19–829202–3.
  pp. 537–59. Multilateral military-related export control measures; and
  pp. 661–708. Chemical and biological weapon developments and arms control.

SIPRI Yearbook 1997: Armaments, Disarmament and International Security. 1997.
0–19–829312–7.
  pp. 345–63. Multilateral military-related export control measures; and
  pp. 437–68. Chemical and biological weapon developments and arms control.

SIPRI Yearbook 1998: Armaments, Disarmament and International Security. 1998.
0–19–829454–9.
  pp. 373–402. Multilateral security-related export controls;
  pp. 457–489. Chemical and biological weapon developments and arms control; and
  pp. 490–500. Entry into force of the Chemical Weapons Convention.

SIPRI Yearbook 1999: Armaments, Disarmament and International Security. 1999.
0–19–829646–0.
  pp. 565–595. Chemical and biological weapon developments and arms control;
  pp. 596–611. Benefits and threats of developments in biotechnology and genetic engineering;
  pp. 667–691. Non-cooperative responses to proliferation: multilateral dimensions; and
  pp. 692–700. Multilateral weapon and technology export controls.

SIPRI Yearbook 2000: Armaments, Disarmament and International Security. 2000.
0–19–924162-7.
  pp. 509–536. Chemical and biological weapon developments and arms control;
  pp. 537–559. Risk assessment of terrorism with chemical and biological weapons;

pp. 560–575. The future of chemical and biological weapon disarmament in Iraq: from UNSCOM to UNMOVIC; and

pp. 667–687. Multilateral weapon and technology export controls.

SIPRI Yearbook 2001: Armaments, Disarmament and International Security. 2001. 0–19–924772-2.

pp. 513–548. Chemical and biological weapon developments and arms control; and

pp. 615–639. Multilateral weapon and technology export controls.

• Other SIPRI publications

Chemical Disarmament: Some Problems of Verification. 1973. 91–85114–20–0.

The Effects of Developments in the Biological and Chemical Sciences on CW Disarmament Negotiations. SIPRI research report 13, SIPRI, 1974.

Delayed Toxic Effects of Chemical Warfare Agents. 1975. 91–85114–29–4.

Chemical Disarmament: New Weapons for Old. 1975. 91–85114–27–8.

Medical Protection against Chemical-Warfare Agents. 1976. 91–22000–44–5.

Ecological Consequences of the Second Indochina War. 1976. 91–22000–62–3, pp. 24–45, 53–55.

Weapons of Mass Destruction and the Environment. 1977. 0–85066–132–3, pp. 31–48.

The Fight against Infectious Diseases: A Role for Applied Microbiology in Military Redeployment. SIPRI, 1979, mimeo. 91–85114–26–X.

Chemical Weapons: Destruction and Conversion. 1980. 0–85066–199–4.

Herbicides in War. 1984. 0–85066–265–6.

Biological and Toxin Weapons Today. 1986. 0–19–829108–6.

SIPRI publications may be obtained through all main bookshops. In case of difficulty, please contact the publishers or SIPRI.